CARNALITIES

MARIANA ORTEGA

CARNALITIES

THE ART OF LIVING IN LATINIDAD

DUKE UNIVERSITY PRESS · DURHAM AND LONDON · 2025

Paperback printed in Canada on acid-free paper.
Casebound edition printed in Canada on
acid-free paper ∞
Project Editor: Liz Smith
Designed by Matthew Tauch
Typeset in Warnock Pro, General Sans, and Sang Bleu Kingdom
by Westchester Publishing Services

Library of Congress Cataloging-in-Publication Data
Names: Ortega, Mariana, author.
Title: Carnalalities : the art of living in latinidad / Mariana Ortega.
Description: Durham : Duke University Press, 2025. |
Includes bibliographical references and index.
Identifiers: LCCN 2024017854 (print)
LCCN 2024017855 (ebook)
ISBN 9781478031277 (paperback)
ISBN 9781478028161 (hardcover)
ISBN 9781478060246 (ebook)
Subjects: LCSH: Phenomenology and art. | Aesthetics. | Hispanic American art—Themes, motives. | Self-presentation in art. | Human beings in art. | Emigration and immigration in art. | Hispanic American photographers. | BISAC: SOCIAL SCIENCE / Ethnic Studies / American / Hispanic American Studies | PHILOSOPHY / Aesthetics
Classification: LCC N66 .O78 2025 (print) | LCC N66 (ebook) | DDC 704.03/68—dc23/eng/20240702
LC record available at https://lccn.loc.gov/2024017854
LC ebook record available at https://lccn.loc.gov/2024017855

Cover art: Mariana Ortega, *Volando al otro lado de la memoria / Flying to the Other Side of Memory*. Acrylic and mixed media, 36 × 36 in. Courtesy of the artist.

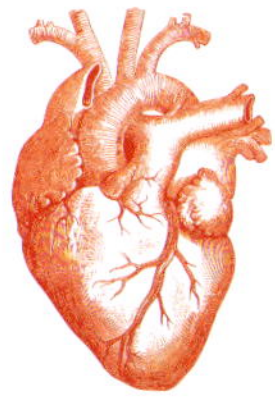

Para Roberto (1937–2023),

Nohelia (1964–2021),

Martha Patricia (1962–2019), y

Kokoro (2006–2024)

Me los imagino
cruzando otros mundos.

Respirando
un aire tierno,
profunda y hondamente,
con un ritmo suave.

Si encuentran nuevos colores,
abrácenlos con cariño,
agárrenlos de las manos,
alúmbrense con ellos.

Que aquí hay menos brillo
desde que se fueron.

To practice the body differently.
LAURA E. PÉREZ, *Eros Ideologies*

I say mujer mágica, empty yourself. Shock yourself into new ways of perceiving the world.
GLORIA ANZALDÚA, "Speaking in Tongues"

I continue to think about beauty and its knowledges.
CHRISTINA SHARPE, "Beauty Is a Method"

The photograph of the missing being, as Sontag says, will touch me like the delayed rays of a star. A sort of umbilical cord links the body of the photographed thing to my gaze: light, though impalpable, is here a carnal medium, a skin I share with anyone who has been photographed.
ROLAND BARTHES, *Camera Lucida*

CONTENTS

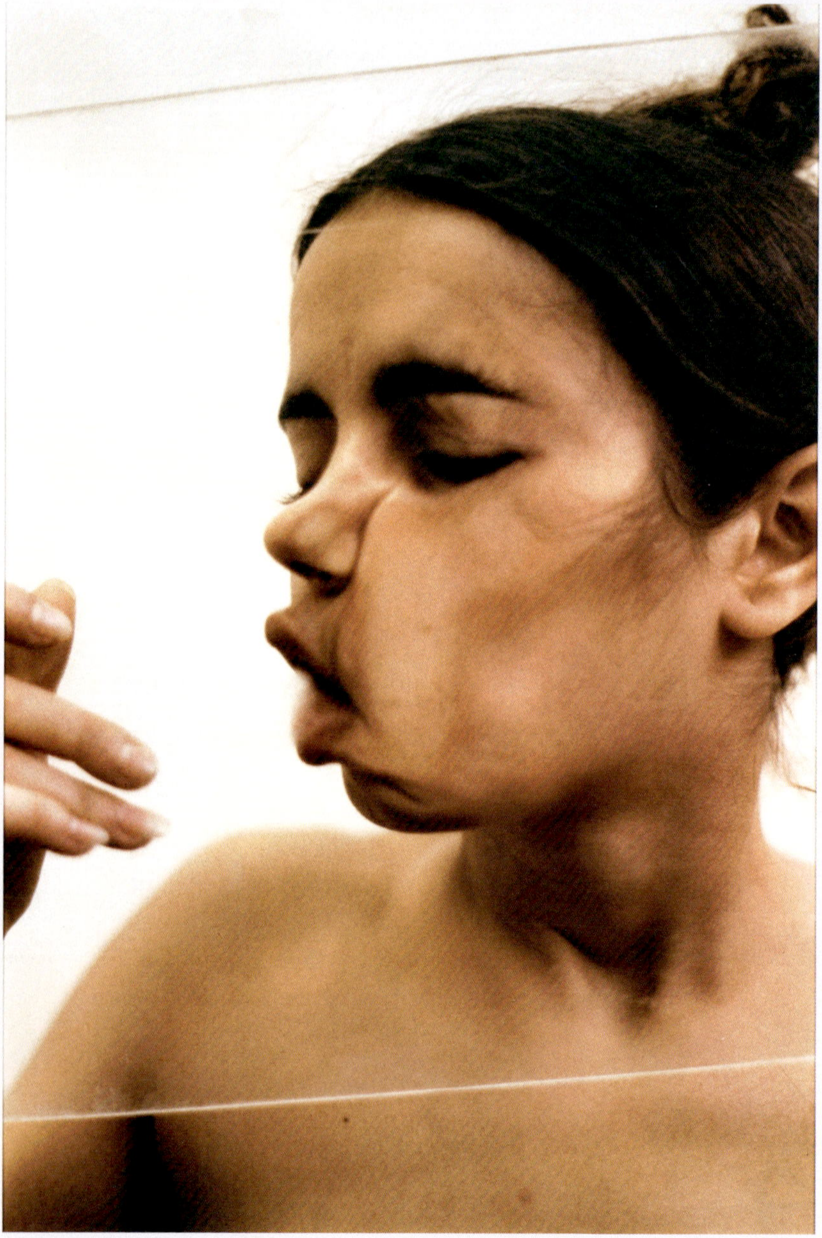

0.1 Ana Mendieta, *Untitled (Glass on Face)*, 1972. Suite of six color photographs, 17¼ × 24 in. Copyright the Institute of Contemporary Art Miami.

PREFACE

Skin of Light

Porous border, living wall,
awakened scars,
as if a graffiti god
created the perfect canvas.

    Let there be skin.

Wounded surface,
written with light,
blood touching invisible sand.
Exile as micro-version of death.

Carnal rays dispersing,
bouncing off eyes,
entering the here, there,
the all and nowhere of me.

An instant screaming of limits,
time that yellows and cracks.
She attempts to cross,
an early skin Silueta[1] interrupted,
touching exilic me.

    This photo is carnal.

ACKNOWLEDGMENTS

Experiences and ideas that influenced this book have been within me for a long time and have taken many twists and turns. They have also been touched and shaped by my interactions with a number of people. If, as Gloria Anzaldúa says, books need to be bathed and dressed, then many students, friends, and scholars have helped me tend to *Carnalities*.

The works of Gloria Anzaldúa and María Lugones, luminous nepantleras and world travelers, continue to sustain my search for the multiple and the otherwise in philosophy. While they have both departed, they live on, visiting us with their images-turned-words that touch and inspire.

Special thanks to Kevin Cedeño-Pacheco, Yi-Ting Chang, Jaqueline García Suárez, Megan Griffin, Erika Grimm, Rawb Leon-Carlyle, Ibis Sierra Audivert, Tiffany Tsantsoulas, Emma D. Velez, and Xalli Zúñiga, all of whom I met as Penn State graduate students but are now working in academia and beyond. I so admire not only their intellect but also their genuine love for learning. I thank Yi-Ting for her valuable suggestions for the first chapters, and Shaila Wadhwani from Marquette University for her help with early stages of manuscript preparation. I thank Rawb Leon-Carlyle for his generosity, patience, advice, and his eagle eye in the preparation of the final version—what a pleasure to work with someone of keen mind and kind heart.

My love of art continues to grow as time passes. It is the type of love that nurtures, allowing me to find joy in the present as well as to drift to other worlds. I am lucky to share this love with amazing scholars and friends, whose regard for art is deep, as is their work on aesthetics. Thank you, Helen Fielding, Laura E. Pérez, and Monique Roelofs, for your friendship and for your inspiring and important writings on art.

Special thanks to those whose analyses on racialization, social identities, and phenomenology have been key in my thinking: Norma Alarcón, Alia Al-Saji, Kathryn Sophia Belle, Antonio Calcagno, Jessica Elkayam Backus, Ellen K. Feder, Emily S. Lee, Linda Martín Alcoff, Jacqueline

Martinez, Helen Ngo, Andrea Pitts, Chela Sandoval, Kris Sealey, and Gail Weiss. Taking part in the Merleau-Ponty Reading Group was a source of delight and wonder. I thank Gail Weiss for organizing us and Bro Adams, Debra Bergoffen, Helen Fielding, Randall Johnson, Ann Murphy, Gayle Salamon, and Dolsy Smith for inspiring conversations.

Colleagues at the Pennsylvania State University have provided much needed support as I embarked in a new chapter of my academic career. I thank Amy Allen, Sarah Clark Miller, Leonard Lawlor, Maha Marouan, Eduardo Mendieta, and Judith Sierra-Rivera. While being part of the Midcareer Faculty Advancement Program in the College of the Liberal Arts, I have had the good fortune of being mentored by Jennifer Hamer. I thank her and the program for all the helpful advice and opportunities to learn about balancing various academic demands. Special thanks to Alicia Decker for her kindness and friendship as well as her leadership of the Women's, Gender, and Sexuality Studies department. Special thanks also to Ekaterina V. Haskins for her friendship and many a writing session.

I carried out the final research for this manuscript while visiting Marquette University in the 2022–23 academic year and the New School in fall 2023. At Marquette, I had the great opportunity to do philosophy and build community with the vibrant and bright Latina thinkers Stephanie Rivera Berruz, Javiera Perez Gomez, and Gabriela Alejandra Veronelli. I thank the tremendous Maria Cooper, who ensured that my stay at Marquette was seamless and whose generosity and laughter were a delight. I remain thankful to the Association of Marquette University Women for supporting my stay at Marquette as AMUW Chair of Humanistic Studies. At the New School, Ellen M. Freeberg and P. J. Gorre gave me the gift of great conversation. I am deeply grateful for their hospitality.

Special thanks to Ryan Kendall for believing in this project. I am thrilled to be working with an editor who has an expansive, multivoiced understanding of feminism. I deeply appreciate her insightful advice, creativity, generosity, and enthusiasm. I also thank Liz Smith and Christi Stanforth for their help with copyediting as well as Matthew Tauch for his book design.

Life (and work) without friends inside and outside academia is not sustainable. I am deeply thankful to all my friends whose love and care keep me afloat: Kate Catanese, Deniz Durmuş, Jonathan Gunderson, Karen Gygli, Robert Kolesar, Jeannette Mohr, Adriana Novoa, Jessica Pfeifer, and Julie Sushytska.

My mother, Norma; my sister Olga; my aunt Sandra; and my prima hermana Martha are the strongest women I know. I thank them for their presence, love, and for all they have taught me; I can only aspire to be as strong as they are. Abrazos fuertes to my generous brother-in-law Hugo, my dear nephews Ronald and Hugo Roberto, as well as to my dear brother Luis and his partner Claudia. Much love to my nieces Nohelia, Celeste, and Gabbie as they make new lives and seek joy without dear Nohelia. I thank Ed, my found family, for showing me that familial bonds are forged with care and laughter. I also remain thankful to Joe and Barbara Bentley for opening their arms to me in such nurturing ways.

To my dearest loving and lovable partner, Nancy Bentley, thank you in red. Your intelligence, kindness, love of words, and your quiet, deep ways make life brighter, airy, joyful. Love to my adored dog Kokoro, whose soulful eyes and tender ways nurtured me as I wrote these pages. He has recently left to other worlds, yet continues to be by my side.

I lost my father, Roberto Ortega; my prima hermana Nohelia Garcia; and my prima Martha Patricia Oviedo while writing this work—I dedicate it to them. *Carnalities* is partly about mourning and carrying our dead with us; this book is my way of carrying them with me.

Earlier versions of sections of chapters 4, 5, and 6 were published in "Bodies of Color, Bodies of Sorrow: On Resistant Sorrow, Aesthetic Unsettlement, and Becoming-With," *Critical Philosophy of Race* 7, no. 1 (2019): 124–43; "Altars for the Living: Shadow Ground, Aesthetic Memory, and the US Mexico Borderlands," in *Thinking the US South: Contemporary Philosophy from Southern Perspectives*, edited by Shannon Sullivan, 113–32 (Evanston, IL: Northwestern University Press, 2021); and "The Incandescence of Photography: On Abjection, Fulguration, and the Corpse," *philoSOPHIA* 9, no. 2 (2019): 68–87.

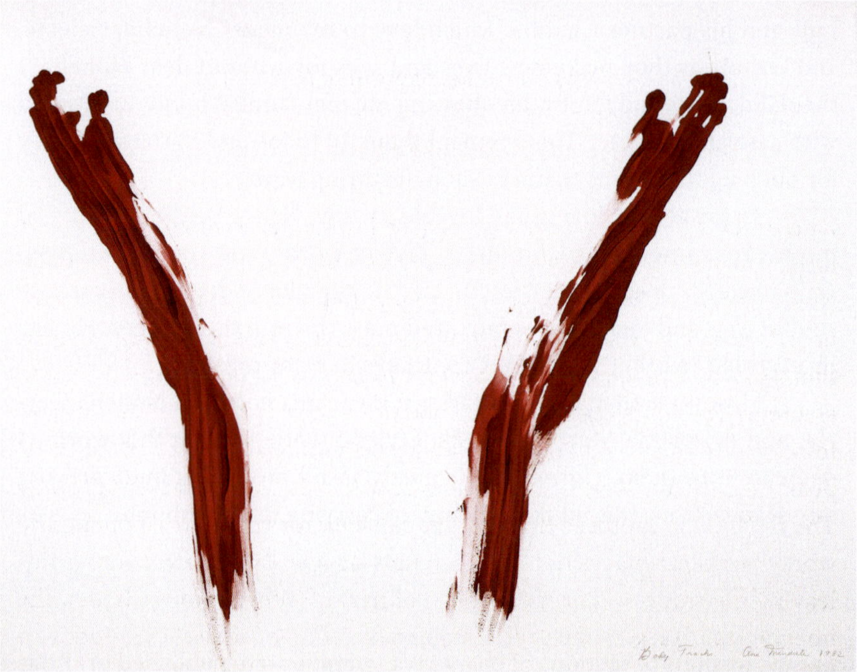

I.1 Ana Mendieta, *Body Tracks (Rastros Corporales)*, 1982. Performance piece; blood and tempera on paper. Copyright the Estate of Ana Mendieta Collection, LLC, and Galerie Lelong, New York.

INTRODUCTION

> This is the sacrifice that the act of creation requires,
> a blood sacrifice.
> **GLORIA ANZALDÚA**, *Borderlands / La Frontera*

I am obsessed with art, perhaps because I think that it has saved me—or, rather, that art has made me more alive. I often find myself noticing the convergences of line, texture, color, tone, light, and sound inside museums, but also in city streets, people's dwellings, and even in those spaces that have been abandoned by beauty. Joined in acts of creativity, these elements fascinate me in their capacity for relation, in their openness to intimacy—with each other and with us who perceive and mold them prompted by our fear, sorrow, and anguished joy. Ana Mendieta's *Body Tracks* (fig. I.1) captures this radiant capacity for relation. To create the work, Mendieta places her bloody hands on a wall and lowers her body, leaving the traces of her movement, of her*self*. What inspires her as she imprints her trace on the wall? The pain of exile, her refusal to ignore violence against women,[1] or her need to create? I think of Mendieta's arms as they yield to the wall, as they touch the surface, her very being connecting to a wall-turned-canvas and blood-turned-paint. This artistic performance forges multiple connections—between Mendieta and the various material elements involved in the performance, with a vexed history of Cuba-US relations, with those who witness the performance, and with the intuitions and forces that inspire her creative process. Her trace is fixed on the wall and paper and written with light in a photograph. More relations become possible, now between Mendieta and those who view the wall, paper, and the photograph, with you as you encounter the work in this book.

Mendieta's trace captured by light pierces me. I wonder how it is possible for this photograph to take me to her trace in such a way that it *affects* me, establishing a relation with me, but also with Mendieta and with that now-wounded wall. Worlds are opened, taking me to the receptivity of a wall, to the force of ritual, to the body's liquid being, to an exilic condition—all bringing forth different feelings, apertures of intimacy, with the photograph itself and with Mendieta's art practice, with all that is entangled in these multiple aesthetic movements. These intimacies, at times inscrutable, can take me to places of joy but also of pain. I think that this is what Roland Barthes means when he says that light is a *carnal* medium, that it touches affectively, that it is registered with the entire body as transmitter and receiver of the emanations of what the image discloses.[2] The photograph is a thing of affect.[3] Barthes, quoting Susan Sontag, says that the photograph of the missing being "will touch me like the delayed rays of a star."[4] While for Barthes the carnal aspect of photography is like a skin shared between the one who sees the photograph and the person captured by the light (recall that his *Camera Lucida* is a work of mourning for his mother), I am interested in exploring how photographs in general have the capacity to affectively touch those who experience them.[5] I am also interested in the aesthetic process itself as a carnal process, whether in writing with ink, light, or any other medium.

In this book I thus write about *carnalities*, creative practices informed by the self's attunement to the material but also to the cultural, historical, communal, and the spiritual—attunement to the interlacing of the self with all these elements for the purposes of gathering possibilities for self-care, survival, and world-making, and for being and sensing anew—for movements of the otherwise. I disclose carnalities Latinxs use for opening possibilities of naming and transforming Latinx life in the face of abjection and violence, for mourning and remembering those who have perished and those who remain in perilous conditions. I do not write about the carnal that is usually juxtaposed to the spiritual but, to use Gloria Anzaldúa's terms, about the "bodymindsoul" touching and being touched by the "Earth's-body."[6] I seek creative processes, practices of art-making, modes of memory-making, and ways of mourning that make it possible for Latinxs to survive, name, construct, transform, and even find joy and love ourselves—despite a life punctured by being-in-sorrow, as so many bodies of color are. By carnalities I mean these creative processes and their results, what is forged by them, whether a sense of well-being, care, protection, inspiration, or even despair that arises through them, or an art object itself, here understood beyond the view that a work of art must be produced by a professional artist or be accepted by the institutions of the art world.

This book is also about *cross*ings—difficult, painful, sometimes impossible crossings—transformations of self within regimes of abjection, as well as literal crossings of borders where a ferocious desert sun or an angry river stop dreams in their tracks, as they so many times do on the Mexico-US border. As we will see, in the crossings of the Mexico-US border, lines of desire for futurity and the interruption of such desire by policies, vigilantes, capitalist greed, and imperial forces intersect, *cross*, in the very body of migrants. I wish to honor those who survive and those who are lost—migrants, refugees, dreamers, risking life and limb for a different present and the possibility of a future, their painful past tethered to those limbs. The carnalities that I describe in this book are practices of the flesh in processes of being and becoming. As Anzaldúa says, "For only through the body, through the pulling of flesh, can the human soul be transformed. And for images, words, stories to have this transformative power, they must arise from the human body—flesh and bone—and from the Earth's body—stone, sky, liquid, soil."[7] I read her as calling for flesh, bone, and blood in their always already entwinement with worlds, with what they perceive. The ardent wish behind these pages is thus to discuss carnalities as connected to Latinx life in its condition of liminal flesh. I want to make visible the perilous yet luminous art of living in Latinidad.

Flesh is expansive in its meaning. In the common phrase *flesh and blood*, the term is connected to blood running in rhythmic cycles binding us to life itself. As such, it becomes an archive of experience and a site of possibilities. In a Christian context, flesh takes on different guises. In the Gospel of John, the Word is said to become flesh, which itself turns into spirit, intertwining the material and the spiritual, while in the epistles of Paul, flesh becomes synonymous with the body and its association with sinfulness. In the writings of Tertullian, flesh is understood as distinct from the body but as "earthy."[8] Flesh also denotes the mere matter of the body, its thingness. In the context of the perverse transatlantic slave trade, it is what the "captive body" turns into, onto which bloody "hieroglyphics of the flesh" are written, as Hortense Spillers so achingly writes.[9] Having become thingness, Black flesh also enters the vicious zone of nonbeing and nonrelationality, although it may still transform into a "vestibule for alternative ways of being."[10] "Flesh," then, paradoxically denotes being, nonbeing, and becoming.

In *Carnalities*, flesh is not equivalent to the material body, to spirit, or to experience as such; rather, it points to the intimacy between all of these in our everyday being-in-worlds. I am particularly interested in carnalities informed by Latina/x writers who understand themselves as producing theories "in the flesh."[11] For Cherríe Moraga, "A theory in the flesh means one where the physical realities of our lives—our skin color, the land or concrete we grew up on, our sexual longings—all fuse to create a politic born out of necessity."[12] We can think of these offerings by Latinas/xs as *carnal theories*, theoretical engagements that go hand in hand with embodied lived experience within complex webs of relations informed by multiple social identities, communities, histories, the earthly and the spiritual. With her writing in black ink, *tlilli*, and red paint or blood, *tlapalli*, symbolic of ancient Aztec codices, Anzaldúa produces stories that she considers "blood sacrifices," that need to be tended as if they were people: "The work manifests the same needs as a person, it needs to be 'fed,' la tengo que bañar y vestir."[13] I wonder, then, about *art in the flesh*, when the "soul makes itself through the creative act," as Anzaldúa makes herself, carves her own bones, face, and heart through writing with the blood that flows from the wounds of the many cuts of her life in the in-between.[14] For her, making art is "making soul," a process that is as personal as it is communal and relational, insofar as it is fused to earthly and spiritual realms as well as to the histories that inform her cultures—a connection symbolized by one of her favorite figures, el árbol de la vida (the tree of life), in which branches, trunk, and roots symbolizing different realms intertwine.[15] Her creative practices, then, are informed by the sensuous attunement to the entanglement between bodymindsoul, earth-body, and what, inspired by her vision, we can call the spirit-body. Soul-making as entanglement-with other worlds becomes blood-writing. Anzaldúa states, "Escribo con la tinta de mi sangre" (I write with the ink that is my blood).[16]

I imagine the redness of blood, its deep, dark but vibrant red spilt over the pages of Anzaldúa's work. I follow the flash of red of her blood, this red, this beautiful color that flows, inspires, overwhelms, and sustains—as blood scares when it gushes out from a cut or when it nourishes when it travels within us. I am reminded of Maurice Merleau-Ponty, the paradigmatic thinker of the intertwining. Of the color red, he says, "This red is what it is only by connecting up from its place with other reds about it, with which it forms a constellation, or with other colors it dominates or that dominate it, that it attracts or that attract it, that it repels or that repel it."[17] What attracts or repels Anzaldúa? What surrounds her—in the midst of other bodies, human and nonhuman, earthly and beyond—such that she cannot be who she is without it? Black ink and red paint write her story—self-writing as carnality. Can soul-making be prompted by light, a light that is heard, touched, a disclosure of the sensibilities and intimacies of the visible and the invisible?

In his later work, Merleau-Ponty famously states, "Between the alleged colors and visibles, we would find anew the tissue that lines them, sustains them, nourishes them, and which for its part is not a thing, but a possibility, a latency, and a *flesh* of things."[18] I am seduced by this "possibility" and "latency" that is flesh. In his view, *I* am flesh and things are enveloped by flesh. When I see things around me, when I see the red of the warning sign, the red of my blood, the red of your lips, I do so because of this flesh: "It is as though our vision were formed in the heart of the visible, or as though there were between it and us an *intimacy* as close as between the sea and the strand" (my emphasis).[19] This flesh is *incarnate possibility*.[20] It is not my skin, my organs, the sum of it all, but what allows for the interlacing of this body with this and that thing, with everything around it. Here Merleau-Ponty discloses a *chiasmic* relation linking my perception with objects around me, connecting objects themselves—interlacing the visible and the invisible, allowing for their reversibility. My body is an example of a chiasmic relation: I touch my hand and my hand becomes subject while the touched hand becomes object, revealing reversibility and possibility of communication.

I wish to follow these intimacies in connection to creative and artistic processes attuned to them, where to see is to touch, where "the vision and the body are tangled up in one another."[21] Yet I find in Anzaldúa's writings more expansive, living intimacies, between perceiver and perceived, between selves, worlds, relationships, histories, cultures, Indigenous myths, meanings, intuitions, images, nature, nonhuman animals, the unconscious, and the spiritual. I read her account as one of flesh*and*blood, as in the blood that carries oxygen to the lungs, heart, and all body tissues, readying them to take that precious breath that ultimately lets the self intermingle with all that is, that makes it possible for the self to exist, readying it for affect, intimacy, and a spirituality that has memory. As Laura Pérez notes, Anzaldúa offers a politics of the spiritual that is also a politics of memory, what Pérez describes as "a politics of the will to remember: To maintain in one's consciousness, to recall, and to (re)integrate a spiritual worldview about the interconnectedness of life, even if it is fragmented, circulating, as its pieces have through colonial and neocolonial relations."[22]

Crucially, Anzaldúa recognizes the irreversibilities of these colonial and neocolonial relations. Writing from the "wound" of the Mexico-US border, she cannot ignore the cracks, the ruptures, the unlacing of perceptions and relations. She must attend to moments in which the perceiver and perceived are not reversible or on equal footing. In her view of a relational, entangled in-between, irreversibility is a constant for those who are othered within dominant regimes of intelligibility and sensibility.[23] In the notion of flesh*and*blood, blood is a reminder of woundedness. In the chiasmic borderlands, Anzaldúa, wearing her flesh as if it were a skin that touches the whole world and beyond—land, culture, myths, histories, community, earthly elements, spirit—becomes a creative, shamanic being: "theory in the flesh" becoming flesh*and*blood art. I thus read her creative practice as a *carnal aesthetics*, an aesthetics guided by flesh*and*blood, an interlacing of self and worlds in which a self becomes attuned to deep perception. It is an aesthetics that follows the mouth that, in Anzaldúa's writings, I interpret as multisensory perception, a carnal bridge between self and worlds.[24] As Anzaldúa states, "Todo pasaba por esa boca, el viento, el fuego, los mares y la Tierra" (Everything passed through that mouth, wind, fire, the seas, and the earth).[25]

Carnal aesthetics is connected to a particular understanding of "aesthetics." The term is derived from the Greek *aisthesis*, which means "perception" or "sensation." I am interested in precisely the sensuous, perceptual moments of creative practices denoted by the notion of *aisthesis*. While some scholars use *aestheSics* or *aesthesics* instead of the term *aesthetics* in order to delink the term from European conceptions of art, I opt to continue to use *aesthetics* but add *carnal* in order to highlight the sensuous, perceptual aspect of artistic practices as well as the entwinement between the body and earthly and spiritual realms.[26] I am very much interested in the decolonial and anticolonial turn in matters of art—as we will see, *Carnalities* encompasses de- and anticolonial movements and processes—but I wish to hold on to the connection to art-making entailed by the term *aesthetic*, to multiperceptual processes specifically linked to creative practices.[27] My interest, then, rests on the sensuous, multiperceptual, affective dimensions of Latinx creative practices.

Anzaldúa's carnal aesthetics inspires me to theorize a specific carnality that I name *autoarte*, an intimate, personal, yet relational creative process in which the self is *affected* by different elements in movements of self-care, self-naming, and transformation. Autoarte captures what Anzaldúa calls the "inner work" that we must do in our crossings, even when acknowledging the interconnectedness between self and others, the natural and spiritual worlds. As noted above, Anzaldúa states, "Todo pasaba por esa boca" (Everything passed through that mouth). There is no escaping all the sea, wind, earth, and fires that come through one's mouth, and that consequently affect the self in a personal, intimate way. Our very bodies and selves are affected. While our bodies are porous and thus entangled with other bodies, human and nonhuman, as well as with the material and beyond, there is still the closeness, vividness of one's experience. As Anzaldúa writes in the preface of her *Borderlands / La Frontera*, a book that has a heartbeat, that needs bathing and dressing,[28] "This book, then, speaks of my existence. My preoccupations with the inner life of the Self, and with the struggle of that Self amidst adversity and violation; with the confluence of primordial images; with the unique positioning consciousness takes at these confluent streams; and with my almost instinctive urge to communicate, to speak, to write about life on the borders, life in the shadows."[29] Autoarte grasps the moments of this intimacy, the inner work but without a metaphysical commitment to a detached, self-sufficient subjectivity.

As a key praxis of carnal aesthetics, autoarte intimately affects, afflicts, and quietly stirs the self that intertwines with worlds. It is in the quiet, says Tina M. Campt, that we may find "quiet frequencies of possibility" as well as of refusal.[30] While she centers the quiet in photographic images, we can regard the quiet within carnal aesthetics in general, which direct us inward while never losing existing, past, and future complex webs of relations. Crucially, a question that arises for Campt is how to think of these movements of quiet in relation to futurity for Black life given a past and present of brutality and sorrow. I am also moved by this question; I wish to ask it in the context of Latinx lives. Campt helps us consider answers to this urgent question when she suggests that a future is not only to be had in terms of actions and political resistance but also in listening for it in "other, less likely places."[31] She finds futural possibilities through *listening* to photographs, a method of "recalibrating vernacular photographs as quiet, quotidian practices that give us access to the affective registers through which these images enunciate alternate accounts of their subjects."[32] Through this careful listening to images, we can find worthy subjects and a present that makes futures while also tarrying with the past, without it stopping us in our tracks. As Kevin Quashie also reminds us, "The inner life is not apolitical or without social value, but neither is it determined entirely by publicness. In fact, the interior—dynamic and ravishing—is a stay against the dominance of the social world; it has its own sovereignty."[33]

Quashie underscores the vibrancy and importance of Black interiority. He does so in order to show that, contrary to public discourses that render Blackness as always in the mode of political struggle and resistance, there is a full range of interiority, of quiet, in Black life. This is a mode that he considers "expansive, voluptuous, creative, impulsive, and dangerous."[34] Inspired by Hortense Spillers's worry that public discourse covers up Black social and human differentiation, Quashie wishes to bring forth the texturedness and multiplicity of Black experience that is found in an aesthetics of quiet.[35] Importantly, his aim is not to undermine political resistance or the multiple relationalities informing Black life: "The quiet subject is a subject who surrenders, a subject whose consciousness is not only shaped by struggle but also by revelry, possibility, the wildness of inner life. . . . The outer world cannot be avoided or ignored, but one does not only have to yield to its vagaries. One can be quiet."[36] A theorization of autoarte is in part an attempt to draw attention to some of the quiet moments of Anzaldúa's aesthetics and of carnal aesthetics in general. Nevertheless, in what follows we will find quiet as well as resonant, sonorous moments in which Latinx carnal aesthetics becomes explicitly resistant.[37]

Carnalities discloses creative practices that avoid acquiescing to the embalming practices of normative, colonial, and neocolonial subjects, imaginaries, and structures. Through sensual attunement to worlds, elements, histories, and cultures, selves of color paradoxically halt time in order to move forward. They destabilize and even negate the temporal and ontological fixity assigned to them that turns them into always already a type and an essence. In so doing, they become futural as it were, opening possibilities for creating themselves and for living otherwise. While destabilizing the rapacious colonial eye within and without is difficult—and sometimes impossible—carnalities do not constitute mere theoretical desires. Through conocimiento (Anzaldúa), and erotics (Anzaldúa, Audre Lorde, Chela Sandoval), bodies of color that are also bodies of sorrow tend to themselves in quiet and sonorous ways, opening new possibilities: incredible feats of survival, self-construction, self-transformation, and joy- and love-seeking. Here I wish to highlight the moments when they do it through carnal creative practices. While the early chapters of the book center Anzaldúa's creative writing practice, most of the chapters pay attention to "light-writing" by Latinx themselves or by those interested in disclosing Latinx experience in difficult crossings. I thus seek flesh*and*-blood art written with light, encounters with carnal photography through which Latinxs nurture our inner lives, transform ourselves, honor our living, and mourn and remember our dead. In so doing, we stand in the face of woundedness: not forgetting it or making a spectacle out of it—the continuation of the spectacle of race that both saddens and entertains the eye trained by coloniality—but remembering that scarred bodies exceed their wounds.[38]

In times in which to be a body of color is to be a body of sorrow, utterly exposed to the whims and the cruelties of racist imaginaries and racist selves who are bolder in their enactment of hate, I move toward an analysis that goes beyond discursive engagements with theories of racialization, oppression, and resistance. In the photograph we find what is beyond the sayable or even the visible. While the photographic image has been primarily understood by its indexicality and by its connection to the regimes of representation and ocularity, here I wish to tell another story of the photograph: its connection to affectivity, its story as an "archive of feeling" that has the possibility of disclosing what exceeds understanding, especially in moments of rupture.[39] Photographic images become enunciations, articulations, presentations, and affirmations, what Rolando Vázquez calls a move from the logic of representation to the relationality of reception.[40] Photographs turn into expressions of who we are and who we want to become-with. In *Carnalities* I explore the nexus of the photographic image, the experience of Latinxs, and carnalities in a critical phenomenological and anticolonial register in order to tell stories with light that capture how creative practices open possibilities for a different present and future, as fragile or precarious that future may be for those whose lives are punctuated by practices of degradation and deadly othering. Writings with light can write many a story. What stories can light write when its radiations touch the lives of Latinxs whose experience is, as late Latinx queer critic José Esteban Muñoz describes, one of *feeling brown*?[41] As we will see, chapter 5 takes up Muñoz's views of feeling brown and brown commons in the context of the flowing of brownness in *crossings* of the Mexico-US border.

With this work I wish to honor those who lost their breath in their perilous journeys to this land in the North believed to overflow with golden opportunity. I also want to remember those who crossed, not to the land of opportunity but to the land of icy infernal cages in detention facilities, brutal working conditions, and constant denigration. I did a crossing of my own in hellish circumstances, but it cannot compare to the ghastly and ghostly crossing of an angry river, of a hellish desert with its deadly heat and animals cravenly roaming, waiting for fallen dreamers. With this flesh*and*blood theory, I want to hold all those Latinxs who made it through their crossings yet find themselves being-in-sorrow, facing the constant shame and humiliations of a life in which your skin or your accent or your ways of being are a problem. I am not deluded about the political and moral efficacy of academic production, especially as it concerns the aesthetic that was so long marked by disinterestedness. I know the limits of books and articles, especially in a society that moves farther away from intellectual discourse and in which education itself becomes commodified. Yet I think of Anzaldúa's blood-writing, Audre Lorde's poetry clothed in *eros*, and, more recently, of Natalie Diaz's postcolonial poem of love and water:

> I am fluent in water. Water is fluent in my body—
> It spoke my body into existence.[42]

I seek to understand the power of art and creative practices moved by a (our) fluency to take in worlds—to let wind, fire, the seas, and the earth through our mouths—in order not only to survive but also to perceive anew, to change our lives, even to find love and joy.

METHODOLOGIES FOR A CARNAL AESTHETICS

In this project I take a multifaceted methodological approach in which Latina/x feminisms, critical phenomenology, aesthetics, and visual studies intertwine to disclose Latinx carnalities, different flesh*and*blood, creative practices of self-care, survival, resistance, transformation, and renewal that register the intertwining of perceiver and perceived, selves and worlds. Since my love and joy affair with photography started long ago, waiting silently for me to feel-with my love of Latina/x feminisms and phenomenology, I highlight photography, the writing with light. In his luminous work *Camera Lucida*, Barthes writes, "As Spectator I was interested in Photography only for 'sentimental' reasons; I wanted to explore it not as a question (a theme) but as a wound: I see, I feel, hence I notice, I observe, and I think."[43] I have been pierced by this comment since the first time I read it many years ago. It has helped me understand my love for photography, why I *feel* photographs—it has led me to these pages.

Carnal Light

Despite the photograph's historically revered function as indexical, as pointing out that "the thing has been there," for me the most salient feature of the photograph is that it stings—that it affectively touches, brings about joy, sorrow, fear, anger, lust, mourning, beautiful and frightful feelings.[44] In her damning criticisms of photography in her now-classic *On Photography*, Susan Sontag also recalls how a photograph "cut" her deeply and sharply as nothing else she had seen before.[45] It is precisely this aspect and ability of the photograph to affectively wound that guides my discussion in *Carnalities*. Here I understand the photograph as carnal, in its flesh*and*bloodness. Taking photographs is itself a carnal process. In his important discussion on art in "Eye and Mind," Merleau-Ponty privileges painting and briefly criticizes photography by recalling Rodin's views on the importance of movement. He states, "instantaneous glimpses, unstable attitudes petrify movement, as is shown by so many photographs in which an athlete-in-motion is forever frozen."[46] While Merleau-Ponty himself privileges painting and does not appreciate the photograph due to its supposed inability to capture movement, in this book I wish to open the space for the photograph's carnality, to find its umbilical cord, its vital connection to those who see it.

A certain kind of alchemy happens with photographs—light turns to affect, transforming pieces of matter into what matters to us, touching us as if they had hands, having the power to caress us lovingly, or to rip us apart, a slow flaying of our skin. My first reading of the meaning of photography as "writing with light"[47] was itself a touching moment—imagining rays of light first calmly, then feverishly writing on metal or paper covered with magic crystals . . . and worlds, people, objects, nature appearing, to be held by us, embalmed for us, as André Bazin would say.[48] According to Bazin, photography's arrival frees painting to be whatever it wants to be, no longer having to represent the world objectively. Painting acquires wings to experiment and move away from the quest of perfect resemblance and realistic representation, moving toward the "aesthetic," and what, according to Bazin, satisfies our need for illusion. Photography, in turn, becomes tied to the object it represents—it itself becomes embalmed as it were.[49]

Almost as quickly as it emerges, the story of photography turns vicious. Due to its evidentiary status, photography becomes the technology that goes hand in hand with the "science" of classifying beings. Photography begins to embalm people in ways beyond freezing them in a slice of time, as it is enlisted in the creation of types of beings whose "essence" becomes marked by inferiority, criminality, childishness, bestiality, abnormality, madness, immorality, and all other manner of inhumanity. The operations of photography become one with colonialist ventures in which the eye of the photographer and of the camera yield an imaginary that includes many variations of othered beings[50] such as "savages" in the corridors of our imagination.[51] This further serves as an "ontological catalyst," *producing* particular kinds of othered beings[52] and becoming indispensable for the new "sciences."[53] As such, photographic practices bolster the reign of ocularity that regards the eye as arbiter of knowledge and becomes the murderous colonizing gaze. They consequently produce aesthetic ignorance and aesthetic violence, the violence and ignorance resulting from aesthetic practices that create imaginaries reinforcing false visions of already othered beings. As a catalyst for material violence against othered bodies, the photographic image, like the word or the knife, cuts through the layers of our skin and exposes our vulnerability, our woundability.

Whether in its ability to connect affectively to a being for whom we feel tenderness or in its ability to create disgust through practices of othering, the photograph becomes a *carnal medium*: "A sort of umbilical cord links the body of the photographed thing to my gaze: light, though impalpable, is here a carnal medium, a skin I share with anyone who has been photographed."[54] In *Carnalities*, I interpret this carnal aspect of the photograph as connected to the photograph's ability to pierce us at both a personal and structural level. The piercing of a photograph is at times tender, loving but it can also be jagged, painful. It can instigate violence, especially when operating in the context of oppressive imaginaries hard at work in the creation of "otherness" in need to be debased, abjected, or eliminated. This "otherness" is not merely an abstract idea or a constructed image of fantastic beings. It pertains living, breathing bodies of color who are shamed, persecuted, harmed, maimed, or killed. Yet this light practice that is used for violence, that cuts deeply and fatally as if with a sharp knife, may also prompt reconfigurations of self and alternative senses of relationality, of being-with and being-in-worlds. This understanding of the photograph as carnal rests partly on a notion of vision in which the eye is not the principal actor, and in which vision, as Anzaldúa and Merleau-Ponty understand, is connected to multiple senses. Together with mouthly perception, the carnal in photography opens the writing with light to practices of self-nurture, affirmation of difference, self-naming, self-transformation, relationality, community, and to practices of counter-visuality that may destabilize the coloniality of the eye that persists in classifying, typing, and essentializing. *Carnalities* seeks the moments in which the carnality of the photography allows for selves of the in-between to move from being objects of monstrosity, criminality, inhumanity, and curiosity fixed by light, to fluid subjects touched by and writing themselves with light in skin-like surfaces.

Latinx, Latinidad, Latinities, and Feeling Brown

Carnalities aims at disclosing the way that aesthetic production, particularly through the medium of photography, expands our understanding of the lived experience of Latinidad at various junctures—in bodily, earthly, and watery crossings, in memorializing those lost in these perilous crossings and those who crossed and yet continue to remain in peril and being-in-sorrow. But I cannot assume that *Latinidad* and *Latinx* are uncontroversial identity categories, because of the tremendous heterogeneity of the group that these terms are supposed to capture—for example, immigrants from Latin America and the Caribbean; those born in the United States but with ties to Latin America and the Caribbean; mixed-race individuals of European, African, and Asian origins; as well as those embodying a multiplicity of intersections of race, ethnicity, gender, sexuality, religion, and nationality with ties to North, Central, and South America and the Caribbean.

Various terms such as *Hispanic, Latino, Latino/a, Latina/o, Latin@, Latinx,* and *Latine* are used to designate individuals of Latin American and Caribbean descent in the United States. The latter two labels have been recently introduced to destabilize the binary that informs traditional understandings of gender, a binary that María Lugones connects to a colonial imposition of gender.[55] *Latinx* is also used to counter the dichotomous gendering of the Spanish language itself. Yet it is a term that has been highly criticized due to what some regard as an imposition of an American academic perspective on discourses regarding identity. *Latine* has thus become the preferred choice for those who wish to avoid this imposition and who consider it an easier term to pronounce for those who speak Spanish. Importantly, the *x* in *Latinx*, a label that first appeared on the internet in the early 2000s, derives its strength from its inclusivity of various genders and sexualities. Nonetheless, Alan Pelaez Lopez reads the *x* as a scar that points to anti-Blackness, settler colonialism, feminicide, and the inarticulation of the Latin American experience.[56] Claudia Milian, however, takes *"LatinX"* as an "expounding concept" and understands the *X* as placeholder for different ways of being and different trajectories and movements of Latinx life.[57] This is the sense in which I interpret *Latinx*, while also understanding that in a different context—for example, a Spanish-speaking context—the term *latine* is preferable. Given that I am writing in a US academic context and value the term's undermining of binaristic gender and sexual categories and its potential for expansiveness, here I use *Latinx*.

Another term used to capture the groups of people that *Carnalities* is concerned about is the umbrella term *Latinidad*. This widely used pan-ethnic term is problematic if deployed to forge a unity out of the tremendous heterogeneity of US people hailing from or having ties with Mexico, Central and South America, and the Caribbean as it is understood by some as not expansive enough to include Indigeneity and Blackness. Moreover, some scholars regard *Latinidad* as a construction that caters to neoliberalism and capitalism.[58] In short, *Latinidad* is riddled with several problems, including unacceptable "internal exclusions."[59] In the following I take a brief excursion into how some theorists have taken up the crucial task of reconfiguring the notion of Latinidad to expand its capaciousness and complexity.

Cristina Beltrán interprets *Latinidad* as a heterogeneous process that must always "remain a question."[60] This understanding of the term is influenced by her critical reception to the idea that there is "Latino" unity in the political sphere, leading her to reject the familiar metaphor of the "sleeping giant" standing for the now largest minority of the United States. Beltrán points out that there is indeed an internal logic to the appeal to the unity of Latinos under the pan-ethnic umbrella term *Latinidad* as this appeal can be strategically deployed by activists to secure federal rights. She also understands that there is also an important emotional and experiential appeal to the use of the term, especially in response to the highly xenophobic and racist US environment. Yet she wants to let the sleeping giant lie—or rather, her view is that there is no sleeping giant. She suggests that we give up trying to make unity out of diversity and that we regard Latinidad as "a site of permanent political contest," "something we *do* rather than something we *are*,"[61] and thus avoid the traps of what she terms "unitary inclusiveness" that has been characteristic of Latino politics in the United States.

While taking a similar route as Beltrán insofar as she is interested in the *process* of "Latining" rather than *categories* of identity, Claudia Milian wishes to find an even more "copious" understanding of "Latin" that is able to go beyond the problems engendered by the notion of Latinidad and other terms used to describe what she calls "Latin" experiences that are prevalent in Latina/o studies.[62] In her view, the term *Latinidad* is still committed to an "ontological grammar" informed by the white/brown binary that does not allow for the possibility of including, following Ed Morales, the "Latin surplus": that is, other ways of being "Latin" that intersect with brownness, dark brownness as well as Blackness, that are not captured by the existing terms.[63] "Morales's overview of Latin surplus," Milian writes, "cannot be wiped off the Latinidad map. It rightfully lacks the social scripting of one Latino, Latina or Latin-American subject as well as a single unit of cultural and geopolitical articulation."[64] Her interest thus lies not so much in "who" Latinxs are but on how they are Latined. Most importantly, she wishes to bring to the fore discussions of groups that have been heretofore ignored, not sufficiently discussed or not captured by the current theoretical understandings offered in Latina/o studies, for example Central Americans, dark brown and Black individuals who are not from the Caribbean, and other "unstable Latined lives."[65] She thus urges us to think about "Latinities."

This development of a trend away from more traditional understandings of categories of identity is philosophically important precisely because of the difficulties associated with firmly rooted theoretical commitments to notions of belonging and unity, whether in individual or panethnic categories. Crucially, what follows from these strategies in which Latinidad is turned into a verb or a process, a Latining, is that the affective dimensions of being Latined are now of a piece with other processes, whether aesthetic, cultural, economic, or historical. One of the principal points of the carnalities that I propose in this work is precisely to show how creative practices disclose affective links and interweavings of Latinx peoples and various worlds. Through these affective links we can understand and name ourselves as well as forge connections with those similar and different from us, not merely in flights of imagination but through specific aesthetic practices.

This affective link in the doing of Latinidad/Latinities is particularly important for Muñoz. His writings on "feeling brown" point to his deep attunement to the affective dimension of Latinidad. Finding the term *Hispanic* "repellent," he refuses to use it and, instead, opts for *Latinidad*, although his thinking about feeling brown is already a movement away from the notion of identity categories. As he states, "Feeling brown, the idea of feeling brown, is my attempt to begin to conceptualize this mode of belonging that I conveniently index elsewhere as the concept of Latinidad."[66] Like Beltrán and Milian, Muñoz engages in the arduous task of finding a way to capture the heterogeneity and complexity of US Latinx experience. In *The Sense of Brown*, I see him struggling to capture something that connects those who are put under the umbrella of Latinidad. He searches for something that differently racialized people have in common without resorting to homogenization and easily prescribed politics. He is affectively pierced by plays and performances by artists such as Ricardo Bracho, Nilo Cruz, Luis Alfaro, Nao Bustamante, and Carmelita Tropicana. In the pages of *The Sense of Brown*, the aesthetic becomes thoroughly carnal insofar as these artistic performances touch him affectively, like Barthes says the *punctum* of a photograph may puncture us.[67]

Through his experience and theorization of the performances, Muñoz captures a shared *feeling brown*. This is a "structure of feeling" that, according to him, is "born out of a shared sense of harm."[68] It captures "different modes of affective struggle," "a certain vulnerability to the violence of property, finance, and to capital's overarching mechanisms of domination," "an 'apartness together' through sharing the status of being a problem," and a "manera de ser, a way of being in the world."[69] There is a Heideggerian tint in Muñoz's characterization of feeling brown as a "being-with."[70] I thus read his account of feeling brown as pointing to a *being-in-sorrow*, an existential characteristic of those who are brown. As an existential characteristic, it captures a way of being in the world, not an essential feature of those under the umbrella of Latinidad. This way of being in the world is attuned to a condition and relationality marked by sorrow, anxiety, not being-at-ease, and the violence felt by bodies of color.[71] What Muñoz captures is the affectivity and vulnerability of what it means to be brown, the way of being in the world captured by those plays and performances that, in turn, touch him and alert him to what he shares with others who feel brown. It is in this sense that the aesthetic becomes carnal for him. Artworks—in his case, performances—reveal not mere sensation or a recording of the experiences of the senses, but the perception-affect nexus in which eye, hand, mouth, ear, skin work in unison to reveal feeling brown.

Despite differences in the rethinking of Latinidad offered by Beltrán, Milian, and Muñoz, these thinkers are motivated by problems associated by the appeal to categories of identity or pan-identity. As we have seen, such problems—flattening of heterogeneity, internal exclusions, unfounded appeals to political unity, and others—do not do justice to the multiplicity of the Latinx community and the variegated ways of being Latinx. As we have seen, for most of these thinkers, the right conceptual move is precisely to step away from identity as a category with essentialist presuppositions, hence their appeal to process and to a Deleuzian rhizomatic approach. My own position shares the same concerns that these theorists have regarding the pitfalls of identity claims, except that I do not regard the notion of identity itself as necessarily tied to essentialist claims, as those who appeal to a Deleuzian approach often do. That is, to appeal to identity does not confine one to an essentialist position or to a sharp dichotomy between views that appeal to identity and those that must jettison such claims. I find appeals to identity to continue to be extremely important for existential and political reasons, especially for members of marginalized communities. As I have previously argued, it is necessary to rethink notions of identity and identity politics precisely in ways that reject essentialist, narrow understanding of these terms.[72] For me, Latinidad constitutes an appeal to identity, but one in which such identity is understood in its complexity, including its process of formation, thus my interest in recent reconfigurations of the term. We can thus think of *Latinidad* as both a capacious noun picking up an incredibly diverse group of individuals as well as a verb that points to historical and cultural processes, and, as Muñoz teaches us, affective components. In *Carnalities*, I follow Muñoz in this momentum leading to a sense of who we are—those of us who are and feel brown—while also considering Latinidad as process, in Milian's sense of Latining. Latinidad/Latinities is something that we are as members of our incredibly diverse community and something we do in the context of how historical, cultural, economic, and affective registers influence our lives.

In *Carnalities* I discuss *our* feeling brown and the skin of the photograph. I am interested in how the photograph touches my own skin and tells me about me and others like and unlike me, who are nevertheless part of a brown commons, those whom Muñoz sees as capable of constructing new worlds and as dreamers of "other planets."[73] The feeling brown as a being-in-sorrow that is shared by people of color points to affective dimensions of Latining that, as Milian seeks, are inclusive of differently racialized bodies of color. That is, the brown commons that is made through feeling brown is not dominated by an account of *mestizaje* that has traditionally informed discussions of Latinidad and is inclusive of Indigeneity, Blackness, and different shades of brownness. In *Carnalities*, the crossings of Mexicans, Central Americans, Caribbeans, and South Americans create a photographic archive of feeling brown. This archive discloses the intimacies among bodies of color with the earth- and spirit-bodies. It also uncovers the very carnalities or creative practices that these bodies of color enact in movements of self-naming and transformation. *Carnalities* is punctuated by a being-in-sorrow that, nevertheless, also points to the resilience, aliveness, and joy of those who feel brown.

A Differential Hermeneutics of Love

Informed by views of Latinidad allowing for multiplicity, heterogeneity, and the processes of being Latined as well as the gestures, enactments, and theorizations of Latinx affective life, *Carnalities* has a certain desire (if books have desires as images have wants),[74] to capture the affective life of Latinidad in the context of our creative endeavors, a desire that I also very much find in the works of Anzaldúa and in the methodology of Chela Sandoval. While the work of Anzaldúa takes center stage in part I of *Carnalities*, Sandoval's theorization of a decolonial erotics as elaborated in her key work, *The Methodology of the Oppressed*, explicitly informs the discussion in chapter 3 and is implicit throughout *Carnalities*. In the following, I provide a brief discussion of her sense of differential consciousness and of erotics that moves my own thinking on aesthetics.

Sandoval envisions love as a technology of social transformation informing her methodology for emancipation from what she takes are neocolonizing forces of postmodernism.[75] At the heart of this methodology is the development of a notion of consciousness inspired by Anzaldúa's mestiza consciousness, a *differential consciousness* that allows subjects to shift technologies of liberation depending on their positions in different maps of power. Sandoval describes differential consciousness as mobile, tactical, kaleidoscopic, and as making possible for the subject to break with dominant ideologies even from within such ideologies: "The differential represents the variant; its presence emerges out of correlations, intensities, junctures, crises" and it has the capacity to "de- and recenter, given the forms of power to be moved."[76] In this book, I enhance the notion of differential consciousness by engaging it in the context of carnalities of Latinidad that are mobilized at different junctures and crossings of Latinx experience. More specifically, I envision carnalities as tactical aesthetic movements of differential consciousness in response to the dominant, hegemonic eye informed by coloniality, the ongoing, present forms of subjugation that are the result of acts of colonialism.[77]

While Sandoval's methodology recognizes that differential consciousness is inextricably connected to aesthetic practices, she nevertheless does not center works of art in her discussion. Yet she states that "differential consciousness is linked to whatever is not expressible through words. It is accessed through poetic modes of expression: gestures, music, images, sounds, words, that plummet or rise through signification to find some void—some no-place—to claim their due."[78] Like Anzaldúa, Sandoval is deeply aware of the generative power of art that yields not merely opportunities for survival but also possibilities for self-creation, transformation, and perceiving anew. She grasps the way differential consciousness senses, reacts, and learns from modes of disorientation in worlds where being brown means being a problem. She understands how such consciousness is affectively tied to social reality, thus capable of reading and sensing maps of power and tactically engaging in different practices to traverse them.

One of the most important and interesting moves that Sandoval makes in her methodology of the oppressed and that informs *Carnalities* is her joining differential consciousness to a hermeneutics of love. In her view, love becomes a *punctum*, a piercing of the self that calls our attention, wounds, or inspires us, a point that, as discussed above, Barthes finds in the photograph. Love also leads the self to a Coatlicue state or a state of confusion, fear, and paralysis that, according to Anzaldúa, precedes transformation and crossing to other ways of being and knowing. Love as *punctum* and the Coatlicue state take the self to an "abyss," opening the possibility of being freed from dominant knowledges and ways of being and sensing. Following both Barthes and Anzaldúa, Sandoval describes love as a "gentle hemorrhage of being" and a painful crossing that opens the possibility for "a passage from language to process, a passage from narrative to an erotics of being."[79]

No longer confined to discourse and to established meanings, this erotics of being becomes a sensory realm in which the self affectively maps herself, becomes attuned to her environments and all the relations within them—textures not previously felt stand out suggesting new movements and relations of things; sounds lose their monotony, calling for new rhythms; eyes, nose, ears, hands, all working together in disclosures of possibilities of being and sensing beyond the colonial norm. Audre Lorde, one of the most important and inspiring theorists of the erotic, connects the erotic to a lifeforce of women that calls for a reclamation of joy in all endeavors—an intensity of feeling and doing.[80] Sandoval, however, takes erotics as a "drifting" of the self toward "that place of life that survives outside and between narrative forms, where meanings live in some free, yet marked and wounded space, a site of shifting."[81] Shifting here has to do with inner work and with changing established, hegemonic, linguistic signifiers as well as ways of being-in, sensing, and reconstructing the world, hence Sandoval's vision of these erotics as embodying a "decolonial love." For her, the methodology of the oppressed becomes a decolonizing theory and method of renewal, social reconstruction, and emancipation. In *Carnalities* I read her decolonial erotics, the sensuous and affective aspect of emancipation, as connected to flesh*and*blood intimacies, to the intertwining of the self and all that is, an in-between realm where there is a multiplicity of touchings between selves and other selves with their various histories and desires, and between self and worlds—a carnal aesthetics turned carnal erotics in order to name and love ourselves, to carry our dead, and to honor those of us who remain in precarious conditions after treacherous crossings.

A Latina/x, Critical Feminist Phenomenological Aesthetics

The remaining methodological approach that informs *Carnalities* is critical phenomenology. In both its transcendental and existential modes, phenomenology is characterized by a description and investigation of first-person experience that has a critical dimension. The meaning of "critical" in a critical approach to phenomenology varies. I am interested in critical approaches to phenomenology that explicitly take up questions related to social identities such as race, class, sex, gender, ability, and nationality.[82] In its transcendental mode as theorized predominantly by Edmund Husserl, phenomenology is a rigorous method that aims for certainty about the structures of consciousness. In its existential mode as theorized most famously by Martin Heidegger, Jean-Paul Sartre, Simone de Beauvoir, Edith Stein, Frantz Fanon, and Maurice Merleau-Ponty, phenomenology moves away from the quest for apodictic certainty about structures of consciousness and moves toward an explanation of the various existential structures of subjectivity praxically embedded in the world as well as a description of key existential notions such as anxiety, fear, death, and authenticity.

Phenomenologists also study everyday perceptual practices—for example, the contradictory movement of presence and absence that characterizes operations of vision insofar as eyes are supposed to see what is really there while, at the same time, they can only capture objects from certain perspectives. Dyads of presence/absence and visibility/invisibility are thus at work in visual perception. What is perceived as given is never completely captured; it never appears in its totality. As we intentionally direct ourselves, for example to a table, what appears is one side of the table or whatever side, depending on the perceiver's location. What allows us to understand that object toward which we are directing our gaze is a background of intelligibility, and, as we will see in this work, of sensibility that makes it possible for us to engage with the perceived in specific ways in the first place.

These perplexing possibilities of presence/absence and visibility/invisibility have been explained by way of the famous figure/ground organization according to which psychologists and various phenomenologists tackle difficulties of perception. What is striking is how these relationships of being/not being, visibility/invisibility, figure/ground can be engaged by phenomenologists to explain not only perceptions of daily objects such as tables, but also of human beings themselves, especially in a context of *othering*—for example, in the fabrication of othered beings that must be abjected, undermined, or eradicated, as well as in the construction of whiteness as the dominant "orientation."[83] That is, the very daily processes of perception, in particular perception of visible differences, are part and parcel of this othering characterized by the objectifying and naturalizing of difference. They play a central role in processes of othering as explained by contemporary phenomenologists. Explaining perceptual practices to show how human beings themselves are perceived in objectifying and naturalizing ways due to their visible differences is, in my view, one of the most important projects of a phenomenology that we now understand as *critical* phenomenology. According to Lisa Guenther, one of the first explicit proponents of a critical phenomenology, this critical approach to phenomenology offers a method that, while rooted in first-person experience, does not privilege transcendental subjectivity, a type of subjectivity that is not relational. Yet she criticizes Husserlian phenomenology for not being critical enough and calls for a critical phenomenological analysis of contingent historical and social structures that shape experience in a "quasi-transcendental way"—structures such as white supremacy, patriarchy, and heteronormativity.[84] Gayle Salamon also calls for a critical approach to phenomenology but takes the critical aspect of critical phenomenology as entailing a reflection of the structural conditions from which it emerges and a description of "what it sees in order to see it anew."[85]

I take seriously Guenther's and Salamon's critical approach to phenomenology. I am also moved by Salamon's urgent call for describing what we see in order to see it anew. It leads me to search how those living under conditions of precarity and oppression find ways to grasp the world and themselves differently, with many eyes, mouths, and ears. In my previous work, *In-Between: Latina Feminist Phenomenology, Multiplicity, and the Self*, my approach entails analyses of existential structures as well as descriptions of the very experience of marginalization *from the point of view* of those who occupy that location. In *Carnalities*, I continue to follow a critical phenomenological approach, in this case in relation to perceptual processes, especially those of racialization, as well as in connection to artistic practices in order to offer a critical phenomenological aesthetics that centers Latinidad.[86]

Informed by Guenther's and Salamon's concerns about the critical aspect of a phenomenological investigation as well as by my previous work on Latina feminist phenomenology where I develop criteria for Latina feminist phenomenology,[87] I take a method of critical phenomenology as involving (1) reflexivity about phenomenology's own operations and aims; (2) a critical examination and critique of major notions or structures as they operate in classical phenomenological texts; (3) a description of lived experience from the point of view of marginalized selves; (4) an engagement with pressing societal issues connected to the entwinement of different social identities such as race, class, gender, and ability; (5) attention to ruptures of everydayness that may lead to new understandings of how social identities affect first-person lived experience; (6) emphasis on concrete, embodied everyday experience; (7) attunement as to how the experience selves from particular social identities are covered up in classical phenomenological analyses; (8) recognition of the multiplicity and heterogeneity of the experience of those embodying specific social identities; (9) critical deployment of experiential knowledge in order to contest or reimagine established notions of the particular social identities being described; (10) attunement to perceptual registers that open possibilities of sensing otherwise; and (11) analysis of possibilities of self-transformation and self-refashioning within the specific context or social identities being described. *Carnalities* expands this vision of critical phenomenology by centering the aesthetic practices of Latinidad/Latinities and by being guided by Latina/x critical feminist phenomenology.

I take one of the central aims of critical phenomenologies as engaged description,[88] not pure description—that is, as attempts to describe everyday experience for the purpose of using such explanations to understand and alleviate pressing societal problems such as racism, sexism, homophobia, and ableism. While I am mindful that description does not constitute explanation,[89] the discussions of Latinx experience I provide in *Carnalities* include descriptions of specific instances of Latinx experience that provide important clues as to how Latinx selves engage in creative practices. I am particularly interested in critical phenomenological discussions of perceptual practices of othering, and in the possibility of countering them in creative acts of self-naming and transformation of communal imaginaries with the purpose of acknowledging, paying respect, and honoring those Latinx selves that have become invisible, have been demonized in the current US American context, or have perished in the *cross*ing of the Mexico-US border.

THE CHAPTERS

Carnalities is divided in two parts, "Carnal Crossings: Eye and Mouth" and "Border Crossings: Sorrow and Memory." Part I, "Carnal Crossings: Eye and Mouth," first centers the visual and progresses to multisensory perception symbolized by the figure of the mouth. In chapter 1 a critical phenomenological analysis of perception of visual difference reveals that seeing race is informed by tacit, embodied habits as well as an intimate connection between perception and affect; that is, seeing race amounts to being affected in particular ways. The colonial eye thus learns to see in such a way that it "cannot" see or feel about bodies of color differently from hegemonic, racist views. Yet an interval of hesitation as explained by Alia Al-Saji is shown as opening possibilities for reconfiguring habits and thus for shifting racist views and for countering the internalized hegemonic, colonial gaze of racialized selves. The movement to mouthly perception or multisensory perception that captures the entwinement between the perceiver and perceived becomes explicit in chapter 2 in a discussion of Anzaldúa's account of conocimiento as affective mapping that translates into a *carnal aesthetics*. While the first two chapters center the transition from eye to mouth, leading to a discussion of the processes informing Anzaldúa's aesthetics, chapter 3 elaborates on the Anzaldúan notion of border arte and introduces an analysis specifically connected to carnal photography, introducing the notion of autoarte as a key carnality of carnal aesthetics. *Autoarte* is shown as a deeply intimate, personal creative process in which the self becomes perceptually and thus affectively attuned to the earthly and the spiritual for the purposes of self-care, self-naming, and self-transformation. The photographic practice and mobile decolonial erotics of Chicana photographer Laura Aguilar are discussed as an example of autoarte through which Aguilar names and transforms herself as well as lovingly intertwines with earth- and spirit-bodies, her body thus becoming a carnal crossing.

Moving from considerations of the body as carnal crossing (as shown by Aguilar's carnal photography) to other earth-water crossings, part II, "Border Crossings: Sorrow and Memory," centers photographic projects on the *cross*ings of the Mexico-US border. In this part of *Carnalities*, photographs show their constructive possibilities in terms of enacting *aesthetic unsettlement*, *aesthetic memories*, and *carnalities of mourning and remembrance*. Chapter 4 introduces the notion of carnalities in the context of *listening* to photographs from the Pima County Office of the Medical Examiner as well as by registering aesthetic unsettlement as *sonic rupture* in the photographs and aural compositions of *Border Cantos* by Richard Misrach and Guillermo Galindo. Bodies of color are shown as bodies of sorrow who become carnal archives in which histories of violence are recorded. Chapter 5 introduces migrant caravans in terms of the notion of flowing brownness. Bodies of color are discussed as sites in which lines of movement prompted by desire and futurity and lines of blockage of such desire *cross* or intersect. The photographs of Verónica Gabriela Cárdenas become an archive of *feeling brown*, a structure of feeling that, according to Muñoz, describes the shared sense of harm that characterizes Latinidad. They also forge a multiracial *brown commons* composed of migrants from Mexico, Central and South America, and the Caribbean. While the first two chapters in this section underscore crossings to the Mexico-US border, chapter 6 is informed by my own crossing to the United States from Nicaragua due to the 1979 revolution.

While not giving up on the constructive possibilities of carnal aesthetics, this chapter highlights the power of carnal photography, specifically the photograph *Cuesta del Plomo* by Susan Meiselas, as having the possibility to undo the self—*my* self. It also reveals why I am distraught by Barthes's readings of some photographs, even though *Camera Lucida* is a key inspiration for this work.

Carnalities presents the photograph as carnal, as a relational surface in which we find and are affected by the lives and *cross*ings of those in Latinidad/Latinities understood as a process of being Latined and a shared sense of feeling brown. Latina/x feminisms, in particular the work of Anzaldúa, point to carnalities, creative practices that register the intertwining of selves and worlds and that open possibilities for self-naming, nurturing, and transformation as well as for art-making as self-and-world-making. These intimacies turned creative acts touch the deepest part of ourselves as well as our relations with the earth- and spirit-bodies, with those with whom we share lives, joys, and sorrow—in moments of quiet and of resonant defiance of the hegemonic eye. In a critical phenomenological approach mindful of first-person liminal experience, of the art of living in Latinidad, *Carnalities* unfolds the vital role of the aesthetic, of writing with light, in its capacity to *affect* us, inspire us, and to illuminate our lives so that we can care for and love ourselves. Echoing Anzaldúa, *Carnalities* is another way of finding luz en lo oscuro, light in the dark.

I CARNAL CROSSINGS

EYE AND MOUTH

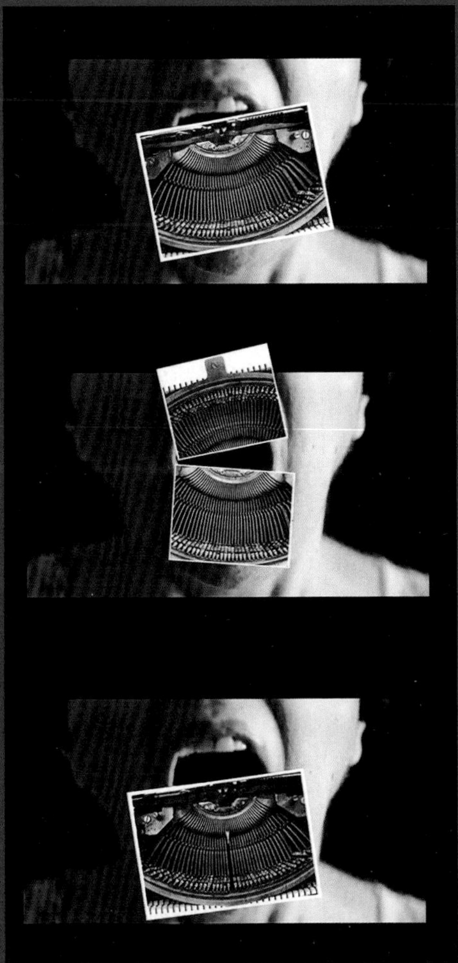

Speak with me, not to me—
not over and through me,
with that hammering tongue
of twisted lead.
        Fire and metal gone wrong.

That is not a clack you hear,
but the contractions
of a bleeding tongue.
Opening, closing,
        Worlds flowing
                through me.

Pl.1 Lenora de Barros, *Saying Almost Nothing.* Three inkjet prints on paper. Copyright the artist.

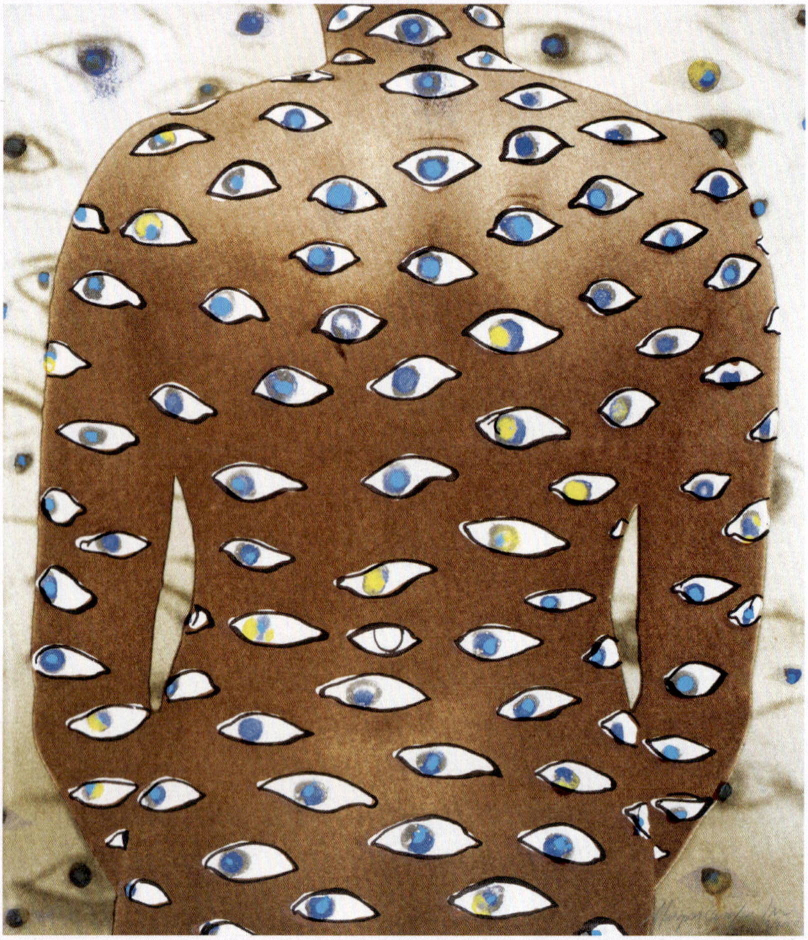

1.1 María Magdalena Campos-Pons, *Untitled (The Right Protection)*, 1999. Lithograph and pulp painting on paper, 20¼ × 17½ in. Edition of 14. Published by the Brodsky Center at PAFA, Philadelphia. Copyright the artist and the Brodsky Center at PAFA, Philadelphia. Photograph courtesy of the artist and the Brodsky Center at PAFA, Philadelphia. Photo by Jack Abraham.

ONE AFFECTED BY THE EYE

A Prelude to a Carnal Aesthetics

> Guidebook to the colony,
> record of each crossed birth.
>
> it is the typology of taint,
> of stain: blemish: sullying spot:
>
> that which can be purified,
> that which cannot—Canaan's
> black fate . . .
>
> NATASHA TRETHEWEY, *Thrall*

> Seeing us as tainted depends on a need for purity
> that requires that we become "parts," "addenda"
> of the bodies of modern subjects.
>
> MARÍA LUGONES, *Pilgrimages/Peregrinajes*

I look at Maria Magdalena Campos-Pons's print of a Black body on whose back and arms multiple eyes have been drawn (fig. 1.1). There are eyes on all the visible parts of this dark body standing straight, like the centerpiece of some anatomical museum that scientists wish to examine, probe, measure, classify, and display to prove animality, inhumanity, immorality, criminality—the familiar descriptors of bodies of color as seen by the colonial eye. Eyes are also drawn on the borders of the print. Who is looking at whom? Although seemingly obvious, the work itself needs to be seen with many eyes, from different perspectives. Is this body of color a sentinel, an arbiter of morality, literally watching out with its many eyes, with its double, triple, quadruple, multiplicitous consciousness, alert to the possible violence that is to come? Is Campos-Pons presenting her own body as a witness? Do the icy blue eyes belong to bodies who watch in wait in order to dominate, conquer, and colonize? What are the eyes outside the frame seeing? While this work appears as "Untitled," there is the addition of a subtitle "(The Right Protection)." A new reading arises:

a series of "evil eyes" are called to protect, to bounce back evil to the evil-doer—these eyes see with the entire self; they are guided by earth-and spirit-bodies.[1]

Let us start with the operations of the eye. When I think about the importance of the visual in practices of racialization, I think of predatory eyes looking for visible differences, wishing to type and categorize selves, as if carving them into stone or forging them into metal plates. This is the familiar story of the colonizing eye, including the eye of the camera, that persists to this day in its various contemporary instantiations. It is an eye that travels well through time and space, morphing into many looks, sometimes even pretending that it does not see skin color, in an altogether familiar story of cruelty cloaked in pretenses of civilization, salvation, and progress. This is the eye that bolsters structures and imaginaries designed specifically to denigrate, abuse, and dominate for the purposes of racial violence, border patrol, settler colonialism, neocolonialism, and extraction of resources. It is a powerful eye, so much so that its unwieldy, unrelenting ways and distorted imaginaries seep into the very bodies of color that it aims to wound.

In this chapter I follow theorists of color who look out for those who are at risk from the colonial eye and who study the operations of negative racial seeing. In particular, I discuss the work of critical phenomenologists Martín Alcoff, Emily S. Lee, Helen Ngo, and Alia Al-Saji, whose analyses of the perception of visible difference are fundamental for understanding racism, especially in the context of the United States. Martín Alcoff's discussion proves to be of special interest due to her claim that visual perception of racial difference rests on sedimented bodily habits that are tacit.[2] Following Martín Alcoff's important analysis, Lee, Ngo, and Al-Saji elaborate on key elements of negative racialized perception, underscoring the integral link between perception and affectivity. Here I first discuss the complex interaction between the visible and the invisible that informs phenomenological analyses of perception, centering on Martín Alcoff's and Al-Saji's analyses of racialized perception as ultimately relying on tacit bodily habits. I highlight Al-Saji's important discussion of the perception-affect nexus in terms of what she calls the "I cannot" of racialization. For Al-Saji, perception is crucially connected to affect—that is, seeing is being affected by the seen. The "I cannot" of racializing perception rests on negative values assigned to visible differences by normative, historical, cultural, and colonial structures. Such negative values are then translated into "natural" ways of perceiving visible differences—the eye seeing racialized difference only as prescribed by dominant norms. That is, black and brown skin are not merely perceived as black and brown; they prompt feelings of hate, disgust, aversion, fear, or pernicious sexual desire for the "exotic." This "I cannot" of racialization is part of the experience of all those who see with colonial eyes, including bodies of color that due to a life marked by constant denigration internalize negative associations about their own visible difference.

In the second section of the chapter, I examine Al-Saji's notion of hesitation as a temporal interval that allows for the possibility of reconfiguring racist habitual perception. Importantly, hesitation is a slowing down of perceptual experience. It is connected to affectivity and provides "room for breathing," a particularly apt description given the sense of suffocation prompted by experiences of ethnocentrism and racism linked to negative racial seeing.[3] For Al-Saji, hesitation opens the door for disremembering and countering how the colonial past continues to affect us.[4] This notion of hesitation informed by the perception-affect nexus, the manner in which perception is tied to affectivity by way of habituation, can also be connected to what I call the medium-affect nexus, the way that certain elements *affect* or *inspire* a self's creativity, artistic practices, and aesthetic experiences. Al-Saji underscores her own experience of hesitation in the context of artworks, which, in my view, may be understood as entailing a moment of deep affective intimacy that can be connected to what Kevin Quashie theorizes as "quiet" and "interiority," that, as explained in the preface, pertains to an "inner life" that is not determined entirely by publicness and that includes a full range of responses beyond the political.[5] Pointing to this personal affective intimacy in relation to "interiority"—or, to quote Anzaldúa, "inner work"—is not meant to reify an isolated subject enclosed in his own mind. Rather, it entails a recognition of the importance and intimacy of personal experience, even if such an experience is crucially informed by relatedness and intimacies with other beings, human and nonhuman. Following Quashie, I also understand interiority in terms of the multifaceted ways that racialized subjects live their lives beyond the public expectation of performing explicitly political resistant acts. While I am interested in these moments of quiet, a consideration of Anzaldúa's notion of germination as prelude to crossing, understood by Lugones as germinative stasis, shows that it is not always possible to draw a hard line between the quiet and what we may regard as resonant moments that can be understood as more explicitly politically resistant. As we will see in chapter 2 when looking at Anzaldúa's carnal aesthetics, inner work that is as deeply personal as it is relational, that affects us at both existential and political levels, sustains us and opens possibilities for "public works," contestations and reframings of the hegemonic, colonial gaze and the treacherous imaginaries it has constructed.

From the outset, it is important to note that in this chapter I do not aim at providing a full critical phenomenological analysis of racializing perception. I take up this issue to call attention to the perception-affect nexus and to the importance of a slowing down of perceptual practices that, as we will see in chapter 2, is also key, albeit in a different context, in Anzaldúa's aesthetic practice.[6] Ultimately, my interest lies not in providing an antidote to a racist, dominant, hegemonic eye but in showing how, despite the racist gaze within and without, bodies of color are still capable of carving their face, their bones, as Anzaldúa says, by way of creative practices. Following Al-Saji's turn toward the affectivity of perception, here I move from the visual that is predominant in phenomenology to what I call *mouthly* perception or multisensory perception. This turn from the eye to the mouth becomes even more explicit in the next chapter's discussion of Anzaldúa's creative practice as a *carnal aesthetics* guided by multisensory, affective attunement to community as well as by material and spiritual elements—by earth- and spirit-bodies. *Carnalities* is, in effect, my attempt to answer Al-Saji's call to look into affective responses to negative racialization. It is also my own gesture to destabilize the reign of the ocular within phenomenological accounts.

PHENOMENOLOGY, THE VISIBLE, AND THE INVISIBLE

Vision continues to be a dominant sense, providing access to shapes, forms, colors, and, according to lore, to our very souls. It has also been historically associated with objectivity and truth. Coupled with the "light of reason," vision has enjoyed the highest status of all the senses—a status, however, that would eventually collapse once scholars pointed to the high price paid for such alleged objectivity, namely, the erasure of vision's collusion with gendered and racialized violence. As critics such as Laura Mulvey, Allan Sekula, John Tagg, Jonathan Crary, Martin Jay, and Nicholas Mirzoeff have shown, visual practices are neither objective nor innocent.[7]

Sekula and Tagg, in particular, show how the interplay of visual practices and technological advances such as photography is key in the deployment of *othering* practices aimed at relegating human beings to classifiable natural types. While art theorists such as W. J. T. Mitchell attempt to shift the conversation away from discussions about image, representation, and violence by redirecting us to think about what images themselves want from us—that is, by considering images on their own terms[8]—vision continues to be understood as complicit with practices of oppression. It is thus of the utmost importance to understand the link between visuality and practices of *othering*, the ways the eye aligns with the sword, the rope, the gun—whatever pain-inflicting object or technology of coloniality—to transform human beings into both objects of representation and bodies to be abjected.[9] Yet the visual as such need not be condemned as inherently oppressive, as visual practices have always been and continue to be engaged in modes of counter-visuality.[10] What is relevant for our purposes is that we still need to understand the processes through which the visual has played and continues to play a role in practices of objectification, especially as it concerns racialization.

By way of critical phenomenological analyses, we can better understand vision's role in these perverse practices of *othering* that aim at categorizing and constructing some beings as inferior because of their visible differences. In her influential contextualist, phenomenological analysis of racist perception in the context of the United States, Martín Alcoff highlights the realm of the visible as a key site for understanding how selves are objectified and differences naturalized. As she states, "Because race works through the domain of the visible, the experience of race is predicated first and foremost on the perception whose specific mode is learned ability."[11] Through her novel use of Merleau-Ponty's phenomenology in the context of racial perception, she alerts us that racism is the result of tacit embodied racializing habits. In other words, our perception of visible differences that seems to register these differences as if they were natural is in fact something learned and informed by cultural views or imaginaries that leads to particular habits of seeing. She thus calls for further analysis of these operations: "Our first task, it seems to me, is to make visible the practices of visibility itself, to outline the background from which our knowledge of others and of ourselves appears in relief. From there we may be able to alter the associated meanings ascribed to visible difference."[12]

Martín Alcoff's appeal to Merleau-Ponty's phenomenology to explain the embodied nature of racist perception has been crucial for critical phenomenologists of color such as Lee, Ngo, and Al-Saji who are interested in the embodied habits of racism. With attention to the ambiguity of racism as well as through an understanding of the self as multiplicitous, Lee questions contemporary accounts of implicit bias that presuppose racism as a matter of individual prejudice. She thus argues for analyses of the social embeddedness of racial meanings;[13] she also proposes a Merleau-Ponty-inspired phenomenology that is more attentive to how notions of multiplicitousness and intersectionality pertain to the lived experience of women of color.[14] Ngo, on her part, considers specific experiences of racism from the point of view of people of color in order to show how racialized bodies stand in "multiple relations to and perspectives upon the self" such that "the spatial cohesion of the body schema" is disrupted, and provides an important analysis of racialized uncanniness that points to not only the experience of pain of racialized selves but also the constructive possibilities born out of that pain.[15] Ultimately, for Ngo, "vision, then, contains the ground for both objectification and its critique, for racialization and for anti-racist intervention into social practice."[16]

While it is important to engage criticisms of ocularcentrism as they reveal the entanglement between perception and power relations as various visual theorists have done, it is also crucial that we consider critical phenomenological analyses of the operations of racializing visual perception in order to understand just how deep negative racialization works within our bodies. These analyses reveal the importance of the practices and micropractices of racialization operating in historico-cultural-contextual backgrounds and in sedimented layers of embodied habits. Such operations are in need of further analysis, whether in the context of the racist, colonial eye of dominant selves or the internalized colonial eye of selves of color. In the context of our analysis, critical phenomenologies reveal a most important feature of experience, the deep entwinement between perception and affect. This perception-affect nexus is crucial for understanding a carnal aesthetics connected to sensuous operations of self-making and transformation that hold openings for movements of the otherwise in the face of the racist eye. The work of Al-Saji is most informative of this nexus.

In phenomenological analyses, visual perception is paradoxically characterized by movements of visibility as well as of invisibility. That is, the eye captures objects in the world, providing evidence, while, at the same time, such objects are perceived only from a specific perspective. An ambiguity of being and nonbeing operates in visual perception. What is given never appears in its totality but only from the perceiver's perspective. Yet what allows the subject to understand an object in front of her is a background of both intelligibility and, as we will see, sensibility that makes it possible for her to engage with the perceived in specific ways in the first place.[17] These dyads of visibility/invisibility and being/nonbeing have been famously discussed by Gestalt psychologists in terms of the well-known figure/ground dyad. These distinctions are particularly important to critical phenomenologists as they help explain operations of racializing perception in neocolonial contexts that account for the objectifying and the naturalizing of difference.

Martín Alcoff thus appeals to the ambiguous operations of perception in which visibility and invisibility are intertwined and a figure becomes visible against an invisible background. She states, "If race is a structure of contemporary perception, then it helps constitute the necessary background from which I know myself. It makes up a part of what appears to me as the natural setting of all my thoughts. It is the field, rather than that which stands out. The perceptual practices involved in racializations are then tacit, almost hidden from view, and thus almost immune from critical reflection."[18] By appealing to the figure/ground distinction common to Gestalt theorists, Martín Alcoff effectively illustrates the movement of visibility and invisibility that informs practices of racializing perception. In Frantz Fanon's terms, it is a "historico-racial schema" that remains hidden in practices of racializing perception.[19]

Inspired by Martín Alcoff, Al-Saji describes the process of racializing vision in terms of a double invisibility. Not only is the historico-racial schema hidden and thus the body is perceived only in biological or naturalized terms, but so is the very process through which this racializing perception takes place.[20] Racialized bodies are completely othered insofar as they are seen as having essential features; they are congealed as it were. Consequently, they cannot be different from the racist's perception of them. As Al-Saji notes, "Racialized bodies are not only seen as naturally inferior, they *cannot be seen otherwise*."[21] Here we can return to Campos-Pons's photograph from the beginning of our discussion. An altogether different interpretation arises: a number of eyes are fixed on and fixing the racialized body, as a chemical solution fixes an image in a photograph. Moreover, as will be discussed in the next section, the watchful eyes can also be interpreted as already imprinted on the body, thus indicating the possibility of their internalization. If they are not evil eyes meant to protect the backs of the racialized body, they now stand for the colonial eyes that have already lodged themselves in that body, prompting the racialized self to see herself from their point of view and thus to undermine herself. This operation of the internalization of the colonial gaze is of great interest precisely because it points to aspects of the experience of negatively racialized selves that are difficult to discuss and to live with. *Carnalities* is meant to show how aesthetic practices can and *are* opening possibilities of dealing with these pernicious consequences of racism, how people of color are still able to find ways of naming and transforming themselves from those eyes within and without that turn them into unwanted, abject types. Yet I wish to dwell a bit longer with the negative operations of racialization given Al-Saji's nuanced analysis.

What is particularly fascinating and important about Al-Saji's account of racializing perception is her attunement to the ways that those whose eyes *cannot* see racialized bodies as other than prescribed by racist imaginaries are not just perceiving differences but are being affected (or have learned to be affected) by those differences. Al-Saji thus discusses the "I cannot" of racialization and explains that this "I cannot" depends on the "receptivity of vision: its ability to be affected, to be touched by that which lies beyond or beneath its habitual objectifying schemas."[22] The moment of invisibility associated with racializing perception, then, becomes a moment of unaffectability—or, rather, of not having the possibility of being affected or touched by the perceived body in a different way from that of the racist perception connected to the modernist historico-racial schema in which bodies of color are objects of distrust, hate, and disgust. For example, consider an individual who cannot see Latinxs otherwise than as "illegals" and "predators," and thus feels disgust whenever they are in his presence. Al-Saji herself provides the example of a teacher's negative physical and emotional response at the sight of a student who usually wears a hijab, even when the student is wearing a high-necked sweater and a bandanna tied at the back of her neck.[23]

The crucial point here is that there is an aspect of racialization that goes beyond the perceptual registering of visible difference and the discursive understandings of such differences—an aspect of racialization that zeros in on the affective response of hate, disgust, and the many other ugly feelings connected to racism that an antiracism law, no matter how powerful, cannot change. This affective component of perception needs to be acknowledged and considered in critical phenomenological analyses of racialized perception. So important is this perception-affect nexus for Al-Saji that she states that "a phenomenology of racialization is a phenomenology of affect."[24] Given these treacherous embodied, affective, yet "invisible" processes, Al-Saji calls for affective responses to negative racialized perception.[25] Lee, following Al-Saji's lead, analyzes how emotions become key in attempts to disrupt ready-made racial associations connected to visible difference.[26] Helen Fielding, another critical phenomenologist committed to finding ways to combat racism, also shifts attention away from traditional rational discourses. As she states, "Attempting to dismantle racist ideology through reason alone is not sufficient for addressing how bodies phenomenally take up racist styles of being that structure the ways they encounter the world and others."[27] We are thus in need of phenomenological analyses that take into consideration the complexity of racialization, including the role of affect in its operations.

Al-Saji's analysis is remarkable in its introduction of the connection between perception and affectivity when grappling with the rigidity and recalcitrance of the "I cannot" of racialization. In fact, as we will see in the next section, it is precisely the affective, specifically an affective hesitation, that Al-Saji sees as opening the possibility for interrupting and transforming racializing habits. In her view, it is an "affective openness" that grounds perceptual habits' dynamism and possibility for improvisation; it is this openness that is closed by the "I cannot" of racialization. In the context of an account of racializing vision, Al-Saji understands visibility/invisibility and figure/ground dyads via a complex perceptual movement in which the eye no longer becomes the main character of the story. That is, while it is still engaged in the operations of vision, these operations are no longer dominated by the eye; they are informed by a more complex entwinement between visual perception and affect. Discourses and imaginaries that stand as the background through which the eye learns to see are tethered to affects, which, in turn, hold the promise for opening "routes for feeling, seeing, and acting differently."[28] There is thus an opening for the possibility for the becoming of affect in the context of negative racializing perception.

Inspired by this critical phenomenological work that points to the crucial connection between perception and affect within specific cultural contexts, I wish to underscore and further develop the role of this affective dimension that, while in these analyses is connected to the operations of the eye at the sight of visible difference, in the following discussions of *Carnalities* is linked to aesthetic practices beyond the visual that support the efforts of racialized, marginalized selves to name themselves despite the colonial gaze. As I write these words, more bodies of color continue to be assaulted, mistreated, and killed in the streets of the United States and beyond. More words are written to denounce and to counter such violence; academic theories on antiracism, antihate, are offered with intellectual rigor as well as with feelings of empathy, distress, and anguish. Yet, as Sartre points out, there is despair in our condition as free human beings insofar as our actions may be undermined by others' choices.[29] In short, while we are making choices that aim at establishing ways of life so that bodies of color are safe and capable of thriving, others are making choices that aim at just the opposite. As we all know (or at least, should be humble enough to admit) our discursive, theoretical interventions only go so far—if they travel at all outside our academic circles. This does not mean that they do not matter. Antiracist work calls for a multipronged approach; an octopus-like approach is needed to combat a multiple-limbed creature of hate. In the next section, I continue to follow Al-Saji's critical phenomenological analysis of racializing perception in its proposal for a slowing down, an affective hesitation, that allows for the possibility of reconfiguring negative racializing habits. Doing so not only reveals the crucial role of affect in forging new perceptual possibilities but also places us in a position to understand how the perception-affect nexus is key in aesthetic practices that make it possible for marginalized racialized selves to name and transform themselves. We cannot afford to bypass the perception-affect nexus, both as understood by theorists of race as well as felt by the very beings that are the object of the racist, colonizing gaze.

HESITATION: SLOWING DOWN AS APERTURE TO THE OTHERWISE

Let us now consider the eyes of Laura Aguilar in her work *Clothed/Unclothed #1* (fig. 1.2) from the *Clothed/Unclothed* series. These are the eyes of a racialized self who, despite a seeming sadness, daringly stares back. These eyes point to a decisive moment in which Aguilar uses the photograph with strength and purpose, effectively producing a counter-visuality that pushes against normative impositions regarding her race, class, gender, and embodiment. As we will see in chapter 3, Aguilar's photographic practice becomes an act of self-making and of communion with her environment as well as a defiance of normative expectations regarding her body, her race, and her queerness. In this instance, though, I would like to point to a particularly interesting feature of the photograph: the way

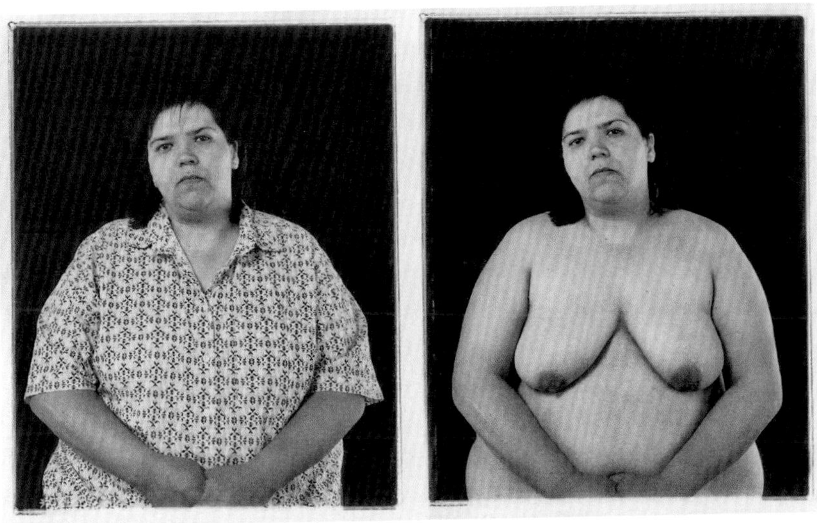

1.2 Laura Aguilar, *Clothed/Unclothed #1*, 1990. Gelatin silver prints. Diptych, 20 × 16 in. Copyright Laura Aguilar Trust of 2016.

aspects of the work prompt a slowing down of perception such that I become more attuned to my expectations and feelings regarding what I am seeing and experiencing beyond the visual.

On the left side of the work, Aguilar wears a printed shirt. On the right side, she is naked. In both images, Aguilar's hands are clasped in the same way, the expression of her mouth is the same, and so is the way her hair falls on her forehead. In both photographs, her eyes are directed to us, viewers, in the same manner: intently, piercingly, daringly.[30] Amelia Jones reads this photograph and others in Aguilar's *Clothed/Unclothed* series as a commentary on race, class, and sexual identification in relation to radical vulnerability."[31] All of the photographs in the series pair photographs of clothed people of color with their unclothed counterparts on the right side. While Aguilar's series indeed displays radical vulnerability insofar as she shows her and her subjects' nakedness in a way that both discloses precarity and strength, for me the nakedness in the photographs also functions at a different level. In this specific example, Aguilar's own nakedness, coupled with her daring look, prompts me to slow down my perception of the photograph. Nakedness here interrupts the multiple familiar expectations of photographic portraits and in so doing slows down perception.

When first encountering the image, I was deeply touched, somehow sensing tremendous sadness in Aguilar but also strength. The way she tightly holds her hands made me nervous. Was she also nervous when taking a photograph of her unclothed self? There are so many rules about not displaying one's nakedness in Latinx culture. Her look—that contemplative look that holds what seems to be a deep sensibility but that is also daring—grabbed me. Her nakedness also made me feel uncomfortable—I was taught well by normative imaginaries and did not expect to see a naked large body, especially that of a Latina/x. So many elements of the work touch me in various ways. Yet the juxtaposition of her clothed and unclothed image, of her holding her hands tightly, of that look, made me pause. How do I affectively react to her nakedness? How am I moved by the contrasts of the clothed and unclothed Aguilar? What is this nakedness in front of me doing? Do I look away, only to look back and start trying to figure out if there are differences between the clothed and unclothed versions of Aguilar? My initial affective responses, including a feeling of being put on the spot, moved me to more engagement with details of the work both affectively and discursively, ultimately, leading me to consider various questions about clothing as a particularized skin of the self, the nakedness of bodies that are traditionally undervalued in society, the relationship between the clothed and unclothed Aguilar, and the dyad of visibility and invisibility as it concerns racialization. But most of all, I found that Aguilar has dared me to slow down, to become attuned to my perception of the work and what it invites me to feel, and to explore.[32]

In her important analysis of racializing perception, Al-Saji makes a crucial intervention in phenomenological discussions on racializing perception, prompting us to consider the benefits of the slowing down of perception. Her analysis is deeply instructive due to her proposal that a perceptual slowing down creates openings for reconfiguring habitual affective responses to visible difference that in racist perception are taken as natural responses to such differences. That is, in her view, the perception-affect nexus not only is a source of negative racialization but also carries with it the possibility for shifting or changing habits. Al-Saji's account of hesitation is consequently vital within the context of critical phenomenology of racialization. As we will see, while for Al-Saji hesitation is ultimately not something that can be directly intended and chosen by us but only indirectly prompted, her proposal is still a daring one, as she recognizes the key potential of hesitation in its connection to affectivity. In this section, I thus center her account of affective hesitation, which she later connects to the aesthetic.

For Al-Saji, the constructive possibilities of the affective rest on the temporal structure associated with affective hesitation or the slowing down of perception which, in her view, becomes the condition for the reconfiguration of negative racialized perceptual habits.[33] Hesitation rests on future possibilities of interrupting racist habits that have been congealed in the past and that inform a subject's lived experience in the present. Inspired by Henri Bergson, Al-Saji understands hesitation as an interval in which there is time for the perceiver to destabilize perceptual habits linked to negative racialization; it is an opening for the possibility of the subject to reconfigure long-held sedimented habits. According to Al-Saji, this interval is opened from within the subject's affective experience rather than coming from without, and it allows for self-awareness, searching, and recollection. That is, hesitation arises when the self registers a perception that is connected to affect. In the slowing down of perception, there is a denaturalization of racializing affect. The feelings connected to the perception of a particular racial visible difference are not registered as the natural way to react. Instead, the habitual perception is interrupted. Thus, Al-Saji states that affect "holds open" the interval of hesitation that opens the possibility for interruption of sedimented habits of perception.[34]

Usually, the ways that we see and feel about racial difference are understood as "natural." Yet in this account the moment of hesitation reveals sociohistorical horizons as part of active embodied processes rather than as unambiguous and incapable of redirection. The interval of hesitation, then, becomes that precious moment of feeling one's way through an experience, the becoming otherwise of the habitual body in an opening that is also a delaying of what is understood as "natural" response, in order to feel and perceive differently from an imposed racist, colonial schema. It is a moment that is also intertwined with memory, with the temporal possibility of destabilizing habits that have become sedimented through time. Recall here how those who hold negative responses to visible differences of racialized selves "cannot" but see these differences in a negative way.

Yet memory becomes key for the critical function of hesitation, for the ability of a self to remember habitual responses of the past and to understand the need to reconfigure these sedimented habits. For Al-Saji, this is the process where affect, as embodied perception, "witnesses" perception and connects it to a memory in the present and to memory in general—which, in turn, links the experience to habits. Habits become occasions to remember as well as events that have the possibility of reconfiguring networks of memories of the past.[35] Memory has a critical function here insofar as it helps to contextualize habits and opens the possibility of interrupting their repetition. Ultimately, according to Al-Saji, temporality both makes habits possible (structuring habits and closing affectivity in racializing habit) and, at the same time, allows for the possibility of their interruption (fracturing habits and opening affectivity in the present during hesitation). Here hesitation becomes "both the ontological ground that makes possible transformations in habit, and the phenomenological opening that can be utilized and supplemented for such change to occur."[36] This is a slowing down in which time, memory, body, perception, habit, affect, and history are intertwined and capable of both further sedimenting colonial visions or stopping, catching a breath, and becoming attuned to that ground of intelligibility, sensibility, and affectability that has heretofore been invisible in racializing perception.

Through the notion of hesitation, Al-Saji answers race theorists such as Shannon Sullivan, who take the possibility of changing racist habits as dependent on a change of environment that creates discomfort and tension for a racist perceiver.[37] According to Al-Saji, a view that holds that a change of habits is dependent on a change of environment needs the possibility of affective hesitation in the first place so as to allow for discomfort and tension. So views that call for a reconfiguration of racial habits such as Sullivan's need to think about the importance of temporality, specifically the working of habits through past experience, not just present experience. This consideration of how habituation is linked to the past is crucial, as racist habituation is linked to specific histories and networks of relations. For a critical stance to be sustained, according to Al-Saji, there needs to be an understanding of "unrecognized attachments and debts to others,"[38] or an understanding of the embeddedness of racial habits in one's relationality and sociality. Critical memory, then, allows for us to consider not just the present but also the weight of the past, while also remaining attuned to the future possibility of interrupting habits.

Al-Saji's account effectively questions the felt immediacy and automaticity of affect that makes it seem as if our habitual responses to difference are simply natural. She ultimately describes two types of hesitation: paralyzing hesitation stemming from internalized habit, which makes the racialized subject expect failure in advance; and responsive hesitation, which has a different relationship to the future, one in which there is indeterminacy in habit that allows for alternative responses and thus the creation of possibilities. Nonetheless, paralyzing hesitation may give rise to responsive hesitation, "a hesitation that makes us think on the way to, and within, action; this hesitation can make us *actional* and no longer *reactional* (to use Fanon's terms), so that 'having taken thought, [one] prepares to act.'"[39] Given the potential to disrupt racist habituation, Al-Saji consequently recommends that the role of hesitation be considered in antiracist practices, fully knowing that it is not sufficient to overcome racist habits but that this affective dimension of racializing perception and its promise for reconfiguring habits must be discussed in phenomenological accounts. She consequently calls for indirect strategies for "fostering hesitation" especially for those who have white privilege.[40]

As we will see in the next chapter, affectivity becomes key in Anzaldúa's analysis of the lived experience of marginalized peoples. She theorizes it as connected to a rupture or arrebato that leads to conocimiento, a complex process of intuitive, perceptual awareness in which there is an intertwining of self and worlds. Importantly, this view can also be expanded through consideration of the ways that slowing down proves to be crucial in processes of self-making and transformation for racialized, marginalized selves, especially with regard to the type of hesitation that is paralyzing for them—those moments when these selves see themselves as always already defined by the colonial gaze. Thus, affective hesitation needs to be understood not only in terms of the perception of dominant subjects but in the very self-perception of negative racialized selves as they continue to experience the ever-present traces of colonialist practices, discourses, and imaginaries. I wish to think and feel-with Al-Saji in order to disclose how, in work such as Anzaldúa's, slowing down is as necessary as it is in Al-Saji's work—despite all their differences in aim and methodology. I also wish to follow Al-Saji's call for critical phenomenology to regard affectivity as a key aspect of perception. I am deeply interested in the role of this temporal interval of affective hesitation, this slowing down that can become an aperture to the otherwise, to other ways of perceiving and being. While my interest in this notion of hesitation is connected to future possibilities in light of the work of Latina feminist phenomenologies such as Anzaldúa's and their view of the aesthetic, in the remainder of this section I take a step back briefly to look at the notion of hesitation in terms of the notion of bracketing, a key element in Edmund Husserl's transcendental phenomenology, but one that critical phenomenologists Lee and Ngo as well as Al-Saji herself question.

When considering racializing perception, Ngo notes that there is a "convergence between representation and phenomena as the figures of 'Latino men as uneducated laborers,' Asian women as 'exotic' and others are 'coded' onto differently racialized bodies." Here I understand this "coding" to have affective responses such as feeling contempt for "uneducated laborers" or desire for "exotic" Asian women. Ngo further states, "If phenomenology purports to return us 'to the things themselves' (per Husserl), then what the analysis of racialized perception shows us is that these 'things' are not simply 'themselves' but are already shaped by, and participate in, discursive practices. In other words, the appearance of a thing and its perception do not occur in some phenomenologically 'pure' way, but rather they are already informed by, and indeed can be put in service of, discursive representations."[41] Transcendental phenomenology is usually described by Husserl's famous dictum "to the things themselves,"[42] which contains a desire for apodictic or certain knowledge as well as a thirst for the discovery of the "essences" of consciousness that are supposed to be the ground for meaning and experience in the first place. To find these essences, Husserl is methodologically committed to a neutralization, bracketing, or "suspension" of the "natural attitude," the everyday, nonphilosophical stance on the world.[43] This methodological move is supposed to guarantee that the essences found are not to be *tainted* by the countless everyday assumptions and presuppositions that subjects hold in the natural attitude. What Ngo makes explicit above is that these so-called "things in themselves" that Husserl is so interested in are already discursively informed. That is, they cannot be understood as pure and neutral and thus detached from social structures; what the eye sees is already informed by cultural discourses and imaginaries. Moreover, we see these discourses and imaginaries as themselves connected to particular affective responses.

According to Al-Saji, the notion of temporal interval plays a significant role in the works of both Husserl and Merleau-Ponty, albeit in different ways. She notes that Husserl's account "insists on the leeway that consciousness feels in relation to the affective pull of 'objects'—without which the free practice of phenomenological bracketing would not be possible."[44] As noted above, this bracketing entails the suspension of the natural attitude in order to carry out a reflection that is to lead to the essential features of consciousness. Moreover, Al-Saji notes that

Merleau-Ponty also needs this leeway when discussing a "scope of life" that allows the subject to step back and distance itself from the world, a type of rupturing with one's familiarity with the world.[45] Al-Saji takes this leeway as presupposed in the activity of phenomenological bracketing in the first place. Yet she is quick to note that Fanon's phenomenology of racialization and anticolonization questions the type of familiarity and comfort of a world in which there is such a temporal leeway where the self can distance itself from the world.[46] Put differently, Fanon's phenomenology shows the deep problems with Husserl's as well as Merleau-Ponty's methodological appeal to a suspension or bracketing of the natural attitude. This point also connects with Ngo's claim above that there is not a phenomenological pure perception that is not already informed by discursive representations that may be demeaning and undermining regarding bodies of color. Not only are the so-called "things in themselves" already discursively informed. They are also affectively informed given that, as Al-Saji notes, the "I cannot" of racializing perception does not refer merely to visual perception but also to the "receptivity of vision: its ability to be affected, to be touched by that which lies beyond or beneath its habitual objectifying schemas."[47]

In previous work, I discuss multiplicitous marginalized selves as not experiencing everydayness by way of a transparent, prereflective being-in-worlds; rather, they are continuously experiencing ruptures of everydayness that lead not only to thematic or conscious reflection but also to a sense of not being-at-ease,[48] a point that aligns with the idea that the experience of everydayness for marginalized selves does not easily allow for a leeway in which we can distance ourselves from the world such that we can bracket or suspend the natural attitude, whether this suspension is thought in terms of content of the natural attitude or in terms of how a subject approaches the world in everydayness. That is, the experience of these selves is not transparent or taken for granted nor can it be put in suspension in order to reflect on the things themselves or the essences of consciousness that Husserl was interested in. As Al-Saji notes, for racialized subjects, sensation is always already informed by the wounds of colonization. When the racialized subject touches a surface, she does not discover her own lived body as Husserl's analysis of touching shows, but, quoting Saidiya Hartman, Al-Saji states that the racialized subject discovers a "carcass" and "hollowed-out stereotypes." She concludes, "Neither can colonization be bracketed to reveal a core of sense, as if racism were an afterthought; nor can it be put out of play to conceive a universalizable subject free of historical violence."[49] The racialized self is already living the wounds of what Al-Saji calls "colonial duration," and it is hesitation with its room to breathe that may allow for reconfigurations of the past.[50]

In sum, Al-Saji's analysis makes explicit a crucial component of a phenomenology of racialized perception: the affectivity that is tethered to habitual perception. She thus reorients the discussion of the phenomenology of racial perception away from an overemphasis on the eye, on visuality, and discloses the role of affect in racialized perception, a disclosure that connects perception to a multivalent field of affectivity. Indeed, for her, Fanon's phenomenology is not a phenomenology of visuality but a phenomenology of affect. It is this attunement to the perception-affect nexus, to the different ways racialized bodies are sensuously connected to the world and thus are wounded by (Anzaldúa) and glued to (Al-Saji) the ravages of colonization, to the wounds of colonial duration, to the humiliation and indignities of all types of racism, that prompts me to consider what for me is a familiar side of the negative connection between perception and affect, the views and practices of the negative racialized self and the ways she is able to name or construct herself despite all that stands in her path—hegemonic social structures, colonial and colonized imaginaries, racist habits, and internalized shame—in particular, the way she can mold herself through carnal creative practices. In the following I begin a discussion of how the aesthetic becomes relevant in the opening of possibilities of the otherwise by way of Al-Saji's appeal to affective hesitation as prompted by works of art.

Affected by Art

Martín Alcoff reminds us that racialized identity is linked not only to one's public identity but also to one's experience of selfhood. Ngo adds that the stress of being the object of constant racism gives rise to an existential instability in which the racialized experience of the body schema is inherently unsettled both spatially and temporally. As Ngo states, "As a racialized body, one stands in multiple relations to and perspectives upon the self, in a way that disrupts the spatial cohesion of the body schema."[51] The result of this experience is the feeling of fragmentation in which a body experiences itself from "this side" *and* "that side," becoming overly reflective of how one's body parts are taking up space. Ngo cites George Yancy's well-known example of the "elevator effect" in which a Black man becomes especially conscious of his Black body as he enters an elevator and a white woman in the elevator responds by tightening her body and clutching her purse.[52] Despite some complicated issues raised by the example, particularly as it engages the intersection of race and gender, it shows how racism is registered in the very operations of the body (of course, in different ways for a Black subject than for a white woman).[53] Not only is the racialized body judged insofar as it occupies a particular spatiality. According to Ngo, the body of color is also temporally affected as it is ahead or "before" itself insofar as racializing perception has already prescribed an essence to it.[54] For example, in a racist society, a Black body is always seen as having a threatening nature or as inferior. This alleged essence in turn is one that a racialized body may internalize, thus becoming thoroughly affected spatially and temporally by racist perceptions from within and without.

If we return to the figure/ground analogy previously discussed, we have a colonialist historico-racial schema that serves as a ground with one's very self as the racialized abject figure. The racist gaze helped by embodied habits connected to this colonialist historico-racial schema is directed toward one's own visible differences as well as one's ability to love, appreciate, and respect oneself. How then can there be a possibility of disrupting the negative affect that flows from the negative racialization within? As we will see, an answer to this question sets the stage for understanding the importance of creative practices for self-care and for destabilizing the power of negative racialization for selves that, like Anzaldúa, have to continually endure the colonial gaze within and without.

Al-Saji's notion of hesitation in the context of works of art offers an initial way to tackle this important question as her critical phenomenology teaches us to pay attention to the crucial perception-affect nexus and to the aesthetic as offering possibilities for reconfiguring modes of racializing perception. I appreciate the way Al-Saji both follows and disrupts the phenomenological tradition in its well-known interest in aesthetic works. Classical figures in phenomenology have provided important analyses of aesthetics—Beauvoir and Sartre highlighting the crucial political role of writing; Merleau-Ponty associating the very idea of philosophy with painting; and Heidegger granting the poet the special status as the interpreter of being. Al-Saji, however, underscores the importance of art for a critical phenomenology invested in countering negative racialized perception. As noted, *Carnalities* is in part an answer to her call for affective responses to deal with racialized perception. In so doing it also offers the point of view of those who experience the wounds and wounding of racism on their own bodies, and who, against the odds, creatively tend to themselves as well as disrupt the normative, racist eye.

Similar to Fanon's example of watching a film and explaining that he waits for himself as he expects the stereotypical Black character to appear in the movie, Al-Saji narrates her own experience while in an exhibition of paintings of Arab women by Benjamin Constant, who portrays these women as highly eroticized and as objects of consumption for the white gaze. The experience is a dizzying one for Al-Saji; she feels she can hardly breathe and feels enclosed by the "tightening of the circles of racialization through sexualization" and is "bogged down in a viscous colonial duration."[55] Yet it is the experience of a photograph by Yasmina G. Bouziane (*Untitled No. 6, alias The Signature*) in the same exhibition that points to the way an artwork may introduce hesitation, even if briefly, as an interval that allows for breathing. Bouziane's photograph portrays an image of herself from her own point of view, which, in turn, momentarily disrupts the suffocating experience created by Constant's paintings that unfortunately continue to dominate the space of the gallery. Nonetheless, the photograph prompts hesitation, a "leeway for reconfiguration," thus creating the possibility for seeing Arab women against the grain of normative colonial imaginaries.[56] Yet another artwork in a different gallery, *This Is General Gordon* by Bob and Roberta Smith, commissioned to be exhibited next to the more traditional, colonialist painting, *General Gordon's Last Stand* by George William Joy, serves for Al-Saji as a more effective example of prompting hesitation.[57] The work is a sculpture made of found objects as well as text recalling the historical events associated with General Gordon's death. In this second example, hesitation is prompted by the viewer walking around the sculpture counterclockwise in order to read the text connected to the history of a colonial past. The circular motion unsettles Al-Saji's body, affectively connecting her to a past in a present that also opens possibilities for reconfiguration.

I take the crux of Al-Saji's analyses of these experiences to be the importance of affect at the moment of hesitation that opens room for reconfiguration of racializing perceptual habits. I would like to expand Al-Saji's account of hesitation in the context of the aesthetic by suggesting that another aspect of experience connected to possibilities of disrupting entrenched colonialist visions is what I consider the medium-affect nexus specifically connected to creative practices. This medium-affect nexus has to do with the way particular elements affectively touch and inspire perceivers or call them to creative endeavors leading to reconfigurations of perception.[58] *Medium* is to be understood in the sense that an element mediates the relation between perceiver and perceived as well as the way in which it may be used as an artistic medium. Here we might think of *unbounded* perception not necessarily connected to sedimented habits. This is the matter of adumbration, inspiration, and spontaneity—it is a moment when the medium touches the perceiver, sometimes leading her to mold, shape, or to simply be led by it in different ways, as if there were a secret communication between them.[59] It is a moment that I take as carnal, as including the intimacy between self and medium. While creative practices are informed by sedimented habits and by reconfigurations of those habits, there are moments in which a slowing down of perceptual experience becomes a moment of deep affectivity, but in this case a letting oneself be moved by wood, stone, light, and so on, or slowing down to register how one is being affected by materials or elements beyond them. Paradoxically, it is a moment of breathing, of deep sensation so as to be affected by a medium that, in turn, may open possibilities for a self who has internalized the colonial eye to attend to herself and to see herself otherwise than the racist eye prescribes. Echoing Al-Saji, breathing stands for the moment of hesitation, a slowing down in which, in my view, perception also heightens.

Al-Saji describes temporality as having texture, weight, and materiality[60]—yet she writes about "hesitation that makes us think on the way to, and within, action."[61] When discussing Fanon, she states, "Fanon's socio-diagnostic shows how phenomenology needs to redress and decolonize social structures, to be world transformation, in order to *create the leeway to reflect*. It cannot assume a transparent, unobstructed interval" (my emphasis).[62] While hesitation is part of a process of embodied habit formation that includes prereflective processes, the disruption or configuration of naturalizing, essentializing racializing habits introduces a more reflective approach. In addition, the critical function of hesitation is, in Al-Saji's view, connected to a memory that in the moment of hesitation may be reconfigured. The medium-affect nexus, however, is not always connected to reflection or memory. An analysis of Anzaldúa's aesthetic practice in chapter 2 will reveal a more complex account of the unboundedness of this medium-affect nexus. Yet it is worthwhile to consider the ways it may be thought in relation to Al-Saji's notion of hesitation prompted by aesthetic works.

While Al-Saji interprets her experience of Bouziane's photograph in terms of hesitation, it may also be read in terms of the medium-affect nexus, in this case an experience of being pierced by an image written with light. As noted in the introduction, following Barthes's characterization of the photograph as a carnal medium, as capable of touching us affectively, I interpret the photograph as carnal.[63] While in the account of hesitation an interval is created in which Al-Saji can become, as she says, unstuck from the colonial past, in this instance, she is grabbed by a particular photograph or by a *punctum* that calls her. For her the photograph becomes a prosthetic that she can carry, promising "a resistant means of revisioning the images I had just walked through and felt swallowed up by."[64] While in her experience, the photograph opens room for hesitation, it may also be seen as piercing her and calling to a moment of deep sensation that is not necessarily connected to the possibility of further reflection. The medium-affect nexus is still connected to the perception-affect nexus insofar as the self is habituated to connect perception with affectivity and is affected by the perception of different materials and their arrangement. The difference is that in this case the self may be moved, inspired, and so on, by the very perception of the medium as a possibility that is difficult to explain and to theorize about but that may nevertheless be an important component of the perception of aesthetic works.

The point here is not to undermine the important work that hesitation, according to Al-Saji, may do by way of reflection prompted by works of art. It is to recognize other layers of perception of artworks that may also be at play. Ultimately, it may be the case that affective hesitation connected to perceptual habitual responses becomes associated with further reflection, especially if the reconfiguration of habit rests on being aware of specific actions in particular circumstances in the past. Even my own response to Aguilar's *Clothed/Unclothed #1*, which I also read as prompting a slowing down of my perception, led to further reflection. Nonetheless, it is necessary to think about the possibility of the affective power of the elements or media themselves (the medium-affect nexus) and their ability to move the one who perceives them. As we will see, for our purposes, the relevance of the medium-affect nexus becomes more apparent as we consider how marginalized selves are able to name themselves and transform themselves through engaging in carnalities, in creative practices informed by the self's attunement to various elements and also to the cultural, historical, and the spiritual.

Despite its well-known function as a mirror of nature and evidentiary medium, the photograph is able to touch the one who perceives it—that is, light can affectively wound or uplift. It may also lead to moments of self-naming and transformation. One of the main aims of *Carnalities* is precisely to disclose the various ways the photograph, as carnal, can be used in processes of self-making, transformation, and mourning by Latinxs. I have lingered with Al-Saji's experience of looking at Bouziane's photograph in order to show how her critical phenomenology appreciates but decenters the reign of the visual by introducing the key perception-affect nexus, and to show how it also captures the importance of the affectivity of perception of art objects themselves, thus suggesting the aesthetic as a vital component within critical phenomenological analyses of perception in general and racializing perception in particular.

In the following, I turn to the view that the experience of looking at Bouziane's photograph stands, as Al-Saji says, as "a resistant means of revisioning the images."[65] While there is sense that such a photograph as well as the experience of it as described by Al-Saji can indeed be considered resonant or resistant—as draining the power of the normative gaze—there are other moments in the experience, quiet moments that are not necessarily connected to resistance but that are nevertheless vital. With the help of Kevin Quashie and Anzaldúa, I wish to tease out how the experience of hesitation may be part of what Quashie calls "quiet." I think of that moment when Al-Saji engages with the photograph, when she is being overwhelmed and suffocated by the orientalist images that she has previously experienced, and her sense of being able to breathe again, even if momentarily, as a deeply personal, intimate moment—a movement from eye to mouth. What does it mean to call the experience resistant? Does the appeal to a notion of resistance determine what the experience is about, namely a resistance that people of color are expected to perform in the context of publicness, as Quashie would say?

In an analysis that is particularly concerned with the association of Blackness with always having to be motivated by strife and a struggle with racism, Quashie questions the association of Black experience with the public expectation of being resistant. Doing so, Quashie notes, flattens Black experience and undervalues the interiority of Blackness that points to Black humanity, "the interior aliveness, the reservoir of human complexity that is deep inside."[66] He thus calls for a consideration of an aesthetic of the quiet, housed in the "interiority" of the self, the aspect of Blackness that continues to be missed and undermined by the association of Black culture and Black identity as always performing resistant acts.[67] As he puts it, "Quiet . . . is a metaphor for the full range of one's inner life—one's desires, ambitions, hungers, vulnerabilities, fears. The inner life is not apolitical or without social value, but neither is it determined entirely by publicness."[68] Moreover, quiet is connected to a sense of "the one" that is not equivalent to the notion of individuality of liberal humanism or to the notion of selfhood. Rather, according to Quashie, "oneness is the human being as a life force . . . the abundance of will, hunger, fear that propels each person through the world."[69] With attention to the crucial differences between Black experience and the experience of other racial, ethnic, and religious minorities, I wish to suggest that we think about Quashie's aesthetic of quiet in connection to other marginalized groups, who, to different degrees, are also expected to translate their experiences of identity to resistant acts, as Quashie points out is certainly the case for African Americans.

I take Quashie's theorization of quiet and of Black aliveness as doing the crucial work of reminding us of the potential for life as well as joy that is not just a matter of futurity for people of color, especially for Black people, but a matter of the present.[70] That is, Quashie is doing the crucial work of not letting notions of "oneness" and "interiority" be confined solely to modernist interpretations in which they cannot be thought as connected to relationality, community, and collectivity. Inspired by Hortense Spillers, he claims that "oneness asserts the right of a human being to be just that—a human being—and this assertion privileges inner life. And yet the interiority of oneness does not correlate with being immune to or isolated from the social world"; rather, it is about "having a license to be of a whole world."[71] This is the human not as the center of the universe or the earth, but in relation to worlds, as complicated as those relations are. In other words, an aesthetics of quiet marked by "the one" and by "interiority" does not preclude the possibility of relationality or of deep connection to the environment and all living beings. It is a matter of tracking features of Black life (and other people of color's lives) that resist the confinement of our lives to death, violence, and woundedness, as this vision may, as Lindsey Stewart importantly argues, perpetuate racism.[72] While in *Carnalities* I will point to bodies of color as bodies of sorrow, I do so while also understanding the features of their quiet life that are both wounding but also have the possibility of aliveness, even joyfulness.

In the context of Al-Saji's discussion of orientalist presentations of Arab women and of her own experience in the gallery, it would be easy to make a connection here between the claim to identity and the need to forge a resistant practice, one that would lose sight of the moment of what

Quashie calls interiority or quiet. Yet I see Al-Saji's experience as pointing to a moment of quiet. While I do not wish to undermine louder or more resonant practices of resistance that follow from the creative endeavors and experiences of marginalized and negative racialized selves, I appreciate Quashie's point that an emphasis on the resistant mode or possibilities of an action may lead to missing or underappreciating other aspects of the experience—namely the intimate and deeply personal, what he calls "interior" moments—that are also so much part of the experience of selves that are constantly navigating oppressive environments.[73] Here Anzaldúa stands with Quashie when in *Borderlands / La Frontera* she states, "The struggle has always been inner, and is played out in the outer terrains."[74] This "inner" work that is so important for liminal, borderland selves, however, does not preclude Anzaldúa's understanding of her connection to other beings, human and nonhuman, including spiritual worlds, that is so important in her work.

As we will see in more detail in chapter 2, Anzaldúa also emphasizes the "inner" when discussing the Coatlicue state, one of the stages of her account of conocimiento, her name for creative, relational, expansive awareness connected to creative practices. In this case she states, "By keeping the conscious mind occupied or immobile, the germination work takes place in the deep, dark earth of the unconscious."[75] María Lugones picks up on the importance of this immobile but constructive moment and develops a view of germinative stasis, an immobility that is productive and may lead to resistant moves or what Lugones regards as "responses."[76] Lugones states that the "quiet *ensimismado* (into one's self)" can be conceived as a state of germination for possibilities of liberation.[77] In an early consideration of the relationship of motion, stasis, and resistance, she also states, "Sometimes resistant movement involves a critical consciousness, although a great deal of resistance springs not from articulations of oppression but rather from strategies of daily survival that often do not involve a reflective stance against oppression."[78] Even though both Anzaldúa and Lugones are committed to understandings of selfhood and subjectivity that are deeply relational, they are nevertheless also interested in the phenomenological experience of the lived experience of a self that, as complex as it is, still experiences life intimately. They recognize the significance of the more immediate and personal inner life of the self. While Lugones's reading of germinative stasis is ultimately concerned with the development of an explicit relational, political resistance, the moment of germination can be understood as quiet.

The point of reading the breathtaking moment of hesitation in light of Quashie's aesthetic of quiet is to underscore the personal, sensuous intimacy or affective dimension of hesitation, although, of course, hesitation does not merely entail this moment. As we have seen, according to Al-Saji, it also encompasses key movements of reflection informed by memory that may or may not lead to a resistant stance. Sometimes the very moment of quiet can be interpreted as an altogether different type of resistance, one that does not require a public or the expectations connected to a specific identity category. These thinkers' consideration of the inner life of the self make possible an understanding of the complexity of hesitation. It also proves helpful in understanding Anzaldúa's creative practice as a carnal aesthetics as presented in chapter 2. While I wholeheartedly agree with Quashie that we must think about quiet moments (what he reads as moments beyond resistance), these moments, as Anzaldúa and Lugones note, may also be germinative and might be associated with actions that may be deemed resonant or resistant to various degrees. Thus, there is a destabilization of a hard distinction between quiet moments and the different types of loudness or resonant potential that our actions carry. Quashie himself states that quiet "may appear public and have and affect social and political meaning, challenge our counter social discourse, yet none of this is its aim or meaning."[79] Thought in terms of the notion of quiet inner work and germinative stasis, hesitation in the context of creative works becomes a carnal act that discloses the complex intimacy between the perceiver and the perceived.

As we have seen, critical phenomenologists show that visual operations of racialization reside deep within our sinews and muscles, in bodily habits that remain tacit. These theorists also point to perception beyond mere sensation, crucially showing what we might call the intimacy of perception, the nexus between perception and affect, thus calling for affective responses to negative racialization. Al-Saji's account of hesitation effectively expands Martín Alcoff's insights about racializing perception, especially as connected to visible differences, and strengthens phenomenological accounts of such perception by offering possibilities of altering negative racializing habits through hesitation. The "I cannot" within and without may be unsettled; "I cannot see Latinos as other than maids and gardeners" and "I cannot see myself as other than what the white eye sees me" do not remain fixed, "natural" viewpoints connected to negative habits of racializing perception. Al-Saji's description of her experience in the museum is striking, both in terms of her explanation of the way that she suffers from what she calls the affective weight of colonization, the dizzying, overwhelming discomfort prompted by racist depictions of Arab women in Constant's paintings, as well as the manner in which another work of art, a photograph, allows for a vital slowing down that gives her room to breathe. Importantly, Al-Saji's analysis paves the way in critical phenomenology for a shift from an emphasis on visibility toward a multivalent approach that highlights affect as a crucial component of perception. Her account of hesitation read alongside the notion of the medium-affect nexus, Quashie's view on quiet, and Anzaldúa's inner work, marks a most complex and intimate, personal experience—one in which a self gets to breathe even if just for a moment. It is also an experience that contributes to the possibility of draining the power of dominant forces, thus sustaining those who constantly navigate unwelcoming environments monitored by the eye of coloniality. Yet we cannot underestimate the paradoxical strength and sustenance of those short, intimate moments—the inner work of being alive—those times when our breathing is not shallow and anxious but measured, deep, and open to mouthly perception.

Al-Saji crucially reminds us that bodies of color do not have the possibility of bracketing colonial duration, the glue that, following Fanon, she regards as adhering to the colonized. Yet racialized selves who continue to endure the wounds of colonization experience a disruption of normative perception in the midst of marginalization—thus affectively and effectively destabilizing not just the colonizing eye but colonizing and colonized ways of being and sensing. I follow critical phenomenologists and other theorists of color in order to show how bodies of color care for, name, and transform themselves in the face of negative racialization practices, structures, and imaginaries both in quiet and resonant ways. In *Carnalities* I wish to point to the carnal practices of Latinxs that are already, against all odds, attending to their inner lives as well as defying the racist gaze, as Anzaldúa does by way of her carnal writing. In chapter 2 I discuss the movement away from the eye that has started in this discussion and direct it to the mouth, or, rather, to an intertwining of eye, mouth, and other senses—to a mouth that touches as it licks, makes sounds as it moves, that is connected to smell as it tastes—to an ever more receptive, sensuous way of being that allows for self-naming and self-transformation, and, as Anzaldúa shows, to creative acts of writing "with your tongues of fire."[80]

TWO

TO BE A MOUTH

Anzaldúan Carnalities

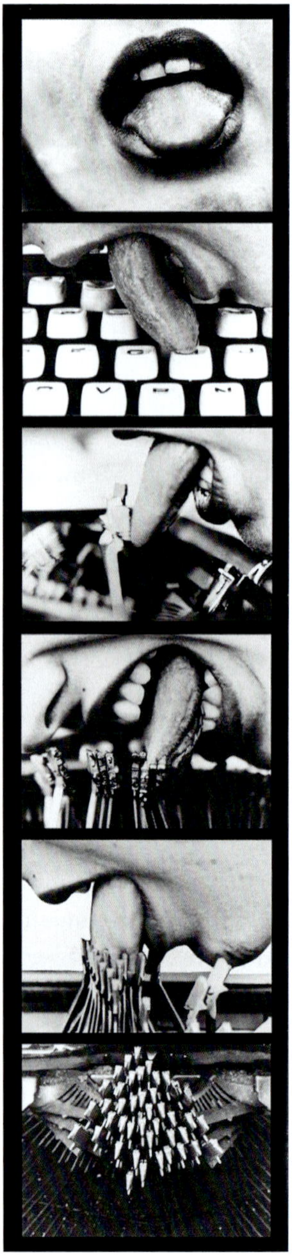

Poem. Tongue as fragile bridge, being-in-*words*, sensing, making self. Sound of typebars, metallic and cold—delicate, powerful tongue. Words will come.

This skin of light speaks to me, calls me, seduces me. It pierces me, the Barthesian *punctum* of a tongue stretched thin, pulled by cutting metal that demands expression. "Poem" paralyzes me—yet also moves me to speak, if not words, other disclosures that bring to light Latina/x bodies naming themselves by way of flesh*and*blood creative practices. As the typebars stand alone, each representing one letter, they must be put together to form arrangements of words that express not only what we see, feel, and think, but who we are. The creative process is one of re-membering—putting together all the parts of our body so as to get a sense of some kind of whole—in the same way that Coyolxauhqui, the dismembered Aztec goddess of the moon, can be put together after she has been torn to pieces.[1] And so many bodies of color are torn to pieces by the prying, racist gaze . . .

The word was born
in the blood,
it grew in the dark body, pulsing,
and took flight with the lips and mouth.
PABLO NERUDA, "The Word," in *Fully Empowered*

My love of images—mesquite flowering, the wind,
Ehécatl, whispering its secret knowledge, the fleeting
images of the soul in fantasy—and words, my passion for
the daily struggle to render them concrete in the world
and on paper, to render them flesh, keeps me alive.
GLORIA ANZALDÚA, *Borderlands / La Frontera*

To be a mouth—the cost is too high—her whole life
enslaved to that devouring mouth. Todo pasaba por
esa boca, el viento, el fuego, los mares y la Tierra.
GLORIA ANZALDÚA, *Borderlands / La Frontera*

Soy la que escribe y se escribe. [I am the one
who writes and is written.]
GLORIA ANZALDÚA, *Light in the Dark*

Everything passed through her "devouring mouth"—wind, fire, the seas and the earth, says Gloria Anzaldúa, the writer of borderlands, bridges, sandbars, and cenotes.[2] This mouth, this point of contact between her embodied self and what exists in this and other realms, interests me.[3] I consider the mouth as a portal and point of intimacy, between selves and earth- and spirit-bodies. In this chapter, I thus write about mouthly or multisensory perception as connected to creative processes that place marginalized selves in spatial maps as well as maps of being—in crossings and journeys of transformation. Here I elaborate on the affective dimension of perception discussed in chapter 1 in order to introduce the notion of *carnalities* that is constitutive of a *carnal aesthetics*. Carnalities are multisensory, multimodal, multivalent creative practices informed by the intertwining between self and worlds, and through which liminal, racialized selves construct, care for, and transform themselves in movements

2.1 (*opposite*) Lenora de Barros, *Poema*, 1979. Six black-and-white inkjet prints on paper, 11¾ × 55 in. Photo: Fabiana de Barros. Copyright the artist.

of the otherwise, in other ways of being and sensing. They are informed by the perception-affect nexus—the way perception in general becomes connected to affective responses through processes of habituation—and the medium-affect nexus—the manner in which an element touches or inspires the self in creative, artistic practices. When Anzaldúa states, "Escribo con la tinta de mi sangre,"[4] her writing with bloody ink is made possible by the mouthly or multisensory perception that informs her path to conocimiento: a creative, intuitive expansive awareness or "knowing" that is deeply relational and highlights the intertwining of self and worlds. Anzaldúa states, "A heightened consciousness or awareness that I call 'conocimiento' and some call 'love' (which may be the same thing) stirs the artist to take action, propels her toward the act of making. This conocimiento initiates the relationship between self-knowledge and creative work. *Because the artist must keep watch on her inner responses, she becomes more aware, more alive, and thus she 'makes' the story of herself as she makes her art*" (my emphasis).[5] For Anzaldúa, conocimiento is about expanded consciousness, a deep spirituality, and intertwining with earthly and spiritual worlds.[6] It is about love and being alive, despite wounds, traumas, whirlwinds, and arrebatos. It is about inner work and "public acts," creative and/or spiritual practices carried out for the purposes of personal and social change understood as spiritual activism.[7] In this chapter, I highlight Anzaldúa's process of making herself through the carnality of writing, while in the next chapter I discuss Anzaldúa's notion of border arte, her explicit discussion on art-making from a place of liminality. I trace the process of being made more alive by conocimiento, which I understand as a mouthly process, as a movement in which all the senses become deeply, affectively attuned to the self's situation, inner life and multiple relationships, human and nonhuman.

In the first section, I discuss how the crucial connection between affect and perception, described in chapter 1 in the context of racializing perception, is connected to what I consider an *affective mapping* in Anzaldúa's "path to conocimiento" as explained in her essay: "now let us shift . . . conocimiento . . . [to] inner work, public acts." I take up the key notion of arrebato or rupture that, according to Anzaldúa, constitutes the first stage of conocimiento. Subsequently, I analyze the possibilities of countering the racist gaze as emerging in nepantla and the Coatlicue state. Of particular importance here is an analysis of Anzaldúa's view that there is a "suspension" of usual frames of reference in this latter state. Conocimiento emerges as a process that opens possibilities of self-perception and of countering the colonizing gaze and the racialization that congeals othered human beings into types and essences. In section 2, I discuss how conocimiento, as affective mapping, provides further insight into the destabilization of normative perception. While critical phenomenologists such as Al-Saji focus on an important reconfiguration of habits, Anzaldúa's view of conocimiento points to additional insights on how shifts in perception happen due to an attunement to the spiritual. The role of re-membering, of putting together the pieces of the self that has been torn apart by violence and oppression—as if we were putting back together Coyolxauhqui the moon goddess—becomes an entry into the perceptually expansive, affect-laden, relational inner work that, according to Anzaldúa, allows for tending to ourselves, transformation, crossings to other ways of being and sensing, and ultimately to what she calls "public acts" or expressions of spiritual mestizaje. As she states, "My struggle has always been to combine the inner work of the soul with outer service in the world."[8] In this view, conocimiento propels the self to create in both germinative stasis and in motion.

In this chapter, we will follow the shift started in chapter 1 from a perceptual emphasis on ocularity to the broader sensuousness of affective mapping, to an aesthetics guided by the mouth—in short, a multisensorial engagement with various elements (yes, the essential ones: earth, water, wind, and fire) and others to forge one's identity through ink and paper as Anzaldúa does and, as we will see in the following chapters of this book, through writing with light. Ultimately, Anzaldúa's creative practice can be seen as a *carnal aesthetics* composed of carnalities, multisensory, multimodal, creative practices of deep perception attuned to the intertwining of self and worlds. By way of carnalities, liminal selves are able to care for and transform themselves in ways that destabilize racializing perceptions that naturalize visual difference for hegemonic, colonizing purposes.

THE MOUTH AS PORTAL TO AFFECTIVE MAPPING

As noted in chapter 1, critical phenomenological explanations of racializing perception by Linda Martín Alcoff, Alia Al-Saji, Emily S. Lee, and Helen Ngo rely on a complex play of figure/ground and visibility/invisibility in which perception of racialized beings is always already informed by a historico-cultural-contextual background informed by coloniality. As Al-Saji shows, the "I cannot" of racialization is part of the experience of racialized perception in which perception and affect intertwine such that *to see* race in differently racialized bodies is also *to feel* about them, to be affected by them in ways informed by a modernist, racist, colonialist vision. This "I cannot" is also part of the negative racialized self's own perception. For example, it lives in Anzaldúa's body, leading her to feel shame about herself, her skin color, her language, and various aspects of her many cultures. It is not only Anzaldúa that feels this way. So many of us, people of color, carry this "I cannot" about our own selves that is such a heavy toll to bear.

Through her creative process, however, Anzaldúa manages to name herself in a way that does not follow the prescriptions of those whose vision sediment her into an othered being, an unwanted type, a problem. She fashions and constructs herself through her writing, not in the kind of creation that happens as if one were to lift oneself by one's bootstraps—we are hopefully beyond such toxic fictions—but in mythico-relational creation.[9] Her writing is informed by her experience, itself connected to her communities and their histories and myths. As she states, "I write the myths in me, the myths I am, the myths I want to become."[10] Through this process, Anzaldúa can be said to disrupt the "I cannot" of her own racialization, the internalized dominant, neocolonial gaze that becomes part of her life experience in the difficult yet fertile life of the borderlands.

Importantly, for Anzaldúa, what is a deeply interpersonal project is also a deeply personal one. Even though in her account there is not a sharp distinction between inner and outer domains, she is still very interested in capturing deeply intimate moments and processes (inner work) in which she experiences wounding. This is one of the most important aspects of Anzaldúa's creative process and of her appeal to readers: her prose disclosing her inner struggles also seems to reach them directly, as if it were being addressed specifically to each one of them. Here relationality and intersubjectivity do not preclude such deep experiences of the personal or the "I." Recalling the preceding chapter's discussion of Kevin Quashie's view on quiet, it is possible to understand Anzaldúa as also capturing quiet moments of life at the limen—although she is also clearly searching for more resonant, resistant possibilities that counter colonial impositions.

Anzaldúa narrates herself into being, her poems pointing to, as Quashie would say, her *aliveness*.[11] Like his important aesthetics of the quiet,[12] Quashie's analysis of aliveness is an homage to the humanity, complexity, richness, fear, and hunger of Blackness in a world that reduces being Black to mere negation or to public, political acts of resistance. I am inspired by his analysis, especially when he takes aesthetics as a "form of life," as "a schema for considering the aliveness of phenomena and the phenomena for aliveness" as well as searching for the "animating capacities evident in the art object."[13] I take Anzaldúa's poems and self-narratives as also pointing to aliveness, to the spirit of Latinx life even in the context of denigration and violence against Chicanxs and other Latinx people in the United States. Here I am interested in the sensibility and affectivity of aliveness. Although as noted in the previous chapters, there is not always a strong distinction between quiet and resonant practices, in this chapter my analysis moves farther away from quiet as theorized by Quashie, as I discuss more explicit resonant attempts at countering the normative eye. Yet I wish to hold on to Quashie's key insights about remembering quietness as well as the need to dwell with the manner in which creative production animates the "to be" of people of color rather than their nonbeing.

Having learned from Martín Alcoff, Lee, Ngo, and Al-Saji about the importance of sedimented habits of perceptions of racial visible difference, and about the key role of affect in such perception—in particular Al-Saji's movement away from the visual in understanding negative racialized perception—it is imperative that we take into consideration the role of affect in the possibility of destabilizing the power of negative racialization in various practices, including aesthetic production. Similar to Martín Alcoff's call for new ways of seeing, we might say that Al-Saji calls for new ways of being affected that become possible by way of the modification of previously sedimented habits as well as by aesthetic experience. She calls for responses to racism at the level of affect, pointing to her experience of artworks as giving her the possibility for hesitation, an interval in which a possibility is open for reconfiguration of sedimented habits involved in negative racialization.

Following Al-Saji's point about the importance of the aesthetic in reconfiguring habituation, I wish to follow the perception-affect and medium-affect nexuses as they inform Anzaldúa's creative practice. I am interested in the "I cannot" of the negatively racialized self, the way people of color view themselves through the internalized colonial eye. I wish to underscore aesthetics, especially when it is no longer conceived in its traditional sense as informed by a European standard of beauty and by disinterestedness but as engaged, embodied, affective, and informed by multisensory perception—as *aesthesis* or perception. Anzaldúa's use of creativity to deal with what Ngo considers the existential and temporal instability of racialized bodies, or what Al-Saji describes as the stickiness of colonial duration, is particularly insightful as she presents a detailed account of her lived experience of fragmented life at the limen and the way her creative writing allows not only for survival but also for transformation and resistance in this precarious space. As Anzaldúa states, "The creative process is an agency of transformation."[14]

In this section, I discuss Anzaldúa's account of conocimiento as carnal and anchored in a mouthly perception that allows for what I call affective mapping. The carnal here is not merely about embodiment but about an embodied self that is intertwined with worlds, what I have described as flesh*and*blood. Conocimiento leads Anzaldúa to affectively map herself within her environment and sense every ache, hurt, and pain that goes through her so as to release words, writing in black ink and red paint, in blood, that makes it possible for her not only to survive, but to name herself and even to transform herself in a way that honors her desires, cultures, and communities as well as unconscious and spiritual elements. Mapping here is not the exercise of cartographers looking into cutting up Earth into sections for the purposes of extraction, settler colonialism, and imperial desires. Instead, affective mapping is a sensuous dwelling with environments and worlds, where the self captures connections or dis-connections with herself, others, and different environments and worlds through affective registers. Moreover, I discuss how the Anzaldúan stages of conocimiento include not just movement but also germinative stasis—a stage that, similarly to Al-Saji's account of hesitation discussed in chapter 1, requires a temporal slowing down of experience so as to be able to engage in deep perception that readies the self for difficult, sometimes impossible, crossings.

Ultimately, the elaboration of a carnal aesthetics as suggested by Anzaldúa's work and further elaborated in this work constitutes a response to critical phenomenologists' call for accounts that recognize the importance of the affective in the context of racializing perception.[15] Unfortunately, I remain pessimistic about our ability to dismantle racist ideologies and perception given the manner in which they suffuse our very bodies as well as so many aspects of society. My aim here is not to propose a political project for the purposes of resisting racism. Rather, it is a pointing to the capacities of the aesthetic, to give us, Latinxs, life. In so doing,

I show that there are disruptions in the fabric of coloniality, even if only for short moments. Nevertheless, these are vital moments for people of color in their daily comings and goings in the geographies of abjection that make up racist worlds. Anzaldúa finds these vital moments through conocimiento, a creative, intuitive knowing that I read as a carnal aesthetics that allows for personal and relational transformation not constrained by the racist eye.

Conocimiento as Mouthly Creation

Anzaldúa's oeuvre is prompted by the deepest attunement to an embodied, affective carnal sense, of the intertwining of her*self*, her environment, and her relations with other human and nonhuman beings—hence her interest in what she calls the earth-body and what I am calling the spirit-body, that which pertains to what is beyond the material whether in terms of spiritual, ineffable, or unconscious elements. As is well known, one of her key contributions is the development of the notion of la facultad, a type of sense that los atravesados, her name for marginalized people, develop as they navigate a world that is constantly threatening.[16] Through la facultad, those at the margins have an instant sense of their surroundings and whether there is immediate danger. This is the realm of an unexplained racing heart, goosebumps, and immediate alertness, except it is not a mere biological fight-flight response. It is difficult to explain sensing what lies in wait for us, ready to pounce. In *Borderlands / La Frontera*, Anzaldúa states, "La facultad is the capacity to see in surface phenomena the meaning of deeper realities, to see the deep structure below the surface. It is an instant 'sensing,' a quick perception arrived at without conscious reasoning. It is an acute awareness mediated by the part of the psyche that does not speak, that communicates in images and symbols which are the faces of feelings, that is, behind which feelings reside/hide. *The one possessing this sensitivity is excruciatingly alive to the world*" (my emphasis).[17] Despite the many benefits of la facultad, such as alerting us when danger is near, it nevertheless also makes us "excruciatingly alive to the world." It is not easy carrying on with a life in which one constantly senses where danger lurks, especially when there are so many threats in the borderlands. Anzaldúa understands the Mexico-US border as a "1,950 mile-long open wound."[18] In *Borderlands / La Frontera* she highlights the pain and woundedness of those who inhabit this terrain. In this text she writes about the "intimate terrorism" of life in the borderlands, where "hatred, anger, and exploitation are the prominent features of this landscape"—where, she says, "pain is the way of life."[19] The very faculty that makes her painfully aware of dangers also helps her navigate difficult worlds while connecting her to creativity. Writing becomes her salve, the possibility of survival, self-naming, self-transformation, and joy. Knowing fully well how Anzaldúa underscores woundedness throughout her writings, I seek the moments in her work that take her beyond survival. They are already scattered in her aesthetic practice of writing in black ink and red paint, but blossom in her specific account of conocimiento that incorporates the earlier notion of la facultad and her view of la naguala, a spirit guide associated with knowledge and creative power.[20]

When describing conocimiento, Anzaldúa states, "A form of spiritual inquiry, conocimiento is reached via creative acts—writing, art-making, dancing, healing, teaching, meditation, and spiritual activism—both mental and somatic (the body, too, is a form as well as a site of creativity)."[21] She also states that the task of conocimiento is "to determine what your life means, to catch a glimpse of the cosmic order and your part in that cosmovisión, and to *translate these into artistic forms*" (my emphasis).[22] While AnaLouise Keating reads conocimiento as a "relational onto-epistemology" and believes that the bulk of Anzaldúa's aesthetics is found in the account of putting Coyolxauhqui together,[23] I read conocimiento primarily as an aesthetics in the sense of *aesthesis* or perception. While there are certainly epistemological, ontological, and ethical components to conocimiento, *aesthesis* is at its heart. It provides the condition for the possibility of conocimiento. It is what allows the gathering of different types of knowledges that happens in the path of conocimiento and that, according to Anzaldúa, direct the self to interconnectedness, a journey of spiritual activism, and healing.[24] The aesthetic, understood in terms of *aesthesis*, then, needs to be understood as fundamental in Anzaldúa's philosophical view. In what follows, I explain conocimiento as affective mapping.

Affective mapping constitutes a self's attunement to what is being affectively registered, not only in terms of perceptual bodily activity but also in terms of what may be intuited and spiritually attended to, including experiences that are ineffable, difficult to understand and describe as well as experiences that may be happening at an unconscious level. This affective mapping helps the self have a sense of where and how she is in worlds. It is also a mapping that can be connected to more cognitive and therefore epistemic understandings—or, as we will see in the next chapter, to understandings of the self's position in relation to structures of power. Affective mapping constitutes a multistage creative process of coming to life in a way that is deeply attuned to worlds, one that also opens possibility to question and defy normative, dominant, or colonial understandings of being and sensing. Rather than a methodology in the sense of offering a systematic development of the tools for creating a domain of knowledge or a linear methodology that includes a bracketing or suspension of the so-called natural attitude (our commonsense view), Anzaldúa provides a nonlinear, multilayered, fluid affective mapping that takes into consideration the fact that as complex, multiplicitous selves, we cannot simply discard, to use Al-Saji's description, the colonial glue that sticks to our lives in our everydayness. Ultimately, conocimiento is to be understood as a carnal aesthetics guided by mouthly perception—what I take to be a perceptual-affective practice guided by all the senses (the five senses and the senses beyond these) and informed by the wounds of a life at the limen in which neocolonial practices and impositions inform everydayness but that, nevertheless, need not fully determine such life. In the following discussion of conocimiento as affective mapping, I underscore two important phenomenological moves: the slowing down that happens in the Coatlicue state and the call for a suspension of usual frames of reference.

Arrebatos and Everyday Wounding

In the following, I consider the stages of conocimiento in detail and with attention to their affective components. While the path to conocimiento is not, according to Anzaldúa, a linear journey, she nevertheless provides a detailed explanation of its stages, an explanation that seems to imply linearity given its very name ("path to conocimiento") and the fact that Anzaldúa provides a numbering of the stages. However, Anzaldúa states that the self may be undergoing any of these different stages at different times. When discussing the árbol de la vida (the tree of life), she points out that it is difficult to get a sense of the interconnectedness of the worlds that the tree signifies because of the up/down linear depiction (the roots as the underworld, the tree as the physical plane, and the branches as the world of noncorporeal energies). She thus urges us to understand that these three levels are not separate but are interconnected and overlapping.[25] This description of the árbol de la vida gives us a clue as to how to understand the stages of the path to conocimiento. These stages are interconnected and overlapping rather than happening in a linear sequence—although it seems clear that for Anzaldúa arrebato is what initiates the journey to conocimiento. Below, I follow Anzaldúa's own sequence of the stages while understanding that a self may be undergoing different stages in different circumstances of her life. Moreover, I do not take the last stage of conocimiento, shifting realities or spiritual activism, as necessarily normative or a stage toward which we ought to move. I take it that while many of us may wish to engage in spiritual activism, it is not always possible. There is an openness regarding our actions as we engage in the stages of the path of conocimiento. I read Anzaldúa as telling us what happens when we do experience the stages and the openings or possibilities of the otherwise that they create. Having experienced the stages in her own life, she is able to provide detailed descriptions of her experience, thus setting an example of her own choice of actions and her spiritual activism. She is alerting us to the various possibilities of ethical life that recognizes the intertwining between selves and worlds without the elaboration of a general normative, teleological ethical stance. Let us look at the notion of arrebato, that which is necessary for initiating the path to conocimiento and that is always already informed by perceptual-affective experience.

Given that Anzaldúa is deeply interested in examining wounds suffered in a life of in-betweenness and informed by the violence of coloniality, it is not surprising that the first stage of conocimiento is arrebato. In *Borderlands / La Frontera*, Anzaldúa brings up the notion of susto/fright and describes it as "a sudden shock or fall that frightens the soul out of your body."[26] However, in *Light in the Dark / Luz en lo oscuro* she opts for the notion of arrebato: what she regards as a rupture or fragmentation in the path to conocimiento. An arrebato is an upheaval, an experience that jolts the self out of familiar ways of being, perceiving, and understanding, thus opening the possibility for new sensations and understandings; it "shifts you into the crack between the worlds, shattering the mythology that grounds you."[27] The experience of arrebato may be so disruptive that Anzaldúa explains it by comparing it to the emotional, psychic, material dismemberment of Coyolxauhqui, the moon goddess. This is a thoroughly embodied experience that is deeply troubling, disconcerting, and painful—a jolt that "jars you out of the cultural trance and the spell of the collective mind-set."[28]

While some of her examples of arrebato are earthquakes and the 9/11 attacks, she also explains arrebatos in terms of more personal experiences—for example, her diabetic attacks. These arrebatos create fear and a sense of estrangement. Here I take arrebatos as constituting ruptures in terms of different degrees: while some may problematize or redirect, others may cause an upheaval and even lead to complete breakdowns. The negative racialized perception that Anzaldúa is constantly subjected to can be seen as continued daily arrebatos. In this case, the ruptures may be of different degrees in terms of how they affect one's self-worth or sense of belonging. Critical phenomenologists discussed in the previous chapter explain that negatively racialized bodies have existential instability, feel spatially and temporally fragmented, experience paralyzing hesitation, and lack a stable body schema or sense of the body's location. Recall the scenario in which a Black man enters an elevator only to see the white woman inside tense and clutch her purse; the experience of Fanon in the theater, waiting to see the caricature of the Black man appear; and Al-Saji's experience in the exhibition of paintings portraying Arab women in a colonialist way.[29] Anzaldúa also describes her own feeling of inadequacy connected to her own visible difference: in her early story "La Prieta," finished in 1981, she recounts how her mother despairs because Anzaldúa is "muy prieta," darker than all her siblings, and tells her not to go in the sun so that she will not get darker.[30] In that same text, she also worries about how "whites are the top dogs and they shit on the rest of us every day of our lives."[31] In "Bridge, Drawbridge, Sandbar, or Island" (1990), where Anzaldúa provides an important discussion about the possibilities of and barriers to coalition-making, she is explicit about race being a key difference between white women and women of color. She states, "Race was the big issue then, as it is now for us. Race, the big difference. When asked what I am, I never say I'm a woman. I say I am a Chicana, a mestiza, a Mexicana, or I am a woman-of-color—which is different from 'woman' (woman always means whitewoman)."[32]

In *Borderlands / La Frontera*, Anzaldúa describes how she navigates the thorny experience of being a new mestiza. Given her intersectional approach, the question of race is always closely connected to the question of gender as well as class, sexuality, ability, and nationality—she says, "for me a woman-of-color is not just a 'woman'; she carries the markings of her race, she is a gendered racial being."[33] While, in her later work, she considers social identities such as race, gender, class, sexuality, and nationality as too constraining and is explicit that the "body is more than the categories that mark you,"[34] she is still very much aware of the deleterious effects of racism and the fact that "my body is raced; I can't escape that reality . . . can't de-race, e-race my body, or the reality of its raced-ness."[35]

Throughout her work, she provides narratives about the consequences of racism on her very self; she carries the shame she is made to feel for being dark-skinned, for having the markings of her race that the colonial, oppressive gaze denigrates. Yet via a creative practice guided by conocimiento, which includes an impulse that she calls the Coyolxauhqui imperative, she is able to find a way to create herself, carving and reconstructing her very self in the face of the violence and fragmentation caused by racism and other traumas: "I am often driven by the impulse to write something down, by the desire and urgency to communicate, to make meaning, to make sense of things, to create myself through this knowledge-producing act. I call this impulse the 'Coyolxauhqui imperative': a struggle to reconstruct oneself and heal the sustos resulting from woundings, traumas, racism, and other acts of violation que hechan pedazos nuestras almas, split us, scatter our energies, and haunt us."[36] The arrebatos prompted by negative racialized perception are a constant reminder to bodies of color of their position of liminality within structures of power. This is a fact that is as close to Anzaldúa as her very skin. That is, arrebatos are felt deep within, in our very self. Arrebatos are connected to our ability to perceive and thus be affected, touched by what we are sensing. They require an attunement to the world beyond mechanical sensation, a sensibility that tells us how we are faring in the world. As Anzaldúa describes la facultad, such sensibility may be unconscious or prereflective, that is, prior to any conscious reflection. While we can say with Anzaldúa that there are indeed major arrebatos, shocks, jolts that are both absolutely life-denying or life-altering—think of going through an earthquake or a war—there are also the arrebatos of the everyday, the daily, cumulative indignities experienced by those who are negatively racialized: arrebatos felt personally and as a member of a community, thus bringing to the fore the sense of personal as well as communal trauma.[37] These daily arrebatos also shatter us, perhaps not in a monumental shock, but in sustained daily ruptures. While in some cases it is not possible to come out of these moments of arrebatos unscathed, negative racialized selves manage to persevere, even against all odds. Anzaldúa's own creative practice is instructive in terms of the possibilities of living a life that is not completely undone by arrebatos.[38] This becomes possible because, for Anzaldúa, the experience of arrebato both contains the wound but also the possibility of treating the wound, especially from nepantla, the place in the middle.[39]

The notion of nepantla is crucial in Anzaldúa's creative practice, as it is in this space where the possibility of reconfigurations, rereadings, reimaginings, inspiration, and transformation happens.[40] Nepantla, as the second stage of conocimiento, is a zone of possibilities and a site of transformation. While nepantla is generally understood as an in-between place in which transformation happens, recent interpretations extend its meaning in important ways. For example, Andrea Pitts reads the notion as encompassing a sense of woundedness as well as a sense of novelty that arises from having simultaneously all or more than one specific racialized and gendered/sexualized positionality.[41] Moreover, Kelli Zaytoun highlights nepantla as part of a process of shifting from what Anzaldúa calls "ego" or "customary point of view" to a compassionate naguala, then to the "neutral" position of nepantla, in which the self "shapeshifts" and thus accommodates differing perspectives and "radically breaks from the categories that defined the old self."[42] Pitts's reading helps us understand how nepantla carries with it the sense of pain that Anzaldúa discusses when being in-between structures or cultures, as well as the sense of openness and possibility that arises precisely at the moment of being caught in this in-between. Zaytoun's reading points to the possibilities of resistance or, for our purposes, an undermining of the racist colonial gaze within and without—although, as we will see below, it is not possible to break completely with dominant, normative, or colonial views.

While Zaytoun underscores that in the neutral place of nepantla it is possible for the self to break from identity categories and thus become a "shapeshifting subjectivity," I wish to highlight the perceptual-affective dimension of the process, which in my view needs to take place for shifting to happen in the first place. Nepantla is absolutely crucial for what we may call movements of the otherwise, possibilities of refashioning and reinterpreting standard views as well as learning to sense differently or anew. In nepantla, the self is able to become attuned to the multiple sensorial openings as well as to intuitions connected to that which is beyond the material. Here Anzaldúa encounters what she calls her "musa bruja," or the imagination that allows her "to use my intuition, to figure things out in images."[43] The affective mapping experienced here allows for a holding together of other ways of knowing, being, and perceiving. The self retains knowledge that is a result of colonial impositions and dominant paradigms but also from other traditions' epistemologies, metaphysics, and ways of being such as that of the Nahua tradition.[44] Yet this act of holding together disparate knowledge systems and ways of being causes pain and turmoil, even terror: it is not easy to face the contradictions, ambiguities, and the multiplicity of questions that arise at this crucial moment. Confusion, and even desconocimiento or unknowing, arises. This is the self's entry into the Coatlicue state,[45] the third stage of conocimiento, a stage that is both frightful and generative. Interestingly, in this stage Anzaldúa suggests a "suspension" of usual frames of reference that is reminiscent of Husserl's suspension of the natural attitude—a suspension that, as we saw in the previous chapter, some critical phenomenologists consider a problematic methodological move.

Coatlicue—"Let the Wound Caused by the Serpent Be Healed by the Serpent"

In *Borderlands / La Frontera,* Anzaldúa provides a powerful description of the Coatlicue state in which Coatlicue (fig. 2.2) "devours" her.[46] She calls the Coatlicue state a "prelude to crossing," "a rupture in our everyday world," and a state where "tongueless magical eyes" and "loquacious rational eyes" are separated by "an abyss, where the self becomes afraid and unable to move."[47] It is a process that begins with "entering into the serpent," into the depths of what is dark and frightful and yet leads to confrontations with one's soul.[48] The self enters the darkness of the underworld, the unconscious, and the possibility of being held in Coatlicue's arms and never letting go, thus remaining a stone forever—the self becomes afraid to "cross over."[49] However frightening, the Coatlicue state is also necessary if the self is going to be able to move forward, to "cross" and become capable of confronting herself in all her fears and contradictions, and if she will be able to defy normative, dominant structures and understandings. As Anzaldúa states, "We need Coatlicue to slow us up so that the psyche can assimilate previous experiences and process the changes."[50]

Having discussed in chapter 1 the importance of a temporal interval of hesitation in Al-Saji's critical phenomenology, I am interested in analyzing how a slowing down of perception also opens the possibility of countering the colonial eye in Anzaldúa's creative praxis. Lugones's interpretation of this slowing down in Anzaldúa's account is instructive. In her second interpretation of *Borderlands / La Frontera,* Lugones reads the Coatlicue state as featuring two moments: a moment of paralysis due to susto (fear, fright) and a moment of germination, a key moment in which the self becomes ready to step out of "ready-made hierarchical worlds of sense" and create a "counter-universe of sense."[51] I read these "ready-made hierarchical worlds of sense" in terms of cognitive meaning as well

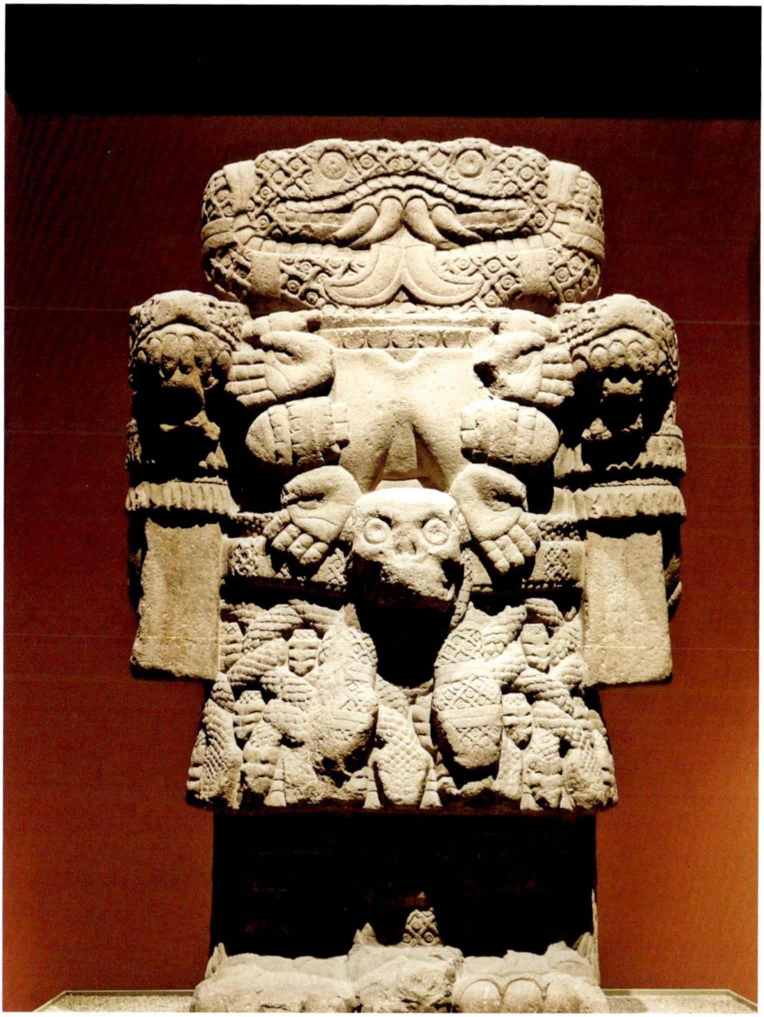

2.2 A statue of Coatlicue. Photo: Bruno Rijsman. Used without alteration under a cc-by-sa-2.0 license.

as perceptual sense connected to the affective. The Coatlicue state, then, constitutes a stage of conocimiento that includes a moment of germination, a slowing down in which the self becomes more sensorially attuned not only to her surroundings but also to bodily intuitions, perceptions, the unconscious and ineffable experiences connected to the spiritual. In so doing, the self becomes ready to question ready-made dominant knowledge, understandings, and ways of being.

In Anzaldúa's later discussion of the Coatlicue state in *Light in the Dark / Luz en lo oscuro*, she emphasizes her own arrebato of being diagnosed with diabetes and her response of fear, depression, sorrow, anger, and the "Sisyphean task" of getting out of bed.[52] Here Anzaldúa is also explicit that, in addition to her depression about her health, there is also the pain and trauma, specifically the "original trauma of this country," the genocide of Indigenous people, the horrors of slavery, and the injustice of climate and animal destruction. A recognition of the evils of coloniality and the devastation of the planet is part and parcel of Anzaldúa's affective mapping of conocimiento. She does not simply cognitively acknowledge these events; she is affectively pierced by them, both personally and communally. As complicated as Anzaldúa's relation to Indigeneity and Blackness is given her appeal to mestizaje, she is deeply affected by past and present histories of racism against various groups and by present neocolonial structures that continue to oppress bodies of color[53]—so much so that she recognizes that her own identification with Chicanidad, her appeal to a category of identity complicates the possibility of coalitions across difference.[54]

Given such attunement to the daily and historical wounds of racism, it is thus puzzling to see that Anzaldúa makes an appeal to a "suspension" of usual frames of reference in the Coatlicue state. Given the importance of this move, I provide Anzaldúa's full description:

> As you begin to know and accept the self uncovered by the trauma, you pull the blinders off, take in the new landscape in brief glances. Gradually you arouse the agent in this drama, begin to act, to *dis-identify* with the fear and isolation. You sit quietly and meditate, trance into an altered state of consciousness, temporally *suspending* your usual frames of reference and beliefs while your creative self seeks a solution to your problem by being receptive to new patterns of association. You observe how stimuli trigger responses from your body and how these reactions function. You urge yourself to cooperate with the body instead of sabotaging its self-healing. You draw a map of where you've been, how you've lived, where you're going. Sorting and re-sorting, you go through the trauma's images, feelings, sensations. (My emphasis)[55]

As explained in chapter 1, following Fanon, Al-Saji points to the fact that racialized selves cannot simply bracket or suspend the effects of coloniality in their lives for the purposes of carrying out a phenomenological reflection of the so-called natural attitude. I take this to be a key point from Al-Saji's analysis and one that indeed has major consequences for critical phenomenology. Given Anzaldúa's thorough attunement to her embodied experience, the importance of arrebatos in her account—as well as a reading of arrebatos that includes racist experiences of various degrees—I take it that what Anzaldúa means by a suspension of usual frames of reference cannot mean a suspension of the marks, wounds, scars, and horrors of colonization on her body and those of other people of color. That is, in my view Anzaldúa cannot carry out a suspension of that which has become part of her very experience of wounding within the borderlands. What can she mean by this appeal to a suspension in the Coatlicue state?

In a Husserlian reading, Jacqueline M. Martinez explains that being in the borderlands constitutes an "involuntary suspension" of the natural attitude itself. She discusses Anzaldúa's sexuality to make her point. For Martinez, it is important that it is in the borderlands that Anzaldúa recognizes herself as a lesbian, even when there are normative views that take such a sexuality as monstrous. Following social-systems theory, Martinez takes borderlands as a boundary in which some energies are different in one side as opposed to another side. For Martinez, Anzaldúa's own recognition of her sexuality is an experience of "unplaced and disjointed energies that loosens normative boundaries," thus leading to a reflection of the difference between her view and that of others who hold the dominant normative position.[56] Yet it is difficult to see how the self of the borderlands who is described by Anzaldúa as continuously gripped by bouts of arrebatos, intimate terrorism, and sustos would experience an involuntary suspension of a natural attitude that includes not merely discursive, ideological views but also wounds that are felt in the very body. I appreciate Martinez's recognition of the importance of borderland as a space where change becomes a possibility. The question is whether the involuntary suspension suggested by Martinez includes the wounds of colonization that intimately mark the life of the new mestiza.[57]

My view is that after the paralysis and fear experienced in the Coatlicue state, Anzaldúa points to a gradual, quiet, meditative moment, what in *Borderlands / La Frontera* appears as a slowing down of the psyche. This is the crucial moment of germination in which the self takes an accounting of past experiences as well as what I am referring to as an affective mapping that becomes crucial for the development of a creative practice. This slowing down may open the possibility of "suspension" that does not bracket the violence of colonization but instead involves a complex process of holding together the wounds and norms of oppressive colonial structures ("the usual frames of reference") and the opening for perceptual possibilities, as well as what Anzaldúa calls a "dis-identification" with the fear and isolation of the Coatlicue state. This dis-identification with fear takes some of the power away from oppressive structures, allowing her to become attuned to what her body and intuitions are trying to convey to her. In this stage, initial immobilization moves toward a shifting—a crossing that is to come—thoroughly informed by affective registers that are not just visual but multisensory in the sense of a mouthly perception that allows for affective mapping in the first place.

What I am suggesting is that this suspension is a slowing down in which there is a holding together of multiple views: normative understandings of the world and of the self are unsettled by bodily, incarnate attunement to spatial, temporal, material, relational, and spiritual elements from other worldviews. The overly rational, categorial, dichotomous understanding of the world and of one's own body as a mind/body sum, along with the normative understandings of difference that it imposes, no longer exerts dominion over a self that has dis-identified with its fear: the fear of not only the damage that these normative views can exert over the self but also the fear of holding disparate views and, as Anzaldúa says, "crossing" to the other side, to a new way of being—to the possibilities of the otherwise. One of Anzaldúa's best-known claims is precisely that the new mestiza's way of being counters traditional dichotomies.[58] Their ground is shaken, unstable; there is possibility of shifting in naguala-like processes that lead the self to cross and to transform. Zaytoun describes la naguala as enacting the shift from the self's inner work to new ways of knowing and being that give rise to coalitional efforts.[59] There is a shift in consciousness in which binaries no longer work and the self is not fearful of the normative system in place, which Anzaldúa describes as heartless, exploitative, oppressive, and thoroughly informed by hierarchies of power.[60]

Through her description of the Coatlicue state, Anzaldúa effectively urges us to become attuned to carnal responses, but not simply in the traditionally understood mechanistic way of bodily stimuli. She is calling for attunement to multisensory perception and to the affective responses derived from this perception. Moreover, when she writes about her attunement to the messages from her body, she is referring to perceptions she feels with her body as well as to the way that her body has an "intuitive knowing" unmediated by mental constructs: "what inner eye, heart, and gut tell you."[61] The carnal here is a spiritual incarnate that for Anzaldúa is at the center of our existence, hence her "spiritual mestizaje."[62] In "Dream of the Double-Faced Woman," Anzaldúa writes, "El espíritu es carne viva."[63] The "suspension" that Anzaldúa calls forth, then, is not a bracketing or disregarding of how everyday experience is colored by the wounds created by coloniality. It constitutes a complex process of holding together those wounds while at the same time not being scared of them or of the openings to the otherwise prompted by affective responses to multisensory perception and spiritual intuitions, openings for recognizing other ways of knowing, being, and sensing that are not tethered to traditional Western metaphysics. Without this process that reveals the importance of affectivity and spirituality, it would not be possible to translate one's life journey into artistic forms, to forge an aesthetics informed by carnalities.

AFFECTIVE MAPPING AND HABITS OF PERCEPTION

> My mouth is a motherload.
> **GLORIA ANZALDÚA**, *Borderlands / La Frontera*

In *Spiderwoman Embrace* (fig. 2.3), Karen Miranda Rivadeneira becomes a motherload—not that vein of metal ore that so many try to find to become

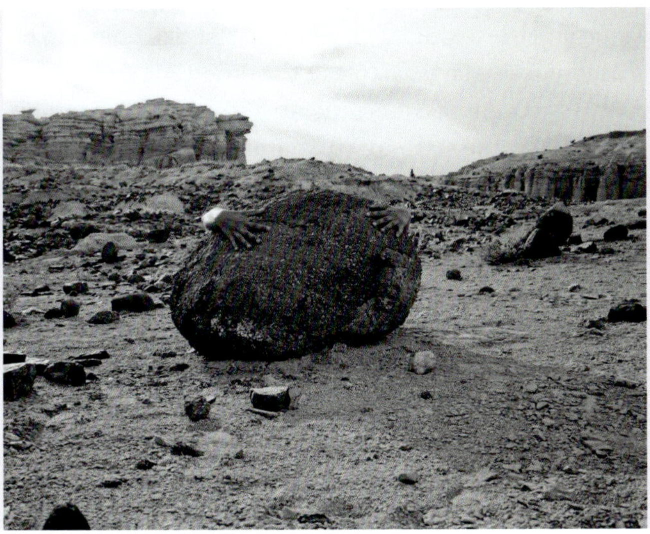

2.3 Karen Miranda Rivadeneira, *Spiderwoman Embrace*, 2019. Archival pigment print, 30 × 24 in. Copyright the artist.

wealthy but that source of multisensory perception that affectively maps our being-in-worlds, that links us to the possibility of conocimiento in Anzaldúa's sense: the whole of Rivadeneira become stone, mouth opening and swallowing earth- and spirit-bodies.

Anzaldúa's affective mapping connects the self to a spiritual incarnate alerting the senses and pushing toward different ways of perceiving, feeling, and knowing. While Anzaldúa's stages of conocimiento do not concentrate on bodily habits and the possibility for their reconfiguration as Ngo's and Al-Saji's accounts do, we can take into consideration the possibility that habits may be refigured in the process of affective mapping of conocimiento. As noted in chapter 1, according to Ngo, habits of perception are not wholly passive. That is, bodily habit entails an ongoing activity and a continual reworking and "reanimation" depending on body experience. If habits are held rather than sedimented, there is an opening for the possibility for reconfiguring them.[64] From a critical phenomenological point of view, it is of interest to see how a shift in bodily habits may also be connected to the various processes of conocimiento. This issue raises the question as to whether an account of redirecting or reconfiguring habits, while deeply important, needs to be supplemented by an understanding of the kind of experience marked by affective mapping that includes attunement to spiritual elements. Although it might not be possible to describe such experience, as it may be ineffable, it is important to recognize how it may still be at play in our embodied practices—perhaps playing a role in reorienting long-standing habits of perception. Anzaldúa's account of conocimiento allows for a consideration of these elements, especially in the process of creative practices. Moreover, given that Al-Saji points to the importance of the aesthetic as playing a role in the unsettling and refiguring of habits, Anzaldúa's account of conocimiento becomes indispensable.

As we have seen so far, the stages of conocimiento include arrebato (stage 1), a "seismic" rupture, followed by an unsettlement in nepantla (stage 2), which holds contradictory views that catapult the self to the blocks and pain of the Coatlicue state (stage 3), which is a prelude to crossing. In this important Coatlicue state, the self can carry out a suspension that, rather than a bracketing of the natural attitude that includes arrebatos related to racism, can be understood as holding normative, dominant visions while also becoming deeply attuned to a multiplicity of sensory and affective registers. Yet despite the constructive possibilities that may arise from the Coatlicue state as explained above—a dis-identification with fear and the unsettlement of normative understandings of the self's racialization by way of affective mapping—these are only part of the path to conocimiento. As such, any consideration of the way the habits of racializing perception are constraining yet also capable of reorientation needs to be supplemented by a more capacious understanding of the complexities and multilayeredness of the processes that allow for self-naming, self-reorientation, and even self-transformation.

I read the Anzaldúan path to conocimiento as both a phenomenological description of her own instances of moving through the process as well as a more general account of the different moments of conocimiento, which may open possibilities for an unsettlement of the normative colonial gaze. In a similar move to Al-Saji's hesitation, Anzaldúa directs us to a slowing down—although in this case, it prompts a productive stasis in which the self has room to expand perceptual-affective awareness. Indeed, for Anzaldúa, the expanded awareness brought about by affective mapping allows for openings in which the self can engage in creative practices that forge possibilities of the otherwise. However, these possibilities are the result of more than rehabituation.

For example, the aural becomes important in Anzaldúa's description of the fourth stage of conocimiento: she tells us that it is a call that prompts the self to cross or to shift from the grip of the normative and the hegemonic. She connects this mysterious call to La Llorona and to la naguala whispering "adelante" to her, prompting her to discover resources within herself and in the world, to take responsibility for creating her life, and to stand at the brink and reconsider crossing, a moment in which there is a self-reorientation.[65] In this stage, Anzaldúa asks herself whether she is ready to face her shadow beast: the parts of herself that hold her failures, her inadequacies, and all the negativities that she has internalized. The "I cannot" of the self's own racialization is here further confronted in a moment that precedes crossing and change. Importantly, in this moment, Anzaldúa highlights the spiritual and connects it to the body. As she states, "You become reacquainted with a reality called spirit, a presence, force, power, and energy within and without. . . . Spirit speaks through your mouth, listens through your ears, sees through your eyes, touches with your hands."[66] A spiritual incarnate continues to inform the moving-across that is to take the self to new visions of itself, to new identities and possibilities of the otherwise. Mouthly sensation is here touched by the spiritual, readying for a process of re-membering, of gathering together all the pieces of the self that has been torn in the violence and trauma of a life marked by colonial eyes.

Let us remember Coyolxauhqui, that Aztec moon goddess (fig. 2.4), "she of the bells on the face,"[67] who is supposed to have been decapitated by her brother Huitzilopochtli, her arms and legs separated as her body rolls down a hill. As she was dressed for war, her limbs are adorned. While, in this most famous rendition of the goddess, her body parts are trapped in stone, they are still ready for battle, almost defying the permanence of the stone—as if this goddess were to start running forward at any moment, arms and legs reattaching themselves in a movement of strength and courage. When Anzaldúa sees a cast of this stone in an exhibition at the Denver Museum of Natural History, she thinks of Coyolxauhqui as exemplifying "women as conquered bodies," yet she also senses a "whirlwind of energy" and a "timeless stillness patiently waiting to explode into activity."[68] Moved by the goddess and identifying with her, she states,

> Coyolxauhqui also represents the "me" tossed into the void by traumatic events (an experience of the unconscious). I disintegrate into hundreds of pieces, hundreds of separate awareness. A plurality of souls splits my awareness so that I see things from a hundred different viewpoints, each with its own intelligence that can "do" a hundred different things (think, feel, sense, observe) in a continuously changing consciousness moment to moment. Yet while experiencing the many I cohere as the one reconstituted and restructured by my own unconscious urge toward wholeness. Coyolxauhqui represents the psychic and creative process of tearing apart and pulling together (deconstructing/constructing).[69]

Anzaldúa's description above is important for understanding both the sense of fragility as well as of strength she derives from this rendition of the moon goddess and why this figure becomes key in her later work. Here disintegration and dismemberment become a source of pain but also, crucially, of knowledges—as a host of sensations, feelings, and cognitions overwhelm her, leading her to understand a multiplicity of ways of knowing, sensing, and being. This depiction of the goddess also leads her to recognize her own urge for wholeness, which she translates into an aesthetic practice of self-writing. As she states, "After being split, dismembered, or torn apart la persona has to pull herself together, re-member and reconstruct herself on another level. I call this the Coyolxauhqui process after the dis-membered Aztec moon goddess."[70]

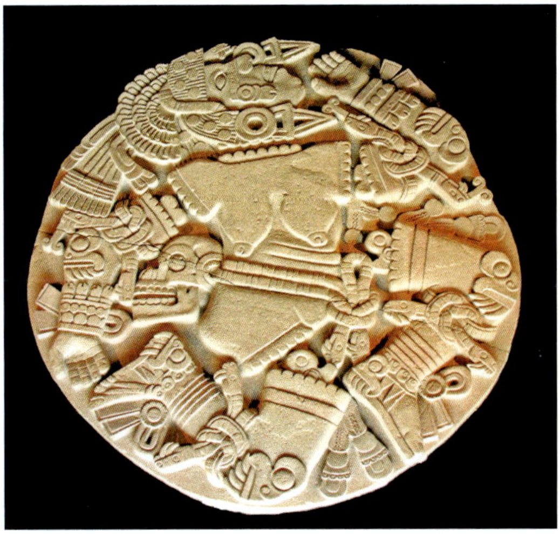

2.4 The Coyolxauhqui stone, found at the temple of Tenochtitlan in 1978. Photo: Dennis Jarvis. Used without alteration under a cc-by-sa-2.0 license.

Putting Coyolxauhqui together, the fifth stage of conocimiento, is crucial in Anzaldúa's affective mapping. It is here where we get to see the power of the creative process in destabilizing standard, dominant, or colonial ways of perceiving and understanding. Anzaldúa herself comments that the essay explaining the stages of the path to conocimiento is the "sister essay" to the essay "Putting Coyolxauhqui Together: A Creative Process," which also appears in *Light in the Dark / Luz en lo oscuro*. The process of putting Coyolxauhqui together is decisive in Anzaldúan aesthetics, as it is here where what has been sensed is creatively processed and translated. The crucial task is to "re-member," understood in terms of translating into language the images that arise from one's body, dreams, and the cenote, the unconscious fountain of conocimiento, which for Anzaldúa constitutes the "mental network of subterranean rivers of information that converge and well up to the surface, like a sinkhole or an opening to the womb of the Earth."[71] Language intertwines with images in the process of putting Coyolxauhqui together. As Stephanie Rivera Berruz notes, Anzaldúa's process shows how language is inextricably linked to embodied identity and thus "orients" self-understanding and relationality.[72] Here re-membering becomes tied to the materiality of language as well as to that which is beyond the material.

In the process of putting Coyolxauhqui together we can also see how Anzaldúa's theory is carnal—that is, how it relies on the intimate relationship between an embodied, sensuous multiplicitous self and the earth- and spirit-bodies.[73] Here this process becomes a flesh*and*blood, carnal aesthetics. Anzaldúa asks us to be attuned to the ways that images derived from dreams, the unconscious, daily life, and spiritual experiences produce physiological reactions in the body and give rise to multiple emotions. La naguala, with her shamanic, shapeshifter powers, appears in order to prompt shifts in perception and movement from "rational to visionary states, from logistics to poetics."[74] To illustrate the process of re-membering, Anzaldúa moves back and forth from theorizing about the epistemic, spiritual, and emotional to "pulling miles of entrails through your mouth."[75] The end result is mouthly creation, the story: she is the story. As she states, "You're the artist scripting the new story of this house/self/identity/essay under construction."[76]

I wish to underscore that putting Coyolxauhqui together or re-membering is for Anzaldúa a "sensuous act" and an "osseous process" of putting *herself* together with pen and ink.[77] Her autohistorias (autobiographical writings informed by the artist's cultural history) and her autohistoria-teoría (autohistorias that include theoretical elements)[78] are the result of an intensive, painful process of sacrificial bloodletting: "Escribo con la tinta de mi sangre."[79] In the later (2015) essay "Putting Coyolxauhqui Together," Anzaldúa extends the imagery of writing as carving bone introduced in *Borderlands / La Frontera* and provides a sustained description of the process. In addition, here Anzaldúa expands on the importance of images as daimonic, as having a spiritual component,[80] and as connected to the sensuous operations of the body and of writing, a view she discusses in *Borderlands / La Frontera*, where she states that "the word, the image, and the feeling have a palatable energy, a kind of power. Con imagenes domo mi miedo, cruzo los abismos que tengo por dentro."[81] For her, "a visual, aural, or olfactory memory of some trivial incident triggers a stream of images. Subliminal events in our body or sensations provoked by its organs appear and vanish like fleeting fish, leaving behind a flash of el cuerpo's knowledge."[82] Conocimiento becomes tied to these images that Anzaldúa captures with her soul's eye and that reside in el cenote, the reservoir of untapped knowledge that includes the unconscious and that which has been covered up by layers of dominant rational knowledge. As Anzaldúa notes in *Borderlands / La Frontera*, "An image is a bridge between evoked emotion and conscious knowledge; words are the cables that hold up the bridge. Images are more direct, more immediate than words, and closer to the unconscious. Picture language precedes thinking in words."[83] This understanding of images and the imaginal is absolutely key to the creative process of putting Coyolxauhqui together, which, according to Anzaldúa, may even "bring into being something that does not yet exist in the world."[84]

Anzaldúa's later text "Putting Coyolxauhqui Together" puts flesh onto the very bones of Anzaldúa's own story about her creative process. We can say that it brings Anzaldúa into being as a new mestiza, a being that had not existed within dominant understandings. In this text Anzaldúa affirms that "creativity requires profound shifts of consciousness and a scattered kind of attention that goes against the habits of thinking."[85] It is through this process that the dominant colonial gaze can be destabilized and that one's internalized "I cannot" of negative racialization may be destabilized as well. Anzaldúa describes the act of creation as one in which images, perception, and affect combine and take her over in the process of putting flesh to the bones of an emerging story. This embodiment of the story is literally a re-membering, a translation of "images arising from your body, the sea, the theater of dreams—allowing them to surface at will and capturing in your net of words."[86] She also calls it an "ensueño."[87]

Key here is Anzaldúa's recognition of the creative process as not agential or carried out by a genius or by an artist understood in a traditional sense, but rather a letting be taken over by a call to create—or in Anzaldúa's case, to write. Writing becomes a thoroughly embodied, sensuous process in which "visual narratives" are produced.[88] Yet it is a bodily act that is accompanied by trances and shifts of consciousness as the self becomes attuned to multiple perceptual inputs. The self in the pangs of creation becomes a naguala, entering into a shamanic state of reception, creation, and transformation. The relationship between image, perception, and affect is key here: "Where does the work of naguala take place? In the body. All emotions and ideas pass through it; writing is nothing if not a bodily act. An image produces a physiological reaction experienced in strong feelings (desire, hate, fear) and manifests itself in neuromuscular, respiratory, cardiovascular, hormonal, and other bodily changes. In other words, an image produces emotion. You can't have an emotion without a corresponding sensory image—and vice versa."[89] However, this particular passage is striking because it might be read as pointing to a reductionist understanding of emotion. Nonetheless, while Anzaldúa connects emotion to bodily processes, she is also linking it to the imaginary. While it is clearly the case that Anzaldúa's account of conocimiento is undergirded by the bodily, it also resists simple materialisms or mere biological explanations. Image, bodily perception, and affect unite to lead the self into a moment of creation, into new visions of herself and of what is. Here images take lives of their own "and walk around as if they choose."[90] They reside in her cenote and she is led by them. Her imagination or "musa bruja" allows her intuition, which she understands as figuring things out in images, to carry out this creative process of not only sensorially reading the material world but also of intuiting that which is beyond the material.[91]

The end result of re-membering is a self that is one and many, a self that is always in process.[92] As Anzaldúa states, "Tu autohistoria is not carved in stone but drawn on sand and subject to shifting winds."[93] Conocimiento becomes an aesthetics—carnal, fleshy, mouthly, and thus an aesthesis. It becomes an intricate, multivalent process of knowing and being tied to carnalities through which marginalized selves are able not only to survive but also to understand themselves and live in worlds in different ways than those sedimented by hegemonic, homogenizing understandings and visions tied to coloniality and other oppressive, violent imaginaries and practices. As carnal, conocimiento's affective mapping is attuned to the intertwining between self, others, and the earth- and spirit-bodies.

Given that the self that emerges out of this carnal practice is a self in the making, a self with an expansive awareness—a bodymindsoul that senses the earth- and spirit-bodies—conocimiento includes what Anzaldúa calls "blow ups," moments in which "contradictions explode in your face."[94] Thus there is a need for "nepantleras," those who are able to see from contradictory sides and engage in a neutral position that allows for coalition-making through spiritual activism, the sixth stage of conocimiento. Here we see the tremendous coalitional desire in Anzaldúa's vision. In this stage, Anzaldúa points to the possibility of engaging in a discussion that includes various points of view in order to "identify common bonds, name reciprocities and connections."[95] This is a moment in which the self does not give up on others even when they are hurtful; it is a "spiritual-imaginal-political vision together."[96] Here we might think of the enactment of what Zaytoun calls "naguala subjectivity" insofar as this is the moment in which there is a shift of consciousness in which the self moves away from a customary point of view to others' points of view and then is able to go back and forth between different views in order to find commonalities and "the humanity of the other."[97] This is a moment of neutrality, one that is very difficult to attain and that only nepantleras (boundary crossers, thresholders, activists) achieve. It is a moment when "the heart es un corazón con razón, with intelligence, passion, and purpose, a 'mind-full' heart with ears for listening, eyes for seeing, a mouth with tongue narrowing to a pen tip for speaking/writing."[98] Writing becomes a type of conocimiento described as "dropping down into yourself, through the skin and muscles and tendons, down deep into the bones' marrow where your soul is ballast."[99] This is conocimiento as spiritual practice.

Let us then return to Anzaldúa's own words: "The heart es un corazón con razón, with intelligence, passion, and purpose, a 'mind-full' heart with ear for listening, eyes for seeing, a mouth with tongue narrowing to a pen tip for speaking/writing. The left hand is not a fist pero una mano abierta raised with others in struggle, celebration, and song. Conocimiento es otro mode de conectar across colors and other differences to allies also trying to negotiate racial contradictions, survive the stress and traumas of daily life, and develop a spiritual-imaginal-political vision together."[100]

I am moved by Anzaldúa's figure of "a mouth with tongue narrowing to a pen tip for speaking/writing," this mouthly aesthetics in which the self cuts through her skin, muscles, and tendons to reveal the soul, the spiritual connection with the earth- and spirit-bodies. Enhancing the possibilities of the spirituality that is highlighted in the sixth stage of conocimiento, Anzaldúa's seventh stage turns to the fusion of bodymindsoul and earth—what I consider a poetics of love, a poetics that, with Kevin Quashie we can call a poetics of aliveness.[101] Anzaldúa states,

> Spirit embodying yourself as rock, tree, bird, human, past,
> present, and future,
>   you of many names, diosas antiguas, ancestors,
>   we embrace you as we would a lover.[102]

In this poetics, Anzaldúa connects East, South, West, and North with the primary elements air, fire, water, and earth. In the last section of the essay, Anzaldúa transports herself (and us) to these cardinal points and, in these movements, the air becomes the reminder of the interrelatedness between us and the earth; the fibers of our spirit extend from our bodies to create the sky, seaweed, serpents, and all humans; the soul catches fire and burns holes in the walls separating us; we walk through flames of transformation and our consciousness speaks to the spirit dwelling in the sea; we ask forgiveness for poisoning the land. Then, completing the circle, she returns to the centro, the center, the underworld, where her (and our) collective creativity becomes strong so as to heal wounds of hate, dissolve divisions, and remember our dead.[103] Finally, Anzaldúa sees herself looking at the sky, offering her book filled with love to the world with the hope that it inspires others to change it, to transform it. She walks back along the circle and makes an offering to the ancestors, to all of us who are gathered in the pages of her book, a work that discloses who she is that also gathers all of us ready to shift to new worlds and new ways of being.

Anzaldúa's conocimiento constitutes not only a poetics but also an erotics of self-making and transformation. We have learned from Audre Lorde about the power of the erotic understood as the life force of women.[104] For her, "the erotic is not a question only of what we do; it is a question of how acutely and fully we can feel the doing."[105] While Lorde theorizes the erotic so as to point to its personal and political possibilities for women in the context of a patriarchy that teaches women to fear their desires, the "yes" within themselves,[106] Anzaldúa's conocimiento as carnal aesthetics is an erotics insofar as it points to the ability of those who are marginalized to rely on their intuitive and sensory powers in order not only to forge themselves but also to love themselves. It is a call for sensuous engagement in creative acts, and specifically for Anzaldúa, in acts of autohistoria and autohistoria-teoría.

Anzaldúa's writing constitutes an erotics and poetics of self-making and transformation, of the bodymindsoul in connection to the earth- and spirit-bodies. It is a process of conocimiento tied to a carnal aesthetics, creative acts in which the self intertwines with the earthly as well as the spiritual in order to carve her face, forge her bones, write with her mouth. Conocimiento as carnal aesthetics arises in and is informed by the cuts and wounds in the condition of liminality and fragmentation. It is here that the bodymindsoul creatively engages with elements, with a medium, be it paint, light, or sound; where the perception-affect and medium-affect nexuses open possibilities for self-making and transformation. For Anzaldúa this medium is complex as it encompasses images that she turns into words with the aid of intuitions, feelings, myths, spirituality, and her in-between lived experience. As she says in *Borderlands / La Frontera*, "Living in a state of psychic unrest, in a Borderland, is what makes poets write and artists create. It is like a cactus needle embedded in the flesh."[107] Indeed, for her, conocimiento is a form of spiritual inquiry that is attained by way of creative acts. While a multipronged approach is indeed necessary to deal with the violence that arises out of the negative racialized perception that is suffered by los atravesados, Anzaldúa specifically appeals to carnalities, to mouthly creative practices arising at the nexus between bodymindsoul and earth- and spirit-bodies: "To be a mouth—the cost is too high—her whole life enslaved to that devouring mouth. Todo pasaba por esa boca, el viento, el fuego, los mares y la tierra. Her body, a crossroads, a fragile bridge, cannot support the tons of cargo passing through it. She wants to install 'stop' and 'go' signal lights, instigate a curfew, police Poetry. But something wants to come out."[108] Something has to come out of Anzaldúa's mouth—screams, sweet musings, sonorous caresses, fleshed words trying to say something, saying something that only her own self can say, words-turned-poetry that put Anzaldúa (and us) in the map of being and sensing.

Moving with Anzaldúa through the stages of conocimiento, while taking into consideration the importance of the linkage between perception and affect, does not disclose a methodology to be housed in the pages of books. Rather, it is an unfolding of life, an affective mapping of Anzaldúa's life, of the lives of people of color, of those who have been marginalized because of their social identities—pierced by arrebatos, everyday upheavals and ruptures that slowly or abruptly chip away at the self, leading it to susto, fear of life, or to feeling as if one has been torn into many parts in the midst of the violence of coloniality. Yet arrebatos are not merely death sentences—although sometimes they can be—but companions to a state of nepantla as a zone of possibilities. Affectively mapping herself in her worlds, the self's perception expands, as does her affective attunement. Paralyzed in the Coatlicue state, Anzaldúa (and we do too) still manages to prepare for difficult crossings. In this Coatlicue state we find a productive paralysis—a freezing of the soul that does not manage to relegate Anzaldúa to oblivion, but instead readies her, prepares her for the difficulties that are to come. The suspension she suggests is a moment of generative stasis—of affective attunement to multisensory perception and multivalent knowings. Anzaldúa cannot suspend the ravages of coloniality that she carries in her body or the rationality of the modern colonial system (the traditional frames of reference), but she can hold them while at the same time affectively opening to multisensory perception, images, feelings, the unconscious—to la naguala, in a process of deep perception *and* communion with others. This is the flesh*and*blood, carnal process of the "inner work" of a self intertwined with her communities, the earthly, and the spiritual—of a self that, despite past traumas, enacts conocimiento as carnal aesthetics, thus making it possible for her not only to name herself in the midst of prying, racist, colonizing eyes, but also to transform herself in bloody, mouthly creation. As Anzaldúa states, "*Escribo con la tinta de mi sangre.* I write in red. Ink. Intimately knowing the smooth touch of paper, its speechlessness before I spill myself on the insides of trees."[109]

THREE

SPILLING HERSELF IN TREES

Autoarte and Laura Aguilar's Queer Erotics

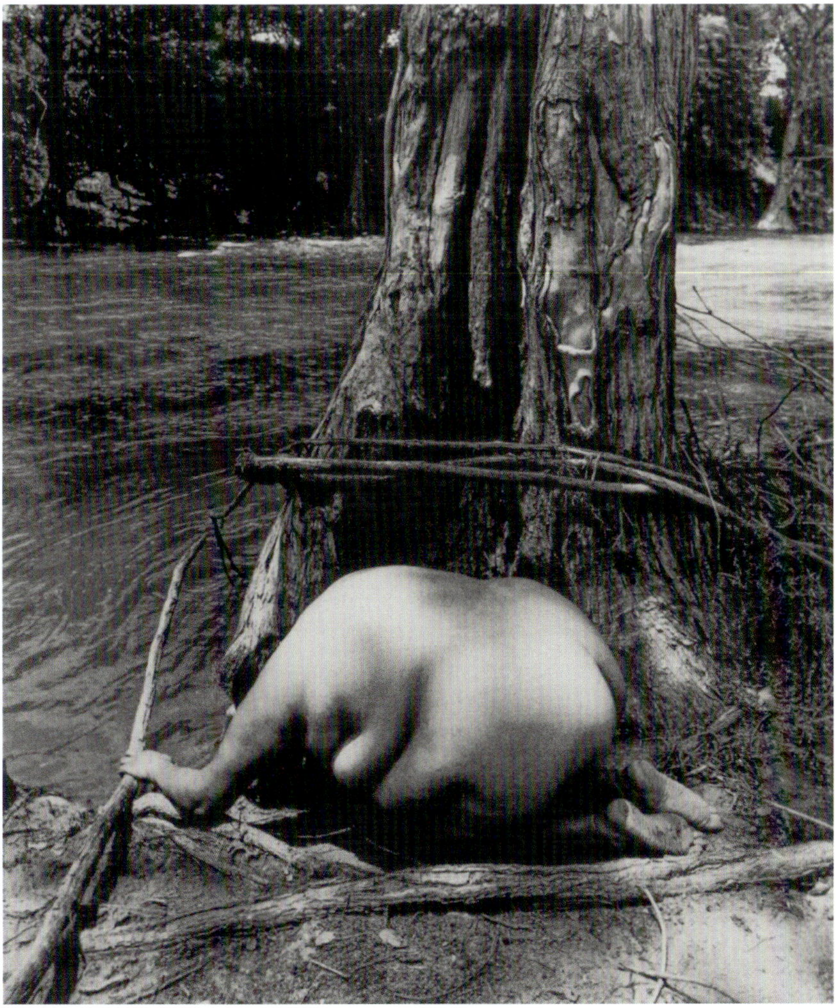

3.1 Laura Aguilar, *Stillness #23*, 1996. Gelatin silver print, 9×12 in. Copyright Laura Aguilar Trust of 2016.

She becomes tree,
bows to it, as if to a forgotten god.
Prescient bark as wounded skin.

Earth womb in paradise lost,
letting her in.
She gives birth to herself.

Light is a witness,
Feels the pangs, hears the quiet scream.
Resplendent flesh*and*blood.

Differential consciousness is linked to whatever is not expressible through words. It is accessed through poetic modes of expression: gestures, music, images, sounds, words that plummet or rise through signification to find some void—some no-place—to claim their due.
CHELA SANDOVAL, *The Methodology of the Oppressed*

Laura Aguilar's *Stillness #23* (fig. 3.1) discloses writing with light as carnality: as embodied, sensuous creation in which the self is intertwined with the earth- and spirit-bodies. In this photograph, this skin of light, the queer Chicana traces her body with light, carrying the weight of her difficult life in the in-between. Between earth and water, Aguilar bends over, holding a branch but also letting go, trusting the tree god. The folds of her skin flow—as the water and the skin of the tree also flow—flesh*and*blood rhythms. How does the texture of that slim branch feel? What sound does the water make? Bark-turned-skin holds Aguilar, tending to her in all her vulnerability. Here Aguilar and light itself encounter each other in a process of both restriction and liberation, in carnal touchings—her body becoming a carnal crossover.

Like Anzaldúa's carnalities, her autohistorias, Aguilar's writing with light constitutes a carnal aesthetics, a mouthly aesthetics guided by the entwinement between perception and affect and the intimacies that envelop her embodied self. Through photography, Aguilar engages in a creative process of self-making despite the colonizing gaze that hovers above and within those in the margins. The aim of this chapter is to introduce the notion of autoarte and to point to Aguilar's photographic self-making as an instance of autoarte and as a queer erotics of light. Inspired by Anzaldúa's carnal aesthetics and Chela Sandoval's methodology of the oppressed, I wish to show Aguilar's writing with light in its differential and decolonial modalities in which perceptual, sensuous practices inform lived experience and creative engagements in a transformative way—in an alchemy of being.

Given that Anzaldúa's carnal aesthetics is characterized by discursive artforms such as autohistoria and autohistoria-teoría, in the first section I discuss border arte as described in Anzaldúa's own narrative of her visit to a museum and being affected by objects representative of Aztec culture, an experience in which she becomes deeply perceptually and affectively attuned to these objects—so much so that her own account becomes an instance of border arte. I point to the various elements of the practice of border arte as it arises in nepantla, the "threshold of transformation."[1] Ultimately, for Anzaldúa border arte becomes a politically resistant practice that allows marginalized groups to produce counter-art, art that destabilizes and counters hegemonic, colonial imaginaries. Subsequently, I introduce the notion of *autoarte* as elucidating the more personal, subjective aspect of the general practice of border arte. Autoarte is a carnality or creative practice through which the self registers intimate, subjective experiences of being affected by different elements—objects, specific materials, human and nonhuman beings, and the spiritual—given an intertwining between the self and worlds. Here light inspires and becomes matter through the photograph. In capturing the intimacies between the self and worlds, autoarte discloses instances of what Kevin Quashie calls quiet or the expressiveness of the interiority of the self, what with Anzaldúa we have described as "inner work."[2] Yet given the intertwining between selves and worlds, these terms do not point to a sharp distinction between subject and object, inner and outer domains. Autoarte is a deeply intimate, personal yet also relational movement in which a self engages in creative practices that make possible self-naming or, as Anzaldúa puts it, self-carving. While the practice of autoarte is not necessarily resistant or political, it may become so as it helps a self counter the colonial gaze or as it translates into artworks specifically designed to depict the experience of life in nepantla. Through autoarte a marginalized self can tell her own story—in Aguilar's case, not with words, as Anzaldúa's autohistorias do, but in writing with light. Autoarte is the carnal process in which a self intermingles with the earth- and spirit-bodies and has the possibility of creatively caring for herself and making herself otherwise than colonial eyes prescribe.

In the second section, I analyze Aguilar's photography as autoarte turned queer erotics of light. Like Anzaldúa's creative practice, Aguilar's photography is deeply informed by an intimacy between the self and natural elements that includes germination, a slowing down that attunes the self to deepened perception. By reading Chela Sandoval's methodology of the oppressed via the notion of affective mapping introduced in the last chapter—in this instance, the way a self sensuously attunes to her location in maps of power—I describe Aguilar's own affective mapping as she translates it into light and, in so doing, makes herself in an act of anguished joy and of love. Autoarte becomes a moment of love—with our selves, others, and what surrounds us—that brings to light new ways of being in worlds. Performed by selves guided by differential consciousness, autoarte becomes a mobile, decolonial erotics of self-care and self-making that may lead to self-transformation and that may be enacted to destabilize and counter normative and colonial imaginaries and discourses. Autoarte stands as a key carnality within a carnal aesthetics in which the artist's body becomes a carnal crossroad to communion with the earth- and spirit-bodies. It remains a praxis of being, doing, and sensing filled with possibilities of survival, self-making, and self-transformation for those who are othered within sociopolitical contexts and epistemic-perceptual regimes that construct hierarchical categories of being. Within a context of perverse violence against bodies of color and bodies of the in-between, autoarte allows for the possibility of intimate self-expression and self-making that may also lead to self-transformation and the countering of the colonial eye. Ultimately, photography as carnality allows Aguilar to become one with the earth- and spirit-bodies, spilling herself inside trees, becoming rock, tree, and earth itself in a different type of shamanic process. With Aguilar, photography-as-intimacy develops into a sensuous writing with light that defies simple, dominant-gendered, and sexual paradigms.

BORDER ARTE, ART OF THE IN-BETWEEN

As documented by AnaLouise Keating, Anzaldúa first publishes on the notion of border arte in 1993 for a catalogue for the exhibition *La Frontera / The Border: Art about the Mexico / United States Border Experience* at the Centro Cultural de la Raza and Museum of Contemporary Art in San Diego.[3] The essay was also reprinted in other venues under the title "Chicana

Artists: Exploring nepantla, el lugar de la Frontera," including the 1998 *Latino Studies Reader* edited by Antonia Darder and Rodolfo D. Torres, and finally heavily revised and reprinted as "Border Arte: Nepantla, el Lugar de la Frontera" in *Light in the Dark / Luz en lo oscuro*.[4] While the original title and publication venue suggest the notion of border arte as art about the border itself and/or produced by border artists along the Mexico-US border, the subsequent titles and publication outlets quickly direct us to a broader understanding of the notion as involving art produced by Chicanas and other selves that are in nepantla or the metaphorical Borderlands.[5] The 1998 version of the article includes the following descriptions of border arte:

> Border art, in critiquing old, traditional, and erroneous representations of the Mexico-United States border, attempts to represent the "real world" de la gente going about their daily lives. But it renders that world and its people in more than mere surface slices of life. If one looks beyond the tangible, one sees a connection to the spirit world, to the underworld, and to other realities. . . .
>
> The border is a historical and metaphorical site, un sitio ocupado, an occupied borderland where individual artists and collaborating groups transform space, and the two home territories, Mexico and the United States, become one. Border art deals with shifting identities, border crossings, and hybridism. But there are other borders besides the actual Mexico/US frontera.[6]

As the first citation above suggests, border arte encompasses a very specific content, art about the "real world" of the people living at the Mexico-US border. Artists are supposed to capture the daily as well as spiritual realities of those living in the borderlands. The second citation expands the sense of border arte to include borders "besides the actual Mexico/US frontera." Hence border arte encompasses art produced by artists from other borders as well as content and production by those with shifting identities, those whom Anzaldúa describes as being in nepantla or in-betweenness in terms of nationality, race, class, or gender or in the metaphorical Borderlands. In this early piece, Anzaldúa ultimately highlights art by women, especially Chicanas, as representative of border arte: "For women artists, nepantla is a constant state; dislocation is the norm. Chicana artists are engaged in 'reading' that nepantla, that border."[7] Yet she immediately states that mestizaje, not Chicanismo, is at the heart of their art.[8] Her insistence on the importance of nepantla and mestizaje for border arte encompasses a major theme in her carnal aesthetics, ultimately promoting border arte as creation characterized by its production within nepantla.[9] As Anzaldúa states, "Border artists inhabit the transitional space of nepantla. The border is the locus of resistance, of rupture, and of putting together the fragments. By disrupting the net separations between cultures, Chicana artists create a new culture mix, una mestizada."[10]

In this section, I interpret the 2015 version of Anzaldúa's essay on border arte. I read border arte as a key creative practice, a carnality, in Anzaldúa's aesthetics and discuss its major characteristics, ultimately pointing to its attunement to flesh*and*blood, to multiple material, spiritual, sensuous, historical, intersubjective relations between the self and earth- and spirit-bodies. In its manifestation as autohistoria and autohistoria-teoría—practices that combine the visual with discourse or visual portraits,[11] as well as other creative production originating from the space of nepantla—border arte is the result of a communal, carnal, aesthetic process imbued with liberatory potential.[12] As noted in chapter 1, as a carnal aesthetics connected to perceptual and affective registers, Anzaldúa's creative practice can be seen as addressing Al-Saji's and other critical phenomenologists' calls for strategies prompting affective responses that might help dealing with negative racialization.[13] Anzaldúa's theorization and enactment of border arte, then, constitutes an important opening for considering practices deeply connected to survival, self-naming, and well-being within alienating, undermining environments.[14]

While in *Borderlands / La Frontera* Anzaldúa discusses her writing in black ink and red paint and highlights the sensuous, anxiety-producing, shamanic processes of putting a story together, in "Border Arte: Nepantla, el Lugar de la Frontera" Anzaldúa expands her discussion on what it means to make art from the limen, from the space and condition of nepantla, what she considers the "threshold of transformation," "the place where we are detached (separated) and attached (connected) to each of our several cultures" and the "midway point between the conscious and unconscious."[15] As noted, she initially describes such art as arising in the specific location of the Mexico-US borderlands, seemingly suggesting that this art needs to be produced in that particular spatiality or by the inhabitants of those spaces. Yet Anzaldúa is also providing a more expansive account of an aesthetics that is performed in other Borderlands, including symbolic, spiritual, and psychic Borderlands. For example, Anzaldúa connects border arte specifically to the tradition of sacred and folk art such as retablos, whose artists she regards as intermediaries between miraculous events and their representations.[16] The moment this folk art is put in museums represents a deep historical break for Anzaldúa. It is the moment when the Western colonizing way relegates the "metate" and "huipil," objects used by Indigenous peoples, to the museum—thus symbolically eradicating Indigenous people from present-day culture. As Kelli D. Zaytoun points out, the discussion of border arte needs to be understood in terms of a decolonizing context in which border arte itself becomes a decolonial practice and project.[17] While at an exhibition of Aztec art at the Denver Museum of Natural History, Anzaldúa goes through an embodied meditation in which she reflects on this relegation of Indigenous peoples and cultures to the past. Through a description of her experience in the museum, Anzaldúa also produces an autohistoria-teoría; that is, she creates border arte about border arte itself.

Anzaldúa's walking meditation, in which she carefully observes Aztec artifacts detached from their original contexts and reflects on the very meaning of art within the colonizing space of the museum, is an enactment of border arte. Her reflections on and writing about whether "this jotita, the queer Chicana, this mexicatejana" will find her "historical Indian identity" in the museum become instances of autohistoria-teoría that is part of her carnal aesthetics. Anzaldúa takes us through the halls of the museum and shares with us her "psychosis" and "double-being," as she feels that her own Indigeneity has vanished but that it has nevertheless become an object of consumption for museum visitors, the museum itself becoming a kind of borderland.[18] In this constructed borderland Anzaldúa experiences different stages of conocimiento that, as pointed out in the previous chapter, include a sense of arrebato, rupture, and fragmentation. As she stands in front of the famous cast depicting the body parts of the Aztec goddess of the moon, her venerated *Coyolxauhqui*, Anzaldúa identifies with being torn apart by the violence of coloniality. She acutely senses her fragmentation. She sees the powerful, yet ruptured goddess in both her fragmentation and in her possibility of being "re-membered"—the term Anzaldúa uses to denote the creative process that allows her to get a sense of herself as a whole, as someone who can create new forms.[19] Anzaldúa stands in front of this goddess made stone, representative of the ravages of colonization—the conquest of women's bodies, land, cultures, and tongues, but not the "underground tongues" of the psyche's images and the unconscious reservoir of el cenote.[20] Anzaldúa's own mouth does not lose all her tongues; they are connected to her Indigenous roots and spiritual attunement to different worlds. Yet in the middle of the museum Anzaldúa stands as a being that has been torn apart, seeking some sort of coming together so as to make "new assemblages" that can change "el punto de referencia" (the point of reference). From this vantage point, however, Anzaldúa also becomes able to see "from a hundred different viewpoints," a vital praxis of border arte.[21]

Anzaldúa's meditation amid objects representative of Aztec culture, her reflection on and connection to her Indigenous past as well as her critique of the commercialization, appropriation, and romanticization of Indigenous culture, art, history, and peoples, are all different forces pushing and pulling her, making her question both her Indigeneity and her own and other Chicanas' possible appropriations of Indigeneity. Yet she also finds strength in works by Chicana border artists such as Santa Barraza, Yolanda M. López, Marsha Gómez, and Carmen Loma Garzas. There is both pride and self-criticism in Anzaldúa's experience at the museum. She becomes attuned to the sound of Edward James Olmos's voice who narrates information about the artifacts in front of her, while also being attentive to her thoughts, doubts, anxieties, fears, and spiritual insights. She stands in front of a glass case trapping the skeleton of a jaguar with a greenstone in its jaw—a powerful animal encased in the glass of coloniality.[22] Still, this animal is representative of "the consciousness that stalks in the darkness" and calls Anzaldúa to tap into her own "unconscious reservoir of meaning,"[23] to be receptive to different ways of being and sensing. Zaytoun describes this experience as Anzaldúa's shamanic journey and her entering into the museum as "a walker between worlds."[24] Torn, anxious but defiant, Anzaldúa stands in the Denver museum—but also in nepantla, the space for creation and transformation, a "contact zone." Anzaldúa herself becomes moon goddess.[25]

Importantly, Anzaldúa is also affected by her encounter with the Coyolxauhqui stone. That is, her experience also points to an intimate relation with objects connected to Indigenous mythology. To expand our insight regarding the importance of the relationship between self and objects, we can appeal to Monique Roelofs's account of relational aesthetics undergirded by a theory of address. That is, we can understand the stone of the moon goddess as *addressing* Anzaldúa and she as addressing it, of course in the constrained context of a museum but also beyond.[26] Doing so is not meant to enact a secularization of Anzaldúa's account or an undermining of a shamanic experience connected to Indigenous practices and spiritualities; rather, I wish to disclose the perceptual, affective connections that are present in Anzaldúa's descriptions of her experience of objects, an experience that does not preclude a connection to the spiritual or to Indigenous cosmologies. Yet here I underscore a reading of Anzaldúa's phenomenological insight regarding the way her perception of objects discloses affective relations. While a phenomenological reading of Anzaldúa has been criticized by Zaytoun as failing to account for naguala processes or shamanic experiences, it nevertheless discloses Anzaldúa's key insights regarding perception and the intimacy between self and objects in creative processes. This is yet another layer of Anzaldúa's description of her experience, one that may not always be connected to shamanic experience.[27] Following Anzaldúa's own methodology that allows for a multiplicity of approaches, there is room for examining how the perception-affect nexus may be understood as playing a role in the intimate relation that Anzaldúa has with the artifacts in the museum. Roelofs's theory of address helps us highlight this intimacy.

According to Roelofs, the aesthetic is intertwined with various modes of living informed by a vast web of relationships that ultimately make our life and our world livable, enjoyable, and pleasurable, or painful, miserable, and dangerous.[28] In *The Cultural Promise of the Aesthetic*, Roelofs offers a living aesthetics in which selves, objects, and worlds intermix and produce ways of thinking, doing, and sensing that defy simple dichotomies and take into consideration complexity, multiplicity, and multilayeredness—not only of our lives and interactions with objects and each other in specific sociohistorical contexts, but also of the ways the aesthetic shifts and morphs in a multiplicity of crisscrossing promises and threats, modes of address, relations, and elements that Roelofs takes as constitutive of the aesthetic. Key to this aesthetics is the notion of address. Roelofs provides a full analysis of this notion in *Arts of Address: Being Alive to Language and the World*.[29] Rather than thinking of address as a form of speech directed at other subjects, she describes modes of address as "forms of signification that we direct at human and non-human beings, objects, and places and that these entities direct at us and at each other," thus reframing the notion so as to connect it with perceptual modalities in subjects but also objects and places.[30] As she states, "On a daily basis, lines of address link us to diverse entities: tunes, screeches, clicks, beeps, cracks, theories, poems, photographs, colors, bicycles, lakes, brooms, effigies, bells, computers, pillows, skyscrapers, trash."[31] For Roelofs, these lines of address keep us alive to the world.[32]

Anzaldúa's process of sensuous, fleshy creativity guided by affective mapping and coupled with Roelofs's aesthetic vision allows for an enhanced understanding of nepantla not only as a zone of painful but creative transformation (a tearing apart and coming together constitutive of border arte) but also as a zone of intertwining between selves and objects—that is, a zone in which there is no longer an understanding of the self in terms of autonomous agency and mastery over worlds. Instead, there is a complex, intricate layering of communication between embodied selves, objects, and places, pointing to both promises and threats across and between worlds of sense, spirituality, materiality, embodiment, and communal histories. Here the perception of objects is always connected to affectivity. What this sensuous aesthetics adds is the call for an engagement with the intricate set of relations, including affective relations, raised by the anatomy of address that, according to Roelofs, discloses possibilities of "agency" not just for subjects but also objects. Such an anatomy of address has five constitutive elements that point to the normative character of modes of address: norms, forms, structures, scenes, and scripts of address.[33] In other words, objects and places, whether natural or artificial, are not simply there for us to perceive them and/or possess them, undermine them, and so on. They are part of a web of relations of address that structure our everyday experience in general, and affective relations in particular. They address selves as much as selves are addressed by them, although not necessarily in a reversible or reciprocal manner.

Now think of Anzaldúa addressing and being addressed by the Coatlicue stone. Anzaldúa first describes her experience of looking at the round stone carving of Coyolxauhqui, the moon goddess, before encountering the jaguar. These cultural artifacts, which in the context of a US museum denote a dead culture, become alive in Anzaldúa's experience, calling her to feel the pain of colonization in women's bodies, the tearing of body, lands, and cultures. She is thoroughly affected by the perception of the stone. Anzaldúa herself becomes Coyolxauhqui, disintegrating into "hundreds of pieces, hundreds of separate awarenesses" considering the pain of the past and how it is carried in the present, even by way of her own embodiment and the way it is oppressed by US white culture and the heterosexism and patriarchy of Mexican culture.[34] Anzaldúa connects to the stone in a movement of the otherwise, differently from the norms and scripts of address associated with a museum. New directions and orientations are opened. Rather than an inanimate, dead museum artifact, the stone takes a life not of its own but in the company of Anzaldúa and of

Nahua mythology. Anzaldúa addresses the stone and the stone addresses her. These addresses are entwined in a web of relations that, according to Roelofs, constitutes a normative web of structures and scripts that has positive as well as negative impacts on the self's present existence (multiple promises and/or threats), and for Anzaldúa also includes the spiritual world and the world of her ancestors. Later, as Anzaldúa encounters the jaguar, it invites her on a shamanic journey to the world of the unconscious and to that which is not easily accessible to the naked eye—the cenote, which as we have noted is Anzaldúa's name for the reservoir of images, symbols, intuitions that are part of conocimiento.

With the aid of Roelofs's living, relational aesthetics, Anzaldúa's connection with the objects in the museum becomes more than a mere seeing of objects representing a dead past but an engaged, sensuous, complex, affective relational self-object experience that takes place within a larger web of relationality informed by various modes of address. At the Denver Museum of Natural History, Anzaldúa addresses and is addressed by Aztec artifacts, is affectively touched by them, and becomes receptive to body, space, matter, spirit, myths, and histories. She lets herself be called—and develops (and enacts) a theory of border arte informed by conocimiento that defies traditional understandings of art-making or the agential, individual artist, creating works of art that represent things, places, and people in the world. Here Anzaldúa defines the practice of border arte and becomes border artist herself. It is a complex process involving her own desires, wants, and intentions but also that which is invoked by artifacts turned addressers that call her to connect to myths and to the spiritual; she gives herself to their calls and to the worlds where they take her. As Anzaldúa states, "Other forces influence, impact and construct our desires—including the unconscious and the collective unconscious forces and residues of those that came before us, our ancient ancestors."[35]

Importantly, Anzaldúa describes border arte as "counter-art," art that moves away from the expected norms and structures of address. Border arte constitutes the creative production of those inhabiting and sensing nepantla, who can shift identities and modes of knowing, thus having the possibility to create anew. Border arte, then, may be politically resistant and may have a critical function of unsettling standard modes of address: "The border artist constantly reinvents her/himself. Through art, s/he is able to re-read, reinterpret, re-envision and reconstruct her/his culture's present, as well as its past."[36] According to Anzaldúa, border arte, rather than pictorially representing the world, "depicts both the soul del artista y el alma del pueblo."[37] The soul of the border artist is one who affectively maps herself, senses the various modes of address of her present situation, and is informed by her present communal relations as well as past histories.

At the end of her five hours in the museum, an exhausted Anzaldúa—with aching feet and buzzing questions in her head—asks, "What direction will el arte fronterizo take in the future?"[38] She wonders about the multisubjectivity and split subjectivity of border artists and worries about polarizing movements that might lead to splits between us/them and insiders/outsiders. Yet she predicts that border artists will refuse to be split. As she puts it, "We are both *nos* (us) and *otras* (others)—*nos/otras.* Art makes a wider community, one that transcends the artist's culture and lifetime."[39] Here a tension in Anzaldúa's account of border arte emerges: while border arte is supposed to capture the "soul del artista y el alma del pueblo," it is also supposed to "transcend" the artist's culture and lifetime. In fact, for Anzaldúa, this transcendence is one of the most important aspects of border arte as it allows for new mixtures, new points of references, as well as shifting identities, border crossings, and hybridism, which she considers decolonizing strategies.[40] Border arte, then, aims to capture specific elements of one's culture while at the same time opening the possibility of changing, rethinking, and reframing them. That is, while anchored in the artist's culture, myths, and histories, border arte also has the possibility of mixing disparate elements and cultures in movements of the otherwise.

With border arte Anzaldúa aims to develop an aesthetic practice propelled by this mixture of disparate elements, a practice that is also capable of offering possibilities of survival and transformation for its practitioners. As a carnal aesthetic, border arte, like the complex subjectivity that Anzaldúa theorizes, remains attuned to the self's needs, desires, hopes, dreams, vulnerabilities, and wounds, but also to this self's possibilities of connection with her community and beyond.[41] As such, the tension that is reflected in the process of border arte as an individual and communal practice reflects the very complex and tense operations of conocimiento itself—which, as we have seen in the previous chapter, includes not only moments of arrebato that are intimately felt in the body in transformations (inner work) but also moments of resistance in connection to one's community (public acts).

Border arte may transfigure and refigure ordinary, dominant, colonial perceptual and discursive operations, becoming a key political practice for those at the margins.[42] Anzaldúa thus leaves us with border arte as a key aesthetic vision that involves the following characteristics that capture both the intimate and communal moments of the process: first, border arte arises in nepantla and involves a tearing apart and pulling together of the artist; second, it is informed by the artist's conocimiento, which is itself an entanglement between the perceptual, the affective, the spiritual, and the epistemic; third, it displays the artist's multiple points of view and shifts of consciousness; fourth, it is dependent on and affected by the artist's sensory receptivity and increased receptivity to the spiritual, including shamanic experiences, as well as to the unconscious; fifth, it has a key communal element and ties to the artist's ancestral and present communities (it is thus haunted by death); sixth, it is a way of creating the history of one's people; seventh, it may produce counter-art; and eighth, both border arte and border artists serve as bridges to groups outside the artist's own community. Having been affectively addressed by the objects in the museum, Anzaldúa has walked her way to a new vision of art and art-making for those in the in-between. Anzaldúa, the border artist herself, walks out of the museum and writes her story—she leaves us with her own border arte. I wish to dwell with the intimacies in Anzaldúa's creative process of border arte, with the way the artist herself is affectively touched in the most intimate ways as she creates border arte such that she becomes able to carve her own face, to make herself through the creative process.[43] This is the movement of autoarte.

THE INTIMACIES OF AUTOARTE

As we have seen, the praxis of making border arte is not only generative insofar as it allows for artistic and creative processes, but it also presents the self with apertures of in-betweenness leading to different and even new modes of thinking, being, and sensing. Anzaldúa's own aesthetic practice, which I have previously described as mouthly and carnal, her flesh*and*blood writings, her autohistorias and autohistoria-teorías, constitute a poetics of self-making: "When I write it feels like I'm carving bone. It feels like I am creating my own face, my own heart—a Nahuatl concept. My soul makes itself through the creative act. It is constantly remaking and giving birth to itself through my body. It is this learning to live with la *Coatlicue* that transforms living in the Borderlands from a nightmare into a numinous experience. It is always a path/state to something else."[44] Recall that for Anzaldúa, writing is "a sensuous act" that allows her to spill herself inside of trees. It is a process of self-formation connected to conocimiento as affective mapping that allows for possibilities beyond survival, toward practices of making and transforming oneself away from the constraints of the colonial eye. In this context, to write is to live,[45] which, in Anzaldúan fashion, also means to commute with the material, the spiritual, the human and the nonhuman, the unconscious, as well as present and past histories of one's people. Writing becomes a carnality, a sensuous creative process, a mouthly aesthetics. Anzaldúa's "blood sacrifices" are informed by the deep intertwining between, as she would say, her bodymindsoul and the earth- and spirit-bodies: "For only through the body, through the pulling of flesh, can the human soul be transformed. And for images, words, stories to have this transformative power, they must arise from the human body—flesh and bone—and from the Earth's body—stone, sky, liquid, soil."[46]

In her ambulatory meditation in a museum-turned-borderlands, Anzaldúa has created an autohistoria-teoría, inviting us to connect her carnal aesthetics specifically to production in nepantla and to relational, communal elements. Inspired by Anzaldúa's polysensory, multifaceted process of creation of border arte, I now wish to introduce the notion of autoarte as a multisensory, mobile creative process of self-making and self-transformation that highlights the intimate, personal perceptual-affective process that is vital for the kind of carnal aesthetics exemplified in Anzaldúa's writings.[47] That is, autoarte captures the intimate nature of the creative practice of border arte. By introducing the notion of autoarte, I wish to further tease out the mouthly, carnal, creative processes that condition the possibility for self-making and transformation as they are intimately felt by the self, and that may also lead to a movement from abjection, dejection, and degradation to possibilities of self-naming, transformation, and even possibilities for joy. This is a process that is intimately experienced by the self and as such is not necessarily done for a public as with more explicitly resistant instances of border arte.

Given the crucial role of arrebato, rupture, pain, and trauma in Anzaldúa's writings, it feels odd to discuss the role of joy in her life and in her work. The word *joy* barely appears in *Borderlands / La Frontera* and in *Light in the Dark / Luz en lo oscuro*. In the preface of *Borderlands / La Frontera*, Anzaldúa says that "there have been compensations for this mestiza, and certain joys."[48] She also says that she felt great joy when she first saw a poem written in Tex-Mex and when writing helps her heal from trauma.[49] Finally, in the section "Invoking Art" in the chapter "*Tlilli, Tlapalli* / The

Path of the Red and Black Ink," Anzaldúa writes that she is almost finished writing the book and describes it in terms of a mosaic with a weaving pattern. When describing the text, she states, "It is a rebellious, willful entity, a precocious girl-child forced to grow up too quickly, rough, unyielding, with pieces of feather sticking out here and there, fur, twigs, clay. My child, but not for much longer. This female being is angry, sad, joyful, is Coatlicue, dove, horse, serpent, cactus."[50] In *Light in the Dark / Luz en lo oscuro,* Anzaldúa mentions that our habitual perspectives change when there is a traumatic or joyful event and that openings to the sacred may also be prompted by "joyful experiences—for example, meditation, epiphanies, communion with nature, sexual ecstasy, and desire."[51] Yet she reminds us that "because most of you are wounded, negative emotions provide easier access to the sacred than positive emotions."[52] Woundedness, according to Anzaldúa, is an opening to vulnerability and being present to others and to one's body—rather than relying on a rational, excessive dwelling on one's wounds, what she describes as a leaving of one's body, a desconocimiento.[53] While Anzaldúa centers woundedness and only considers joy explicitly only these few times, I seek joy in her words. I sense that it is there—precisely in her carnal aesthetics.[54] Autoarte is a notion meant to capture the intimacies of the creative process that open the possibility for self-naming and self-transformation in both its woundedness and moments of joy.

Autoarte involves two major movements that the reader will see can be connected to border arte but that, in this instance, highlight the personal, intimate, subjective affectivity of a particular though relational self. The first movement is that of the self affectively responding to sense perceptions due to the perception-affect nexus previously discussed. The second movement is that of the self intimately registering how different elements or media creatively inspire her, what has been described as the medium-affect nexus. The first movement may involve the first through fifth characteristics of border arte listed above, albeit without following a linear sequence; it is thus a complex, polysensory, multivalent process. The second major movement connected to autoarte involves what we may consider an aesthetic translation of the affectivity prompted by a medium, be it word, light, sound, paint, stone, and so on—a process of translation that *may* open the possibility for the self engaged in the creative process to "carve" and transform herself in ways distinct from normative, hegemonic visions. In autoarte, the multiplicitous self constructs herself while she paints with light, molds with touch, seduces with sound, delights with taste. It is a mouth that speaks, screams, hums, kisses, touches, bites, and leads the body to write with light, sound, taste, and touch.

In the practice of autoarte, the body serves as a crossroad to ways of being, sensing, and knowing that are constitutive of affective mapping, self-making, and self-transformation. Here the perception-affect and medium-affect nexuses move the self toward a creative process or practice. While such process or practice need not be a traditional artistic practice nor require expertise or a final product that is to be considered an artwork in the traditional sense, it nevertheless opens the possibility for the self to name and construct herself in moments of intimacy or intertwining with others and earth- and spirit-bodies. With its double movement, autoarte is a carnality, a sensuous, creative process that translates the affective responses of perception into creative processes of self-making and transformation within a chiasmatic in-between. Autoarte entails moments not just of communication but of intimacy. If understood within the context of the Anzaldúan praxis of border arte, autoarte is that personal, subjective moment in which the maker or artist can be torn apart but also pulled together, a Coyolxauhqui moment of self-construction that may counter the prying colonial gaze. Even though the creative process and content of autoarte (or of border arte) are not to be thought as the answer to alleviate negative internal or external racialized perception or other types of violence and oppression, we cannot disregard the opportunities, even if elusive, in which bodies of color can name themselves and, in so doing, care for themselves.

In the practice of autoarte, the affective component associated with perception and intuitions is registered by a particular self, prompting different creative translations—hence the "auto" of autoarte. Importantly, the Greek prefix *auto-* is usually translated as "self" and has traditionally been understood in terms of self-movement, self-acting, or self-creation—for example, *autopoiesis,* an important concept that has been understood in terms of its biological implications as well as narrative and political possibilities.[55] It is also commonly understood as simply denoting one's own experience, such as in the term *autobiography.* Anzaldúa herself uses the term *autohistoria* to point to the stories she writes about her life—except that in her usage she is already destabilizing the traditional meaning of *autobiography* as her autohistorias combine both real and fictive elements and depict the "I" of the *auto*biography as one that is deeply relational and cannot be understood as separate from particular communities or histories, as traditional understandings of subjectivity are. Similarly, I intend the "auto" of autoarte to stand for an intimate, personal embodied experience, a movement that is being registered, sensed, *suffered* (as in "experienced") by a particular self, but must be always understood as relational and in connection to a larger web of personal relationships and addresses in Roelofs's sense. As such, autoarte is profoundly important for marginalized, multiplicitous selves, especially when they are in the grip of hostile, dominant environments.

Given autoarte's two main movements that sensuously connect the embodied self to elements, objects, and so on, in particularized personal experiences, autoarte is a key practice of carnal aesthetics, one that is highly personal, intimate, and thus involves "inner work." Autoarte can be connected to what in previous chapters has been explained as quiet, Kevin Quashie's term aimed at capturing movements related to the "expressiveness of interiority." As he puts it, "Quiet, then, is the inexpressible expressiveness of this interior, an expressiveness that can appear publicly, have and affect social and political meaning, challenge or counter social discourse, yet none of this is its aim or essence."[56] In my view, autoarte encompasses this expressiveness of interiority that is so important for Quashie, although in this instance it highlights the embodied aspect of the experience in the context of an intertwining of selves and worlds. Consequently, autoarte is a thoroughly embodied practice in which one's body becomes a carnal crossroad to aesthetic self-making.

To say that the body becomes a carnal crossroad in autoarte is to acknowledge how the body is the direct connection between the maker, artist, or self in-between who is affected, and that which affects this body, be it an object, natural elements, or specific materials. Here we find a chiasmatic relation, an interlacing between self and worlds that defies traditional boundaries between objects and subjects, leading to intimacies of the in-between. These intimacies are felt deeply within one's body, although they are always already informed by the communion of selves and worlds. Autoarte as creative practice, with its double movement of perceptually and affectively registering worlds and its translation of such experience into a creative object in different media, does not move from the inside to the outside as if these two realms were separate. The personal, subjective element of the practice already has relational ties, with objects, the human and nonhuman, and the spiritual. Yet autoarte highlights that intimate, subjective moment when, through the body, the self engages in the creative process and affectively maps herself in an environment for the purposes of self-naming, which is not necessarily connected to an audience. As such, it is quiet. As Quashie says, "The aesthetic of quiet is watcherless."[57] In other words, autoarte is not necessarily a political practice done for the purposes of explicit public political resistance that needs an audience. However, autoarte is indispensable.

While autoarte may be a fulfilling moment in its quietness, as a sensuous, mouthly process, it may also reveal possibilities for affective mapping as well as self and communal constructions different than those dictated by colonial impositions. That is, it may also prompt the self to enact a communal making of the history of one's people, produce explicit counter-art, or serve as a bridge to other communities (the sixth through eighth characteristics of border arte above). In both its more and less quiet moments, autoarte is already part of the lives of people of color, even if they are not professional artists but everyday selves engaging in hometactics,[58] finding ways of being-in-worlds that help them, as Anzaldúa says, re-member some of the pieces of their selves that have been scattered by experiences of arrebatos. Autoarte can consequently be thought as an aesthetic hometactic: specifically, as one in which the aim is not to attain familiarity or sense of belonging to a group or to a place, but in the sense of an aesthetic self-tactic in which one's sensory, affective registers are engaged in deep perception that helps a self name and even transform herself by way of creative processes—including processes that may open possibilities of transformation away from the prying colonial eye. It is important that this notion of aesthetic self-tactic is not taken to mean that the self can create or transform herself in absolutely any way she wants, as if there were no bodily or structural limits.[59] The importance of the "tactical" here is not meant to undermine material conditions and constraints but to capture the sense of the multiple openings for survival and self-naming, self-transformation away from dominant imaginaries that become possible in different circumstances of one's life. As such, this tactical character of autoarte points to its mobile character.

Since the construction and revelation of selves is dependent on an entwinement between the self and the earth- and spirit-bodies, it is also important to point out that autoarte is something that *happens to* the self-turned-artist, as well as a practice that can be intentionally cultivated. For example, Anzaldúa describes autohistoria as not completely agential since it is created in different places and times when she is creatively *moved* by different elements (the medium-affect nexus), be it unconscious elements from el cenote or affective responses to objects and situations. How does the attunement of this intertwining take place? Without wishing to categorize that which defies categorization and which is sometimes ineffable—for example, the way a piece of wood calls the artist to shape it, or light shows itself to the photographer, painter, or whoever is moved by light, or the pigment red inspires one to construct a form on a canvas—it is important to note that selves constantly experience these moments of affinity, intimacy, communion, with the earth-body and beyond. Such experiences are, in my view, carnal openings in which the self flows with the elements, open to different possibilities of connection and affectivity. Yet there is also a more intentional or active engagement in the practice of autoarte in which the self explicitly, actively reads and creatively interprets the various images, signs, affects arising from various sources. In both its moments when autoarte happens to the self or when the self actively seeks autoarte, this tactical, mobile carnality can be practiced in different contexts and for different reasons. In this latter active sense, autoarte is no longer a quiet practice but can be said to become more resonant, searching for louder ways than the institutional or dominant manner in which we are supposed to respond to the world and all that is in it.[60] In these openings—which, according to Anzaldúa, are cracks, ruptures, or tears of the "membranes surrounding, protecting, and containing the different cultures and their perspectives"—new possibilities, new forms, new ways of being emerge.[61]

Through these cracks the marginalized self that has been directed to see herself in specific ways—ways that may also be denigrating and undermining—can be moved to artistic creation to see and present herself in a different light. Autoarte registers flesh*and*blood, the entwinement of self and worlds, and presents a potentiality that is key in the process of self-making. Anzaldúa lets us see how it influences her own writing such that it allows her to "re-member" herself, to make herself after she has been torn apart by the processes of coloniality. It is her autohistorias and autohistoria-teorías that emerge from her close communion with the earth- and spirit-bodies and el cenote that help her carve her own face. While autohistoria and autohistoria-teoría highlight writing, autoarte can be connected to any process of mouthly creation including and beyond black ink and red paint.[62]

Thinking with Roelofs, I would like to connect this mouthly process of autoarte with what she considers the double movement of the aesthetic: the fact that it is deeply tied to injustices, hierarchies, and threats but also harbors constructive possibilities for desire, sociality, and meaning—it is imbued with promises.[63] Autoarte is crucial for staying alive in two senses: as being alive to the world in a way that one notices its richness, complexity, and the multiple relations of flesh*and*blood, and as surviving worlds that do not allow for much dignity and respect, as living in worlds in which, every day, one is constantly reminded of the gestures, worlds, and habits of racism as well as sexism and other violence. Yet for some there will not be the opportunity to engage in practices of autoarte, as they might not have the opportunity, time, or resources to do so. As mobile, autoarte is not guaranteed or does not guarantee a seeing of oneself otherwise or being-in-worlds differently than dominant powers allow. There is no fixed methodology or requirement necessary for practicing autoarte, no prescription as to how it is to be done. My point is that autoarte is already being put in practice by countless marginalized selves even when they are not artists in the traditional sense; they are already affectively and creatively mapping themselves in the face of hostility and worlds sutured by racist structures. As Anzaldúa shows with her own practice of writing autohistoria-teorías, and as we will see in the case of Aguilar's photography, it is indeed possible to use light for the purposes of creating oneself away from expected abjections and indignities connected to a life of liminality and marginalization and in order to seek joy. I thus wish to underscore the capacity for creative processes as being key to the lives of those who are marginalized and living in in-between-worlds. While the practice of autoarte is neither inherently resistant nor political, it persists. At moments it thrives, despite obstacles to liberation and attempts at denigration of bodies of color, who despite their sorrow, are able to create, and to write themselves into being, even with light.

AGUILAR'S BODY AS CARNAL CROSSROAD, AN EROTICS OF LIGHT

It's hot. She rests in Sandy's room (fig. 3.2). Is it a day of leisure or of anguish? Is it too hard to live the life of a young, lesbian, working-class Chicana artist? Perhaps that cold drink, the soft wind touching her skin, caressing her preoccupations, can give some respite. She is extremely shy and has a disability that has made her life difficult. She feels shame because of her sexuality and her large body. Yet she takes a camera and discloses herself, shows her vulnerability to the lens, in a way that we never thought a shy woman would. This writing with light has been interpreted as "a personal yet feminist response to the many women's fitness,

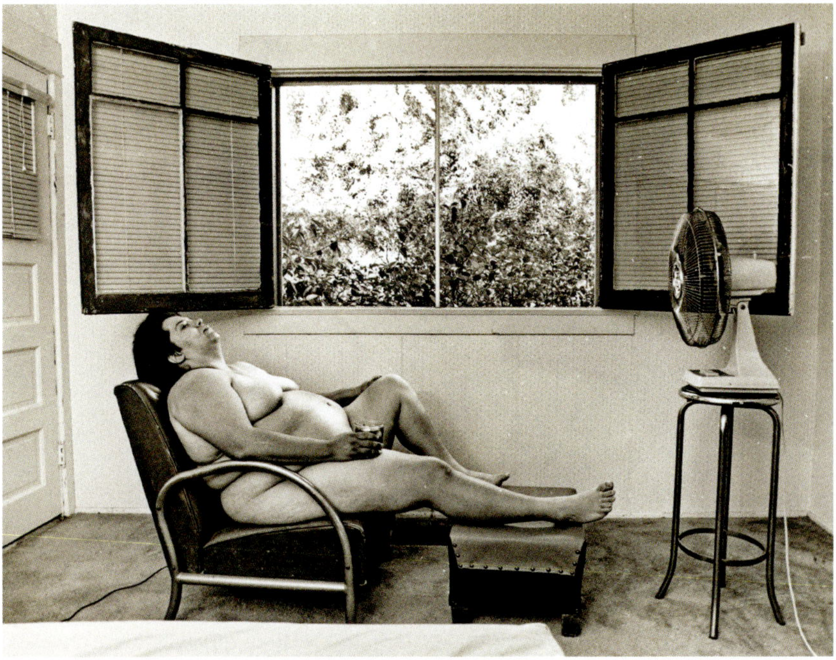

3.2 Laura Aguilar, *In Sandy's Room*, 1990. Gelatin silver print, 16 × 20 in. Copyright Laura Aguilar Trust of 2016.

clothing, and glamour magazines she came across while housesitting for her friend Sandy."[64] For me, it shows Aguilar's body as a carnal crossroad, as a bridge to other ways of being and sensing. The camera will take her to deep intimacy with the earth- and spirit-bodies. It's 1989. From that open window, trees are already peeking in, calling her to commute with them by way of her skin and light.

As we have seen in the previous section, autoarte as the intimate dimension and process of border arte is a vital component of carnal aesthetics. It highlights the self's intimate, subjective affective responses to perception and translates elements into creative works. In so doing, it discloses the intimacies of the creative process. Autoarte captures movements of sensation when the body is touched, affected, moved, wounded, inspired in sensuous ways within a context that recognizes the intertwining of the self with the earth- and spirit-bodies—as in the case of Aguilar's *Nature Self Portrait #5* (fig. 3.3). As if looking for company, in the midst of a life filled with anguish and sorrow due to society's controlling hegemonic visions of beauty, race, class, sexuality, and ability that reject her,[65] Aguilar

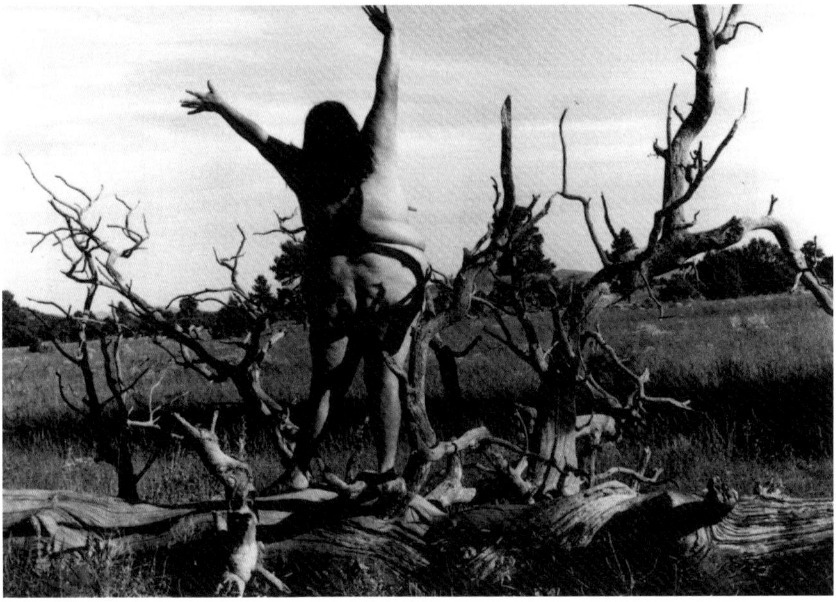

3.3 Laura Aguilar, *Nature Self Portrait #5*, 1996. Gelatin silver print, 20 × 16 in. Copyright Laura Aguilar Trust of 2016.

finds the tender company of twisted yet defiant branches rhizomatically dancing, inviting her to become one with them. Aguilar lets light capture her communion with trees, grass, sky, and light. I wonder, what sensations animate her? Is there an ever-so-slight wind touching her skin as she sprouts roots to ground herself in a world that rejects her because of her gender, ability, sexuality, ethnicity? What goes on in her as she extends her limbs toward a sky that welcomes her? Her writing with light is her autoarte.

As a carnal practice, autoarte is informed by the intimacies between the self and the elements in terms of the perception-affect and medium-affect nexuses; it senses that compelling, sometimes dynamic, sometimes subtle movement, in which the self is personally affected. It may involve a Coatlicue moment, a moment of dread, fear, self-dispersal, and wounding as well as *a* Coyolxauhqui moment of *re-membering,* a coming together in an act of self-naming, self-creating, self-transformation away from the destructive dominant colonial gaze. Autoarte captures the intimacy of the self in the moment of being touched by the earth- and spirit-bodies toward a creative act. As a mobile creative process that engages the self's embodied, spiritual, earthly, and communal experiences with intuitions, needs, desires, and longings in a process of a sensuous art-making, autoarte is a creative praxis that grants marginalized selves an aperture to self-making and self-transformation, revealing the body as a carnal crossroad.

In this section, I wish to consider Aguilar's light-writings in connection with Sandoval's vision of erotics. Inspired by Audre Lorde, Sandoval recognizes the power of art-making not only for one's very survival but also for one's attainment of joy, for a life in which the self is not really absent, lost in a sea of imposed norms, but instead lives a life informed by sensuousness and the erotic. This is not the simple joy associated with happiness but an anguished joy, the joy of those whose histories and lives continually intersect with the woundedness and sorrow created by the way that coloniality continues to structure worlds. As previously noted, Audre Lorde reminds us that "the erotic is not a question only of what we do; it is a question of how acutely and fully we can feel the doing."[66] Anguished joy is this acute feeling. Here I consider autoarte in the context of Aguilar's writing with light to disclose what Chela Sandoval describes as an erotics and hermeneutics of love that, in Aguilar's work, is transformed into a queer erotics of light, unveiling Aguilar and others in an affirmation of sexuality that defies traditional Catholic mores. Aguilar's photography is a queer seeking of joy as can be had by a body that has already been denied an existence full of pride and self-assurance, a life without shame of her sexuality, but a body that nevertheless does not give up on love or futurity—a love that as we will see below, may be both quiet and, as Sandoval notes, a way of "*re-forming* the self and the world."[67]

Not giving up on love informs Sandoval's important methodology of the oppressed, a methodology that enables a *differential* mode of social movement and consciousness that allows subjects to attain the skills necessary to read and counter oppressive capitalist ideologies.[68] In her response to Fredric Jameson's claim that postmodern subjects are trapped and lack a type of "cartographic proficiency" of knowing how to cognitively map themselves so as to understand their particular positionalities within local, national, and global contexts saturated by capitalist mechanisms and ideologies, Sandoval points to US Third World theorists "taking and using whatever is necessary and available in order to negotiate, confront, or speak to power—and then moving on to new forms, expressions, and ethos when necessary."[69] That is, tactics of survival and resistance, or technologies of the methodology of the oppressed, as Sandoval envisions them, have been continuously at work even though they have been made invisible, tokenized, or undervalued in an academic setting marked by what Sandoval calls "academic apartheid."[70] As Sandoval states, "US peoples of color have long acted, spoken, intellectualized, lived out what Cherríe Moraga calls a 'theory in the flesh,' a theory that allows survival and more, that allows practitioners to live with faith, hope, and moral vision in spite of all else."[71]

With a vision toward the future, Sandoval wishes for new technologies for a methodology of the oppressed. She calls for "new ways of reading, thinking, behaving, hoping, imagining, from the simplest activity . . . to the most obtuse, understanding the differential form of oppositional consciousness and social movement as the methodology of the oppressed that can generate a hermeneutics of love in the postmodern world."[72] Inspired by Lorde and Barthes, Sandoval calls for a hermeneutics of love and an erotics in which love is "reinvented as a political technology, as a body of knowledges, arts, practices, and *procedures for re-forming the self and the world*" (my emphasis).[73] These exercises in survival, self-naming, and self-transformation that marginalized selves enact are not mere epistemic exercises guided by differential consciousness. In my view, those at the margins are able to engage in *cognitive* mappings in the first place because they are already *perceptually and affectively mapping* themselves in their environment, their bodies affectively tracking the self's location in cartographies of power. These mappings are the body's affective attunement to their location in the spaces that they inhabit, which are saturated by power relations. Sandoval's methodology, then, can be seen as enhanced by what here I have been calling carnalities, creative practices in which selves affectively map themselves and engage in an aesthetics of self-making and transformation in a context in which self and worlds intertwine.

Aguilar's writing with light is prompted by perceptual operations that are themselves informed by affective responses. Such perceptions are not mere physical sensations that can be reduced to the interaction of physical and chemical reactions but affective mappings connected to mouthly perception—to feeling one's way in one's environment while being touched by worlds.[74] Given Sandoval's interest in "new ways of reading, thinking, behaving, hoping, imagining,"[75] I opt to center creative practices and consider the affective mappings of Aguilar as illustrated in her photographic autoarte through which she finds herself. Her photographs become skins of light, and her autoarte translates to a practice of love.

Aguilar's Autoarte as Affective Mapping

Aguilar's early photographic practice centers the capturing of marginalized national, racial, and sexual identities—for example, the series *How Mexican Is Mexican*; *Latina Lesbians*; *The Plush Pony*; and *Clothed/Unclothed*.[76] She later photographs the intimacy between her body and nature, her body absorbing light as much as the camera so as to write her story with it. When first encountering her work, I found her early self-portrait to be revealing.

"I am not comfortable with the word Lesbian," writes Aguilar below her own photo (fig. 3.4) for the *Latina Lesbians* series, consisting of photographs of Latinx lesbians in their everyday environments, accompanied by notes by those photographed. Aguilar feels discomfort with the word *lesbian*, which points to an uneasiness about her sexuality or with being encased in a particular sexual identity.[77] This discomfort with her sexuality contrasts with the relaxed posture of her body and her smile. Yet a print of an austere, grave Frida Kahlo stares back, creating a palpable tension within the photograph. It is the tension and contradictory moment of a smiling Aguilar and a serious Kahlo while surrounded by what I take to be objects that Aguilar cared for—books, masks, a puppet, a photograph, toy horses, a scary but funny stuffed monster hanging from the ceiling, and the game of lotería that so many Latinx children grow up playing. Yet Frida becomes a Barthean *punctum* here, recalling Aguilar's own woundedness. Aguilar's discomfort jumps to the fore, especially in light of the various difficulties of her life and her struggles for self-acceptance. Seriousness, discomfort, and pain do not escape this photograph, although Aguilar attests that each day she is becoming more comfortable with the word *LAURA*. Despite her struggles, she does not let go of the child within her, of her playfulness. "I will be damned if I let this part of me die!" she writes under her portrait. She must remind herself. She must do the work that it takes to keep her joy, as she is well aware of where she fares with others who merely mistake this joy for childlikeness and naïveté.

Through a photographic practice that specifically highlights the very sexual identity with which she is not comfortable, Aguilar affectively maps herself in the difficult terrain that does not accept lesbians or those who are playful. She does so in an act of vulnerability that is also her strength, as she cannot deny her own discomfort in her sexuality—doing so would negate her even more. An attunement to her environment, to

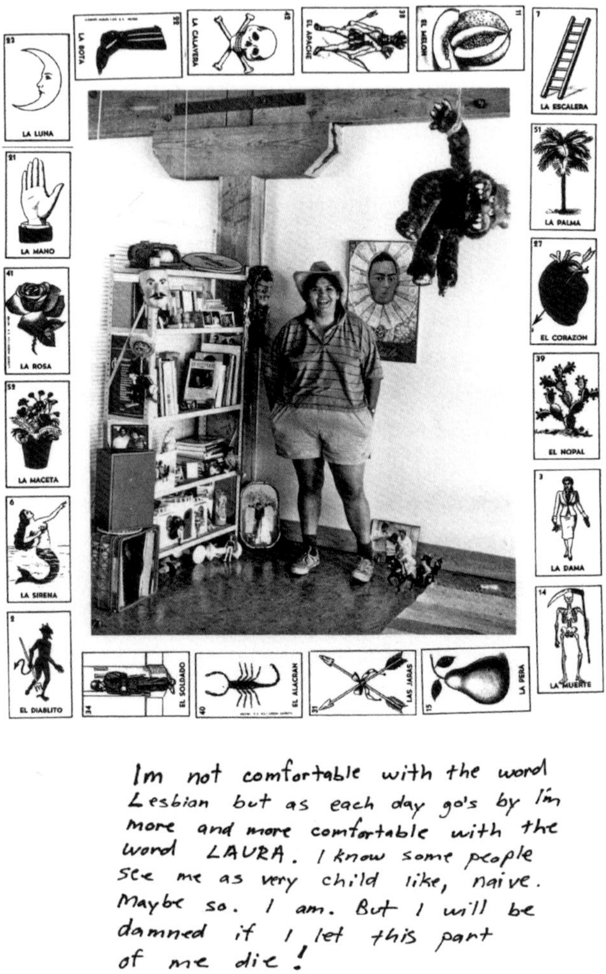

3.4 Laura Aguilar, *Laura Aguilar* (*Latina Lesbians Series*), 1987. Gelatin silver print, 11 × 14 in. Copyright Laura Aguilar Trust of 2016.

how others see her, to her own pain—but also to the joy, however tenuous, that games and toys bring her—is shown by her photographic practice that itself becomes a way of capturing this affective mapping with light, not in order to document or represent her life but to forge herself. Aguilar effectively and affectively uses photography to define herself, even when she is not quite comfortable with who she is. Moving from this affective mapping to a creative practice that itself registers this attunement, to a carnality, Aguilar will be damned if she does not commute with light in order to forge her bones or re-member herself as Anzaldúa would do. This is an enactment of queer carnality, of a creative process in which the queer artist asserts her being in the context of antiqueer normative environments. This is autoarte that becomes resonant, resistant. Similar to the Mexican artist Nahum B. Zenil (whose ex-votos paintings I have also analyzed as queer autoarte),[78] Aguilar's use of creative practices such as writing with light is a positing of her very existence as a queer within normative contexts that invisibilize, undermine, and do violence to LGBTQ2S+ individuals. What matters here is the queer artist's ability to affectively map herself in order to translate such mapping into an artistic practice that allows her to define herself, thus making queer autoarte not a "queer artwork" or a work about queerness, but an artwork that is the result of the artist's sensibility and ability to define herself and members of her group against the grain of normative, life-denying, invisibilizing, oppressive forces (figs. 3.5 and 3.6).[79]

Aguilar's two series that center Latina lesbians, *Latina Lesbians* and *Plush Pony*, are remarkable insofar as they affirm Latina lesbian existence. They are nevertheless very different, not only in terms of form and composition but also in terms of the social identities they highlight and the affective connection that Aguilar has to the works. While *Latina Lesbians* (figs. 3.4 and 3.5) features mostly educated lesbians in the late 1980s, *Plush Pony* (fig. 3.6) presents a small community of working-class Latina lesbians who frequented the bar called Plush Pony in El Sereno, a neighborhood of Los Angeles. The *Plush Pony* series was also done in 1992, a key year in the history of Los Angeles given the riots that erupted after four police officers were acquitted of all charges of the assault against Rodney King. As such, James Estrella urges us to understand the *Plush Pony* series in its complexity: the unlikely combination of lesbian pride and joy in the photographs and the political and economic events happening in the city at that tense time, a combination of hope and despair.[80] Estrella's archival work with Aguilar's documents points to Aguilar's "emotionally laborious experience while working on the *Plush Pony* Series."[81] Aguilar herself writes that, in downtown Los Angeles and East Los Angeles, she sees "a lot of despair, and a lot of apathy on the streets and in the people" while in Pasadena, the wealthier suburb, she notes the different, more comfortable life.[82] She is also not able to connect with the women who visit the Plush Pony and is deeply aware of the difference between this series and

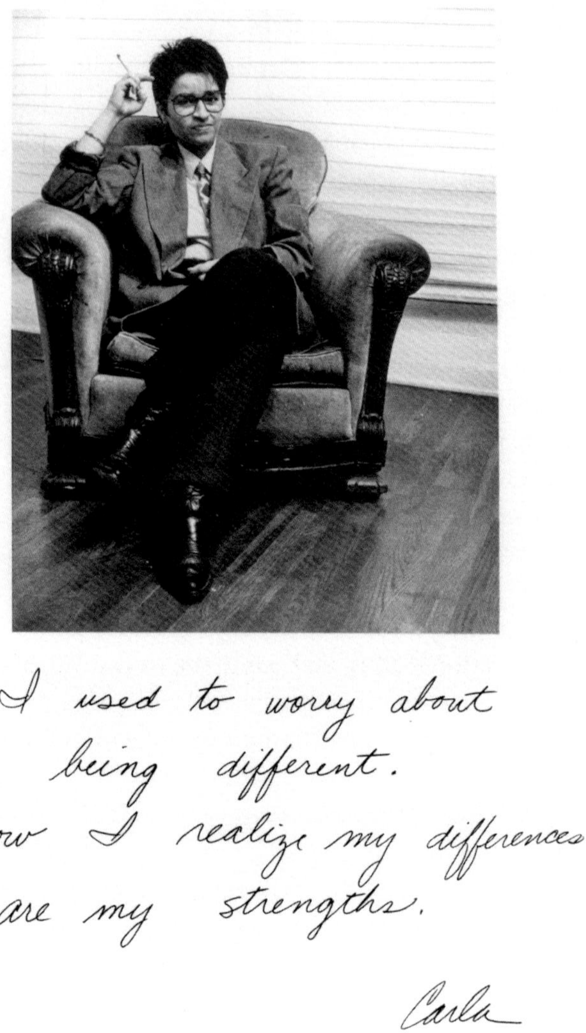

3.5 Laura Aguilar, *Carla Barboza* (*Latina Lesbians Series*), 1987. Gelatin silver print, 11 × 14 in. Copyright Laura Aguilar Trust of 2016.

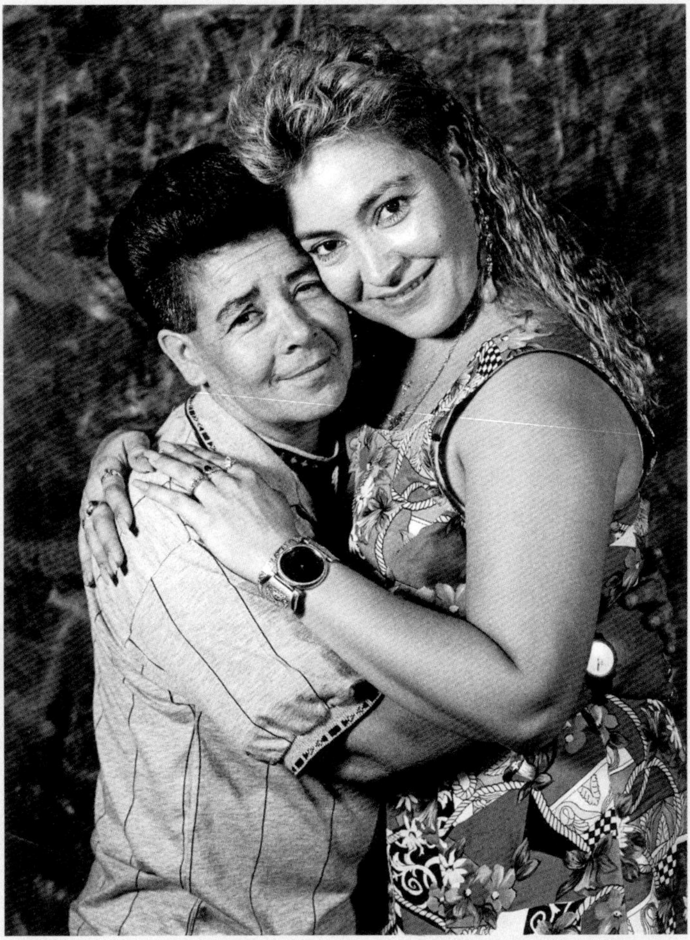

3.6 Laura Aguilar, *Plush Pony #15*, 1992. Gelatin silver print, 11 × 14 in. Copyright Laura Aguilar Trust of 2016.

Latina Lesbians, in which she says she was showing "one side of my community."[83] Aguilar is here affectively attuned to her environment as she produces her photographs, subsequently mapping herself within the context of the relations of power in the places she visits. She states, "I am referring to East Los Angeles; although, it doesn't have to be East Los Angeles. It can be anywhere there is a feeling of despair. In these types of areas there is a feeling in the air. You can see it, yet you can't touch it. It is a feeling of despair like there is nothing left of one's dreams to destroy."[84] Despite the emotional turmoil involved in the creation of *Plush Pony*, by way of her camera, Aguilar performs what might have seemed impossible given her comments about the feelings of despair that she feels in working-class communities and impoverished areas of Los Angeles such as East Los Angeles and El Sereno: she captures glimpses of joy and affirmations of life and futurity in these lesbian Chicana women for whom the Plush Pony is the "only place of community."[85] Importantly, as Macarena Gómez-Barris notes, the plush view becomes a makeshift studio that gives rise to a "plush view archive" rather than a normative archive. For Gómez-Barris this plush view archive is a "brown queer archive" that "has an entirely different condition of possibility precisely because displacement, dislocation, movement across borders and spaces, fragmentation, and its 'uncollected' quality necessarily define it as provisional."[86]

Of course, Aguilar knows that art can only do so much in "giving a voice" to those of color who take pride in themselves and their culture. "Don't tell her art can't hurt," Aguilar implores in the title of another photograph (fig. 3.7), defiantly looking at us, her hands tightly holding a gun aimed at her mouth, the "devouring mouth" that for Anzaldúa is the entrance of wind, fires, sea, and earth.[87] Let us remember Anzaldúa's warning, "To be a mouth—the cost is too high"—so much so that life itself is at stake. As a woman of color who takes pride in herself and her culture, who as she says, uses her art to give a voice to herself and culture and to build bridges, what does it mean for Aguilar to have door after door slammed in her face? She has managed to do autoarte despite all odds, learning disabilities, racism, sexism, financial precarity, self-doubt, pain, abjection, yet here she is—a contradiction in terms—defiantly asserting herself, putting herself in the map, while at the same time conceding that the cost might indeed be too high, that it hurts too much to be that woman of color who is trying to survive by way of her art when the artworld doesn't even notice her. "The believing can pull at one's soul," says Aguilar. Her photographs become skin of light, both registering her experience of vulnerability and pain in

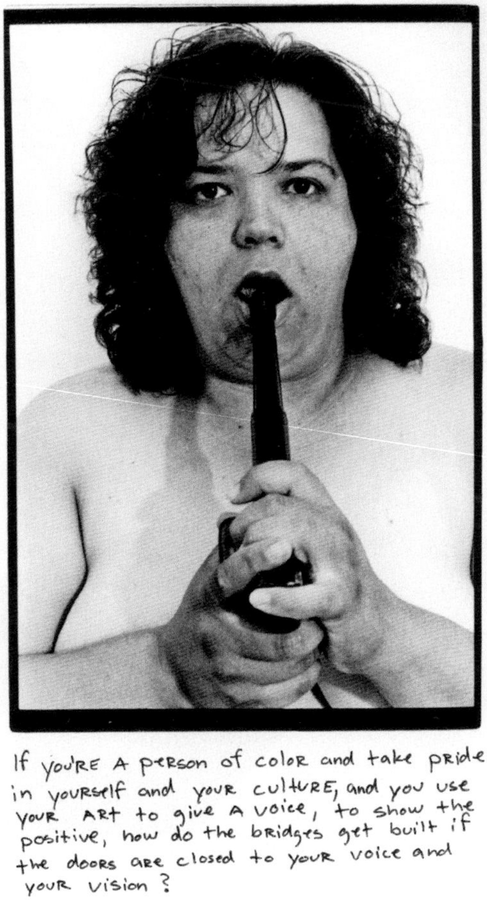

3.7 Laura Aguilar, *Don't Tell Her Art Can't Hurt (Part C)*, 1993. Gelatin silver print, 40 × 57 in. Copyright Laura Aguilar Trust of 2016.

the face of abjection as well as affectively touching the one who experiences them, inviting her to enter into Aguilar's world.[88]

In her heart-wrenching videos, Aguilar captures her pain in moving images. Slowing down and halting these images reveals frightening stills from the video *The Knife* (fig. 3.8) that disclose Aguilar's anguish-turned-blade seeking her own blood. In a piercing moment in her video

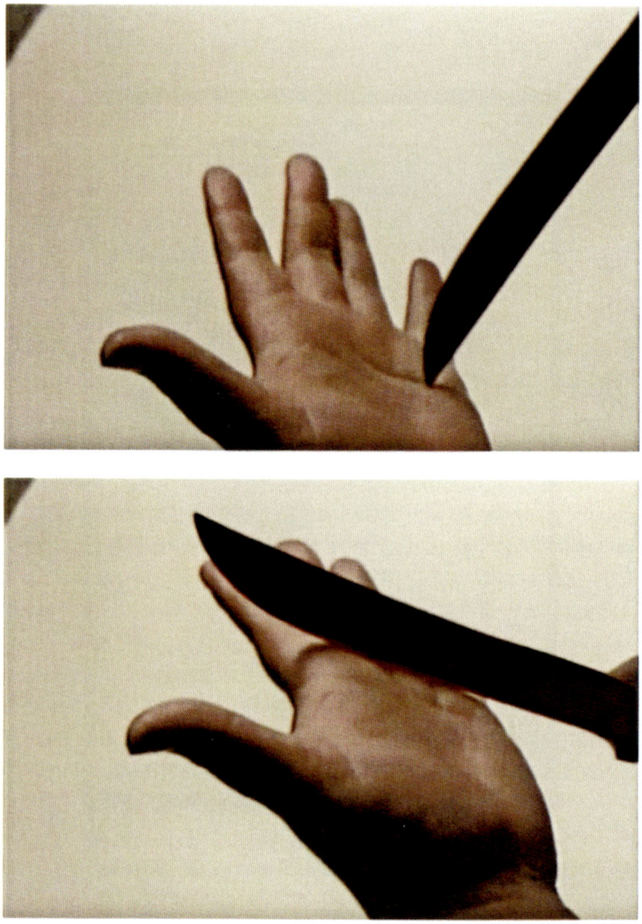

3.8 Two stills from Laura Aguilar's *The Knife* (1995).

Talking about Depression 2 (1995) Aguilar speaks wounded words: "As long as I can remember, I've felt like I should be dead."[89] How does one live while knowing that one should be dead or that so many would not even twitch an eye if one did die—because they don't even know one is there in the first place and would not care if they knew? Aguilar constantly faces this Sisyphean dilemma of whether to keep living under difficult circumstances. Yet so many of those who are marginalized, who are atravesados, continue living in spite of it all. In her *How Mexican Is Mexican* series (1990) Aguilar takes a portrait of herself and below her image writes, "My father told me, if asked say your 'Mexican-American.' My mother told me whatever you do in life, all people will see is the color of your skin. I spent 20 years feeling ashamed, but that was then."[90]

It is so common for the lived experiences and intellectual production of people of color to be invisible or undervalued within many contexts, including academia. Sandoval thus criticizes Fredric Jameson for not recognizing the moments of dissidence and resistance among US feminists of color.[91] Yet, as it is clear in Sandoval's work, the cognitive mapping of marginalized multiplicitous selves is not all there is to the story, hence her desire for a hermeneutics of love within the context of the methodology of the oppressed. In my view, a key moment of this methodology is the moment of affective mapping, when through the perception-affect nexus the self is wounded and thus becomes attuned to her position in the maps of power. For Aguilar, these affective mappings become *apertures* of self-making—even when the gun is in her mouth, the knife is ready to cut her skin (fig. 3.8), or her hand slaps her own body, as in her video *Talking about Depression*.

Gun, knife, or wounding words don't stop Aguilar. Like Anzaldúa does with her pen, Aguilar somehow finds her way through her camera, following that light that guides her not simply to represent herself by way of photographs—a mere indexing that Aguilar was there—but to sensuously situate herself, her bodymindsoul, with all its folds, nooks, apertures, scars, and blemishes in a world, even within those four walls turned studio, turned stone forest (fig. 3.9).

In *Nude Exercise #3* (fig. 3.9) we see her, armadillo-like, cocooning, unable or unwilling to face the camera, her form becoming stonelike, turned mere object in a brutal society enamored with slim, white, taut bodies. This body turned stone is lonely, stones her only companions. In a beautiful composition of skin-turned-stone and stone-turned-skin, Aguilar in her inertness follows the path of conocimiento that for Anzaldúa happens via creative acts. Is this moment akin to what Lugones would call the moment of germinative stasis that precedes a response to hegemony in Anzaldúa's work? Lugones states, "For Anzaldúa, the Coatlicue is preparatory to becoming a full-fledged member of the borderlands, a new mestiza. It is a state of stasis, of motionless, a standing still. The Coatlicue state has two simultaneous 'moments': in the first moment the focus is on the self afraid, terrified of abandoning the conventional construals of the self. The self is afraid of not being anyone after all."[92] As noted in the previous chapter, while Lugones is initially critical of Anzaldúa's description of the state of intimate terrorism because it seems to be too confined

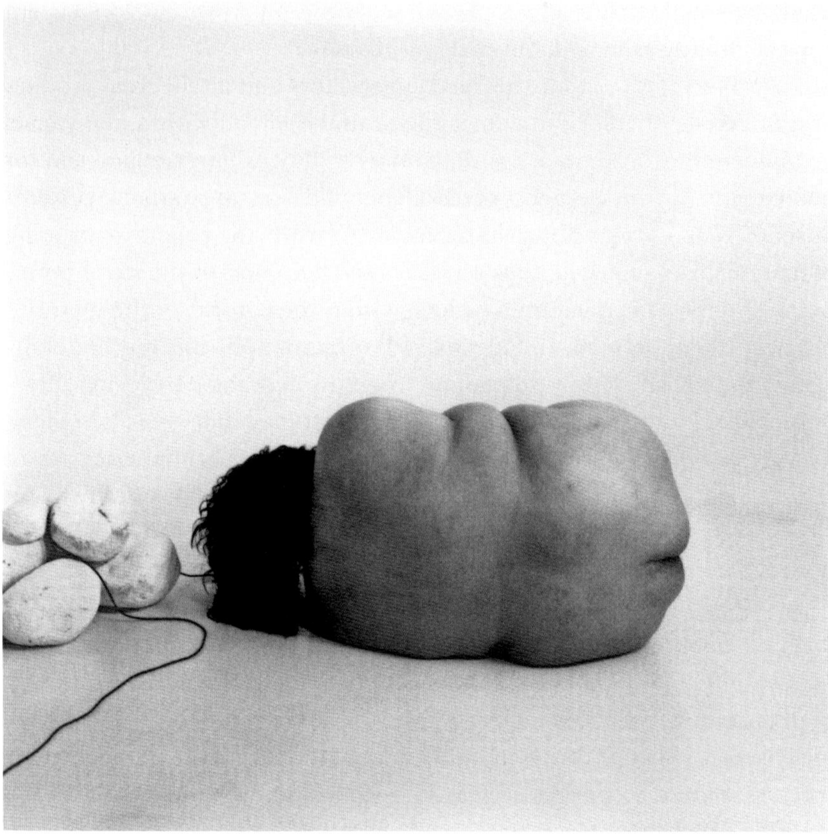

3.9 Laura Aguilar, *Nude Exercise #3*, 1990. Gelatin silver print, 11 × 14 in. Copyright Laura Aguilar Trust of 2016.

to the inner psychic world of the self and thus unable to yield a sociality of resistance,[93] Lugones later recognizes this inner passivity as part and parcel of a moment of germination, in which the self undergoes a quiet, passive preparation for resistance that is not merely reactive but responsive and thus "thoughtful, often complex, devious, insightful response, insightful into the very intricacies of the structure that is being resisted."[94] It is a moment Anzaldúa describes thus: "One remains ignorant of the fact that one is afraid, and that it is fear that holds one petrified, frozen in stone."[95] Is Aguilar at this moment preparing to give birth to herself, the camera's manual shutter release cable turning into an umbilical cord tethered to Aguilar's body? There is more work that Aguilar will do with light in order to make herself via autoarte. As you might have already noticed, she will leave this room and spill herself into trees.

Photography, which in its standard reading is merely a practice that indexes something that is there or has been there, becomes carnal in Aguilar's hands. How can a mere piece of paper that captures light (or pixels) touch in such a way that it peels sedimented layers of feelings—despair, grief, exasperation, indignation? The power of the photograph is its strength not as a medium of verification due to its revered power of indexicality but to its power as a carnal medium: the photograph has the ability to pierce us, and the photograph itself is a relational surface that is chiasmatic, as it touches me and I can touch it. In other words, the photograph is fleshy; it serves as the surface, moment, space in which self and worlds intertwine. I see Aguilar's *Nude Exercise #3* and I am affected; feelings are stirred in me that I cannot avoid, that take me to further moments of sensibility. I see, I feel with my entire body. I see Aguilar as a body of color that is a body of sorrow, mapping herself in a world that rejects her. In so doing, her carnal autoarte produces an art object that points to the very entwinement of self and worlds, and, as Anne Marie Leimer notes, that turns space into place.[96] The photograph as spirit animal, the photograph as shamanic, captures Aguilar's own body as a carnal crossing—she is becoming one with the stones in a moment of stillness that, as we will see, later transforms into a movement in which Aguilar ventures out and communes with the natural world and other selves, the photographic act not merely robbing the moment in order to represent it in pieces of paper holding chemicals that capture light, but actually sensuously engaging with the elements in a moment of erotic fusion, Aguilar-turned-pond, turned-tree, tree-turned-Aguilar, Aguilar-turned stone, Aguilar becoming-with others (figs. 3.10–3.12).[97] We see a beautiful, sensuous movement from germinative stasis to communion with others and the earth- and spirit-bodies. This is light-writing as love.

A Note on Love and the Differential

Inspired by Anzaldúa, Sandoval understands a hermeneutics of love as connected to an unnamable process akin to making soul.[98] Her own methodology of the oppressed is a result of her being pierced by the work of Lorde, Anzaldúa, and other theorists of color who write "theories of the flesh," and by European thinkers such as Barthes who theorize the *punctum*, that piercing moment that opens the gates of sensibility.[99] Thus, her

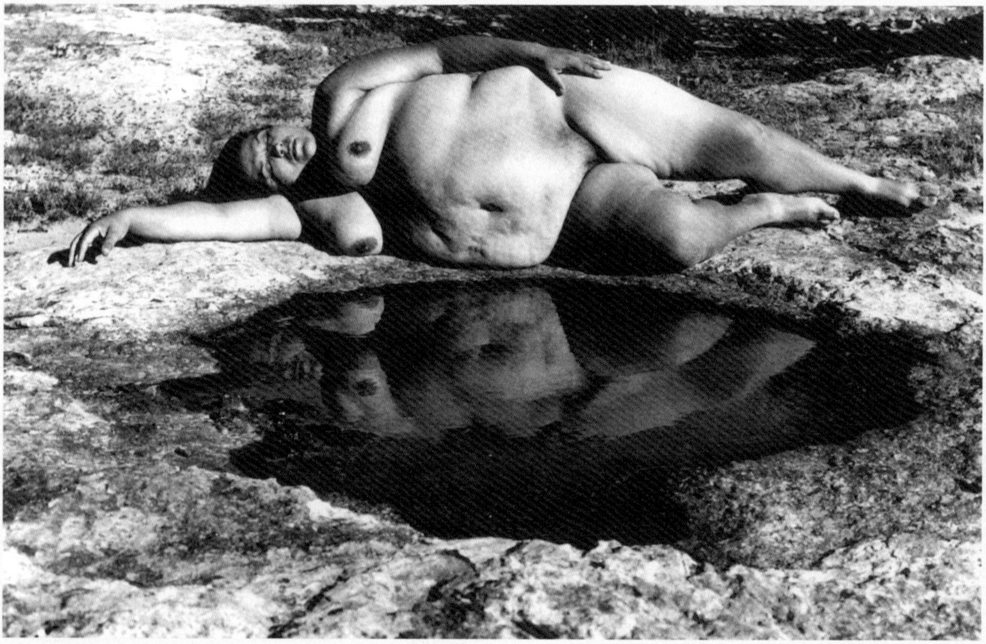

3.10 Laura Aguilar, *Nature Self Portrait #4*, 1996. Gelatin silver print, 20 × 16 in. Copyright Laura Aguilar Trust of 2016.

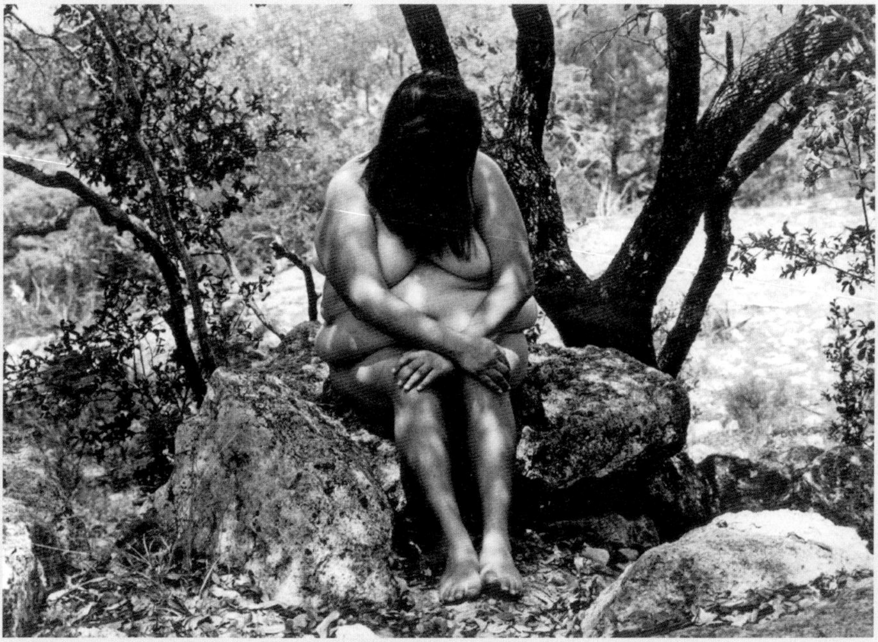

3.11 Laura Aguilar, *Stillness #18*, 1999. Gelatin silver print, 12 × 9 in. Copyright Laura Aguilar Trust of 2016.

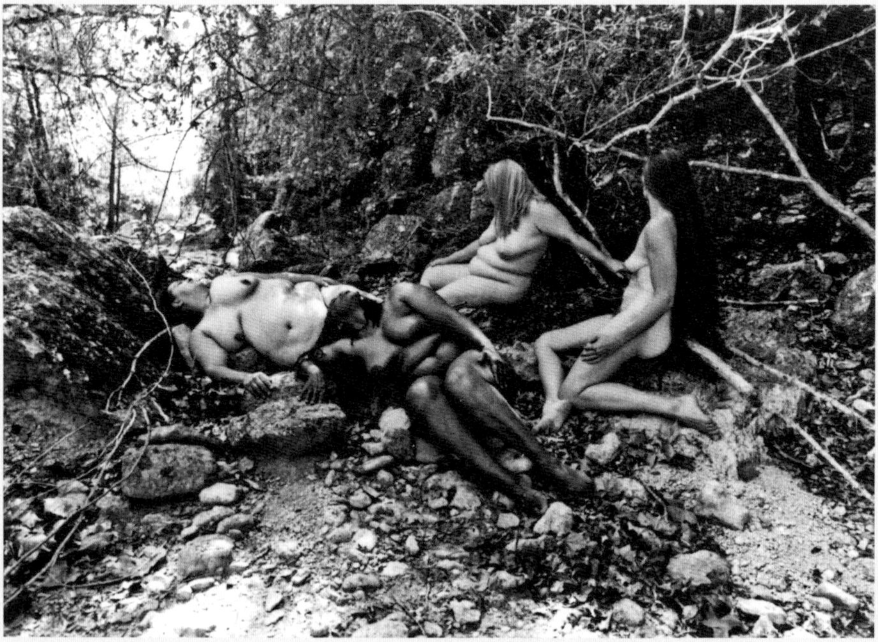

3.12 Laura Aguilar, *Motion #58*, 1999. Gelatin silver print, 51 × 40.5 in. Copyright Laura Aguilar Trust of 2016.

work is one of wounds and how to tend them lovingly with the aid of differential consciousness.

This differential consciousness that guides all citizens confronting the wounds of "late-capitalist, postmodern, neocolonial globalizing systems of exchange" is, according to Sandoval,[100] the key "technology" that arises within conditions of oppression and that guides subjects in four major forms of oppositional movements: the equal-rights, revolutionary, supremacist, and separatist forms.[101] Through differential consciousness the subject chooses "between and among" oppositional ideologies. When describing this consciousness, Sandoval states, "I think of this activity of consciousness as the 'differential,' insofar as it enables movement 'between and among' oppositional ideological positionings in order to disclose the distinction among them. In this sense, the differential mode of consciousness functions like the clutch of an automobile, the mechanism that permits the driver to select, engage, and disengage gears in a system for the transmission of power."[102] Through the guidance of differential consciousness, the subject is able to discern which form of opposition she is to commit herself to and where to apply it in a tactical manner. Importantly, such application is connected to a *democratics*, to the practitioner's "ethical commitment to justice and to the equal distribution of power," to a "principled conversion," and, consequently, it is not to be understood as a willy-nilly taking up of identities.[103] Some might think that Sandoval's analogy, however, is too mechanical, thus seemingly covering up any sensuous aspect associated with the shifting of ideological positionings. Yet as anyone who has learned to drive a car with a manual transmission understands, it is precisely the sensory attunement with the automobile that allows for a successful shifting of the gears so as not to turn the automobile into an awkward, jumping horse that cannot trot smoothly in the terrain. This bodily attunement to the various elements involved, this sensing of the circumstances that includes driver, automobile, road, and destination is of particular interest, as it highlights an affective mapping; it unfolds in a personal moment of attunement. Artistic or creative practices are about this sensory unfolding: when the sensing body interacts, is addressed by and addresses gesso, paint, light, sound, metal, wood, paper—both matter and spirit—in order to engage in an erotics of being.

Differential consciousness engaged in the praxis of making soul—the key moment that allows the subject to affectively map herself—is, according to Sandoval, "kaleidoscopic," weaving in and out of different oppositional forms, of seeing with multiple eyes, seeing and sensing different forms, understanding multiple meanings, and transfiguring meanings and ideologies even from within normative ideological systems.[104] This connection to semiotics and to the possibility of changing meanings turns out to be crucial in the opening up of the sensuous, carnal possibilities found in Sandoval's methodology. That is, when following the erotic in Sandoval's own text and vision, we are directed, surprisingly, to the discursive and to ideology.

Ideology, which has been shown by Louis Althusser to be the powerful instrument of control by the state and structures that he calls ideological state apparatuses, is successful due in part to its connection to sensibility. The sign, which is the result of the relationship between the operations of the signifier and the signified—a relationship that according to Althusser becomes understood as naturalized when in fact it is not—carries with it not simply meanings that are to be associated with the mental; they are meanings that have "a sensory reality" and that provide affective, sensuous satisfaction. Sandoval states, "Barthes's radical aim in *Mythologies* is to challenge this formation through which Western meaning, consciousness, and ideology are produced, and thus to rescue the irreproachably good, compliant citizen-subject of Western culture as she/he unerringly *enters this sensuous experience*, this living prison house of meaning" (my emphasis).[105] The process of meaning-making associated with ideologies propagated and enforced by ideological state apparatuses is one that produces patterns of meaning-making that affect our understanding of reality. Yet it is also a thoroughly sensuous process. Meaning becomes "conjugal, erotic, and satisfyingly naturalized."[106] I read the words *conjugal* and *erotic* and I resist their association with operations of the science of signs. Yet semiotics is precisely a site where we can find the intertwining of sign, meaning, and sensation. Immediately I think of the colonizer: the colonizer that gets such satisfaction from seeing the cross; the delight that he must feel in his envisioning his satisfaction as he sees "heathens" being converted into Christianity. The world of semiotics is also a sensuous world, and I wonder whether it is this sensuousness that gives it such power.

It is precisely Sandoval's recognition of the importance of sensuousness, of the interaction between discourses and bodily sensation and affect, that is one of her major contributions in her methodology of the oppressed. It is what turns her methodology into a hermeneutics of love and an erotics of being. While it is Barthes's view of semiotics and prophetic love that are explored in detail in her analysis, it is US women of color theorists who have informed her understanding of the urgency of theories "in the flesh." Sandoval has learned from Anzaldúa, Lorde, Moraga, and all those women of color who, throughout the 1980s and 1990s, were putting themselves on the pages of their writing—who were offering, as Anzaldúa would put it, "blood sacrifices."[107] Recognizing the alignment between white European thinkers and theorists of color, as she so skillfully does throughout *The Methodology of the Oppressed* and in an ultimate move toward an erotics rather than a discursively informed methodology, Sandoval takes us to the Barthesian "zero degree of meaning,"[108] the point where signifiers have become emptied of traditional meanings and there is room for resignification and lovemaking; where affective mapping and autoarte unite in a process of carnal creation that makes and transforms the self by way of a communion with elements. In this space of the zero degree of meaning, "the obtuse, third meaning emerges to haunt all we think we know."[109] It is a space of poetry, where we have the possibility of sensing, being, and understanding otherwise. This is the moment of falling in love, the moment where "I fall, I flow, I melt."[110] At this point, lover and beloved disappear, leaving the lover dispersed, drifting, no longer belonging to a lover/loved binary, but inhabiting a "third space" in which new possibilities are encountered, including possibilities of resignification or, in Sandoval's terms, meta-ideologizing.

This moment of falling in love, what Sandoval transforms into a *punctum*, fascinates me. For me, it is the moment where the creative self has the possibility of sensuously commuting with the elements (medium-affect nexus) in order to create in such a way that she intervenes in reality but in doing so, also changes and transforms herself. It is a moment of alchemy, of taking elements and luminously transforming them. This is a mouthly moment of a self in communion with what is. It is the moment of autoarte. Within this luminous moment of autoarte, a self connects with what she finds in the world, be it ink, paint, sound, light, stone, water, earth, in order to name herself and put herself in the map of being, even if only for a moment, a moment in which no matter what the colonial gaze dictates, she belongs in the world and can be earth, pond, tree, stone (see fig. 3.13) . . . and, as we will see, eagle (see fig. PII.1, beginning part II).

Border arte is a carnality that arises in nepantla. For Anzaldúa, it points to the soul of the artist and that of her people. Her own autohistoria-

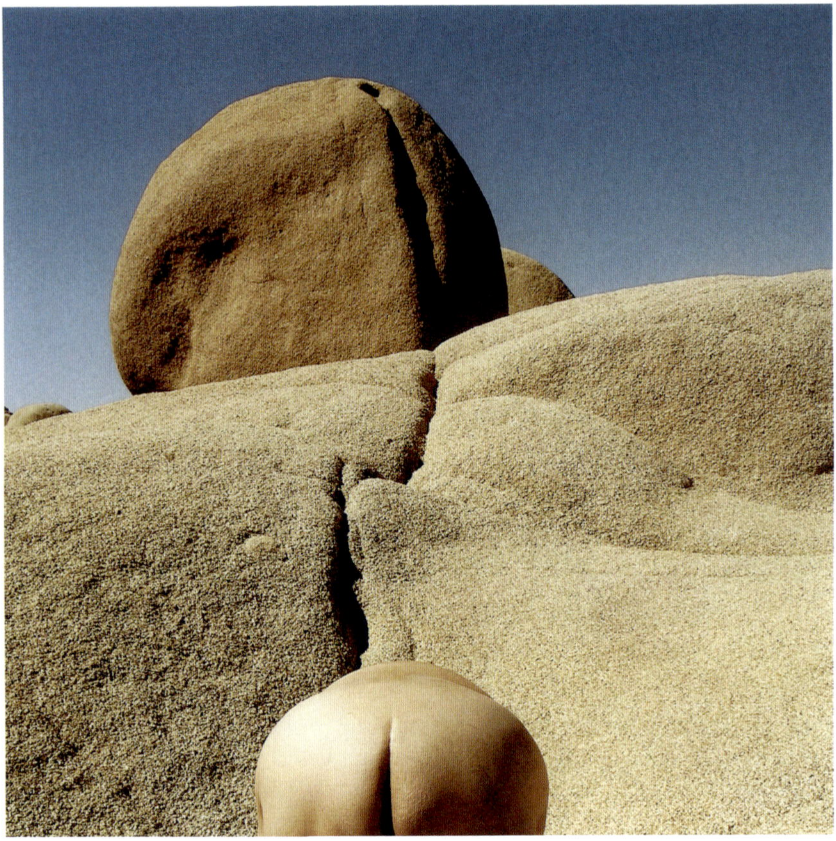

3.13 Laura Aguilar, *Untitled* (*Grounded* series), 2007. Inkjet print, 16 × 16 in. Copyright Laura Aguilar Trust of 2016.

teoría, developed as she walks through the exhibition of Aztec cultural objects, is an example of border arte. Through being addressed by the Coyolxauhqui stone and through a shamanic experience in which she listens to the jaguar spirit, Anzaldúa's awareness expands so as to create with black ink and red paint. Her border arte is informed by conocimiento as "inner work" and "public acts" in which both sensual intimacy and affective mapping with her environment as well as a connection to her cultures, histories, and Indigenous heritage lead her to creation. She is torn apart and also gathers her pieces by way of her story that, while inspired by her culture, myths, and histories, can also create something new. Autoarte, in turn, points to the more intimate and personal aspect of the resonant practice of border arte. It encompasses the act of being inspired and affected by an element and the subsequent translation of that moment into a creative work, leading to movements of self-naming and possibly self-transformation, as Aguilar translates her experience and affective mapping into another kind of writing, the writing with light. Her creative photographic practices thus point to a deep attunement with the elements so as to produce portraits of nature that are portraits of herself, and portraits of herself that are portraits of nature in moments of aliveness, anguished joy, and love. Audre Lorde says that "poetry is not a luxury"; neither is autoarte.

II BORDER CROSSINGS

SORROW AND MEMORY

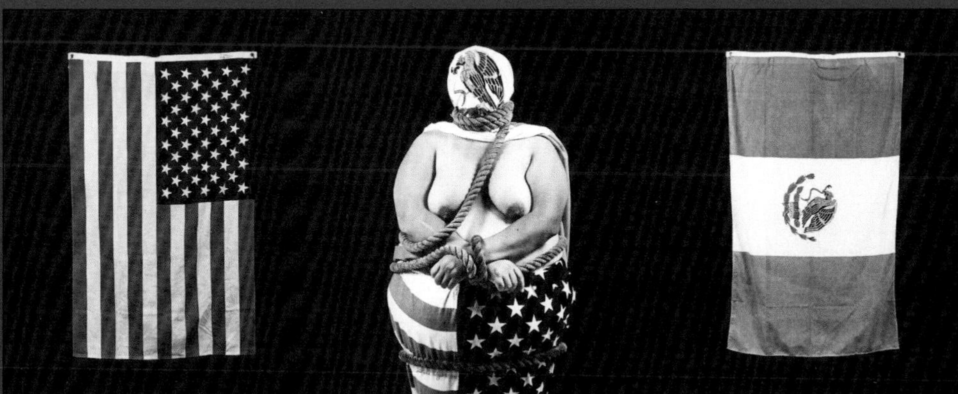

Eagle draped over face, mouth bound—rapacious being stealing poetry, song, and calls for love. Another mouth, that of desire, hidden away by the stars and stripes of colonizing "America." Thick rope, poisonous snake, threatening life—Aguilar in her way to crossing, to becoming águila. I want her to fly. Predators will not consume this body. But they will feed on so many others along the long wound of the Mexico-US border.

PII.1 Laura Aguilar, *Three Eagles Flying*, 1990. Gelatin silver print. Each image 20 × 24 in. Copyright Laura Aguilar Trust of 2016.

FOUR

SORROW, AESTHETIC UNSETTLEMENT, AND SONIC RUPTURE IN THE MEXICO-US BORDERLANDS

> I have been in Sorrow's kitchen and licked out all the pots.
> **ZORA NEALE HURSTON,** *Dust Tracks on a Road*

> Perhaps we cannot bury our dead until justice is realized.
> Maybe we must carry the rotting bodies of the fallen
> through the streets.
> **KARA WALKER,** *After the Deluge*

In this chapter I shift from the ways that bodies of color perform carnalities—to name and transform themselves away from structures, discourses, and imaginaries anchored in coloniality—to a consideration of tarrying with sorrow, as if sorrow flowed in the veins of bodies of color. An analysis of a carnal aesthetics of flesh*and*blood creative practices that includes autoarte turns to an examination of carnalities enacted to honor, mourn, and remember those Latinx and Latin American lives who, even as I write these words, walk, swim, run, hide, survive, perish in perilous crossings, including that border that Anzaldúa calls a "1,950-mile-long open wound."[1] As Aguilar's autoarte has shown, carnalities are exacting, heart-wrenching. Recall her photograph *Don't Tell Her Art Can't Hurt* (fig. 3.7), where she photographs herself holding a gun to her mouth. I shudder when I sense that she means it, that she might hurt herself—life is too hard to bear given the constant racism, classism, ableism, sexism, and homophobia. Yet her photographic autoarte gives her strength that, similarly to Anzaldúa's creative practices, allows her to define herself amid so much pain.

I think of Anzaldúa when she says, "A paradox: The knowledge that exposes your fears can also remove them."[2] This Anzaldúan insight carries some truth. Yet we cannot forget all of those bodies of color who have perished in so many crossings, whether forced or voluntary. Tarrying with sorrow means holding on to difficult histories, that despite their pastness continue to hold sway over us, in a temporal trick in which the past refuses to become a *has been*. Instead, somehow, whether we want it or not, a simple gesture, a slur, a glance, a law or worse, a beating, a violent death (and more and more death . . .) brings that history of pain, sorrow, and woundedness to the fore. It does not go away, no matter how we as individuals or groups want to take its power away. In the context of Black life, a painful, brutal past becomes the "afterlife of slavery," and life "in the wake" as "keeping watch with the dead."[3] In the context of the heterogeneity of Latinx lives and imperial histories, a painful past is a sorrow that so many carry as if it were another layer of skin. For Anzaldúa it becomes connected with arrebatos; for Lorgia García Peña it fosters "vaivén" / "ElNíe" (a sense of being neither here nor there, belonging and not belonging);[4] for José Esteban Muñoz it is linked to a structure of feeling, to "feeling brown."[5] To write about sorrow, then—and I suspect to read about sorrow as well—prompts feelings of ambiguity and uneasiness and carries the risk of reifying it, whereas ignoring it fosters naïveté or cruelty.

I thus choose not to ignore thinking about and feeling sorrow, as so many are apt to do, even in the face of the many deaths caused by a pandemic. We live in a society structured to cover up pain and sorrow, including a history of racist brutality against African Americans, a brutality that Kara Walker compares to the "muck" left after Hurricane Katrina.[6] While sorrow understood as sadness, grief, and affliction—the kind that strikes deep in our chords—touches all of us at some point of our lives, the sorrow from this muck intimately touches the lives of people of color. "Muck," murky, toxic, filthy waters, is Walker's name for racist pathology, the kind that is always suspicious of bodies of color—especially Black bodies—that leads to so much death, destruction, and abjection of these bodies. The sorrow that I write about here is one that flows from this muck and is associated with the injustice arising from racism and xenophobia. The bodies that I wish to speak about are bodies of color marked by the muck of racism and xenophobia. These are the bodies on which historical, cultural, aesthetic, and economic systems converge, relegating them to the status of "alien" and "illegal."[7] In this discussion, bodies of color are not meant to be understood as metaphors for pain and sorrow. They are real, actual bodies that suffer the consequences of racism and xenophobia. I write about their sorrow not merely to pour salt on open wounds; to extol woundedness; to relegate the sorrowful to a permanent, essentialist condition of despondency; or to be trapped in a tired "grammar of woundedness."[8] As noted in the previous chapters, a life of woundedness does not preclude the possibility of quiet strength and perseverance. Here I discuss quiet as well as more resonant aesthetic practices, carnalities that make possible for bodies of color as bodies of sorrow, to mourn, to honor, to carry their—our—dead.

I conceive of bodies of color as *bodies of sorrow*, as carnal archives, as sites in which histories of injustice and practices of racism and xenophobia are held. In these folds of skin histories of violence are written and precarious and treacherous crossings are recorded. Mindful of the various meanings of "flesh" in terms of its being, nonbeing, and becoming—here I continue to understand flesh not as material embodiment nor lived experience but in terms of the intimacies between bodies and various earthly and nonearthly elements—in terms of flesh*and*blood. I wish to honor these bodies of color in their condition of bodies of sorrow insofar as they are marked by "otherness" and difference and continue to be relegated to precarious edges, violent margins, and brutal crossings but also as they continue to survive, to make it against all odds. Yet how do we honor those who succumb to the violence of racism and xenophobia—those whose crossings proved fatal? Bodies of color keep falling, Keenan Anderson, Tyre Nichols, Alonzo Bagley, Herman Whitfield III, Jayland Walker, Trayvon Martin, Rekia Boyd, Miriam Carey, Michael Brown, Eric Garner, Tanisha Anderson, Yvette Smith, Walter Scott, Tamir Rice, Natasha Mckenna, Sandra Bland, Aiyana Stanley-Jones, Freddie Gray, Alton Sterling, Philando Castile, George Floyd, Ahmaud Arbery, Breonna Taylor, Pearlie Golden, Oscar Grant III, Pedro Villanueva, Melissa Ventura, Vinson Ramos, John Crawford III, Atatiana Jefferson, and so many more, including those who are unnamed, whose remains become "John Doe" in their attempt to cross the Mexico-US border.

There is so much violence against bodies of color, particularly Black men and women, that making a list of those who have been killed by police may seem disrespectful. What does it mean to provide a mere list of those who have perished because of racist violence? It is a list with no end in sight. Yet their names must not be forgotten. Here I also wish to think about those whose names we will not know, who have been consumed by the desert, drowned, or suffered violence in their crossing of the Mexico-US border. It is estimated that there have been more than nine thousand deaths on this border since 1998 due to exposure, hypothermia, dehydration, drowning, vigilante killings, transport in vehicles, and violence carried out by the Border Patrol. In 2021 alone Border Patrol reports 568 remains found, while in 2022 there were 895 remains found, the deadliest year so far; between October 2022 and August 2023, the remains of 640 migrants have been found.[9] In the context of Latin American and Latinx lives, racism is also tied to specific policies and practices connected to a racial history of upholding and protecting whiteness.[10] As we continue to witness brutality against bodies of color, let us be clear that we cannot forget these bodies and that we need to recognize how the muck of history is very much part of present storms.

In the first section of this chapter, I am guided by the question of how we remember and mourn those who perished in their crossing, whose deaths and names are not even known. To answer this agonizing question, I choose a set of photographs from a different archive than the ones that I have discussed in the previous chapters. Here I do not engage aesthetic photographic works; rather, I look into photographic records from those who are closely documenting the deadly crossings of migrants but that, as we will see, perform more than a documentary function. Here I seek the carnality of the photograph. I discuss photographs from the Pima County Office of the Medical Examiner in Tucson, Arizona, depicting objects left by various Latin American and Latinx immigrants who perished crossing the Mexico-US border. The photographs are of images of mundane objects that might perhaps not have much meaning for many viewers, but that move me deeply as a Latina who is painfully aware of the circumstances in which Mexicans, Central Americans, and other Latin Americans cross the brutal Mexico-US border. The photograph as carnal medium, as relational surface comes to the fore here: I see these images and they wound me. I wonder if others are wounded or moved by them in the same way, perhaps unsettled by them. I thus elaborate further on the notion of carnal aesthetics introduced in the first part of this work by following the methodology of *listening* to photographs by Tina M. Campt, in which the mode of listening to supposedly quiet photographs leads to perceptually rediscovering them and their subjects. Photographs from the coroner's office that are meant simply to serve as evidence of objects carried by "illegals" become transmitters of the sorrow as well as of the humanity of those who perished in the crossing. With the help of Alfred Frankowski's understanding of the political sense of sorrow of W. E. B. Du Bois's Sorrow Songs, I take the sorrow disclosed by the photographs as an interruption of a broken present.

In the second section, I elaborate further on the carnal role of the photographs given that they prompt or disclose sorrow. Following this disclosure of sorrow in connection to an interruption of the present (even if an already broken present) leads me to think of the notion of *aesthetic unsettlement*. Such an aesthetic unsettlement constitutes a destabilization, disruption, interruption, and, as we will see, a rupture of expected perceptions and ready-made affective responses. Within a carnal aesthetics, it is important to remember this aesthetic unsettlement in terms of the notion of *aesthesis* or perception rather than a traditional understanding of the aesthetic as concerned with the notion of the sublime or providing standards for beauty. With the help of Monique Roelofs's relational aesthetics, aesthetic unsettlement can also be understood as promising or threatening, depending on the different modes of address between things, people, and places that are involved in the experience. As such, this unsettlement is key to the possibility of reconfiguring not only perceptual responses but also discursive and cognitive views associated with them. Whether photographs prompt aesthetic unsettlement is dependent on many factors, including the personal, affective, cultural, and political views of the viewer, the contexts in which photographs are experienced, and what the photograph itself captures. I thus cannot make a general claim as to how certain photographs will impact the viewer. I can only show how the photographs from the Pima County Office of the Medical Examiner impacted me and suggest how they might prompt aesthetic unsettlement.

In the last section of the chapter, I deepen the analysis of listening through a discussion of the exhibition *Border Cantos*, consisting of Richard Misrach's photographs of the Mexico-US border wall, landscapes, and objects found in the area as well as aural compositions that Guillermo Galindo plays with instruments he constructed with objects discarded by those crossing the border. I discuss my own response to the exhibition, in particular my experience of listening to the composition *Efigie|Effigy*, which enhanced the perceptual power of the exhibition, leading me to have a more immediate, bodily response to the photographs, further highlighting the sorrow carried by those crossing the border and pointing to the continuous brokenness of the present. I provide an interpretation of the experience by way of Alia Al-Saji's notion of hesitation introduced in chapter 1, which I subsequently enhance with Anzaldúa's notion of rupture and germination in order to present an account of *aural unsettlement* and *deep listening* as *aesthetic unfolding*. I let the sounds of Guillermo Galindo resound in the sonorous being of my body and discuss what such an experience discloses in order to learn about what the aural reveals that the visible does not.[11]

BEING-IN-SORROW

In this section I discuss photographs from the Pima County Office of the Medical Examiner in Tucson, Arizona, where forensic anthropologists try to identify those who perished crossing the Mexico-US border.[12] While the photographs are not part of an art photography series one might see in a museum, what they disclose may be revealing in terms of how the visual goes beyond mere representation and is connected to various aesthetic modes that disclose the photograph as a relational, affective medium—as carnal. I am guided by Tina M. Campt's methodology of *listening to images* that discloses the photograph's capability to discover the photographed subject beyond the normative confines of controlling images, as well as by Monique Roelofs's important rethinking of aesthetics as connected to modes of address, promises, and threats, and a complex web of relations between people, objects, and places, as introduced in chapter 3. In addition, in this section I discuss the intersection of bodies of color and the sorrow specifically prompted by racism and xenophobia carried out by those who engage in racist racial projects. I follow Michael Omi and Howard Winant in their description of a racial project as "simultaneously an interpretation, representation, or explanation of racial dynamics, and an effort to reorganize and redistribute resources along particular racial lines."[13] In this case the redistribution of resources as well as the relevant interpretations and representations are used to uplift whites and undermine bodies of color. We can also think of xenophobic projects in which interpretations, representations, and redistribution of resources *other* particular beings in order to undermine them. Racist and xenophobic racial projects at the macroscopic and personal levels suffuse the pages of the history of this country as well as the pages that are being written now. Here I highlight the body of color as an ontological site of sorrow prompted by racism and xenophobia, as the *there* of the pain, grief, hurt, anguish, and affliction rooted in racist and xenophobic practices. With the aid of Alfred Frankowski's analysis of a political sense of sorrow, I show that these photographs point to, as he would say, "a broken present."[14]

My discussion of bodies of color as bodies of sorrow is not intended as a metaphorical or an essentialist description. Bodies of color are certainly not a mere metaphor for pain and sorrow; they are also not essentially defined by victimhood. Rather, bodies of color are being-in-sorrow, a way of being in the world attuned to the sorrow, anxiety, and the not being-at-ease that are part and parcel of liminal, marginalized existence. As we will see in the next chapter, being-in-sorrow is a way of being in the world that is connected to what Muñoz calls "feeling brown" or having a "shared sense of harm."[15] Cultural, historical, material, and discursive circumstances have inflicted and continue to inflict wounds on bodies of color, in particular Black bodies whose present pain cannot be separated from the terror of slavery.[16] Again, following Omi and Winant, I wish to be mindful of the particular contexts in which wounds associated with racial violence arise. To consider bodies of color as bodies of sorrow is not to condemn such bodies to suffering, but it is to bring to light, to make visible, what so many do not want to see—even when it is staring us in the face: their suffering, their mistreatment, their dislocation, their status as disposable, as invisible bodies, as bodies that don't matter.[17] In order to disclose the carnality of the photograph and to learn to listen to photographs, let us consider three photographs (figs. 4.1–4.3) from the Pima County Office of the Medical Examiner.

The Vicks VapoRub container stands out to me in the first photograph (fig. 4.1). In this context, it becomes symbolic of the possibility that any pain encountered will be lessened. Latinx readers of this text might understand this point well. In Latinx culture Vicks stands for a cure-all—if only it were the case for the woman who carried it in this particular journey. I find both the visible and the invisible in these photographs. Visible are the daily objects carried by those attempting a treacherous journey, a journey that cannot be simply called "illegal" but one on which perhaps the whole livelihood of a family in Honduras or México or El Salvador depended, a journey of life and death. These are photographs of objects from forgotten dreams, forgotten in a double sense: the dreams will never become true for the travelers, and the public will not know of these border crossers. They will remain nameless. Invisible are the bodies of color who carried these objects and who held their dreams close to their heart in the hope of being able to cross for a better life. These invisible bodies are bodies of color that are also bodies of sorrow. They hold not only the sadness of their stories and their failed efforts but also a history of failed dreams as their lives are interconnected to a series of cultural and historical events that have set their journeys in motion. After all, we cannot and should not forget the history of US-Mexico and Central American relations. These histories of racism and xenophobia go hand in hand with colonialist, imperialist histories.[18]

There is a long history of US involvement in Latin America, and specifically in Central America, a history marked by military interventions and

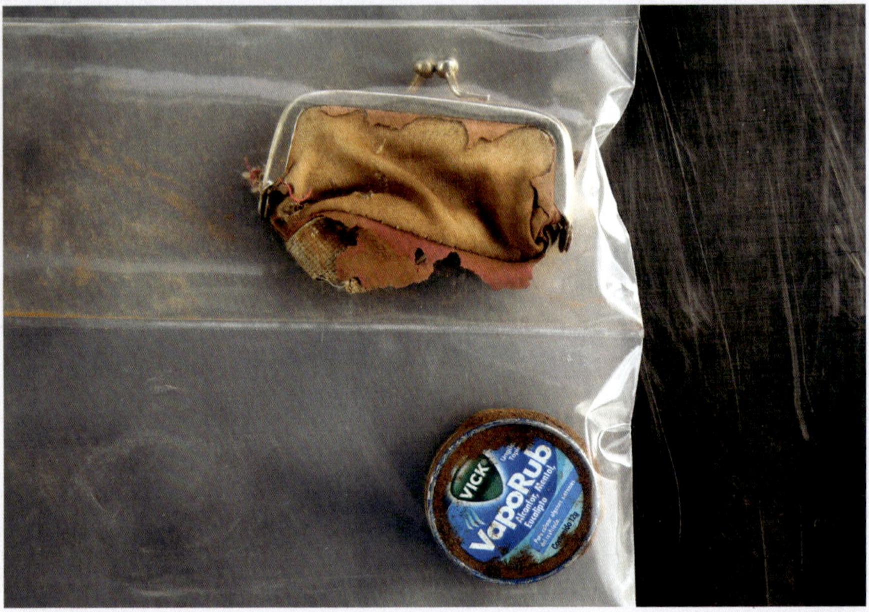

4.1 (*above*) A change purse and container of Vicks VapoRub are kept in a sealed bag of personal effects at the Pima County Office of the Medical Examiner on December 9, 2014, in Tucson, Arizona. The items were found with the skeletal remains of a person discovered in the Arizona desert on September 23, 2014. Photo: John Moore / Getty Images.

4.2 (*right*) A Spanish-language Bible and other personal items are kept in a sealed bag of personal effects at the Pima County Office of the Medical Examiner on December 9, 2014, in Tucson, Arizona. The items were found on the mummified remains of a Guatemalan male discovered in the Arizona desert on June 19, 2014. Photo: John Moore / Getty Images.

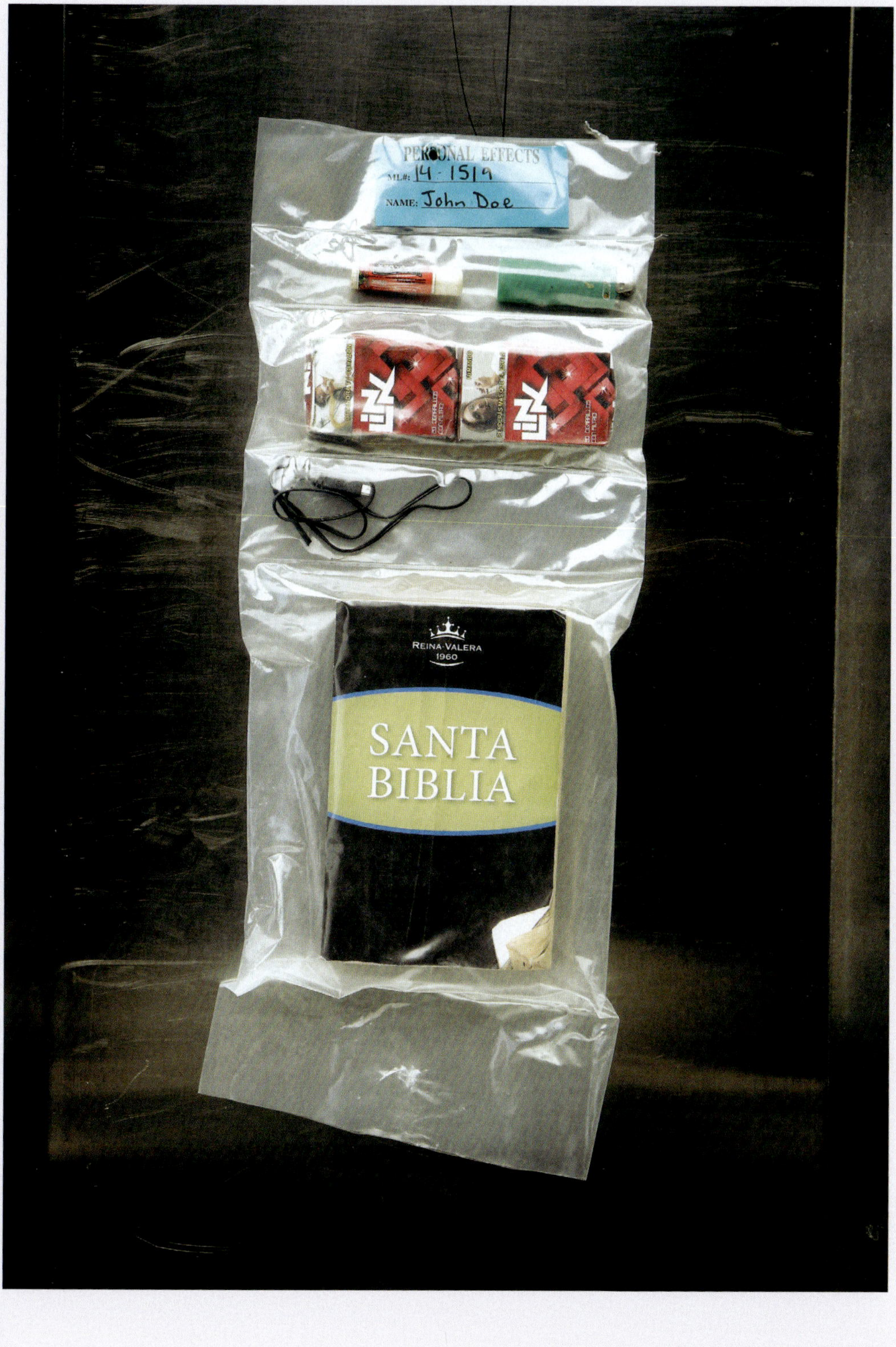
PERSONAL EFFECTS
ML#: 14-1519
NAME: John Doe
REINA-VALERA
1960
SANTA
BIBLIA

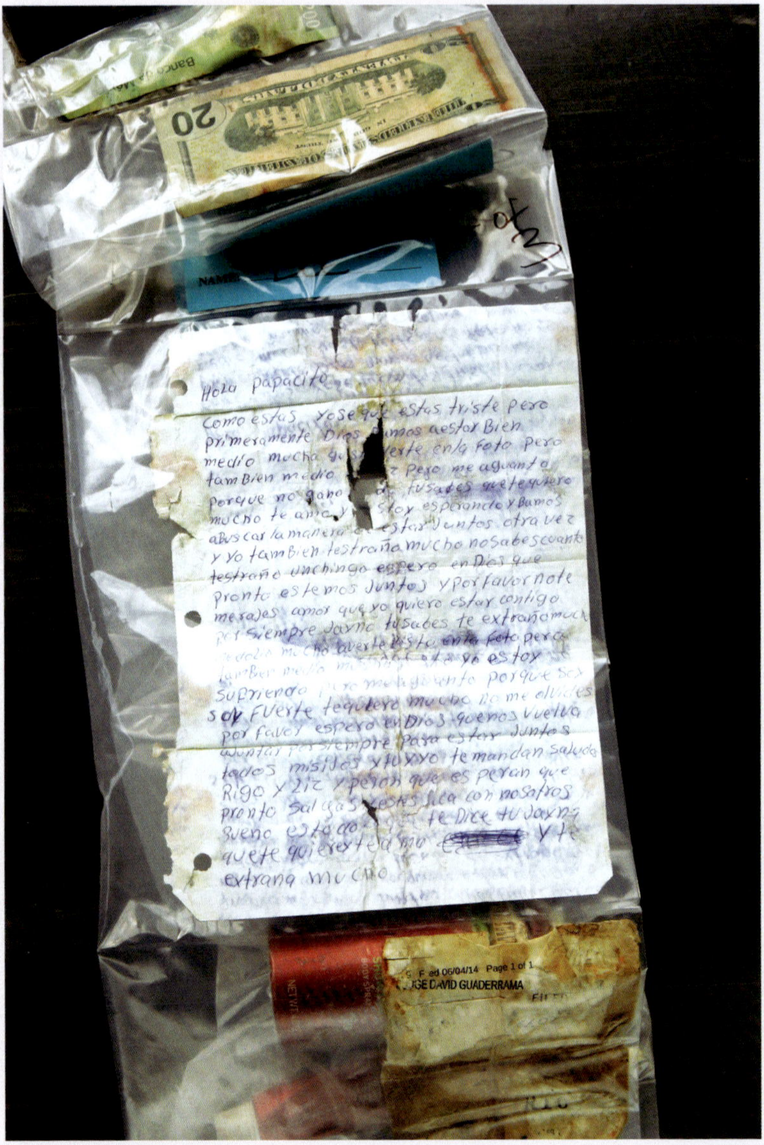

4.3 Money and other items, including a letter to a loved one that reads, "I know you're sad. . . . It made me very happy to see you in that photo, but it also made me sad. . . . I love you and I'm waiting for you and we will find a way to be together again, I also miss you a lot, you don't know how much, I miss you so fucking much. . . . I'm suffering but I'm holding on because I'm strong. . . . Please don't forget me." The items were found on the decomposed remains of a man discovered in the Arizona desert on October 9, 2014. Photo: John Moore / Getty Images.

support of oppressive governments: for example, the US Marines' occupation in Panama from 1903 to 1914 to safeguard the interests of the United States during the construction of the Panama Canal; the occupation of Nicaragua from 1912 to 1933 and subsequent support of the Somoza dictatorship; the 1954 CIA-backed armed overthrow of Jacobo Arbenz Guzmán in Guatemala in order to protect landholdings of a powerful US corporation, the United Fruit Company; the 1980s involvement in the civil war in El Salvador, in which the United States fought against the rebel group FMLN (Farabundo Martí National Liberation Front); support of the Contras in order to destabilize the government of the Sandinistas in Nicaragua after the 1979 overthrow of the dictator Anastacio Somoza Debayle; and actions not to reinstate the overthrown Honduran president Manuel Zelaya after the 2009 coup in that country.[19] Wars, treaties, and subsequent economic development that transformed geographies and governments for the gain of US control and empire continue to affect thousands of people, as Mexicans and Central Americans and, more recently, South Americans and Caribbeans dare to risk their lives in order to reach the Mexico-US border.

I wish to engage with these images by following Campt's methodology of *listening* to images, in which quotidian images that are seemingly quiet can be used as unlikely archives that "give us access to the affective registers through which these images enunciate alternate accounts of their subjects."[20] But how does one *listen* to images? For Campt, the answer rests in redirecting our understanding of sound away from a primarily scientific view of sound and learning a new kind of attunement to the photo, an attunement that in my view is dependent on the very carnality of the photograph. She invites us to be attuned to the lower frequencies of the images that have much to say. Photographs that in normative contexts are used for governmental operations of tracking, classifying, and thus controlling individuals—for example, the passport photos of Black Caribbean men in postwar Birmingham that Campt analyzes—can be read, or rather listened to, otherwise. Campt hears in these photographs the middle-class aspiration of these Caribbean men and "the quiet frequencies of futurity, of their aspirations" and "right to come, to go, and to stay, as well as to arrive and return over and over again."[21] These photographs are something other than what they were meant to be; they are no longer mere representations of specific Black individuals within the context of the control of Black Atlantic mobility. While these photos are set within specific parameters of composition and utilization, if listened to in terms of their haptic, affective qualities, they reveal futural possibilities. Campt states,

"These photos were both instrumental *and* affective conduits of the aspirations of thousands of new Commonwealth migrants who had already arrived and were beginning to contemplate new journeys. . . . [They] register a quiet insistence on forms of diasporic dwelling that demanded the right to come, to go and to stay, as well as to arrive and return over and again."[22]

Campt is interested in registering the various levels of perception and audibility of the unexpected archive of sound and feeling that she has chosen. Importantly, she registers the frequency of the photographs as a refusal: "The quotidian practice of refusal I am describing is defined less by opposition or 'resistance,' and more by a refusal of the very premises that have reduced the lived experience of Blackness to pathology and irreconcilability in the logic of white supremacy."[23] Rather than engaging in movements of opposition or resistance—the more likely political options when facing conditions of oppression—Campt looks for the more tenuous but not necessarily less powerful, sounds of these photos. Doing so constitutes "nimble and strategic" creative practices of refusal pointing to fugitivity in the images, the fugitivity of these individuals who refuse to be relegated at the edges of the metropole or contained within it. Here I take Campt to be sensing the carnality of the photographs, the way there is a relationship between them and the one viewing them—in this case listening to them. That is, these photographs are also *touching* Campt affectively. A haptic listening arises such that it opens the possibility for Campt to encounter the sounds of the fugitivity of the men in the photographs that points to "transient zones of freedom."[24]

I return to the coroner's photos of the objects found next to the remains of those who were crossing in search of a better future for them and their families. I wish to *listen* to these photos. I am touched by them in ways that are somehow disconcerting. How can a set of photos of objects cataloguing mundane evidence wound me so deeply? And what are the reverberations of these photos, the quiet or lower frequencies that Campt is directing us to learn to listen to? While there are no photographs of people here, the objects disclosed can tell us about those who carried them. Within the dominant anti-immigrant US imaginary, they are supposed to be "illegals," "rapists," mothers of "anchor babies," "gangbangers," those seeking to disrupt the peace and steal all the precious resources of well-regulated, welcoming, peaceful US cities. Of course, this vision of the US city is yet another element of such an imaginary. For many who are steeped in this normative anti-immigrant imaginary these mundane objects will have no meaning—if objects can be said to be guilty, they will be seen as merely aids to "illegality."

Yet when becoming attuned to the photographs, I listen—I hope you do as well—to the lives that carried the objects in those photographs: money, a Bible, lip balm, anything that might help in the crossing. With Campt, I think of refusal. The refusal of those crossers to stay put in situations that negate them and confine them to lives of fear, abjection, and violence. This is a refusal to be overcome by paralysis in the face of brutal governments, merciless militaries, ruthless gangs, and disastrous economic conditions. In figure 4.3, there is also a love letter with the message "I love you and I'm waiting for you and we will find a way to be together again. . . . I miss you so fucking much. . . . Please don't forget me." This is a different kind of object as it carries with it the discursive and it is thus filled with signifiers tied to cognitive processes. Yet this letter reverberates; it can be listened to. While we can point to high frequencies that can be connected to obvious and loud expressions of love and loss, there is also that humming behind the words.[25] It is the humming of a quiet love that is nevertheless as strong as what is stated in that piece of tattered piece of paper traveling with the same desires of the one making the perilous journey. The quiet hum of this photograph is connected to all those movements a lover makes but does not disclose as loudly as a love letter can do: the gestures and caresses to the loved one while they are not even noticing, the many moments of affection constantly orienting the lover's life. And there is the pointing to the loved one, the "illegal" that comes to steal precious resources, but that in reality is someone loved, cared for, missed. Let's not forget them.

The fugitivity of these border crossers, however, has been abruptly interrupted, as the heat and perils of the desert have taken them, dreams and all. Now all of them have new names: "John Doe" and "Jane Doe." This detail is a slap in their faces and a negation of them as cultural, historical beings.[26] All the objects intended to provide support for their bold and courageous movements across different worlds, this time a material, deadly crossing, may become (as we will see below) inert objects, mere evidence. In their lively relations to those who carried them, however, they provided advice, solace, spiritual strength, and a reminder that love was still possible even from the other side. Still, the low humming and frequencies continue to emanate and can be listened to by those attuned to the carnality of the photographs that, in this instance, moves the viewer through listening, disclosing what Alfred Frankowski understands as the brokenness of a present that refuses to remember the past and present violence against African Americans. It is also a present that does not acknowledge and remember Latinx life and death.

In his reflections on the history of violence that is so much part of the present and past of African Americans in the United States, Frankowski brings to light a political sense of sorrow that, in my view, is key for thinking about the meaning of sorrow in the midst of a present that continues to inflict wounds on bodies of color. In his elaboration of a critical aesthetics in the work of W. E. B. Du Bois, Frankowski takes Du Bois as opening the space for an aesthetic and political sense of sorrow that can be used as a strategy for a more resonant response to ongoing oppression.[27] Frankowski analyzes Du Bois's *The Souls of Black Folk* in light of the importance of the Sorrow Songs in the text. In an often-quoted passage, Du Bois says that the Sorrow Songs "are the music of an unhappy people, of the children of disappointment; they tell of death and suffering and unvoiced longing toward a truer world."[28] Frankowski reads these songs not as representing sadness, but as the interruption of forgetting. Importantly he points out that in the supposedly postracial time of the Obama presidency, memorialization—for example, monuments to honor African Americans and the civil rights movement—serve not only to memorialize but also to forget the current violence inflicted on Blacks. That is, the memorials appease as they acknowledge a racist past but they are also taken to confirm that violence against Blacks was a thing of the past. Postracial discourse thus turns memory into forgetting.[29] The Sorrow Songs, then, have special significance according to Frankowski, because they introduce memory as sorrow, but in order to interrupt the forgetting of a history that has been left out, the history of those who suffered the brutality of slavery.

I am moved by Frankowski's call to memory, to memory of loss, and I am interested in how a carnal aesthetics can answer such a call. What I find most meaningful in Frankowski's analysis is that he reads the Sorrow Songs as the interruption of forgetting,[30] not as a reminder of sadness but as a recovery of a past that is lost and as an exposure of a present that is broken. In other words, our very present is shaped by past violence that we do not wish to acknowledge, hence the need for keeping memory alive. Like the Sorrow Songs, recovering bodies of color as bodies of sorrow, as sites in which racism and xenophobia leave their mark both materially and discursively, points us to a present whose brokenness cannot be evaded, even though dominant discourses attempt to do so. Even though Frankowski's analysis concerns African American experience, his analysis helps me understand the condition of other bodies of color who suffer at the hands of racist and xenophobic people and structures. It is certainly not my aim to make all the experiences of bodies of color equivalent. This would make a mockery of the specific history of brutality that is part of the African American experience. I am also not interested in a competition of wounds, wounding, and victimhood, especially when there is a misunderstanding about identity politics as essentialist and of appeals to justice as calls to victimhood.[31] I am interested in understanding the experiences of other bodies of color by way of what philosophers such as Frankowski reveal regarding the relationship between aesthetics and racialization.

Like the Sorrow Songs, these sorrowful photos disclosing the remaining objects carried by those who wanted a chance in the mythical "land of the free" point to bodies of color as bodies of sorrow that interrupt a broken present. It is a present in which countless migrants from Latin America die or remain at risk in their crossings to the Mexico-US border. Yet there is no memorialization here, since they are nameless and considered merely "illegals." There is no room for memory to honor these specific bodies, no room to honor "illegals" and lawbreakers. They are thought as not deserving of respect; they have become unmournable in the eyes of dominant selves who hold racist and xenophobic narratives that have turned even more explicit and hateful. Yet despite different histories of violence and varying influences of these histories, Black and brown bodies share a history of violence marked by US colonialist, racist, and imperialist desires and practices that must be called out and must not be forgotten.

When I think of these border crossers—in search of safety, of a better economic future, in their attempt to survive, in their fugitivity—I cannot help but think that if these immigrants had the fortune to cross and to find a way to live in their new country, they would probably be also stuck in the muck of racist and xenophobic habituation. It does not matter that they pick the strawberries we eat, that they build the buildings we inhabit, that they take care of precious children of those who can have a splendid life because their children are taken care of. They are supposed to be part of an invisible background—not the invisible background of intelligibility that philosophers talk about, but the background of privileged lives. They need to be in place in order for others to thrive. Yet we live in a present in which many of these bodies are gone and those that survive remain in the background, also invisible. The sorrow connected to these photographs—which are themselves connected to bodies of color as bodies of sorrow, even when they have perished—is a reminder of a past history of US involvement in Latin America. It is also an interruption of a present that continues to be broken. These photographs cannot be the Sorrow Songs that Du Bois calls forth in his reminder of the spirit that Blacks have given to this country, but they are nevertheless an evocation of a sorrow that is *haunting* a broken present, a present that must be interrupted.[32]

AESTHETIC UNSETTLEMENT

The evocation of sorrow and the haunting that arise from these photographs—which were meant to record mundane objects but, as we have seen, turn out to hum to those of us who are willing to listen to them—points to the carnal dimension of the photographs, to their prompting an affective reaction in us. It is a piercing and haunting sorrow that precludes the possibility of the constant need to forget the past of violence against bodies of color so as to paint a picture of a sanitized, normal present. They allow for an opening, both to sense the humanity of those crossing the border and to sense a halting moment in the midst of the brokenness of the present. As such, perceiving these photographs, this unexpected archive of feelings,[33] prompts an aesthetic unsettlement—a destabilization, interruption, and, as we will see, a rupture—of expected, ready-made perceptions and sensations. In this instance, what is unsettled pertains to the kinds of perceptual-affective responses one is to have to evidentiary photographs from a medical examiner's office. That is, the photograph's ability to touch us—to move us affectively given the relationship between the one who perceives it, with eyes, ears, and mouth, and the photograph itself—opens possibilities for sensing otherwise. In its relational, intimate encounter with those who perceive it, the photograph ceases to be a representational medium and grows that umbilical cord that is so evident in Barthes's *Camera Lucida* in which the feeling of mourning overflows from its pages. The photograph, then, goes beyond its capabilities of showing that something is or was there and, instead, becomes an aperture for numerous affective relations between it, what it discloses, and the one experiencing it. Despite Barthes's interest in what he takes to be the essence of photography, its indexicality, he nevertheless recognizes that the photographic encounter is an affective encounter. Let us return to Barthes's words: "The photograph is literally an emanation from the referent. From a real body, which was there, proceed radiations which ultimately touch me, who am here; the duration of the transmission is insignificant; the photograph of the missing being, as Sontag says, will touch me like the delayed rays of a star. A sort of umbilical cord links the body of the photographed thing to my gaze: light, though impalpable, is here a carnal medium, a skin I share with anyone who has been photographed."[34] In its carnal mode the photograph touches us, *affects* us. In order to provide a sense of aesthetic unsettlement that accompanies photographs from the Pima County Office of the Medical Examiner in their mode as archives of feelings, I now return to Monique Roelofs's aesthetics comprising three major elements: promises and threats, modes of address, and relationality.

In her multifaceted and rich account of aesthetics, Roelofs reminds us of both the cultural promises as well as threats of aesthetics. As she states, "We organize our aesthetic relationships, in part, around promises and threats that we discern and lend multisensory, intercorporeal forms of articulation. Many are the ways in which we endeavor to put into effect and fulfill such pledges and menaces, or, as the case may be, try to undermine, abandon, and alter them. Undertaking aesthetic activities and projects—as we do in virtually all realms of life—we juggle tensions between promises and threats."[35] In addition, she highlights the important workings of the notion of address within the context of aesthetics. Reframing the notion of address away from its traditional understanding as connected to speech, Roelofs importantly understands address in terms of its perceptual modalities. The notion of address, defined by Roelofs as "forms of signification that we direct at human and non-human beings, objects, and places and that these entities direct at us and at each other,"[36] now directs us to the crucial notion of aesthetic unsettlement that arises when encountering the photographs from the medical examiner. One of the most powerful aspects of Roelofs's account is precisely how the aesthetic is a practice involving a complex web of relationalities between objects and selves such that objects *address* us in a myriad of ways, both in normative alignments to structural systems and away from them, thus creating promises and threats.

As noted in the previous chapter, Roelofs's "anatomy" of address encompasses norms, forms, structures, scenes, and scripts of address that allow for interpretations of artworks and practices that are keenly attuned to the sensory happenings at the nexus of bodies and objects. Multiple aesthetic possibilities are thus opened that help Roelofs forge a multisensory, intercorporeal aesthetics that discloses the intimacy and intertwining among people, objects, and places. Quotidian objects, then, become major characters in the play of her interpretations of artworks and practices. In particular, Roelofs highlights the question of difference within the context of this vast "assembly of conceptually inflected, socially situated, multimodal, embodied practices" of the aesthetic.[37] That is, a key aspect of her account is the elucidation of the ways the aesthetic is tied with injustice and hierarchy and consequently with the problematizing, countering, and resisting such injustice. Unsettlement, then, becomes a key element in this aesthetics that is so closely tied to the ethical and the political.

We can now ask, as Roelofs does, "How do unsettlement and continuity, contestation and common ground, go together in aesthetic territory?"[38] Similar to the crucial role of the notion of arrebato in Anzaldúa's carnal aesthetics, unsettlement plays a vital role in Roelofs's aesthetics insofar as her various analyses of artworks and aesthetic theories reveal promises, openings for perceiving and understanding anew, but also threats and reification of dominant, oppressive structures and understandings. While her analyses of artworks disclose various unsettlements of norms of address that open possibilities of being and sensing otherwise, a key discussion of this unsettlement pertains to what she regards as a "critical encounter" with ignorance, specifically the absence of knowledge supported by aesthetic means.[39] Understood in the context of the multiplicity of promises and threats, modes of address, and relationalities within specific cultural contexts, however, this ignorance is the product of multiplicitous operations that yield "states of knowledge and ignorance that materialize in the contours of aesthetic habits, desires, values, institutions, discourses, and forms."[40] These co-constitutive relations between the aesthetic and epistemology can be considered *aesthetic practices of ignorance* that are themselves connected to political violence and abjection. As such they need to be understood as capable of producing *aesthetic injustice*, or the injustice that flows from the intertwining of the aesthetic, epistemic, and political.[41] Her work, then, makes a crucial connection between aesthetics and, among many fields, epistemology. Unsurprisingly, for Roelofs, cultural artifacts can "make infringements on ignorance" and exercise what she calls an *epistemic destabilization* or unsettlement that reveals the dynamic interaction between forms of knowledge and ignorance as supported by the workings of address in quotidian objects and artworks as well as aesthetic practices.[42]

Inspired by this relational aesthetics in which the sensory, cognitive, and affective intertwine to disclose a multiplicity of openings for the destabilization of norms and parameters of what is aesthetically, politically, and epistemically acceptable, including "diminutive sites of critical resistance,"[43] I understand the carnality of the medical examiner's photographs by how they *address* and *unsettle* affectively those who experience them. That is, the photographs address us beyond the context of a representation that is to be cognitively understood. While indeed there are objects represented in them, those objects are not mere representations or data to be stored in a cabinet of consciousness. Rather, the photograph as a carnal, relational medium addresses us in in visual and auditory modes that touch us affectively. Following Campt, I have suggested how becoming attuned to these photographs' mode of address in terms of sound removes them from the context of mere data and evidence so as to disclose objects helping not "illegals" but those who refused to stay in conditions of abjection, poverty, and violence—dreamers, lovers, believers in possibilities of earthly transformation.

Listening to the photographs ultimately reveals the humanity of those crossing as well as their condition as bodies of sorrow. Here aesthetic unsettlement may also move toward an epistemic destabilization of the message photographs such as the medical examiner's aim to provide. Yet this destabilization is crucially linked to the moment in which the viewer is affectively addressed by the photograph. There is a double movement in which aesthetic as well as more cognitive modes of address work in tandem to reveal a different possible understanding of what this photograph is capable of doing (besides providing evidence) and what kind of people border crossers can be (besides being criminals and "illegals"). Those experiencing these photographs, those who listen to them, become intimately attuned to how these photos address them, to what the photograph makes them feel—a key moment in the possible reconfiguration of more thematic understanding of the meaning of the photograph and their content. If we take seriously the important entwinements between perception and affectivity discussed in previous chapters, then this moment of aesthetic unsettlement as perceptual-affective possibility of the otherwise, of an intimate sensation that opens the possibility of disruption of pervasive, settled modes of perception, becomes a key moment, as it may give rise to an opening for a subsequent cognitive reassessment of those who carried the objects shown in the photograph.[44]

Of course, it must be noted that this aesthetic unsettlement is one that may or may not happen. There is not a normative claim here. Whether photographs prompt aesthetic unsettlements or not is dependent on various factors, including personal, affective, cultural, and political views of perceivers as well as the photographs' ability to capture relevant contexts. The key issue is that the aesthetic moment promises openings for an engagement with the photograph that leads to alternative aesthetic and cognitive possibilities. It may also, as Roelofs reminds us, lead to threats arising at the moment of address. In the case of the series of photographs from the Pima County Office of the Medical Examiner, the photographs may not enact the kind of aesthetic unsettlement that leads to an affective attunement to the sorrow of those whose belongings, the things of their lives, now appear in sealed plastic bags on the surfaces of papers in which light has written.

Instead, these images may actually foreground the very indexicality of the photograph that has historically been associated with the mere there-ness of an actual object in the world—an indexicality that has placed the photograph as proof of reality, objective knowledge, and scientific wonder, in the service of a will to truth that has been committed to practices of othering intertwined with ideologies of power marking bodies of color as inferior, unwanted, unmournable. In this instance, the photos may in fact be understood in their mode as mere forensic evidence, or following Barthes, as "unary photographs" that shock but do not create a disturbance,[45] thus relegating the owners of the objects to the background—their experiences and lives not affectively touching the viewer in a promising way. That is, the photograph's indexicality allows for the possibility of the naming of a particular kind of abject subject. As Ariella Azoulay explains when discussing the interpretation of the phrase *this was there*, which is associated with the indexicality of the photograph,

> The interpretation of this phrase, however, has always been inspired by the claim "*this is X*" latent with it. "*This is X*" already constitutes a form of naming of the "*this*" that "*was there*." When "*this is X*" is linked to "*this was there*," a representation is distilled from the photographed event and is grounded in the photograph itself. Thus, in many archives photographs are filed under categories including "refugees," "torture," or "expulsion" in a way that turns the photograph into a representation of phenomena or situations such as "refugees," "torture," or "expulsion." The representation annuls the excess and lack that were inscribed in the photograph, subordinating it to one, supposedly factual, point of view, thus enabling the photographs to determine that "this is a table" or "this is a refugee."[46]

In the case of these photographs, their indexicality may simply point to "this is an illegal," thus giving rise to a number of threats: the condition of unmournability, the undermining of humanity, the ignorance of the conditions of pain that leads people to go on a treacherous journey in order to seek a better life or simply to survive. In this case the photograph, as explained by Azoulay, becomes a mere representation conforming to what she sees as "a highly reduced template of polarized relations such as inside/outside, photographer/photographed person, spectator/subject of observation" rather than a nondeterministic encounter, an "open encounter in which others may participate."[47] That is, the power of indexicality freezes specific meanings of and reactions to the photograph and precludes the possibility that spectators may engage not only with what the photograph is supposed to be indexing—in this case objects carried by "illegals" and "illegals" at the border—but also with a whole host of affective possibilities arising from the image that may bring forth alternative understandings of the lives and journeys of these border crossers.

While the threat of a primarily indexical reading is indeed possible, I would like to suggest that what we may interpret as the promise of these photographs, the opening to perceiving and understanding border crossers otherwise, becomes more feasible in the context of the photos of the medical examiner despite their status as evidentiary photographs. Consider an altogether different set of photographs from the series *El Sueño Americano* by artist Tom Kiefer, who worked in a Customs and Border Protection center in Arizona and used objects discarded in his series.[48] The question here is whether perceiving the photographs prompts an aesthetic unsettlement that may lead to seeing border crossers anew or whether the encounter with the images reinforces already-made scripts regarding these objects and those who carried them.

Tom Kiefer's photographs in his series *El Sueño Americano* fail to prompt a promising aesthetic unsettlement. For example, in *Tuny*, the neatly arranged rows of canned tuna against the clean and neat background of plastic turf remind us of an advertising for the brand rather than the food that immigrants were carrying in a perilous journey. This is not surprising as Kiefer himself worked in advertising. In *Belt Labyrinth* we find less the touch of advertising and more of an artistic arrangement with beautiful form. Unfortunately, Kiefer's beautiful composition of belts neatly staged in a circular labyrinth does less to remind us of their owners than an appeal to a sense of order that a circular composition calls forth. The photograph that seems the least concerned with the humanity of the bodies of color crossing the border is *Extra Migrant Clothing*. In the context of our discussion on the sorrows of bodies of color, it is a particularly puzzling image. A long-sleeved pink, black, and white shirt with printed words—*design, joy, fish, love*—and other random arrangements of letters shrouds a shiny brown fragmented mannequin. No head. No arms. No legs. A peaceful light greenish-blue background accentuates the brownness of the mannequin. Were there to be a political significance to this photograph, it would have to be with the fact that bodies of color are indeed fragmented by brutal racism and xenophobia, by so much muck. Yet this particular photo—which could very easily be part of some clothing catalogue that at least honors different shades of skin in mannequins—does not leave a trace of the brown bodies about which it is supposed to be about. As Laura Pérez notes, "The use of representation of dress and body ornamentation in visual, installation, or performative art practices is, similarly, both symbolic and productive. . . . Whether they attempt to appear natural within a given culture or to create a spectacle of difference within it, clothing and body decoration signal the nature of membership within a given culture, be it normal, privileged, marginal, in opposition, or ambiguous."[49] In my view, the "extra" in *Extra Migrant Clothing* does not refer to the additional clothing found by Kiefer but to an "outside," the Latin root meaning of the word, the outside to which brown bodies of sorrow have been relegated in this image. The photo is disturbing, because it is representative of the status of these selves within US culture—made invisible, pushed outside, forgotten, and unmournable if they perish. The photo itself is part of a threatening aesthetic production that, rather than honoring border crossers, erases them in the very attempt of making them visible. While Kiefer may have good intentions in his photographic practices, the unsettling that these photographs perform is a threatening one given that the lives of those crossing ultimately remain outside their frames.[50]

When we think about the ways we can be addressed by objects left by those crossing the border, an interesting issue that arises is whether the context captured by the images plays a significant role in the possibility of creating promising or threatening aesthetic unsettlements. As we have seen with the photographs of the medical examiner, the objects shown in them have been thoroughly decontextualized from the very site marked by loss. However, different attunements to the photographs' address can be seen as opening possibilities of promising unsettlement. Of course, here I have been disclosing the carnality of the photograph that displays the objects carried by border crossers in ways that destabilize an understanding of the photograph as merely *representing* these objects, especially as evidence. Instead, photographs as carnal, relational objects themselves present us with a perceptual experience linked to affective responses to objects not simply proven to be "there" but as things connected to a larger web of relationality between them and humans in specific contexts. Possibilities for aesthetic unsettlement, then, may be

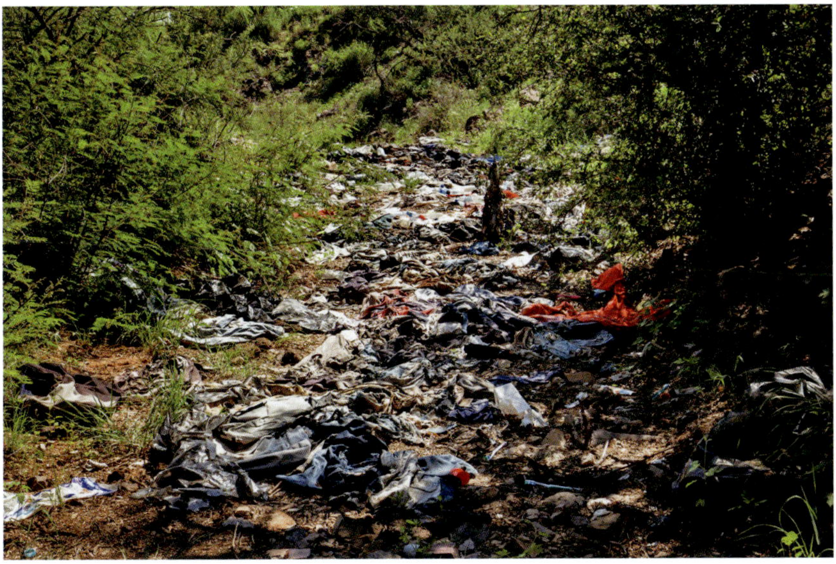

4.4 Debris field left by migrants on the US side of the US-Mexico border, 2012. Photo: Richard Barnes.

connected to the specific ways the images point to these larger webs of relationality.

As a point of comparison with Kiefer's photographs, let us briefly look at a photograph that also presents us with objects connected to those crossing the Mexico-US border, in this case articles of clothing (fig. 4.4). This is a photograph that is part of the exhibition *State of Exception / Estado de excepción*.[51] This exhibition includes work by artist Amanda Krugliak, videographer and photographer Richard Barnes, and is based on the work of anthropologist Jason De León, who has written on the border;[52] De León also created the Undocumented Migration Project, which has a large collection of objects left in the desert by border crossers.[53]

This photo of numerous articles of clothing scattered in an area of the Mexico-US border has possibilities of aesthetic unsettlement that may pierce the viewer in such a way as to develop an affective response to the plight of those crossing the border and to prompt the viewer to seek more knowledge of their condition. There is a question as to the extent of the role that the context in which the objects are found plays in this experience of unsettlement. Given the complexity and multilayeredness of relations, it is not possible to predict how the photograph's capturing of the larger context will effect aesthetic unsettlement. In this example, the context in which the clothing is found matters. Compared to Kiefer's project, there are different aesthetic openings here. Rather than decontextualizing the objects from the painful experience of crossing the border that might, in fact, have led to death, this photograph may prompt a promising aesthetic unsettlement leading the viewer to affectively respond to the magnitude of the problem—there are just so many articles of clothing pointing to a large number of people—or to the difficulties that can be encountered in the particular terrain that border crossers have to traverse. For me, the photograph turns sorrow into a river of clothing that flows in the muck produced by racist pathology. Yet we cannot predict whether someone else will see the photograph and feel disgust about all the trash left by those crossing the border. That is, it is not clear whether the use of these objects in order to decry the injustice of events will reify the very negative associations already associated with migrants.

Importantly, this photograph is one of various objects in the exhibition and needs to be experienced in connection to the rest of the exhibition, which also includes actual objects from De León's collection of things left by those crossing the border. In the exhibition, the visitor may walk on a narrow passage and encounter a large print of the photo and then move to the next room and be faced by a wall of seven hundred backpacks recovered by De León and his assistants (fig. 4.5). As opposed to Kiefer's photographs that, in my view, cover up or keep out the humanity of the border crossers—and most likely do not elicit the need to know more about the existential, cultural, political, and economic situation of those crossing the border—Barnes's photograph and the installation of the wall of backpacks as exhibited has the possibility of aesthetically unsettling the viewer. Yet, as Roelofs's relational aesthetics would highlight, it also harbors a threat: it runs the risk of creating a spectacle of the plight of these immigrants when their belongings are taken from their original context and staged so as to create an *experience* for the gallery viewer.

Does this photograph of seven hundred backpacks affectively pierce us or merely reproduce an instance of the spectacle of race that is so much part of the history of this country?[54] Does the photo hum to us or does it scream at us?[55] Does it undermine the sorrow that the owners of these backpacks carried? Again, a viewer's reaction to the work cannot be predicted, expected, or demanded. In a sense, this is a part of what I take as a result of the intimacy between perceiver and perceived in the perception-affect nexus and the medium-affect nexus—the aesthetic possibilities

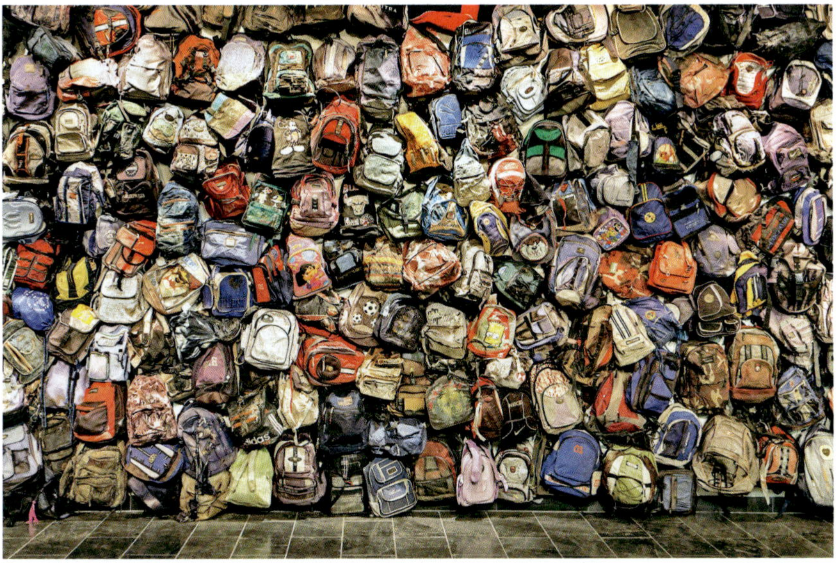

4.5 Richard Barnes, *Installation of Backpacks Left Behind by Unauthorized Border Crossers along the United States–Mexico Border*, 2012. Photo: Richard Barnes.

generated by encounters between people, objects, places, artworks, and so on are immersed in deep webs of relations and cannot be reigned over or completely controlled. While an artist or cultural producer may try to manipulate us via particular shapings of the work themselves, the affective quality of our responses cannot be guaranteed.

What we can be certain about is the addressability of objects to us and how some modalities of address affect some people more than others. Such modalities matter and may make the difference between promising unsettlements or mere threats that perpetuate perceptual structures. But as we have seen, aesthetic unsettlement constitutes affective attunement at the moment of perception that discloses openings that may redirect us to other ways of being, sensing, and knowing. Aesthetic unsettlements carry promises and threats. While they may not be the arrebatos, the earthquake-like moments that place Anzaldúa in moments of paralysis but also of readying to cross to the other side, they nevertheless may quietly take us to the sorrow carried by bodies of color, which is itself a type of unsettlement or, as Frankowski puts it, an interruption of the forgetting of a history of violence and what is for me an interruption of a broken present. It is the promise of this interruption that interests me, that I seek in *Carnalities*.

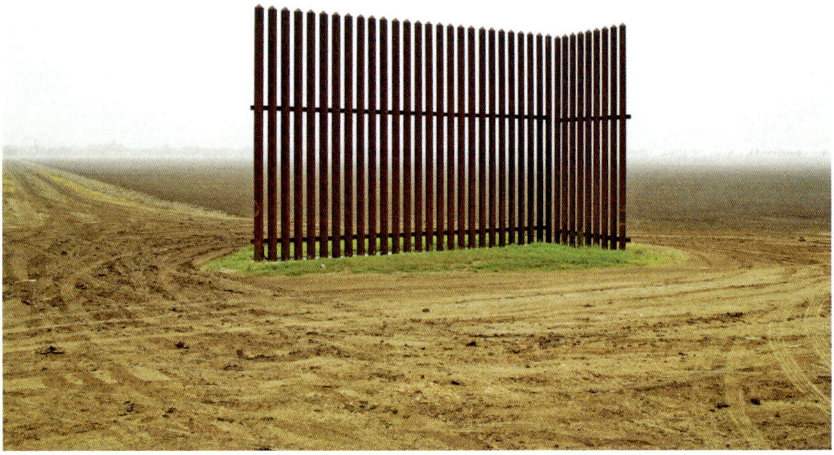

4.6 Richard Misrach, *Wall, Near Los Indios, Texas / El muro, al este de Nogales, Arizona (Border Cantos* series), 2014. Pigment print, 80 × 60 in. Courtesy of the artist and the Fraenkel Gallery.

This is what sorrow sounds like—eerie flute sounds, anxious birds calling for help, afraid of being forgotten. Flutes made of bottles, Cokeflutes, Pediaflutes. These flutes could save your life.

Two sections of border wall stand aimlessly in the middle of the desert. Life does not stand this straight. It softens, sways with the wind, cares for other life.

***Agitanques*. Jugs filled with gravel and sand create new sounds of old sorrows. Sand in the throat, in tired veins and arteries—soft, vital organs in danger. Jugs shaken violently. Parched bodies struggle with all this sand, with this gravel forcing itself through moving flesh. The end is certain to come. Find the blue barrel turned blood.**

***Agua*. Water is like a precious metal here. The flaying cloth of a blue tattered flag leans to the right, wanting to touch the lonely tank.**

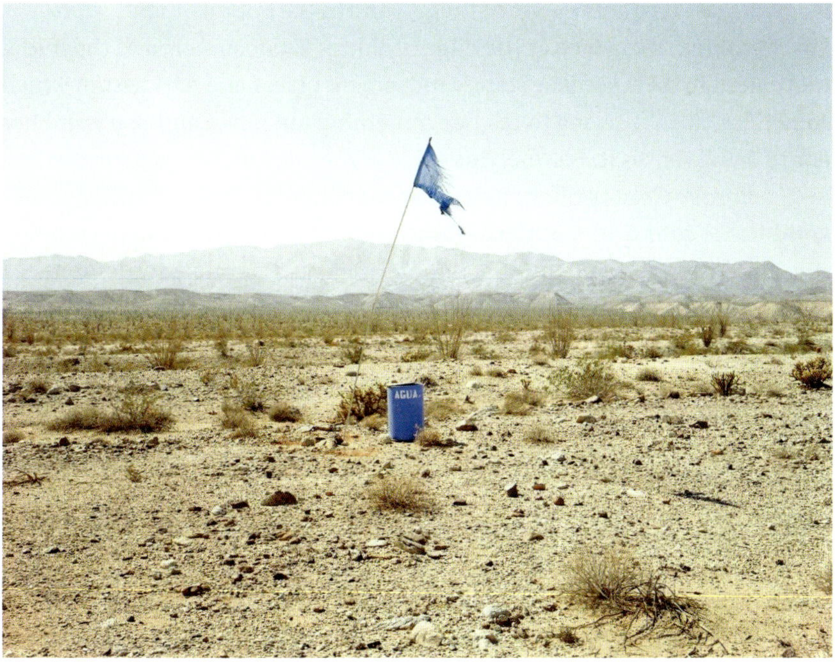

4.7 Richard Misrach, *Agua #1, near Calexico, California / Agua no. 1, cerca de Calexico, California* (*Border Cantos* series), 2004. Pigment print, 72 × 60 in. Courtesy of the artist and the Fraenkel Gallery.

The photographs of the Pima County Office of the Medical Examiner can be listened to in a way that discloses the humanity of those daring to cross that bleeding wound that is the Mexico-US border. They also reveal the sorrow that is tethered to these courageous beings in their journeys of both refusal and futurity. This is a sorrow that continues to flow in the present but is linked to past injustices, a history subject to what Jacqui M. Alexander calls a deep forgetting.[56] Yet the sorrow that flows from photographs can interrupt a broken present thirsty to forget. To expand on the notion of aesthetic unsettlement, in this section I engage with the works from the exhibition *Border Cantos* by Richard Misrach and Guillermo Galindo (figs. 4.6–4.9). I do so in order to deepen the analysis of *listening*. In this case, however, the listening that I discuss is connected to photographs of the Mexico-US border by Misrach and to compositions by Galindo performed with instruments made of objects left by those crossing the border.[57] I aim to discuss *aural unsettlement* as connected with the carnality of the photograph, an aural unsettlement that takes me to, in Anzaldúa's words, "that voice at the edge of things," and to the notion of *sonic rupture*.[58] For Anzaldúa, this voice at the edge of things is encountered at the initial movement in the Coatlicue state, a movement of fear and darkness in which something alien is trying to tell her something unknown and scary and her entire being senses it. For me, this voice at the edge of things is sorrow.

Border Cantos offers its visitors aesthetic possibilities that go beyond those found in standard photographic exhibitions. Experiencing this exhibition is to encounter the possibility of aural unsettlement.[59] I follow Helen Fielding's phenomenological analysis of works of art as offering possibilities for perceptual *encounters* rather than as illustrations of theoretical views to explore my experience with various works of the exhibition that led me beyond the visual toward an encounter with the power of the aural.[60] I do so with the intent to posit an account of *deep listening* that involves *aesthetic unfolding* or a slow attunement to the affectivity of the senses that discloses the intertwining between self and worlds.[61]

In the exhibition, Misrach's stunning photographs are accompanied by Galindo's powerful compositions. One of the questions that immediately arises for me in the context of this exhibition is how we may approach *Border Cantos* from a phenomenological perspective in order to show how it allows for aesthetic openings that have the possibility of reorienting not only how we perceive the exhibition's works but also the discursive normative frameworks associated with the imagery of the photographs—namely, images of sections of the wall built along 269 miles of the almost 2,000-mile-long Mexico-US border (figs. 4.6 and 4.8), the landscapes of the border (fig. 4.7), and effigies found in some areas (fig. 4.9). As it is not possible to discuss the many perceptual encounters I had with the photographs and different compositions, and since I cannot fully capture my experience of the exhibition in a discursive manner, I will concentrate on one of the most gripping experiences I had while at the exhibition: the moment when I immersed myself in the disturbingly beautiful yet threatening photographs by Misrach while at the same time listening to Galindo's composition *Efigie|Effigy*.[62]

The effigy as instrument, whose chest resonates with deeper tones from the top two strings, conveys the sense of a beating heart in the midst of danger, tries to beat "in sympathy" with the sounds of those upper strings, which themselves first produce scary screeches, changing to a hurried tone, a mounting sense of danger, one that conveys fear and desperation, while the *Zapatófono*, made from a shoe worn by an immigrant and gravel, walks on its precarious crossing. The composition itself

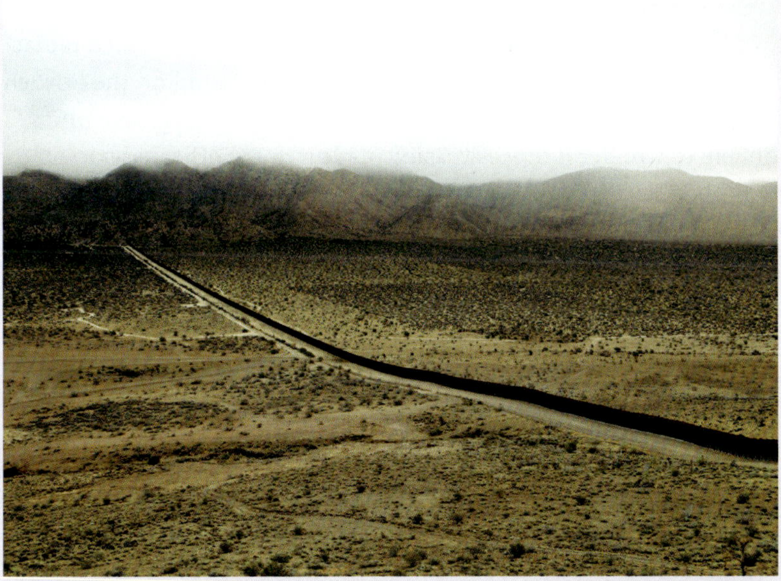

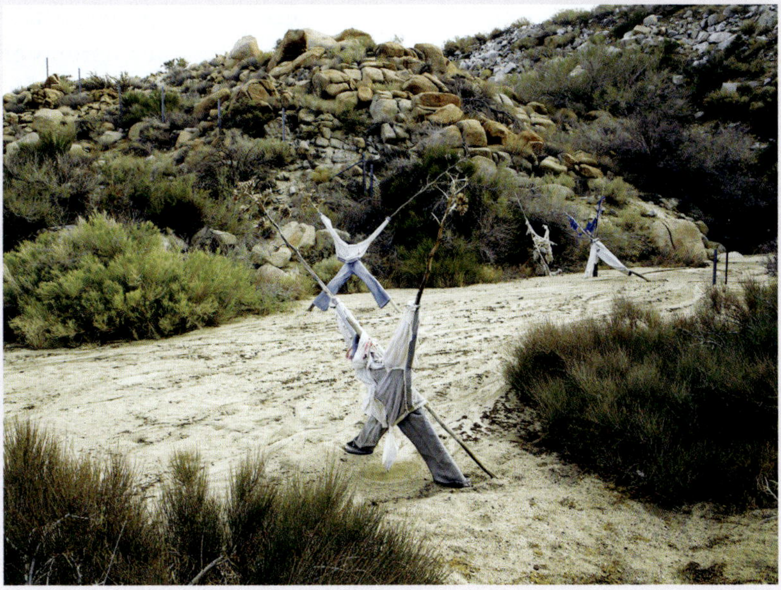

4.8 Richard Misrach, *Wall, Jacumba, California* (*Border Cantos* series). Pigment print, 80 × 60 in. Courtesy of the artist and the Fraenkel Gallery.

4.9 Richard Misrach, *Effigy #10, near Jacumba, California* (*Border Cantos* series). Pigment print. Courtesy of the artist and the Fraenkel Gallery.

filled me with anxiety and a certain tightness in my own chest, which increased more at the moments of dissonance and discordance radiating from the strings. Here is a collection of objects found on the border, objects-turned-persons, turned *someone*, walking, running, screaming. I cannot help to wonder if those crossing made it to the other side or if they avoided the *hieleras*,[63] those cold cages in US detention centers that, as we will see in the next chapter, leave them in a purgatory, in abeyance in a deplorable present and an unimaginable future.

My response to *Efigie|Effigy*, both as composition and as instrument, is one that I can only describe as overwhelming and shattering, opening a series of affective responses to the intertwining of not only the visual and the aural but all that my body as a being-in-worlds was sensing.[64] The addition of the aural component changed the manner in which the photographs addressed me: somehow the landscapes in them became more threatening and hostile, the skies more ominous. The sonorous box that is my body was keenly attuned to the reverberations of the composition. A series of aesthetic unsettlements followed that cannot be neatly circumscribed given the complexity and richness of the experience. Returning to Frankowski's analysis of the Sorrow Songs as interruptions of the forgetting of racial violence against Blacks, as well as my own sense of the photographs from the Pima County Office of the Medical Examiner as evoking a sense of sorrow that interrupts a broken present for brown bodies, *Efigie|Effigy* paradoxically also conveyed a continuous brokenness of the present and the anxiety that it provokes. That is, listening to the composition while surrounded by large photographs of the landscapes of the Mexico-US border produced a feeling of confinement and desperation as I was also overwhelmed by sorrow. The sense of threat dominated the experience enveloped in piercing, sounds and images of a long wound.

This experience of a multifaceted aural unsettlement was for me akin to a conjuring up of not only the past wrongs against Latin American, Caribbean, and US Latinxs peoples but also the continuous state of threat in which so many migrants find themselves in the United States, even if they manage to cross. This latter sense is reminiscent of Frankowski's view of the function of the Sorrow Songs as connected to memory. Yet by means of Galindo's gripping composition, this brokenness surfaced as a continuous wound, a haunting of our very broken present. I suspect this is the case, because I am someone who, having had a difficult migration to the United States, am deeply aware of the plight of migrants in this country and, in particular, of the continuous misrepresentations and mistreatment of them that continues to be either unnoticed or not taken seriously enough such that so many people, including children, are left in deplorable conditions in cages in detention centers. Yet I still wonder whether this experience may also count as an *aural unsettlement* that yields promising possibilities destabilizing sedimented perceptual habits as well as opening room for critically engaging with discursive understanding of notions such as "migrant," "the wall," "illegality," and so on. In other words, how do elements of *Border Cantos* such as the ones I describe reorient our aesthetic sensibilities, which may also open a room for a reorientation of more thematic discursive or cognitive notions?

Phenomenologically, the experience could be understood in terms of the notion of hesitation explained in chapter 1—an experience that, for Alia Al-Saji, provides a temporal opening that allows for a type of disremembering of the colonial past and a disruption of habitual practices. In this interval of hesitation, perceptual practices slow down, giving the self the opportunity to denaturalize habits (including, in the case of Al-Saji's early account, racial habits) so that sociohistorical horizons are revealed as processes that are constructed rather than seen as "natural." For example, habits of racialization such as reactions of disgust at the sight of racialized visible difference are then no longer to be understood as natural reactions but as constructed ones, and thus there may be room for reorientation. Yet what would it mean to think of hesitation in light of the listening of *Efigie|Effigy* while also experiencing Misrach's photographs? This is a difficult question, especially in light of the fact that photographs are involved and that there are no racialized subjects in them. But I hope it has become clear that here I engage the photograph as a carnal, relational medium that is not confined to mere visibility or representation. Instead, I follow both the affective and aesthetic (perceptual and thus affective) possibilities that can be found in the photographs.

In this instance, we can say with Campt that there is the humming of the photographs of the border connected with the sounds of Galindo's composition. In my view, it is possible to connect all these perceptions, which themselves are linked to affect via the perception-affect nexus and the medium-affect nexus, to an *aural unsettlement* that opens the possibility of a temporal slowing down akin to Al-Saji's notion of hesitation. Yet I wish to add an Anzaldúan perspective. Al-Saji rightly and importantly notes the need for a temporal slowing down at the moment of perception of artworks so as to make possible both the registering of the affective dimensions that are opened up by perception and a possible further critical reflection of sedimented habits.[65] I am thus interested in how this multivalent *aural unsettlement* can lead to a tarrying with the manifold affects awakened by the different ways some of the artworks address the perceiver and become intertwined with conocimiento, the intuitive knowing that Anzaldúa also considers a type of soul-making.[66]

As we have seen, Anzaldúa's carnal aesthetics, which is informed by a seven-step process of conocimiento, takes aesthetics to be indispensable for the purposes of self-creation, affective mapping, and transformation—so much so that, as we have seen for her, conocimiento entails a translation of the meaning of one's life into artistic forms, just as Anzaldúa translates her life into autohistorias. An important element of conocimiento is the suspension of usual frames of reference in the sense that rather than following normative, dominant understandings and structures, the self becomes attuned to an intuitive knowledge or, in Anzaldúa's words, to "what inner eye, heart, and gut tell you."[67] Particularly interesting is the way that this intuitive knowing is fundamentally connected to arrebatos or experiences that jolt the self away from familiar patterns. They are ruptures in the fabric of our everyday existence that open possibilities for shattering what for Anzaldúa are the mythologies that inform everydayness. She concentrates on images and takes these images as very special sorts of bridges. Recall her important comment about images: "An image is a bridge between evoked emotion and conscious knowledge; words are the cables that hold up the bridge. Images are more direct, more immediate than words, and closer to the unconscious. Picture language precedes thinking in words."[68]

While Anzaldúa prioritizes the translation of images into words in her own self-making creative process, her view constitutes, as I have shown, a mouthly, carnal aesthetics open to all the senses. Her aesthetics leaves room for an elaboration of what here I call *aesthetic rupture*, specifically a sonic rupture. In my view, it is the sonic rupture caused by *Efigie|Effigy* that led me to be so thoroughly affected by *Border Cantos* and to be taken to a place of vulnerability in the midst of the brokenness of a present for Latin American, Caribbean, and Latinx migrants. That is, aesthetic unsettlement, read from an Anzaldúan perspective, constitutes an *aesthetic rupture*. In the case of *Border Cantos*, *Efigie|Effigy* in connection with the photographs leads to a *sonic rupture*.

Anzaldúa's discussion of conocimiento briefly touches on the aural in stage 3: the Coatlicue state, the stage in which one enters a state of paralyzing fear, faced with writing blocks, but also the stage that amounts to a preparation for a shift in which pain and grief force one to face a difficult situation. It is in this stage where she listens to La Llorona's wail: she states, "La Llorona's wail rises, urging you to pay heed. All seven ojos de luz blink 'on.' Your body trembles as a new knowing slithers up like a snake, stirring you out of your stupor."[69] It is fitting that it is the wailing of La Llorona that prompts Anzaldúa to hone her intuition and prepare her to cross. La Llorona (or the weeping or wailing woman) is very much part of Mexican and Central American mythology. She is the ghost of a woman who has killed her children and has been punished to roam the earth, crying and looking for them. It is the wailing sounds of her sorrow that prompt Anzaldúa to pay attention, to hone her sensible faculties. In so doing, Anzaldúa enters a state of gestation or what Lugones reads as a state of germination:[70] "We need Coatlicue to slow us up so that the psyche can assimilate previous experiences and process the change. . . . Those activities of the Coatlicue States which disrupt the smooth flow (complacency) of life are exactly what propel the soul to do its work."[71] The sounds of unbearable sorrow, then, constitute the sonic rupture that Anzaldúa specifically ties to emotion as she takes conocimiento as entailing a "breaking out of mental and emotional prison and deepening the range of perception."[72]

The deepening of a range of perception prompted by sonic rupture is, in my view, an *aesthetic unfolding*, an unfolding of all senses as they become heightened and register the various perceptual and affective modes prompted by the work's address to us. In the case of my experience of *Border Cantos* (as connected to various compositions but especially *Efigie|Effigy*) the sonic rupture led to the artworks prompting affects in me that lingered, gripping me in such a way that I could not let them go, a melancholic grip leading me to tarry with sorrow. The importance of sonic rupture is its possibility in opening up a range of perception beyond the visible: that is, of showing us or alerting us to that which resists visuality, to the invisibility within the visible, an instance of moving beyond the eye—to the ear and mouth. While Misrach's photographs and Galindo's compositions could very well be capable of raising a number of emotions on their own, the aural component heightened the experience given that my own body felt the vibrations of the sounds, becoming itself a kind of receptive effigy.

The difficult question, however, is whether this sonic rupture may lead someone whose relationship to migration is quite different from mine to experience aesthetic *unsettlement*, which heightens the senses and allows for being affectively moved by the works, which itself opens the possibility for a further moment: that of reconfiguring the discursive, cognitive modes associated with notions such as "wall," "illegality," "migration." In short, could the experience of the exhibition touch viewers in such a way as to develop the intuitive sense that is so important for Anzaldúa? Could it open the possibility for perceiving and thinking otherwise? Anzaldúa states, "This visual intuitive sense, like the intellect of heart and gut, reveals a discourse of signs, images, feelings, words that, once decoded, carry the power to startle you out of tunnel vision and habitual patterns of thought."[73] Clearly, she thinks that once the intuitive sense is heightened, there is a possibility for different feelings, perceptions, understandings, and ways of being. Given the primacy of the aesthetic in her account of conocimiento and in the way that she resorts to creative acts to forge her very bones, Anzaldúa takes artworks as being able to have these effects on those who experience them. So far, my own interest in carnalities in this book have led me to point to the possibilities of artworks to prompt aesthetic unsettlements with promising possibilities of the otherwise. I understand carnalities as precisely creative practices of art production and art reception that help bodies of color cope with the sorrow they carry and that may also help with processes of self-naming, transformation, and relational world-making against the tyranny of the colonial gaze. Bodies of color as bodies of sorrow are already engaging in these practices. With Anzaldúa, I can only point to the possibility of aesthetic ruptures prompted by artworks as capable of reaching those in dominant positions. It will be in their being experienced that openings may be created, as it is at the moment of rupture that the self is transported to a moment of nepantla as a transitional state that opens possibilities of critical reflection and demythologization, of seeing "through the fiction of the monoculture, the myth of the superiority of the white race."[74] Adding an Anzaldúan moment to the notion of hesitation thus prompts us to look into the ruptures that allow for the possibility of slowing down and of aesthetic unsettlement in the first place, because they transport the self to nepantla, a "site of transformation" where one can no longer live "according to old terms."[75]

In the case of sonic rupture, which highlights the aural but also involves multiple senses given the complexity of our experiences (whether of other people, places, objects, or artworks), the aural element adds to the complexity of the layering of perception as it may pick up that which is resistant to visibility. Here aesthetic rupture in its sonic mode may be understood as having a double movement: that of literally rupturing the complacency of sonic expectations and of bringing forth bodily reverberations of sounds, leaving one in a sonic nepantla that subsequently leads to the moment of Coatlicue fear. In *Border Cantos*, the aural dimension of the exhibition by way of Galindo's compositions elevates the sonic capabilities of our bodies as they are affected by the vibrations of piercing sounds, leading to a slow unfolding or deepening of perception. The sounds made with those objects left by those engaged in this deadly crossing—wailing, thumping, screeching, moaning, and, if I may say so, sorrowing—also make the museum itself a sonorous box in which we cannot expect a sanitized silence or the sounds of the usually inane description of recorded guides to artworks. In this instance, listening becomes an experience in which there is an engagement with the world and, as Salomé Voegelin would say, listening as a method of exploration.[76] For me, this can be a temporal slowing down that allows for deep listening as aesthetic unfolding that involves a moment of being pierced as if with a sonic *punctum* that connects us to the work affectively—a tarrying with that experience; a Coatlicuan plunging into the experience of sorrow, fear, and anxiety; and a possible reconfiguration of previously understood discourses in connection to what we are experiencing, a prelude to "crossing" to new ways of sensing and understanding. As Anzaldúa says, "In the deep fecund cave of gestation lies not only the source of your woundedness and your passion, but also the promise of inner knowledge, healing and spiritual rebirth (the hidden treasures), waiting for you to bear them to the surface."[77]

My perceptual encounter with *Border Cantos* touched me deeply, prompting me to consider the importance of aural unsettlement in looking for that which resists the visible. The aural component of the exhibition intensified my experience by way of a sensing of the vibrations of tension, hurriedness, fear, and danger that cry in *Efigie|Effigy*, further taking me to an experience of the utter sense of brokenness that remains in the present for Latin American, Caribbean, and Latinx peoples. Adding an Anzaldúan perspective connected to conocimiento led me to the notion of aesthetic rupture or the arrebato (stage 1 of conocimiento), in this case sonic rupture, in which the everyday modes of sensing and being are disrupted and one is affectively pierced; nepantla (stage 2), the movement to a space of possibility and transformation and to the Coatlicue state (stage 3 of conocimiento and prelude to crossing). It is in this Coatlicue stage of blocks and fear where one faces the voice that comes from "the voice at the edge of things," what I interpret as the voice of sorrow, the sorrow that accompanies bodies of color in their journeys. *Border Cantos*, in its multivoice, multilayered modalities of perceptual address, allows for an aesthetic unfolding in which I and hopefully others have the opportunity of tarrying with this sorrow that bodies of color cannot let go as if it were one of those tattered pieces of clothing or objects left in the desert. We who care about the plight of these courageous border crossers cannot let go, not even of these objects as they continue to hum about the lives of those who carried them.

To conclude my discussion of aural sorrow in light of quiet and resonant carnal photographs, I would like to engage with the notion of melancholia, which, as compared to mourning (a gradual letting go of a loved object), is understood as a pathological mourning that does not know how to stop. According to queer theorist José Esteban Muñoz, both mourning and melancholia are "riddled with queer possibilities."[78] Following Raymond Williams, Muñoz sees melancholia as a "structure of feeling" that is necessary and not always counterproductive and negative.[79] As he states,

> I am proposing that melancholia, for Blackness, queers, or any queers of color, is not a pathology but an integral part of everyday lives. . . . It is this melancholia that is part of our process of dealing with all the catastrophes that occur in the lives of people of color, lesbians, and gay men. I have proposed a different understanding of melancholia that does not see it as a pathology or as a self-absorbed mood that inhibits activism. Rather, it is a mechanism that helps us (re)construct identity and take our dead with us to the various battles we must wage in their names—and in our names.[80]

Ultimately, for Muñoz, melancholia is an ambivalent structure of feeling that retains the problematic object and taps into the energy that is generated by the contradictions and ambivalences that arise at the loss of the object.[81] There is so much loss for communities of color in general and LGBTQ communities of color in particular. Muñoz quotes Jeff Nunokawa on the history of the gay male reading like a book of funerals.[82] The loss is not just of a history made through art but of actual bodies succumbing to the deadly disease of AIDS and violent homophobia. Mourning for Muñoz, then, takes a different turn—it is one in which one mourns for oneself, one's community, "for one's very history."[83] Such mourning does not end, as if it were directed in a linear manner, with a final letting go of the lost object. As Muñoz says, "Whereas lives that are either/or/and Black and queer remain on the line, there is no 'normal' teleological end in sight for mourning."[84] Here mourning becomes life affirming or a resistant melancholia as it allows for a (re)construction of identities that were not meant to be.

Muñoz's vision of melancholia—not a melancholia that remains pathological but one that is both painful *and* resistant—interests me. It has been a *punctum* for me in his work as it captures the fact that the past, present, and future of queers of color are in a sense always full of loss but also imbued with creativity. Taking up a racialized identity is a melancholic act in itself, as theorists such as Anne Anlin Cheng, David Eng, and Shinhee Han have noted.[85] The loss and the trauma that queers of color carry in everydayness is not something to be gotten over, something mourned and then replaced. The loss and the trauma that bodies of color carry with them cannot be simply overcome. As bodies of color, we are haunted by this sense of loss. Yet the point of the melancholia, if we follow Muñoz, is to see the possibilities of how this sense of loss can move us to have a present that is mindful of the past, moving us to attempt to make new worlds, worlds in which there will still be loss and shame and in which we will carry our dead with us.[86] It is a melancholia that resists erasure of the past, no matter how painful a past, while at the same time refusing the brokenness of the present and defying the closure of the future. As Muñoz states in his later work in which he develops a concrete utopian vision of futurity even in the face of heartbreaking reality, "We must vacate the here and now for a then and there. Individual transports are insufficient."[87]

As we have seen, the photographs from the Pima County Office of the Medical Examiner—an unlikely archive of feelings—paradoxically take us to an aesthetic moment marked by sorrow: the sorrow for those who perished in their crossing of the Mexico-US border. If listened to, these photographs disclose the humanity of those border crossers willing to risk life and limb to make it to the other side. In turn, *Border Cantos* by Misrach and Galindo augments the perceptual encounter by adding a sonic layer to the experience of Misrach's photographs that, in my own encounter with the photographs and compositions such as *Efigie|Effigy*, led me to a moment of utter brokenness for the present and futural possibilities of Latin Americans, Caribbeans, and Latinxs in the United States. As such, the works enact aesthetic unsettlements or a destabilization, disruption, interruption, or rupture of expected perceptions and ready-made affective responses that, following Roelofs's aesthetics, can be promising or threatening. That is, aesthetic unsettlements may open the possibility for a perceiving otherwise that can subsequently be engaged in a critical assessment of discursive and cognitive understandings associated with perception, or they may reinforce dominant modes of perception and understanding. While it is not possible to predict how artworks may or may not aesthetically unsettle perceivers, it is possible to point to the potential of artworks to do so and to actual experiences of such an unsettlement. With Anzaldúa, we can further understand aesthetic unsettlement in terms of ruptures of everyday modes of perception that take us to the Coatlicue moment of fear and confusion, but also of crossing and transformation, in which perception slowly unfolds toward deep listening: sorrow calls, wounds, and brings forth that melancholia that, as bodies of color as bodies of sorrow, we carry with us—not only when we wail for our dead but also when we find the strength to carry them in our attempt to resist the muck, the filthy muck of racism, and attempt to perceive anew and to make new worlds.

FIVE

*CROSS*ING AND FEELING BROWN

Verónica Gabriela Cárdenas's Carnal Light

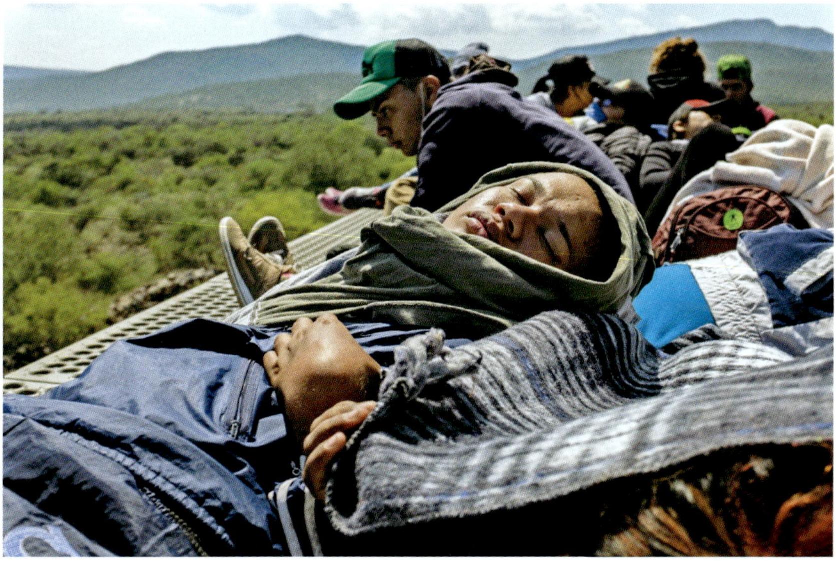

5.1 People travel on a freight train collectively known as La Bestia (The Beast) toward Tijuana, Baja California, Mexico, where many of them would be turning themselves in to US Customs and Border Protection at the San Ysidro Port of Entry to begin their immigration process in October 2017. Photo: Verónica Gabriela Cárdenas.

La Bestia

Moving north
Swollen limb
tearful skin,
rides this ruthless beast.

Living cargo.
Moving north

Angry metal,
Train of death
Interrupted childhood.
Moving north

> Those brown feelings are not the sole province of people who have been called or who call themselves brown. It is, instead, and more importantly, the sharing out of a brown sense of the world, a flowing into the common, that nonetheless maintains the urgencies and intensities we experience as freedom and difference.
>
> JOSÉ ESTEBAN MUÑOZ, *The Sense of Brown*

> This tombstone of the "world" . . . is situated at the edges of what exists, between the shadows and the light, between the conceived (abstraction) and the perceived (readable/visible). Between the real and the unreal. Always in the interstices, in the cracks. Between directly lived experience and thought and (a familiar paradox) between life and death.
>
> HENRI LEFEBVRE, *The Production of Space*

> I will etch visas on toilet paper and throw them from a lighthouse.
>
> JAVIER ZAMORA, *Unaccompanied*

As shown in the previous chapter, the unlikely archive of photographs from the Pima County Office of the Medical Examiner and the exhibition *Border Cantos* by Misrach and Galindo disclose sorrow as aesthetic unsettlement. They also point to the sorrow that is tethered to bodies of color in their crossings along the wound that is the Mexico-US border—some migrants never making it, as they are ravaged by the desert or an angry river, the Rio Grande, known to Mexicans as el río Bravo. In this chapter, I move with the flow of this sorrow disclosed by carnal photographs and sounds of migration, a flowing of bodies of color attempting impossible crossings in order to have a future in the United States. It is a flow that does not run smoothly as water through a peaceful stream. Rather, it is the anxious, broken flow of bodies of color as they trek some two thousand or more miles for up to three months under dangerous, violent conditions or ride La Bestia (The Beast), several freight trains moving from Mexico to the United States. I am thus referring to a flow that doubles—into the sorrow of bodies of color as well as the bodies of color themselves as they form caravans, large groups of migrants engaged in *cross*ings, contemporary stations of the cross, as they demand justice and a future. I wish to connect this flowing of sorrow with a "manera de ser," a way of being in the world, that José Esteban Muñoz calls "feeling brown."[1] For Muñoz, feeling brown is a structure of feeling in which there is a "shared sense of harm" that nonetheless is also "the shared flourishing that transpires and unfolds despite systemic harm."[2] Through Muñoz's theorization of feeling brown, it becomes possible to understand not just the personal way that bodies of color are affected by their experiences in worlds in which they are made abject, but also how Black, brown, Asian, and other bodies of color can feel "together in difference."[3] Continuing the analysis of photographs as carnal, given their affective power and the disclosure of the intertwining of selves and worlds, in this chapter I follow the flow of Verónica Gabriela Cárdenas's carnal photographic practice that *brings to light* and transmits *feeling brown.*[4]

In the first section of this chapter, I introduce the notion of *flowing brownness* by way of a photograph from Cárdenas's latest series, *Del Rio,* which documents the 2021 migrant caravan of Haitians as they settled in the Acuña–Del Rio International bridge across the Mexico-US border. I explain flowing brownness as a literal movement of bodies of color, as when they form caravans and traverse multiple territories in order to reach the Mexico-US border where they can apply for asylum, as well as the feeling of brownness that, according to Muñoz, is shared by bodies of color across different races. I read these caravans, originally connected to Las Estaciones del Viacrucis, the Stations of the Cross or Way of Sorrows, as contemporary *cross*ings of bodies of colors, in which the cross symbolizes different aspects of migration. Moreover, I discuss Muñoz's notion of feeling brown with attention to two main issues: brownness as shared sense of harm and brownness as commons. I read Cárdenas's photographs as carnal insofar as they are the sensory circuits through which feeling brown is transmitted. This reading of the photographs, informed by Muñoz's notion of feeling brown, opens the possibility for a promising aesthetic unsettlement in which the Mexico-US border can be reinterpreted so as to avoid the invisibilizing of Black Latinidad in discussions of the Mexico-US borderlands. It also highlights the heterogeneous, communal, and coalitional aspect of feeling brown.

In the second section, I continue to explore the figure of the cross, in this instance by way of Cárdenas's *Traveling Soles* series highlighting the crossing of Central American migrants, especially children. I analyze the photographs in the series as well as the spaces Cárdenas constructs to honor these migrants. I present Cárdenas's practice as a carnality, an aesthetic practice informed by the entanglement of selves and environments, in this case for the purposes of honoring and mourning border crossers. I also read the photographs in their series as instances of descansos, what are now described as spontaneous memorializations, memorials constructed in highways and urban areas when there has been a sudden death. In addition, I consider the sites transformed by Cárdenas in order to take the photographs and the photographs themselves as altars for the living. Here photographs become *aesthetic memories* to honor immigrants and *memento vivere*, reminders to live in such a way so as to not forget the lives of migrants who survive but that, nevertheless, remain at the edge between life and death given the racism, abjection, and economic struggles they must endure in their new land.

"KEEP THIS COUPON": FLOWING BROWNNESS

In a photograph from Cárdenas's latest series, *Del Rio*, two hands showing two tickets are captured by light (fig. 5.2). They are the hands of Joseph Niclas and Calypso Marie Chalissia, who patiently wait to apply for asylum in the United States. Two generic, unremarkable tickets, the kind usually distributed in county fair raffles, are now worth life, a future. The couple has flown, ridden other forms of transportation, and walked with so many others probably coming from Brazil or Chile, countries that saw a great influx of Haitians after the 7.2-magnitude earthquake of 2010 that took the lives of 217,000 and left more than 1.5 million homeless in Haiti.[5] To reach the Acuña–Del Rio international bridge, connecting the US border cities of Del Rio, Texas, and Ciudad Acuña, Mexico, this couple must have endured arduous, brutal conditions. Thinking about the terrain that must be traversed from Brazil to the Mexico-US border is overwhelming. Now consider the miles traveled and walked, the violence endured. Then there is the exhaustion, anxiety, and fear. In the context of the harrowing migratory experience of this couple, this image of hands holding their precious tickets is piercing.

In its portrayal of hands holding these "tickets" full of promise, the photograph almost effaces the enormity and precarity of the couple's situation. After their treacherous travel, this couple arrived at the border with approximately fifteen thousand people also seeking asylum in the United States. "KEEP THIS COUPON" is printed on one of the tickets, as if doing so

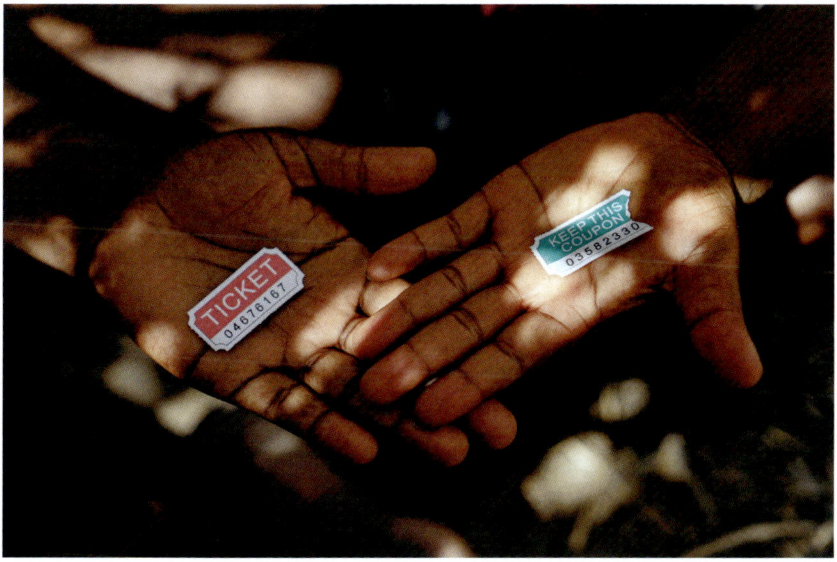

5.2 "A Haitian couple that has been waiting for four days near the Acuña–Del Rio International Bridge show the tickets that they were given by Border Patrol to wait for their turn to turn themselves in to continue with the asylum process in Del Rio, Texas on Friday, Sept. 17, 2021." Photo: Verónica Gabriela Cárdenas for the *New York Times*.

will indeed guarantee that their dreams, desires, and hopes will come true and that their sacrifices in their perilous journey north will have been worth it. Yet this private moment between Cárdenas and the couple is sealed in an intimate light that falls on the words *KEEP THIS COUPON*. It is during this captured slice of time that we are reminded of the particular lives of these two people. Cárdenas opens their lens to the liberatory possibilities of the couple's journey. Do their tickets not guarantee a screening for asylum?

Of course, this is too hopeful a reading. The particularity of these two people is lost in the midst of fifteen thousand others whose desire for asylum they share. Their hands could be the hands of so many others who flowed into the Mexico-US border in September 2021. The photograph captures the desire of these two people as they wait for their turn, KEEPING THEIR COUPON, but also reminds us that these hands could be those of the thousands of people also waiting for their turn. There are so many lives at stake here. We can keep an anxious hope despite knowing that these pieces of paper could lose their value in an instant due to immigration policy changes, economic conditions, and pandemic fears, while recognizing how deep sorrow flows in these movements of dreams, desires, and futurity.

In this section, I begin with a discussion of migrant caravans read as *cross*ings and *flowing brownness*. While the cross is a problematic symbol given its association with colonizing religious structures and histories, here I take up the figure of the cross in the religious sense that migrants have assigned to the caravans, as a call for justice. The cross also becomes symbolic of different moments of migration: crossing from one place to another; the migrant body as the site of intersection between desires for futurity and forces that negate their lives; as well as the movement of being-crossed-out, of perishing. Subsequently, I move on to discuss the caravan in terms of flowing brownness inspired by Muñoz's account of feeling brown.

As pointed out in the last chapter, due to violence, poverty, climate change, as well as a history of US military interventions and support of oppressive governments, migrants from the Northern Triangle of Central America (Guatemala, El Salvador, and Honduras) as well as Mexico continually risk their lives crossing the Mexico-US border in search of safety and better opportunities. In recent years, however, there has been a new way of crossing, a crossing-with-others by way of caravans. In the fall of 2018, a group of two hundred Hondurans gathered in a bus station in San Pedro Sula in order to walk together to the United States. They called the event "La Caminata del Migrante" and circulated a flyer through social media with information about their departure and the statement "No nos vamos por que queremos, nos expulsa la violencia y la pobreza" (We are not leaving because we want to; we are driven out by violence and poverty).[6] As they moved forward, they were joined by migrants from Guatemala, El Salvador, and Nicaragua, and a week later the group had grown to five thousand.[7] These flows of migrants and asylum seekers labeled "caravans" continued to arrive at the Mexico-US border after the 2018 caravan and are now regarded by some as the start of a new social movement.[8] Conservative pundits moved swiftly to condemn these caravans, calling them "invasions," leading former US president Donald Trump to put into effect Title 42 at the outbreak of the COVID-19 pandemic, allowing Customs and Border Protection officials to swiftly deport migrants from the border without giving them the opportunity to apply for asylum. With the change of presidency, caravans continued to move north. While the caravans have traditionally consisted of migrants from the Northern Triangle, recent caravans include Haitians and Venezuelans. The change of the racial composition of the caravans is deeply important as it points to the need for a more expansive understanding of the Mexico-US border experience. With attention to the possibility of coalitional possibilities, I wish to discuss this shift in terms of flowing brownness as connected to Muñoz's notion of feeling brown and the brown commons. Before I turn to this flowing brownness, however, I note the importance of the figure of the cross in the caravans as the "passion" of these migrants—that is, their pain, sorrow, and suffering as they walk and have been forced to migrate, what Muñoz would refer to as a "shared sense of harm."

CROSSING

From 2013 to 2018 there were groups of migrants marching in Central America and Mexico to call for justice for migrants by comparing their processions to the Viacrucis (the Stations of the Cross or Way of Sorrows), with immigrants dressing as Jesus and carrying a cross. The Stations of the Cross are an integral part of Christian religion and consist of fourteen images depicting fourteen stations symbolizing Jesus Christ's different stages as he walks to his crucifixion. It is the "passion" of Jesus, his suffering and sorrow as well as his endurance, that is being exalted as believers engage in their own pilgrimages guided by the Viacrucis. Hence, there is a significant religious aspect even in the most recent caravans, as migrants continue to appeal to the Stations of the Cross and the Passion of Christ and to invoke the figure of Jesus Christ as a migrant. For example, a 2022 caravan carried a sign with red letters spelling out "Viacrucis Migrante 2022" (Migrating Stations of the Cross / Way of Sorrows 2022), signaling that they saw themselves as involved in a pilgrimage in contemplation of the passion or the suffering of Christ (see fig. 5.3). Given that these migrants sometimes trek up to two thousand miles while enduring dangerous and violent conditions,[9] it is indeed a passion (as in *passio* or suffering) that marks these bodies; the bloody letters of the sign they carry are a reminder of this precarious, carnal flowing.[10]

I interpret this flowing of bodies as *cross*ing insofar as many of these migrants believe themselves to be engaging in a type of religious pilgrimage, a politico-religious one in which they advocate for their lives and the lives of other migrants living under precarious conditions—their very bodies becoming the sites on which the entanglement of religious practices, laws, policies, conditions for citizenship, political structures, economic structures guided by neoliberalism and coloniality, leave their

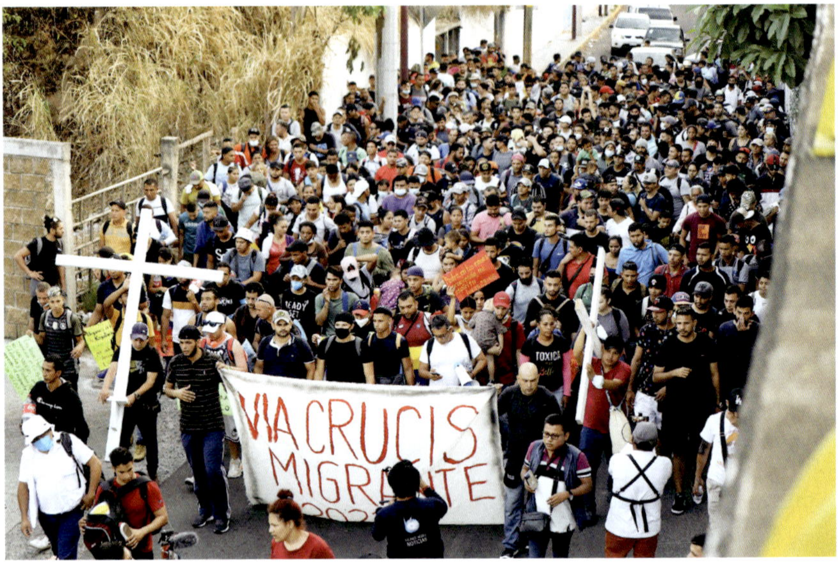

5.3 The Viacrucis caravan before being stopped on April 16, 2022. Photo: Jacob Garcia / Anadolu Agency via Getty Images.

bloody marks. There is passion here—passion as in suffering but also as in powerful feeling, indicating the ambiguous character of the Christian beliefs that guide them that both demands a redemptive suffering for their sins and provides a powerful impetus and support in their endeavors. Here, however, I wish to highlight the figure of the cross in terms of movements and sites of migratory experience. The first movement is the literal crossing of a border, which may or may not happen. While these migrants walk under unimaginable conditions—I think of their moving across the deadly jungle trek, the Darién Gap at the Panama-Colombia border—with the dream of reaching the Mexico-US border propelling them, there is what we may regard as an accompanying movement, all that stands against their journey, including environmental conditions, legal policies, anti-immigration and racist sentiments, vigilante violence, lack of resources, and multiple other factors. I see these two ambulatory lines intersecting or crossing in the very migrant body. Finally, there is the deadly interruption of the journey, a being-crossed-out that is always a possibility for these migrants enduring treacherous conditions. This understanding of crossing in terms of these various possibilities of embodied migrant movement brings forth the linkage between specific spatialities of the border, temporality, coloniality, and the migrant body, which as a site of sorrow is also the site of the convergence of lines of abjection and violence but also of futurity.

Reading the migrant body in terms of *cross*ing, as carnal intersection, however, does not entail that this body is a mere site of victimization. While I take bodies of color to be bodies of sorrow as explained in chapter 4, this is not to relegate them to a realm of pain and nonbeing. This intersection, this *cross*ing that is the migrant body in the flowing brownness of the caravans, can, according to Blanca Laura Cordero Díaz and María Georgina Garibo García, be understood as an "acuerpamiento en movimiento" (embodied movement) that rests on the political character of migration as "desobediencia civil" (civil disobedience) and "derecho de fuga" (the right to flee).[11] While their success is not guaranteed, part of their political strength and possibility of safety lies in numbers, in the very flowing, embodied movement that they enact toward the Mexico-US border. Through this tactic, migrants, especially women, children, and the elderly, are able to cross, as are those who cannot afford the high fees that smugglers (coyotes) charge to accompany them in their crossings. The movements of *cross*ing are thus complex and need to be understood in their personal as well as political possibilities, openings as well as closures in a context of what Muñoz calls the brown commons.

Feeling Brown

I wish to return to Cárdenas's series *Del Rio* that captures the flowing of the 2021 Haitian caravan at the Acuña–Del Rio International Bridge. I see their work as *bringing to light* feeling brown. Here I take "bringing to light" not merely in its usual meaning as revealing and disclosing but as a specific carnal aesthetics, an aesthetics of flesh*and*blood, that writes with light; the photographic act that, in this case, captures flowing brownness and feeling brown. Their photography does not merely document or point to the presence of the migrants in Del Rio, the "that-has-been" that, according to Barthes, is the essence of photography, its indexicality. As we have seen, despite Barthes's intention to find the essence of photography, Barthes himself gets caught in a subjective methodology: he examines the photographs that animate him, and, importantly, the photograph that moves him deeply is that of his mother in the now-famous "Winter Garden Photograph." This is a crucial aspect of his discussion given that his mother had just died. The text thus discloses a double movement: that of a philosophical, phenomenological analysis in search of the essence of photography, as well as Barthes's own affective needs given his own mourning for his mother. What I find most moving in the text is precisely the manner in which affect spills out of the pages of *Camera Lucida*. Recall his point that "a sort of umbilical cord links the body of the photographed thing to my gaze."[12] While, as we will see in the next chapter, I will part ways with Barthes given problematic readings of race in his analyses of the *punctum*, what he considers an element of the photograph that pricks or bruises the viewer, I deeply appreciate his recognition that what is supposed to be a medium defined by its indexicality is nevertheless thoroughly carnal and thus has an affective pull. In their series *Del Rio*, Cárdenas *brings to light* this affectivity. While they capture the literal flowing of brownness in the sense of Black and brown bodies moving-with each other, they also *bring to light* the structure of feeling that Muñoz refers to as feeling brown that has so far only appeared in terms of the notion of sorrow. As such, the archive of feeling that is being created by Cárdenas is an archive of feeling brown. In the following, I discuss this feeling brown that for Muñoz is a structure of feeling, a manera de ser, a way of being, that Black, brown, and other bodies of color share, what Muñoz calls a "feeling together in difference."[13]

Del Rio by Verónica Gabriela Cárdenas

One of Cárdenas's most important photographs (fig. 5.4) in their series *Del Rio* shows a line of immigrants forming a straight line crossing a shallow area of the Rio Grande. We see these migrants moving in both directions, as they continually cross to the Mexican side in order to bring supplies that will help them survive while they wait on the US side for their turn to request asylum. The photograph is striking because of its compositional beauty of sky, foliage, water, and people arranged in a balanced, almost symmetrical gesture—with its blues and greens punctured by specks of red, yellow, and pink—in contrast with the experience it discloses: that of fear, desperation, and willingness to be part of an impossible journey. The river is cut by a line seemingly taming the waters so as to allow these dreamers to make their crossings, as if these waters knew the urgency of their situation—river and human intertwined in a moment of survival. Yet we know just how angry this river can get—there is a reason its other name is el río Bravo—and how many have perished in its waters.[14]

When I study this photograph further, I see it as capturing the flow of Black and brown migrants coming to the Acuña–Del Rio International

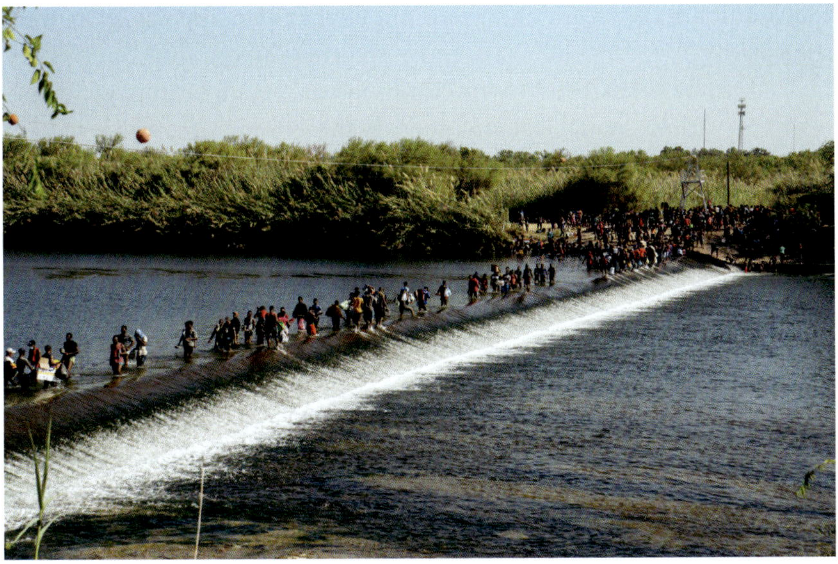

5.4 "Migrants, mostly Haitians, cross back and forth between both countries through the Rio Grande to buy food and things that they need while they wait for their turn to turn themselves to Border Patrol to continue with their asylum process in Ciudad Acuña, Mexico on Friday, Sept. 17, 2021. It is estimated that more than 10,000 migrants are waiting to seek asylum on the U.S. side as of this day." Photo: Verónica Gabriela Cárdenas for the *New York Times*.

Bridge. My sense of bodies of color being bodies of sorrow intensifies. It also prompts me to consider this sorrow in terms of Muñoz's sense of feeling brown; more specifically, the photograph discloses a sense of what Muñoz calls the *brown commons*. While Muñoz's writings on the notion of feeling brown highlight "first and foremost . . . brown people in a very immediate way, in this sense, people who are rendered brown by their personal and familial participation in South-to-North migration patterns," he appeals to a brown commons, which he defines as "the commons of brown people, places, feelings, sounds, animals, minerals, flora and other objects."[15] I wish to add "river" to this list. The sense of which a brown commons is brown has to do with, first, there being brown people in this commons, suffering and flourishing together, even though there are always structures trying to devalue them; and second, with their sharing what Muñoz calls an "organicism that is not solely the organic of the natural as much as it is a certain brownness which is embedded in a vast and pulsating social world."[16] This is an organicism in which objects touch and are copresent and there is a flow and an impulse away from subjectivity.[17]

Muñoz takes the brown commons as organizations of feeling brown in various spatial instantiations. In these commons, which according to Muñoz already exist,[18] people of color find themselves as sharing a sense of harm due to oppressive norms. He takes feeling brown as "indexing a certain vulnerability to the violence of property, finance, and to capital's overarching mechanism of domination."[19] For Muñoz, the brown commons hold moments of endurance, resistance, refusal, and futurity for brown people. While he highlights social worlds as brown commons, here I emphasize the Rio Grande as brown commons. Given that its waters continually hold the flow of brown bodies crossing, and that these are *cross*ings marked by a series of economic, political, and environmental forces, the river—painted with light by Cárdenas—becomes brown commons where "there is a kind of uncanny persistence in the face of distressed conditions of possibility."[20]

Zooming in to capture the migrants' experience up close, Cárdenas presents us with their walking-with in an embodied flow and precarious traversing of this river (fig. 5.5) that, rather than being a natural commons in a traditional sense, becomes a brown commons where bodies of color share their feeling brown. This feeling brown is connected to the precarity of their situation and the way their very bodies are *cross*ings themselves as they are the brunt of the violence of empire and coloniality. We can also see these migrants and the things they carry: water bottles, bags, coolers, buckets, a mattress, boxes, shoes, clothes, food—not to mention their hopes, dreams, as well as their sorrow—in the midst of the sky, water, and land that receives them, as entangled in collective embodiment in search of the otherwise. This is a photograph of flesh*and*blood, which, as discussed in the introduction, points to a disclosure of the intertwining between bodies of color as bodies of sorrow and worlds. These bodies of color marked by being-in-sorrow, however, also embody opportunity, civil disobedience to multiple national policies, and enactment of the right to flee. However, I opt not to use the term *flourishing*, which Muñoz aligns with the shared sense of harm of feeling brown—I take flowing brownness as defiant and in search of the otherwise.

Even as we recognize the defiance of these migrants, however, it is difficult not to remember what they are against: the possibilities of bodily and psychological harm that are always lurking in their caravan-experience. Such a possibility of bodily harm is captured in an utterly

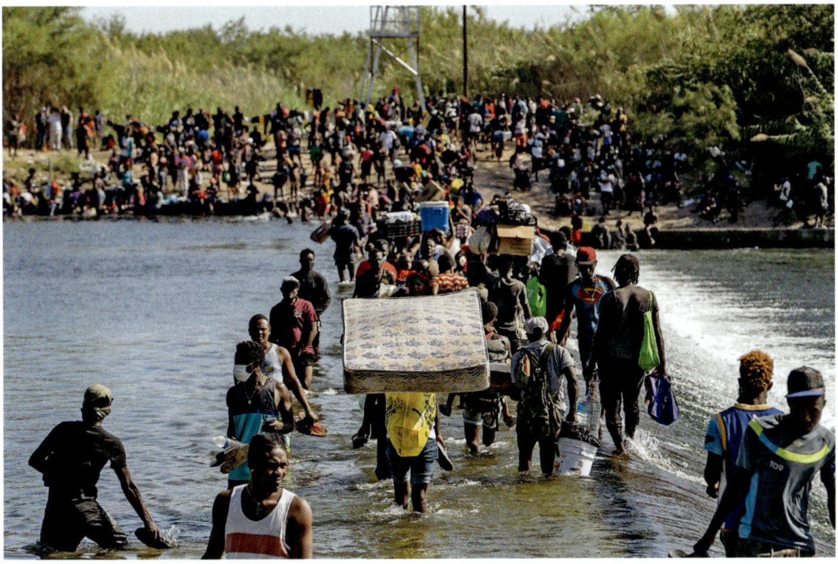

5.5 "Migrants, mostly Haitians, cross back and forth between both countries through the Rio Grande to buy food and things that they need while they wait for their turn to turn themselves to Border Patrol to continue with their asylum process in Ciudad Acuña, Mexico on Friday, Sept. 17, 2021. It is estimated that more than 10,000 migrants are waiting to seek asylum on the U.S. side." Photo: Verónica Gabriela Cárdenas for the *New York Times*.

distressing photograph by Paul Ratje. Ratje's photograph (fig. 5.6) became the subject of scandal and criticism, as a number of people thought that the Immigration Patrol agent on horseback was using a whip to control a Haitian immigrant returning from getting food across the river. The photograph turned out to have been taken at an angle that made the long reins in the agent's hand look like a whip.[21] Nevertheless, it still caused uproar from liberals who thought that the photograph was "horrific" and from conservatives who criticized liberals for their quick condemnation of Immigration Patrol agents when they did not have all the information regarding the photograph. What is striking is that anyone could have taken the photograph as the usual state of affairs—even if whips were *not* being used. A *Los Angeles Times* headline gets to the heart of the matter: "Latinx Files: The Photo That Captured the Decades of Failures of US Border Policy." The article's author, Fidel Martinez, put it simply: "The cruelty is the point."[22] Cruelty in the hands of Immigration and Customs Enforcement (ICE) and the US Customs and Border Protection (CBP) against those trying to enter the United States from the Mexico-US border is well

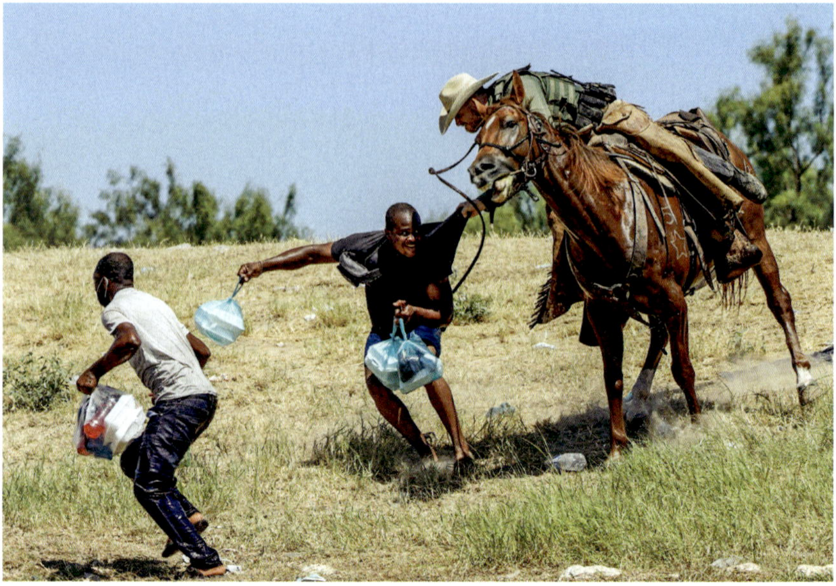

5.6 A US Border Patrol agent on horseback tries to stop a Haitian migrant from entering an encampment on the banks of the Rio Grande on Sunday, September 19, 2021, near the international bridge in Del Rio, Texas. Photo: Paul Ratje / AFP via Getty Images.

documented and, according to political theorist Cristina Beltrán, supports a vision of American democracy that is tied to white supremacy.[23]

As noted in the previous chapter, when considering photographs of the objects found near the remains of migrants or other photographs pointing to migrant experience, Cárdenas's photographs of the caravans as well as Ratje's photograph may very well fail to prompt feelings of sorrow for these migrants and instead suggest confirmation that hordes of migrants are coming into the United States to take its resources and engage in violent behavior. The constructed imaginary in which immigrants are merely "illegals" and "rapists" may very well rear its ugly head. As also noted in chapter 4, according to Monique Roelofs, the aesthetic harbors both promises and threats. Cárdenas's photographic works, then, may prompt this threat that, in the context of rising US nationalism and anti-immigrant sentiment, precludes the possibility of viewers ever feeling any distress for those who make up the caravans on their journey northward.

Here I must reiterate my point that *Carnalities* is not to offer a normative account of how artworks are political or how they must be perceived or experienced. Doing so would undermine the very fluidity and openness of carnalities, of creative practices themselves as well as the tactical use of these practices as marginalized bodies of color engage with them in different contexts. I may point to what Roelofs calls the promise of the aesthetic, to the possibility that artworks of various kinds, including photographs, may prompt aesthetic ruptures of the dominant, colonial eye. I can also indeed show that creative practices have been crucial in the lives of those who are marginalized. Recall the vital role of the creative practice of writing for Anzaldúa and of photography for Aguilar. From them, we have learned of the tremendous potential of carnalities for those who practice them and for those who are able to experience the artworks produced by them. Similar to Muñoz's conviction that there is already a brown commons, it is my view that carnalities are already being practiced by bodies of color for various purposes, including self-naming, self-care, transformation, refusal, and even resistance. One of the aims of this work is precisely to honor these practices as they have sustained aliveness in the context of Latinidad. To impose an abstract normativity upon flesh*and*blood creative practices in order to satisfy a need for simplicity and for political and ethical guarantees misses the complexity of the experience of both creating and experiencing artworks, especially in a context in which such practices are performed by bodies of color marked by being-in-sorrow and the possibility of violence.

Considering the body of color as the site on which violence is always a possibility—and on which violence materializes in the context of caravans crossing the Mexico-US border that has been deemed an "abjection machine" and a "genocidal machine"—underscores Muñoz's key point that feeling brown is a way of being in the world connected to a shared sense of harm and a being-in-sorrow.[24] In the following, I continue to engage with Cárdenas's photography: I discuss two photographs, one from their *Del Rio* Series (2021) and another from their *Migrant Caravans* (2017) series, with the help of Munõz's claims that "different kinds of brownness touch but do not fuse" and that "some people's sense of brownness may potentially touch other people's sense of brownness."[25]

Touching Brownness

While in the first photograph (fig. 5.7), Joseph, Calypso Marie, and their daughter Sarah rest in a migrant shelter in Acuña, Mexico, in the second work (fig. 5.8) various Central American migrants of different ages ride one of the deadly La Bestia (The Beast) freight trains. These trains

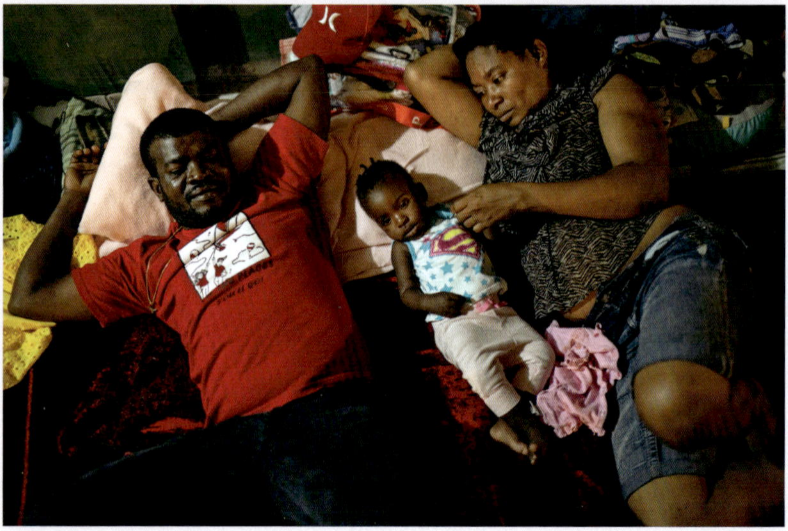

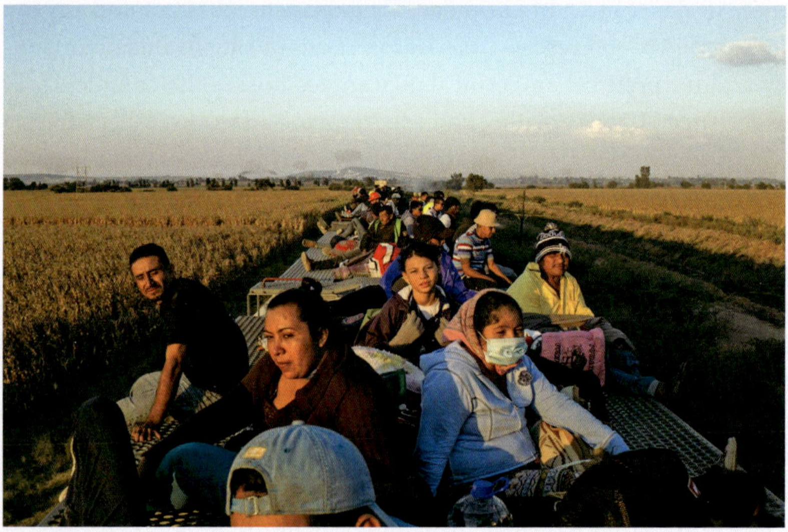

5.7 "Joseph, 42, left, and his wife Calypso Marie, 41, along with their nine-month-old daughter Sarah, get ready to go to bed at a migrant shelter in Acuña, Mexico on Monday, Sept. 27, 2021. Most of the people at the shelter are Haitians who had been waiting under the Acuña—Del Rio International Bridge to turn themselves in to Border Patrol in the U.S." Photo: Verónica Gabriela Cárdenas for the *New York Times*.

5.8 People travel on a freight train collectively known as La Bestia (The Beast) toward Tijuana, Baja California, Mexico, where many of them would be turning themselves in to US Customs and Border Protection at the San Ysidro Port of Entry to begin their immigration process in October 2017. Photo: Verónica Gabriela Cárdenas.

go through at least thirteen Mexican states to reach the North, where migrants are exposed to robbery, rapes, gang violence, bodily injury from falls, turning the train into a "microcosmo de violencia, movilidad humana e (in)seguridad" (a microcosm of violence, human mobility and [in]security).[26] What immediately struck me in my experience of the first photograph is what we may think of a threefold *punctum*: not three different points that pierce the one who experiences the photograph, but the *punctum* of sorrow that lives in the faces of Joseph, Sarah, and Marie, their eyes looking away to some other place where one looks when in the midst of an impossible situation while also knowing that one must try to get through it. I see the same look in the women and children riding La Bestia. I see little Sarah's shirt with the Superman logo and various feelings are raised within me. I cannot ignore its irony slapping me in the face given the situation of this family and of this girl who must not completely understand what is happening but can still feel fear and pain that will mark her for life. Yet I also feel that these migrants are the real superheroes given what it must take not only to leave one's home, no matter how fraught, but also to endure the brutal journey north.[27]

I also think of how these two photographs depict different groups of people, with their particular journeys and reasons why they have been forced to join caravans in search of asylum in the United States. Different histories inform the nations they hail from, although we can safely say that such histories are indeed connected to US imperialism and economic extraction in the region. The way these histories affect these migrants' bodies and lives makes it possible to say that their feeling brownness affectively registers a sense of shared harm and the sense of feeling like a problem.[28] Their lives touch but do not fuse. That is, even though all these bodies of color find themselves in conditions of flowing brownness, a condition of precarity that they clearly share, they cannot be understood as being able to take each other's place. Despite experiences that make them part of the brown commons, they nevertheless have their own particularities as well as their specific histories. Following Lugones, we can say that they come to inhabit liminality and a border-dwelling situation from different journeys and thus cannot be considered homogeneous, form instant coalitions, and have a transparent view of one another.[29] The histories of Black and brown peoples in Latin America and in the United States cannot simply be subsumed under a category or a coalitional project that effectively erases their heterogeneity. With his account of feeling brown and the brown commons,

Muñoz is looking to open the possibilities for coalitions by way of affectivity or of "sensory circuits" rather than through a notion of identity that, according to him, homogenizes and is too closely connected to notions of liberal subjectivity.[30]

This coalitional approach is guided by the structure of feeling brown, by sensory circuits to be transmitted, as Muñoz thinks W. E. B. Du Bois's use of the Sorrow Songs transmits brownness at the level of affect for African Americans and those who read his influential *The Souls of Black Folk: Essays and Sketches*. In my view, Cárdenas's photographic practice as carnality and their various series of photographs of crossing *bring to light* and transmit feeling brown as well as disclose the brown commons. This transmission happens at various levels. Those who are touched by the photographs of the caravans are invited to experience a promising aesthetic unsettlement as described in the previous chapter, an affective experience that has the opportunity to open possibilities of the otherwise. In this case, experiencing the photographs allows for a different understanding of the Mexico-US experience as well as of Latinidad itself. In other words, the Mexico-US border is no longer to be seen in terms of the standard paradigm, as a region that is traversed only by Mexican and Central American migrants (here read as mestizo peoples). The experience of Black Latinidad is also very much a border experience and a *bordering* experience as understood by Lorgia García Peña. Understanding the Mexico-US borderlands as not confined to the experience of mestizo bodies allows for a reconfiguration, a rethinking of Latinidad that does not invisibilize Black Latin Americans, Latinxs, and Caribbeans. It is on Muñoz's part a gesture, as he states when borrowing from Cherríe Moraga, of "dreaming of other planets."[31] Feeling brown as a structure of feeling and a way of being in the world allows for a relationality that does not conform to hegemonic conventions or a dominant logic of essentialist views on race and identity categories. As noted in the introduction, my own view of Latinidad, as both a noun capable of capturing the heterogeneity of Latinxs in terms of their race and other social identities and as a verb or process attuned to historical, economic, and cultural contexts, is very much informed by Muñoz's attunement to the affective component of our existence that allows for coalitional possibilities.

In bringing to light how the transmission of feeling brown through Cárdenas's photographs allows for a rethinking of the Mexico-US border, I do not wish to reify this border as the central issue within US Latinx studies. The crucial work of Lorgia García Peña here must be taken into account, especially in the current moment when theorists are engaged in reconsidering and reinterpreting the notion of Latinidad and the field of Latinx studies. As García Peña points out, Latinx studies centers the Mexico-US border experience at the expense of discussions of Black Latinidad. In *The Borders of Dominicanidad*, García Peña offers a genealogy of Dominicanidad that takes into consideration national narratives of what it means to be Dominican as well as contrasting archives that are not part of these official narratives, what she calls contra*dictions*.[32] She offers a key discussion of the role of the United States in the creation of racial formations in the Caribbean as well as of the importance of geographical and symbolic borders in connection to the United States, Haiti, and the Dominican Republic in the construction of Blackness and Latinidad in the United States. The Haiti–Dominican Republic border remains "linked to the US through the body of the Dominican racialized immigrant/minority subject."[33] This enacts what García Peña sees as a disruption of the current understanding of the US category of "Latino/a" by decentering an understanding of the border in terms of location (as in the Mexico-US borderlands). Instead, García Peña proposes a reading of the border as active, as *bordering*, the activity of bordering that produces the embodied location of living in El Nié (neither here nor there), "where the multiple impositions of the nation-state and the imperial-colonial discourses coexist—that is, racialized bodies."[34] García Peña thus effectively expands the range of Latinx studies by calling for us to look at how nineteenth-century US imperialism affected important relations of border and bordering in connection to the Dominican Republic, Haiti, and the United States in order to understand present processes of racialization, bordering, and exclusion. Such an analysis presents a more expansive understanding of the relationship between Latin American and Latinx studies. As seen above, Muñoz's theorization of feeling brown and brown commons also allows for this more expansive vision, while also highlighting the affectivity that is alive in what I have here referred to as *cross*ings and flowing brownness.

In addition to prompting an affective response that may lead to a promising aesthetic unsettlement leading to a more expansive understanding of the Mexico-US border and thus of Latinx studies, another way Cárdenas's photographs transmit feeling brown is by showing that Black Mexicans, Central Americans, and Caribbean people are part of the brown commons as understood by Muñoz. Despite their heterogeneity and multiple histories, they, to use Muñoz's terms, may touch each other's brownness without fusing. What I take as brownness-with is, according to Muñoz, born out of a shared sense of harm and about a lack, a sense of feeling like a problem. While I highlight the important characteristics of feeling brown, a shared sense of harm and feeling like a problem, another aspect not yet discussed but important in Muñoz's account is that feeling brown is also about an "affective excess," or the view that we who are brown are louder, angrier, excessive in our comportment.[35] Muñoz makes the key point that this supposed excess makes whites uneasy.[36] Ultimately, the three aspects of feeling brown, a shared sense of harm, feeling like a problem, and an affective excess, may allow for what Muñoz calls intraracial empathy. The extent to which different shades of brownness and Blackness are able to lead to inter- and intraracial empathy due to their registering of feeling brown is a difficult issue, not to speak of critiques associated with the notion of empathy itself.[37] Nonetheless, even if the notion of intraracial empathy turns out to be too hopeful in the context of Latinidad, it is important to regard Muñoz's theorization of feeling brown as opening the door for a more expansive and complex understanding of Latinidad that recognizes the key role of affect in a forging of coalitions across difference and that does not invisibilize Black Latinidad.[38]

Cárdenas's photographs disclose caravans as embodied flows of brownness that in their *cross*ings turn what started as Viacrucis or the Stations of the Cross in defense of migrants into massive movements-with of migrants to the Mexico-US border. As we have seen, the cross itself becomes symbolic of different aspects of the migratory experience. It is symbolic of the literal *cross*ing of borders, one that may or may not happen but that nonetheless gives migrants strength to continue the perilous journey, as survival, asylum, or better economic opportunities may wait on the other side. It is also symbolic of a different *cross*ing, the intersection of lines of movement propelled by hope, refusal, and a sense of futurity with obstacles created by policies, structures, laws, and actions on the part of immigration agents, smugglers, vigilantes, and others that undermine and harm their attempts and sometimes even cross out their journeys, even their lives. Cárdenas's photographs serve as the sensuous circuit through which feeling brown is transmitted in those experiencing the photographs as well as in the photographs themselves. Feeling brown, understood in terms of a shared experience of harm, the sense of being a problem, and an excess of feeling, opens possibilities of coalitions across differences, allowing bodies of color to touch each other in their brownness without fusing into one another, thus opening room for a more expansive vision of Latinidad that does not invisibilize Black Latinidad. The Rio Grande itself becomes brown commons not in terms of the usual ways a natural environment provides resources to be shared by those inhabiting it, but as a site where bodies of color share not only their feeling brown but also their determination, strength, and courage to undertake that most arduous *crossing* to take them to the other side. Ultimately Cárdenas's carnal aesthetics *brings to light* an archive of feeling brown. In the next section, I continue to follow movements of *cross*ing, in this instance by showing how Cárdenas's photographic carnality points to the transformation of spatialities around the Rio Grande and other border areas into altars: altars for those migrants who have perished in their journeys north, but also for the living, those who remain but whose lives are marked by precarity and abjection.

ALTARS FOR THE LIVING: *TRAVELING SOLES*

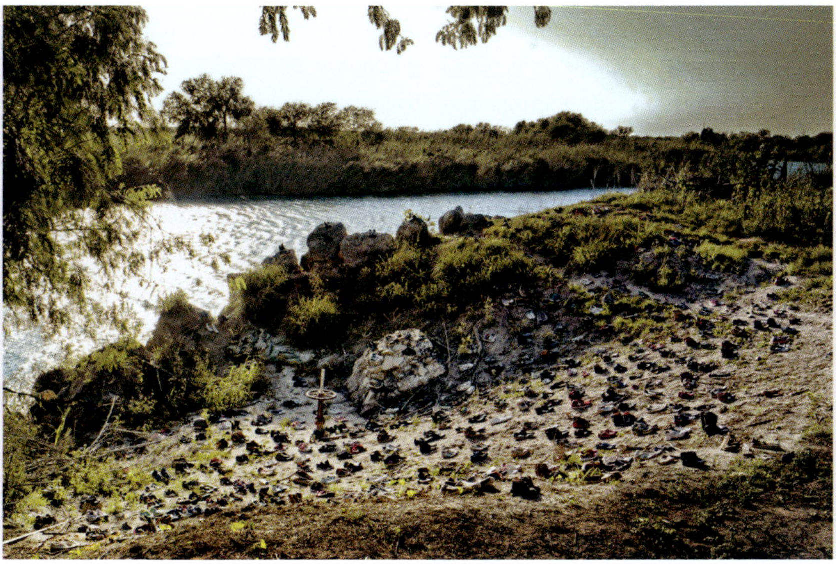

5.9 From the *Traveling Soles* series: 433 soles enter the United States after crossing the Rio Grande in 2017 near Peñitas, Texas. Photo: Verónica Gabriela Cárdenas.

A photo (fig. 5.9) from Cárdenas's series *Traveling Soles* (2014–17) captures a spontaneous altar constructed by Cárdenas with shoes that migrants wore as they entered the Mexico-US border.[39] Four hundred and thirty-three soles/souls stand at the bank of this angry river, standing for the bodies of color who wore them and for the many other migrants who will also dare this *cross*ing. These embodied soles/souls of rubber and leather—which not long ago held the bodies of older and young migrants, helping them in their perilous journey—seem alone, abandoned. Yet they stand together and are being called to do memory work. They have thus acquired a new life, as sometimes objects are bound to do in their connections to our lives and our memories. Now these soles/souls call us not to forget the *cross*ings and flows of brownness into the Mexico-US border.

Cárdenas started collecting shoes at the beginning of 2016 from the Humanitarian Respite Center in McAllen, Texas, whose aim is to help the increasing number of asylum seekers entering McAllen after being processed by authorities. Asylum seekers are provided clean clothes and shoes upon arrival at the center. Seeing that migrants' old shoes were discarded, Cárdenas got the idea to create *Traveling Soles* as early as 2014. With the aid of friends, they were able to place the shoes in different areas, including the bank of the Rio Grande, water tanks, and the port of entry in Hidalgo, Texas, and other important locations, removing them as soon as the photographs were taken so as to not get caught by immigration authorities. They then gathered the shoes and stored them, keeping the now-sacred objects. By altering the grounds with the very shoes that carried migrants through their difficult journey, Cárdenas brings to the fore the intimacy between those selves that walked, trekked, and swam, and the very river and its ground. This entanglement between bodies of color, water, and land, as well as sorrow, anger, anxiety, distress, desire, hope, refusal, indignation, strength, and all those feelings that migrants carry—as they also carry water bottles, tuna cans, Bibles, and other objects—is re-created by Cárdenas in a gesture that transforms the terrain from shadow ground, a ground with a past, present, and future connection to pain and death, to sacred ground, a spatiality that holds the memories of our dead as well as desires for futurity.

This Rio-Grande-turned-altar is now sutured as it were with desiring and striving migrant bodies. By photographing it, Cárdenas is both stopping time to capture a moment symbolic of *cross*ing that most of us will never witness. Cárdenas is also honoring that flowing brownness that constitutes their existence. The photograph itself and the act of photographing both become carnal insofar as they *affect* us, touch us, but also disclose the intimacy between selves and worlds. As we have seen through Muñoz's notion of feeling brown, we can read Cárdenas's photographs as constituting an archive of feeling brown. Through their photographic carnality, Cárdenas also intervenes in spatialities in order to create altars for those lost in the crossings and for those who survive but remain in conditions of precarity and abjection. As Cárdenas states,

> **I think that when the shoes are placed there, it is a way of making the place come back to life. By placing the shoes, missing their owners, it is a way of not showing their absence, but it is more of a reminder that there are people continuously taking the same paths. It is a non-stop flow of people coming seeking asylum, evading Border Patrol and also dying. So when we place the shoes, I think of a large group of people that was passing by those places and then they stopped so that I could take their photo to document that small fragment of their journey.[40]**

The spatialities produced, then, intertwine the individual with the communal, the sacred and the material, presence and absence, and memory and forgetting—they are altars for the living and for those who perish in their migration—and they are living paths insofar as they signal actual trajectories of flows of brownness that forge possibilities of survival.

In this section, I continue to think of the figure of the cross as it merges with the *cross*ings, the migratory movements of bodies of color, and their flowing and feeling brown. I would like to think about the production of spaces of mourning in connection to memory practices—but not only for the dead. I seek memory practices for the living, for those who deserve to be remembered even as they survived their journey north. With the help of Cárdenas's carnal photographic practice, I develop the notion of *aesthetic memory*, the forging of memory through creative practices in order to honor all of those immigrants who have become invisible as humans and hypervisible as "criminals" and "illegals" in the current US imaginary that continually attacks migrants coming from Mexico, Central and South America, and, as we have seen, increasingly from the Caribbean. Instead of discussing grand memorials in honor of those who died in grand battles or events, traditionally used to exalt nationalism, the use of *our* dead against "evil" forces, I turn to spontaneous memorials. I discuss how Cárdenas's makeshift memorials also become altars for the living—for undocumented border crossers, especially Central American children, whose names we don't even know and who do not fill the pages of our newspapers, social media, or radio waves—unknown altars for those whose crossing is the result of a painful history connecting the United States, Mexico, Central America, and the Caribbean.

Inferno

In the liminality between the public and the private we sometimes find spaces that have been produced explicitly to memorialize the dead. Consider roadside memorials, now described as "grassroot memorials."[41] These are spaces marked by white crosses and all manner of unsophisticated memorial objects: the plastic flower, the discolored ribbon, the tattered stuffed animal. They are spaces produced by mourning and pain as they are meant to remind us that someone tragically died in that now-sacred ground. They are also performative in that they have the function of making-remember and bringing-to-light lost loved ones as well as resisting not only death but also traditional spatialities of mourning, as if graves, cemeteries, and churches were not enough to hold those who found their being-in-worlds halted in a tragic instant. They are the spaces of the dead for the dead and for the living that remain and find themselves angry, grieving, desperate. Can these spatialities be more than shadowed grounds that have been marked by death, violence, or violence-to-be? Can they help us honor those who walk on those grounds without collapsing to the unexpected finality of a flying bullet, or the violence of a coyote or an ICE soldier,[42] or the wrath of the elements in a burning desert or an angry river?

The soles/souls that *cross*ed the Mexico-US border at the port of entry in Hidalgo, Texas, traveled under hellish circumstances. Here I continue to follow the flow of brownness, both in terms of their very bodies engaged in *cross*ing, their shared sense of harm, as well as the feelings of sorrow evoked by disclosures of their experience. In particular, I am pierced by the fact that Cárdenas's *Traveling Soles* highlights Central American children, including unaccompanied children, as part of this flowing brownness.[43] It is heartbreaking to think of these children trekking what Jason De León describes as the "massive open grave" of the Mexico-US border, where he spots a complete tooth lying on top of a rock, where he picks up a small piece of bone only for it to crumble to dust.[44] The desert is highly efficient in pushing bodies to the limit, especially when they are not well prepared for such a treacherous journey—the scorching heat, the dust, the animals waiting patiently for the will to give up. So are the angry waves of an angry river, both respected and dreaded by those who know the stories of those who have managed to swim to their new land. It is a hell of sand and water. Sadly, it is also a hell that many do not know about, one that is not part of news cycles unless there is a particularly horrific story to tell, such as the story of the death of forty-six migrants who died in and around a tractor-trailer that was abandoned in the outskirts of San Antonio, or the drowning of Oscar Alberto Martínez Ramirez and his twenty-three-month-old daughter Valeria, whose bodies were found in the bank of the Rio Grande.[45] Yet Cárdenas's carnal photographic practice centers this migrant experience, writing an archive of feeling brown with light, an archive of South-to-North migration that constitutes one of the most important transnational and geopolitical events tied to power plays of corporations and governments as well as to histories of trauma, especially in connection to Mexico-US relations and, as noted in the last chapter, to US interventions in Central America.

*Altar*ities

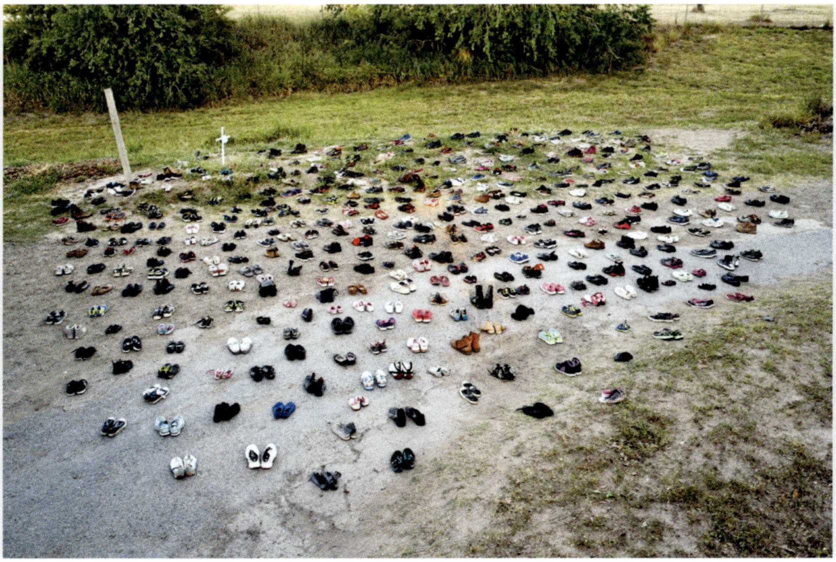

5.10 Four hundred thirty-three soles visit the temporary grave for an undocumented migrant in 2017 in Falfurrias, Texas. The person buried was later identified as Yoni from Guatemala. Photo: Verónica Gabriela Cárdenas.

Returning to the symbolic power of the cross in terms of its appeal to justice for migrants and to its pointing to different aspects of the migratory experience, I now wish to discuss the soles/souls' visit to or veneration of a white cross—rather, to their honoring the migrant that has been buried at the site marked by the cross. The image (fig. 5.10) is powerful in its double relational movement between cross and soles/souls, the cross watching over these soles/souls as they watch over it. Their visit to this sacred ground discloses the intimacy between the spiritual and the material. Through the photograph Cárdenas opens room for both mourning and remembrance—of both the living and the dead.

This carnal photograph enacting a *cross*ing between the material and the spiritual recalls *descansos* that are so prevalent in highways in Mexico but that are also part of the US landscape, the "grassroot memorials" that we find along highways where there has been a tragic death, what scholars formerly called "spontaneous memorials."[46] They consist of simple white crosses growing from the ground like some type of strange plant looking for sun. They are found in highways and streets in rural and urban areas in various US states.

They also become beautiful art installations to honor those tragically lost; for example, they are particularly ornate in New Mexico (figs. 5.11 and 5.12). Hearts, plastic flowers, and religious statues accompany and transform the white cross and the ground that it occupies into an artistic installation, not so much in the sense of museum art installations, whose spatialities are particularly designed for such creative practices, but rather as a creative gesture of love meant to honor the ones lost tragically in spatialities that defy the public and private divide—in a carnal practice of mourning.

I see the nexus between descansos in their loving instantiations in the spatialities where lives were lost and Cárdenas's *Traveling Soles* in terms of the production of multifaceted spaces. These are spatialities that become "sacred," given that life perished at the site, and we are now led to consider the ground's connection to death and to spirituality. They also become "counter-space" and "differential space" in the sense that Henri Lefebvre notes, in their challenging of normative capitalist senses of space. Moreover, they are "liminal," "in-between," "borderland" spaces as informed by Anzaldúa, in their holding possibilities from multiple cultures and stances. In particular, I am interested in the manner in which the production of these spatialities as well as the spatialities themselves open possibilities for memory-making. Because they are between the public and the private, the sacred and the profane, the visible and the invisible, these sites are haunting. Cárdenas's *Traveling Soles* not only discloses an archive of feeling brown connected to the history of Latin American/Caribbean/Latinx migration to the United States but also creates altars for the living in these sites. These altars for the living are themselves *memento vivere*, an intertwining of the earth- and spirit-bodies with different chosen

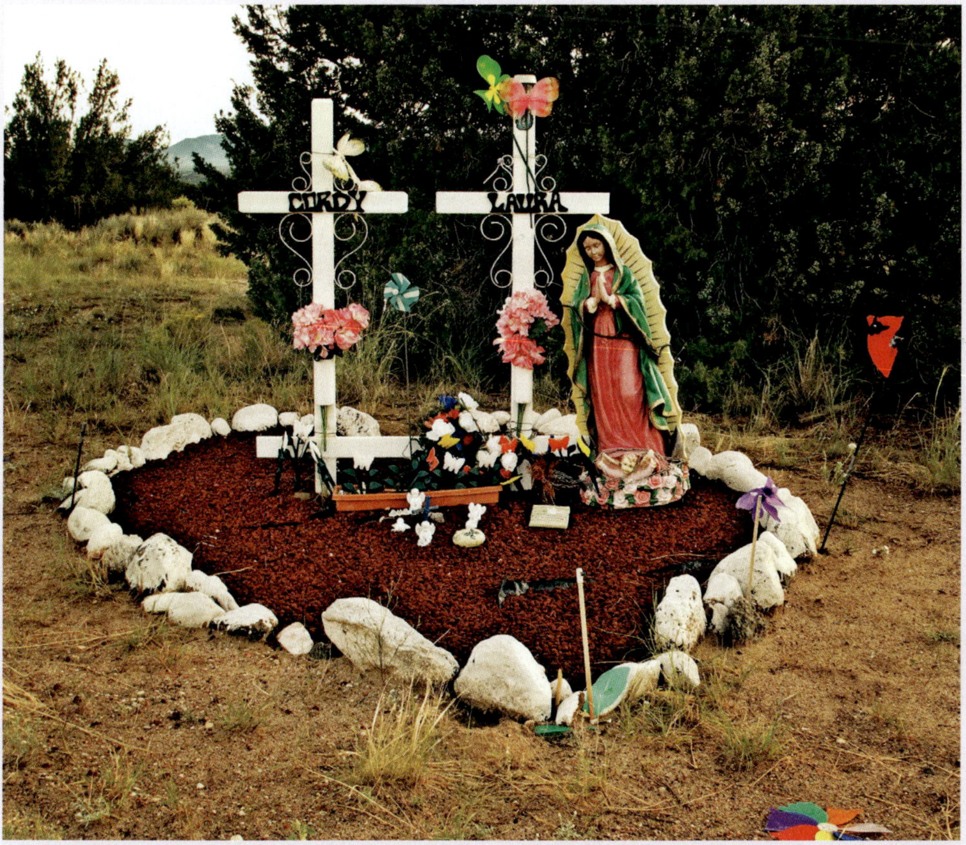

5.11 Memorial around mile marker 13 on US 550 West out of Bernalillo, New Mexico. Photo: John Fowler.

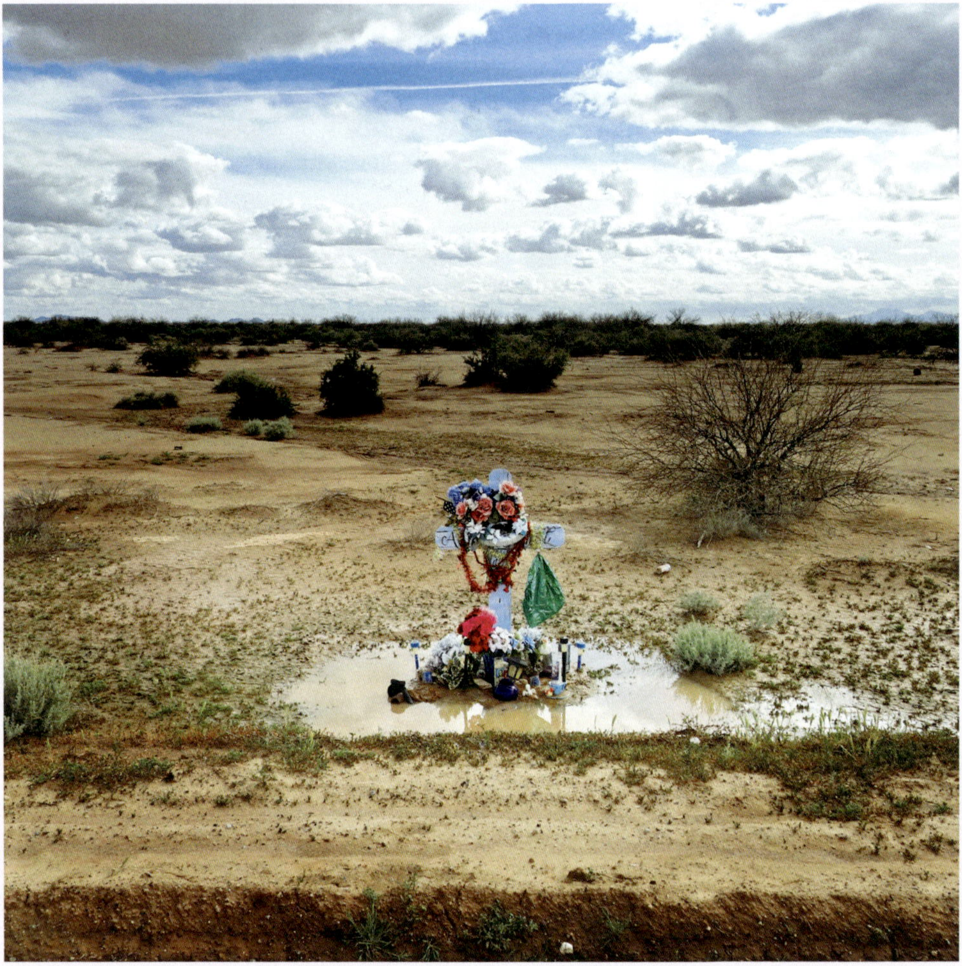

5.12 Roadside memorial, Riggs Road, Gila River Indian Reservation, Arizona. Photo: Kevin Dooley.

objects that serve as reminders to live in a way that does not forget the lives of those injured by tragic historical circumstances in which coloniality, empire, capitalism, and neoliberalism collide, forcing countless people into dangerous migrations. *Traveling Soles* thus honors these migrants and border crossers whose lives have been tragically impacted by US colonial, imperial, and economic interests. Next, I discuss the production of descansos or roadside memorials in terms of their becoming spaces that are haunted and haunting.

Ghostly Spatialities and Remembering with Light

Descansos prompt a meditation on the power of landscape and place. In his analysis of roadside memorials, Robert M. Bednar quotes W. J. T. Mitchell's view of landscapes as constituting "a dynamic medium" and "a process by which social and subjective identities are formed."[47] Following Anna Petersson, we can see the material world as an "important media for expressing, communicating, and experiencing, understanding and even debating different experiences of loss and bereavement."[48] In a play of absence and presence, ritualistic practices are carried out to call forth the memory of a loved one lost too soon. A cross is placed where it is not supposed to belong, and this very act designates the space as sacred. Through symbolic elements and other chosen objects, primarily the cross, public spaces become private spaces of mourning while at the same time remaining public, in what, again inspired by Barthes, we could call a public *punctum* that calls those driving by that road, by that street, to remember to stop drinking and driving, to stop texting and driving, or to simply remember the dead. The symbolism of the cross is powerful. It is thought to prevent the soul of the deceased from getting lost or staying at the place of death,[49] or keep the ghost of the deceased from haunting the location. There is also the Spanish tradition in which crosses were placed by the side of the road to mark resting places (descansos) for those carrying a coffin to the burial ground. In Catholic tradition, the cross is supposed to be a reminder for those walking by the site to pray for the deceased as souls in purgatory need the prayers of the living.[50]

The production of spaces of mourning and of memory-making is marked by a disruption of instituted modes of spatiality. As Henri Lefebvre notes, capitalist modes of production seep in through all aspects of experience, including spatiality—thus leading to the imposition of homogeneity and transparency everywhere we go. Spaces are broken up for practicality and visibility: what he calls the modernist trio of readability-visibility-intelligibility takes over and logics of visualization and metaphorization rule.[51] Highways become part of that modernist machinery of space with its specific functions: they are to transport us in our pilgrimages of productivity; they are not supposed to be places of mourning. Yet Lefebvre calls for counter-spaces, spaces that, as he notes, "[shake] existing space to its foundation."[52] I see descansos as radically rupturing established rules of the meaning and purpose of specific spatialities while, at the same time, producing alternative, liminal spaces suffused with mnemonic power.[53]

These liminal, in-between spaces of memory-making disrupt the distinction between the public and the private, as private rituals of mourning mark public roads aimed for practical purposes. They reconfigure presence and absence insofar as present objects point to absent loved ones. They mix the sacred and the profane, intertwining the spiritual with the material. Finally, they problematize the distinction between the visible and the invisible given that what is seen in these spaces is not what is there. Insofar as these liminal spaces call for practices of mourning that both recall the spiritual and the worldly, they can be considered altars as well as memento mori—not the discrete death masks, or pieces of bone or tufts of hair of the beloved hidden inside a portrait, but a shifting ground, earthly but sacred, of prayer and remembrance.

Yet Cárdenas offers an altogether different type of sacred, haunted, and haunting ground in this series. While the cross is the key element in descansos, explicitly connecting the ground to *altar*ity—to that which is spiritual and ineffable—Cárdenas's practice leads to an alternative altar, one lacking the heavily religious symbolic object of the cross, where we, instead, find a water tank (fig. 5.13). Four hundred and thirty-three soles/souls surround this life-giving water container turned cross. This is an object to be venerated, to be prayed to, to be consumed if one is to be able to make it through the brutal journey, especially in the hell of the desert that migrants traverse to reach the United States. As the cross protects sacred spaces, the water tank turns the ground into sacred ground, inasmuch as it is what allows for the possibility for these migrants to live. Water, not blood, becomes the sacred element here. It is the element that watches over these soles/souls, as much as they watch over it.[54]

In these makeshift sacred grounds where crosses and water tanks are prayed to, there is a logic of spectrality—that is, these are places haunted and haunting insofar as they are shadowed ground. They are

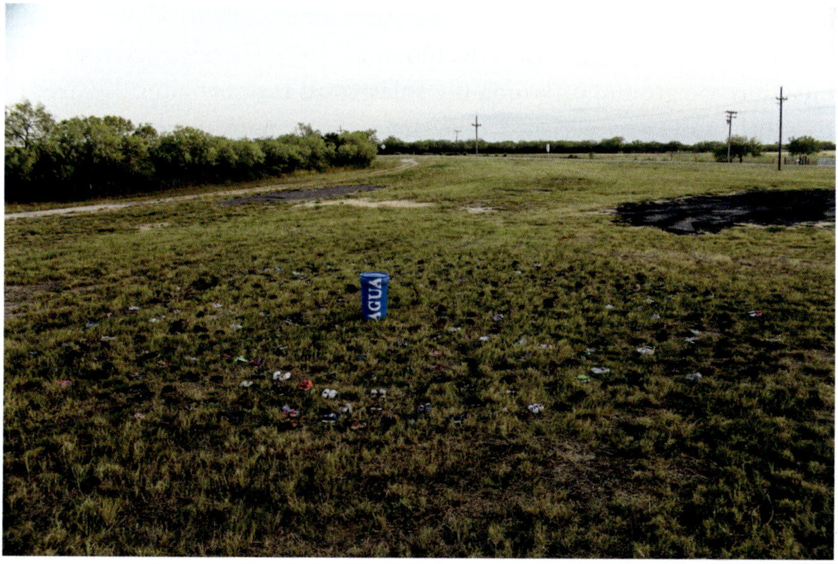

5.13 From the *Traveling Soles* series: "433 pairs of shoes surround a container with water bottles, representing those that try to evade getting caught while crossing the checkpoint in 2017 near Falfurrias, Texas." Photo: Verónica Gabriela Cárdenas.

grounds that harbor histories of violence. For *Traveling Soles*, Cárdenas specifically chooses spaces that are indeed haunted, not just by those who cross and do not make it, but by the very histories of US imperialism in the various regions where migrants hail from. While discussions about ghosts and haunting are pervasive in part due to Avery Gordon's moving and influential analysis in *Ghostly Matters* (and, of course, the work of Toni Morrison, Marx, Derrida, and others), here I wish to attend to the importance of ghosts, particularly in the context of Cárdenas's makeshift *altar*ities. As Gordon explains, "The ghost, as I understand it, is not the invisible or some ineffable excess. The whole essence, if you can use that word, of a ghost is that it has a real presence and demands its due, your attention. Haunting and the appearance of specters or ghosts is one way I tried to suggest, we are notified that what has been concealed is very much alive and present."[55] For her, there are three important characteristics of haunting: first, ghosts add strangeness into space and thus "unsettl[e] the propriety and property lines that delimit a zone of activity or knowledge"; second, ghosts are symptoms of what is missing—as such, they represent loss but also future possibilities; and third, a ghost is alive, so we "must reckon with it graciously, attempting to offer it a hospitable memory out of a concern for justice."[56] Cárdenas's *Traveling Soles* unsettles the ground on which the soles/souls rest, conjures the lives of those migrants who perished, and, importantly, performs memory work precisely out of a concern for justice for migrants flowing into, *cross*ing the Mexico-US border.

What memory work do these photographs—and the sacred ground that Cárdenas has created—enact? The most obvious answer is that they call forth the memory of those who have been lost, who succumbed in their journeys north. But this is not an easy feat. As María del Rosario Acosta López notes in her discussion of the nexus of art, trauma, violence, and memory, there is an important fragility to memory that we cannot forget.[57] That, is memory cannot be produced by works of art so as to provide explanations and resolutions of injustices. In a sense, the work of art has come too late as the past cannot be redeemed; it is but a fortuitous encounter between memory and forgetting.[58] Yet the work of art enacts a call for us who encounter it to engage in memory work. As such, Cárdenas's photographs hail us. They demand that we remember the dead.

These photographs, however, also call us to remember the living. This is a crucial aspect of Cárdenas's series *Traveling Soles*—they also call on us to remember the migrants who were successful in reaching the border or being granted asylum, but who nevertheless remain in perilous conditions. While these migrants did not perish, they might suffer "social death" in the future.[59] In particular, the photographs prompt us to think of the many children whose lives have been affected by their *cross*ings. For Gordon, ghosts carry the departed in the present and point to a longing in the future. For me, the ghosts in these photographs carry those that survive. While for some, the shoes photographed by Cárdenas might be simply understood as mere objects—and those viewing the photographs may become mere spectators—for me, these soles/souls are transformed in the context of the altars Cárdenas has created. Given my own history of migration, I cannot simply look at the photographs with some detachment about the specters they conjure. The soles/souls become animated in Cárdenas's photographs, even though in the current imaginary they have become ghostly subjectivities.[60] So many have literally been left in limbo, in purgatory, stuck in *hieleras* (coolers) with no knowledge of what will happen to them, lest the US immigration system decides to do justice to them.[61] We have, then, these souls not floating in an ethereal, transcendent limbo but in real, brutal, inhumane spaces in which their health does not matter and their future matters even less. Their condition in holding facilities is inhumane, with reports of hungry, cold immigrants with only a thin metallic sheet to warm themselves, sleeping on the floor, being maltreated by guards. Additionally, family members were separated from each other. The Trump administration's "zero tolerance" implemented in April 2018 proved to be devastating for migrants, while the Biden administration also passed legislation that put migrants at risk.[62] As one of those detained, Rafael Martinez comments about his experience in the detention facility: "There we were, caged up like animals, and they were laughing at us."[63] Imagine, then, the horror of this cold, grim purgatory holding so many souls in need of altars.

The photographic altars, as well as the spatialities that Cárdenas's intervention has turned into altars, honor both the living and the dead. They also mark difference. In her influential analysis of Chicana aesthetics, Laura Pérez notes that Chicana altar art is *alter* art, a production of altars of alterity. As she notes, the altar has been "a site for the socially and culturally 'alter,' or other, to express, preserve, and transmit cultural and gender-based religious and political differences."[64] Altar art is created by those who have been othered in order to disclose the lives of Chicanas at the margins as well as their spiritual politics. When considering Amalia Mesa-Bains's altar art, Pérez explains that Mesa-Bains's table-like altars are places "for the care of the self."[65] Cárdenas's carnal photographic practice and photographs constitute *altar*ities for migrants who have been othered. Like migrants themselves who construct altars in the desert,[66] Cárdenas creates sacred spatialities that are haunted and haunting, that call for communal care; their *altar*ity, alterity, and in-betweenness prompt us to remember not only those who perished but those who made it to the other side but that nevertheless are in detention facilities, deported, or in the precarious condition of the undocumented self. These sites work as mnemonic sacred spaces in the name of both the dead and the living.

The Absence and Presence of Soles/Souls

While the sites created by Cárdenas become sacred ground and perform memory work, Cárdenas's carnal photographs themselves become art objects that forge aesthetic memory, memory that is both prompted and preserved through the aesthetic work and its experience. Photographs of those shoes—those soles/souls waiting for water, looking at the waters of the Rio Grande, at the grave of an unidentified border crosser—point to those who *cross*ed, are *cross*ing, and will continue to *cross*, their very bodies the sites of the intersection of futurity and the violence of capitalism, imperialism, and racism. Yet these photographs mark an *empty* index—empty because the border crossers are no longer in the places photographed; they are marked by empty shoes. The index of these photographs cannot be simply, as Barthes would put it, the "that has been" of soles, of shoes.[67]

While Cárdenas's photographs point to absence, they become an emptied index that, with the help of Lisa Saltzman, we may understand as emerging "as a compelling form for concretizing and commemorating loss, for marking and memorializing absence."[68] They thus point to "spectral presence."[69] That is, they mark an emptied index that nevertheless takes us to the presence, in this case, of those who are being forgotten and remain in cold purgatory—if they have not been already deported and facing the violence that they were running from in the first place. These photographs constitute aesthetic memories that perform memory work at a time when usual practices of memory-making either fail or are not called on—and what remains is a forgetting—a forgetting that thousands of Central American children crossed the perilous border, many of them unaccompanied, and they now remain in the United States in cold cells, detention centers, or the difficult foster care system.[70]

Remember the Children

When discussing their project, Cárdenas states, "I wanted for people to imagine what the owner of those shoes went through." This is a particularly important point when considering the more detailed photographs featuring pairs of children's shoes (figs. 5.14–5.16). How can we imagine what it took for the wearers of these tiny shoes, many of whom were suffering from hunger and dehydration, to arrive at the Mexico-US border after traveling in dangerous La Bestia and then walking miles and miles on different types of terrain? Without wishing to reify the image of the child here (and thus heteronormative understandings of the role of children) it is of the utmost importance that we consider these children's experiences in terms of the way their bodies and minds are being pushed to the limit.[71] We must think about their exhaustion, hunger, thirst, confusion, fear, dread—a complete displacement of quotidian modes and spaces of comfort. It is not the case that the perilous travel that adult border crossers experience is any less brutal. Yet, echoing the sentiment of Ivan Karamazov in *The Brothers Karamazov*, the suffering of children does not make sense. While in the text Ivan is concerned about the suffering of children in a religious context and thus exploring the problem of evil as understood in the philosophy of religion, we can still consider the suffering of children in any context and draw attention to its utter incomprehensibility and injustice. We must then imagine *and* remember what the owners of these soles/souls have gone through in their perilous travel and *cross*ing of the Mexico-US border.[72] As these small shoes, dirty and tattered, stand emptied of the souls that accompanied them, Cárdenas this time provides us with their presence by way of explanations of their lives and their journey. I am thankful to learn more about the lives of these children, although this information confirms the being-in-sorrow that led to their journey north in the first place and that may still be very much part of their current ex-

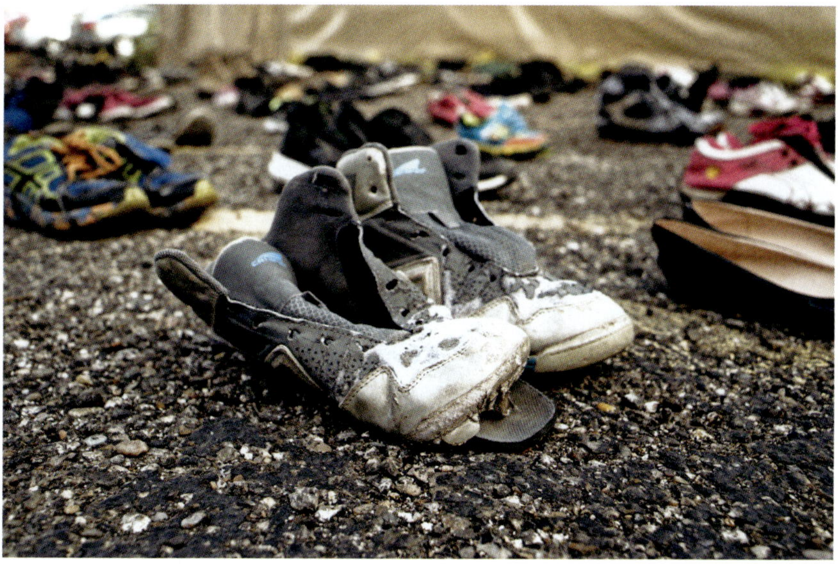

5.14 From the *Traveling Soles* series: "Luis, Honduran, age 8. His father says that Luis's mother left him when he was only two years of age adding that 'violence gets worse every day.' As early as 10 years of age, gang members start recruiting them to work for them. His father opted to give him a better future by taking him to the United States. Since they did not have the economic means to travel differently, they had to board La bestia, The Beast, that is the cargo train that some migrants take in order to get to the northern part of México to subsequently cross into the U.S." Photo: Verónica Gabriela Cárdenas.

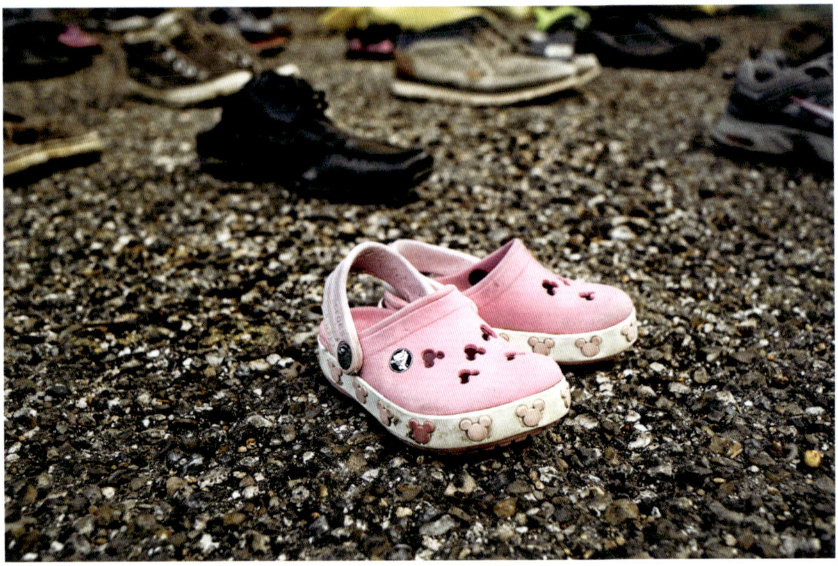

5.15 From the *Traveling Soles* series: "Alondra, Honduran, age 3. There were complications as she was being born, and as a result, she cannot walk. The prognosis for the next two years looks promising. Her father lost a leg when he was run over by a vehicle in their country. Alondra's mother along with her older sister moved to the U.S. three years ago. Her father did not tell her mother that he would embark on this journey along with their youngest daughter. Despite their physical limitations they were able to arrive to seek asylum in the U.S." Photo: Verónica Gabriela Cárdenas.

istence. And what does it mean, I wonder, to live in a society where it is easy to forget their plight?

This forgetting of not only these children's plight but also thousands of other migrants that have survived and perished, both identified and unidentified, is not a simple forgetting or failure of memory practices. It is a sustained forgetting, an intentional practice better understood as part of a project of epistemic ignorance fueled by lack of care, privilege, coloniality, and racism. It is also a deep forgetting, as Jacqui Alexander would call it.[73] Knowledge of these selves as well as of their imprisonment and their brutal deaths at the border is intentionally covered up. If it is not covered up, it is transformed and folded into a narrative that upholds hypernationalist, xenophobic standards that consequently tells their story as that of "illegals" who come to this country to "milk" the United States—think here of the unfortunate tale of mothers who come here to have babies in order to drain the American system.[74] These migrants, even the

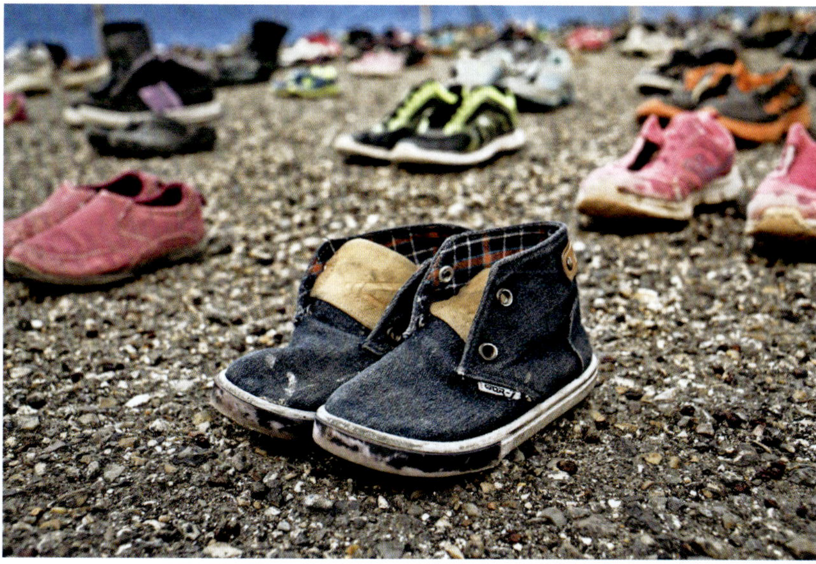

5.16 From the *Traveling Soles* series: "Fernando, Guatemalan, age 4. He and his mother left their country to seek a better life since they had lost their home and his father abandoned them. They were able to escape alive after the federal police in Mexico shot the trailer where they were traveling. He spent his fourth birthday hiding from Mexican immigration agents in the bushland." Photo: Verónica Gabriela Cárdenas.

young, are also described as "criminals," "gang members," and "rapists." We thus encounter a double-edged process in the national imaginary regarding these border crossers. On the one hand, they are made invisible, their lives and deaths of no consequence to the nation. On the other hand, they are made hypervisible by way of a narrative of criminality.

Given this double-edged sword that doubly injures the migrants to whom Cárdenas builds altars and sacred grounds, the function of aesthetic memory becomes key. In addition to being an archive of feeling brown, Cárdenas's photographs serve both to negate these narratives of invisibility and hypervisibility and to preclude the possibility of these selves and their stories being relegated to oblivion. Even though, as we have seen, the photographs index spectral presence and a certain void and emptiness, they nevertheless carry with them crucial mnemonic possibilities. As the products and recorders of altars of alterity, they may help us—or rather *haunt* us—not to forget. Such is the nature of spectrality. And what remains when the shoes are removed from the sites chosen by Cárdenas? More voids. Yet as Margry and Sánchez-Carretero point in their analysis of grassroot memorials, a void—the void of a nonpresent memorial that reflects absence—adds a powerful affective quality to the emptiness.[75] It is an invitation to memory-making and mourning. Cárdenas's carnal photographic practice ultimately discloses a spectral presence, a play of both presence and absence, that serves to memorialize both the dead lost in their *cross*ing, and the living, those who risk their lives in order to flee violence and/or to find the so-called American Dream. As such these photographs become *memento vivere*. They are reminders that others should live—and that we should live in such as way so as to not forget.

There Is No Heaven

Cárdenas's carnal photographs are sites of memory that push us to confront a reality that, in the current US imaginary, has been relegated to forgetting. They become altars for the living and aesthetic memories, whose purpose is not only to record the lives and experiences of border crossers but also to preclude the possibility of us forgetting their plight. Cárdenas's archive of feeling brown turns into altars for the living and aesthetic memories that, in some cases, may serve as a call to conscience, even if only for an instant. However, they are not to supplant the daily reality of those whose crossings are memorialized. Their mnemonic function is not a simple "let's remember and life is better" or "art saves." Like my view of hometactics,[76] the production of spaces of memorialization in the in-between, between the shadow and the light, in the cracks, between life and death, are memory-tactics à la Michel de Certeau. Those of us who are part of the brown commons already enact such tactics as a way of dealing with the forgetting that is so much part of worlds ruled by imperialism, coloniality, and the rule of capital. This is a forgetting that remains etched in histories of violence—if only we could indeed etch visas on whatever paper we find and gift them to all those running for their lives,[77] their lives as children cut short not by death but by having to grow up too fast in a cold hell or a brutal, indifferent purgatory, as heaven does not exist for them.

Following the flow of brownness in its various meanings—as the literal movement of bodies of color as they trek toward the Mexico-US border in search for a future, as the flowing sense of shared harm in their experiences—discloses the migratory experience of Mexicans, Central

Americans, Caribbeans, and South Americans as *cross*ings, movements of migration in which their very bodies become the site in which the push for futurity and the pull of negation and abjection intersect. That is, while these flows of brownness do indeed have a sense of shared harm and of being an excess, they nevertheless push forward, endure the imaginable despite the sorrow and melancholia they carry—despite the laws, policies, and structures set up to harm them, to scar them. Cárdenas's *Del Rio* and *Migrant Caravans* disclose these *cross*ings in their possibility of creating the brown commons where, according to Muñoz, differently racialized migrants can be together in difference, and can experience feeling brown without fusing into each other, thus unsettling readings of the Mexico-US border experience that invisibilize Black Latinidad.

Cárdenas's carnal aesthetics of light transmits feeling brown, thus creating an archive of this manera de ser, or way of being in worlds. Yet the power of their carnal photography goes beyond capturing the flowing and feeling of brownness. It transforms spatialities such that they can become sacred ground, not in terms of traditionally understood religious spaces but in terms of the creation of altars both for those migrants who perished in their *cross*ings and for the living, for those in detention centers, for those living the difficult existence of the undocumented self, for those who live in El Níe, for children who endure La Bestia and trek difficult terrains, for children who remain captive, for children without childhoods.[78] Following the figure of the cross, a reading of descansos and *Traveling Soles* together ultimately discloses the power of Cárdenas's photographs as hauntings, as objects of memory-making, and as altars for the living. In the intertwining of presence and absence, the material and the sacred, and the individual and the communal, Cárdenas's photographic practice discloses a carnal aesthetics that defies deep forgetting.

SIX SOMETHING VERY EXTRAORDINARY

Incandescence and the Wounding Photograph

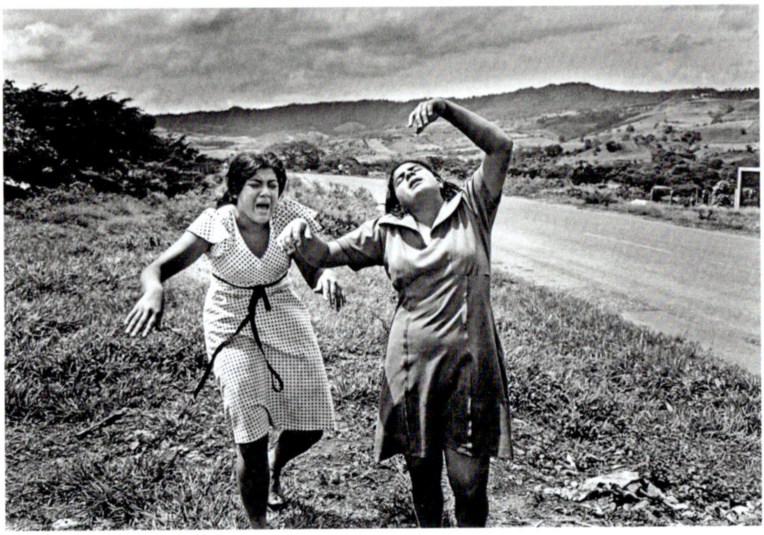

> Here a mother and daughter sob over the father's arrest (Baudelaire: "the emphatic truth of gesture in the great circumstances of life"), and this happens *out in the countryside* (where could they have learned the news? for whom are these gestures?).
>
> **ROLAND BARTHES**, *Camera Lucida*

In the epigraph above Barthes is describing a photograph from Koen Wessing's series on the armed conflict in Estelí, Nicaragua, in 1978. In *Camera Lucida*, Barthes discusses some of Wessing's photographs from this series. He says that he was attracted to them because of a "certain duality," for instance, the mother and daughter in the photograph in figure 6.1.

6.1 Koen Wessing, *Estelí, Nicaragua*, 1978. Gelatin silver print, 16 × 12 in. Courtesy of the Stedelijk Museum of Modern and Contemporary Art and Design.

When commenting on the photographs from Wessing's series that he does not specifically discuss in *Camera Lucida*, Barthes says, "They were fine shots, they expressed the dignity and horror of rebellion, but in my eyes they bore no mark or sign: their homogeneity remained cultural: they were 'scenes,' rather, *à la Greuze*, had it not been for the harshness of the subject."[1] Jean-Baptiste Greuze was an eighteenth-century French painter known for his portraits, historical paintings, and *genre scenes*, paintings portraying everyday life.

For Barthes, photographs of the war in Nicaragua are fine shots. They express the horror of rebellion. They do not bear a mark or sign. They would be like everyday scenes, were it not for the harshness of the subject.

Barthes's comments on Wessing's photographs stunned me. In his eyes, this is not a special photograph except for the curious duality. It is very different for me. My body feels the photograph—the grimaces of these women *fulgurate* me.[2] They stab me.

> Somos la orquídea del acero,
> florecimos en la trinchera como el moho sobre el filo
> de la espada,
> somos una vegetación de sangre.
> Somos flores de carne que chorrean sangre . . .
> JOAQUÍN PASOS, "Canto de guerra de las cosas"

> Keep Writing
> Because memory.
> CRISTINA RIVERA GARZA, *Grieving*

The grimaces on the faces of the two women in Wessing's photograph (fig. 6.1) express the sorrow and pain they endure as their loved one is arrested. Given the atrocities committed by Anastacio Somoza's Guardia Nacional, it is not surprising that their gestures are overflowing with anguish, despair, and heartache. Who knows whether their loved one will return? Yet Barthes wonders, "For whom the gestures?" as if the two women were performing in a play and there were no spectators. Barthes takes this photograph as depicting the everyday life of these women in this rural town of a tiny country. Following Sontag's discussion of photographs documenting the pain of others, we could say that for Barthes this photograph merely confirms "that this is the sort of thing which happens in *that* place."[3] But I come from *that* tiny country—no longer my home in the familiar sense but still a home one longs for (exiles will understand this strange and yet chronic condition). The photograph, then, punctures me in a way that is difficult to describe with signs on a page, as the memories are acutely painful.

While there is a deep anguish that is stirred within my body by this photograph of sorrow, there is also a more measured perception of some of its details—for example, the way the pattern of those ominous clouds seems to be reproduced in the woman's forehead. It is as if she had a sad sky on her forehead, one that contrasts with what I take to be the festive polka-dot pattern of her dress. The contrast is jarring, especially as my eyes center on her mouth, agape in shock. In *Carnalities* I have taken you, dear reader, in a movement from the colonial eye to the multisensory mouth, to practices enacted by those who feel brown in order to register their inner life, to transform themselves, to open futural possibilities but also to mourn. What does this woman's mouth say if we listen closely? What sounds does this photograph make? The one who has taken the photo is a stranger, a documentary photographer. As such, the image carries the traditional intent of representing the horror of precarious political circumstances in other places. The women here are not enacting carnalities in the sense that Anzaldúa, Aguilar, or Cárdenas do. Yet the carnality of the photograph itself calls for affective registers and its ability to point to an entwinement of worlds—different worlds, bodily, earthy, spiritual—that sky on her forehead, that screaming mouth disclosing the precarious being-in-worlds of these Nicaraguan women. Recalling Anzaldúa, what torturous winds, fire, seas, and earth pass through these women's mouths?

As the grieving, screaming woman with the polka-dot dress points her arms downward, as if pulled to the ground by sorrow, the second woman, head tilted, eyes closed, also in sorrow, lifts her arms—and it seems as if she is going to fall backward, as if the anguish is too much to bear. I want those lifted arms to be grabbed by something out of the sky, steadying her, making it possible to live a different life. This photograph that apparently did not puncture Barthes but that pierces me in so many ways helps me move into the final chapter of *Carnalities*, one in which I shift from a consideration of Mexico-US border *cross*ings and the flowing of brownness to exploring my own difficult *cross*ing to the United States that, despite being so long ago, it sometimes feels as if it was yesterday (again, exiles will know what I mean).

As I proceed, I know that what follows places me in that realm where one is looking too closely at one's omphalos—I apologize in advance. The way I am moved by the photograph of these two women, along with my distress about Barthes's lack of strong affective reaction to this photograph, points to the fact that the carnality of the photograph, its ability to pierce us affectively, is a function of the histories we carry with us. My reaction not just to this photograph of these two grieving women but to a number of Wessing's photographs in this series on Nicaragua is so strong as to take me to a precarious memory-space, a moment of remembrance that is afflicting rather than joyous as so many acts of remembrance are. I am immediately transported to a chilling experience in connection to the carnality of a very specific photograph, Susan Meiselas's *Cuesta del Plomo*. While in previous chapters, we have seen the possibilities of self-naming and transformation as well as mourning and remembrance enacted by carnal photography, here I wish to tell of another side of the story of the carnality of the photograph: when it can undo us. Writing about *Cuesta del Plomo* became a tarrying with a ghost, but one that is paradoxically also about corporeal excess.[4] This chapter is thus about the possibility of the carnality of the photograph to puncture so deeply that the self is at risk of being undone—except that it is me that is taken to this limit of subjectivity. Following Barthes, I call this aspect of the photograph *photographic incandescence*, the affective and carnal possibility of a photograph to undo subjectivity, to take the self to the limits of its humanity.

Photographic incandescence refers to the fiery, suffocating moments in which inside and outside, subject and object, lose meaning; the moments when the excesses of the body reveal both our mortality and liminality. In the first section, I discuss the haunting photograph *Cuesta del Plomo* (fig. 6.2) in terms of the Barthesian notion of fulguration and Julia Kristeva's notion of abjection. I explore how incandescence is connected to the corpse, which Kristeva regards as the "most sickening of wastes."[5] I explain how my "I" is overcome by the corpse—the corpse in a photograph—and engage this horror with Barthes's notions of piercing and fulguration.[6] In the second section, I discuss how the ambiguity brought forth by photographic incandescence is, in my view, productively engaged by returning to Anzaldúan carnal aesthetics and the imaginal encounter with the dismembered Coyolxauhqui that opens the possibility for re-membering. As we will see, the attempt to put Coyolxauhqui together is an experience that is not without pain, not without possibility of failure, of unreconcilable excess. I wish to close *Carnalities* by returning to *Cuesta del Plomo*, as my experience of it encapsulates in the most intimate way the very carnality of the photograph that has so far informed this book.

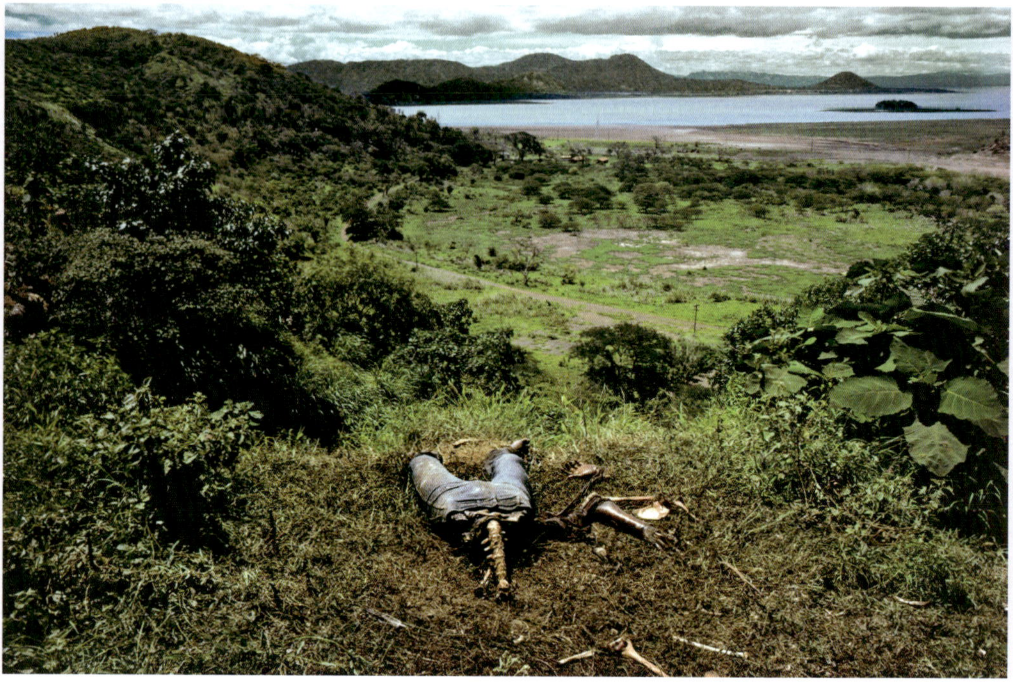

6.2 Susan Meiselas, *Cuesta del Plomo*, 1978. Copyright Susan Meiselas / Magnum Photos.

Piercing. Pricking. Cutting. Stinging. Bruising. These are all ways of describing how a photographic *punctum* affects one that views a photograph—or rather, one who feels it. There are various degrees of intensity to all of these sensations. But seeing *Cuesta del Plomo* for the first time took me beyond the limits of words themselves. So deeply was I stabbed by this photograph that I thought I would vomit. I still flinch when I see Wessing's photographs of Nicaragua. I am very much affected by Wessing's photograph of the two grieving Nicaraguan women discussed above. I also remember visiting a gallery and seeing large-format photographs of Sebastião Salgado's series *Migrations*, and feeling as if I would faint. I remember writing a paper on Ana Mendieta's photographs of her *Silueta* series and crying while I was writing, as I could feel the sense of exilic melancholia in them. I have thus experienced the intensity of the carnality of the photograph many times—but not with the sharpness I felt when I saw Meiselas's *Cuesta del Plomo*. The utter horror of the photograph coupled with my experiences at a time of violence in Nicaragua transformed my encounter with *Cuesta del Plomo* into one pointing to the limits of subjectivity and of sense-making. Barthes's notion of fulguration and Kristeva's view of abjection and horror help me, however imperfectly, describe this most intimate and disconcerting experience of the carnality of *Cuesta del Plomo*.

FULGURATION AND ABJECTION

Cuesta del Plomo was taken by Susan Meiselas in 1978 as she documented the events leading to the Nicaraguan Revolution in 1979, in which the dictator Anastacio Somoza was ousted. In its denotative meaning, it points to the transformation of a *who* into a *what*: a corpse half eaten, probably by vultures—remains of one of the many who lost their lives opposing Somoza's brutal regime.[7] Eduardo Cadava documents the place of the photograph as Cuesta del Plomo, a hill where the National Guard assassinated and dumped rebels and where Nicaraguans searched daily for missing persons.[8] Yet considering the carnality of this photograph takes us to its connotative meaning, to the multiple contextual layers informing it and its experiencing it. For me, *Cuesta del Plomo*'s carnality is intertwined with the particular life-changing history of my *cross*ing, my difficult experience of leaving Managua and settling in the United States under dire economic conditions and without knowing the language. To experience the photograph, then, is to feel it as it punctures me in terms of its horror and in terms of my experience as a Nicaraguan whose life was radically changed due to political upheaval, violence, and relocation. Following Barthes, I thus point to this photograph as *fulgurating* me and as disclosing the incandescence of photography. Inspired by Kristeva, I also point to how the carnality of *Cuesta del Plomo* takes me to the edges of myself.

Besides using the terms *piercing*, *pricking*, *cutting*, *stinging*, and *bruising* to describe what the *punctum* does to the viewer—or, in my view, the way the carnality of the photograph *affects* us—Barthes introduces a most compelling term, *fulguration*, what he calls "an intense mutation of my interest," that detail that "overwhelms the entirety of my reading."[9] Yet when I see *Cuesta del Plomo*, fulguration overwhelms the entirety of my *being*. I am no longer "reading" or "interpreting" the photograph in a specific way; I am being touched (wounded) by the photograph with an intensity that I cannot call a "tiny shock," as Barthes sometimes calls the *punctum*.[10] For him, fulguration is connected to a detail in the photograph that he sees as a detonator and an explosion that "makes a little star on the pane of the text or the photograph."[11] Yet I wish to explore fulguration in connection to an "incandescence" that produces a big shock within my being. The word *incandescence* is beautiful; it is itself a Barthean *punctum* made of letters, capturing strong affect and nauseating emotion—fiery light arising out of some sort of being that has succumbed to desire itself or to horror. It is a being burned by those rays of light that, according to Barthes, emanate from the photograph.

While in his early work on photography Barthes explains the differences between the denotative and connotative messages of the photograph, in *Camera Lucida* he embarks on a phenomenological quest in search for the essence of the photograph, which he ultimately explains as the photograph's pointing to a "that-has-been," to the undeniable fact that some being has been there or existed.[12] Yet, as noted, this exercise in search of photographic essence nevertheless opens the floodgates of affect by way of his experience of the "Winter Garden Photograph," a photograph of his mother when she was five years old standing next to her brother in a winter garden. In my view, Barthes is fulgurated by this photograph. We must remember that *Camera Lucida* is a work of mourning, and feelings seep out of its pages. Barthes cries with words in this text, trying to make sense of his mother's death, a death that also takes him to his own mortality, to love, as well as to a most carnal incandescence: "The Winter Garden Photograph, however pale, is for me the treasury of rays which emanated from my mother as a child, from her hair, her skin, her gaze, *on that day*."[13] The rays from this photograph of his beloved mother take him to the limits of his being.

I read his experience of the Winter Garden Photograph as a fulguration prompted by those rays emanating from his mother in the photograph, lighting a fire within him so intense that he feels existential dread as he recognizes not just his being-toward-death but his complete end, since he does not have any children.[14] This fulguration disclosing his being-toward-death both denies and confirms his being—it paradoxically individualizes and generalizes him as a *who* that is to die and a material corpse-to-be: "From now on I could no more than await my total, undialectical death. That is what I read in the Winter Garden Photograph."[15] The Winter Garden Photograph that piercingly and fulguratingly individualizes him as a body that is to become excess also connects him to his beloved mother who is no longer. It is a photograph that can only pierce *him* with the intensity that it does precisely because of his love for his mother and his past with her. As he says, "I cannot reproduce the Winter

Garden Photograph. It exists only for me. For you, it would be nothing but an indifferent picture, one of the thoughts and manifestations of the 'ordinary.' . . . At most it would interest your stadium: period, clothes, photogeny; but in it, for you, no wound."[16]

Incandescence and fulguration can be understood as two sides of the coin of deep sensation, of the type that may burn your being to the point of no return. For Barthes, fulguration arises from looking at a piece of paper—not any piece of paper, but one on which light has written and from which a real body emanates. The radiations of a body, his mother, captured by light, fulgurate him and touch him "like the delayed rays of a star."[17] This sense of fulguration, of being taken to the limits of being, happened to me when first encountering *Cuesta del Plomo*, although, of course, for different reasons and circumstances. I did not know the person whose remains lay in this sacred ground. I did not know of his circumstances. Yet the rays emanating from this carnal photograph still fulgurated me (and continue to do so) given my difficult experience leading to my *cross*ing to the United States. While for Barthes it is the rays of the loved one that fulgurate, for me it is the rays not of a particular loved being but of a self, now a half-eaten corpse, that point to the limits and fragility of being a self.

Fulguration as intensity that overwhelms the self, placing her in close connection to being-toward-death, is also fueled by the utter abjection which, following Kristeva, I take as leading to the path to an abject boundary-subjectivity or the destabilization of order, system, and identity prompted by it. But it is not just identity in general, but *my* identity that becomes both *I* and *not I* when looking at *Cuesta del Plomo*.[18] The incandescence of abjection, the fiery light arising out of the paper and suffusing my being as I succumb to the image, is a vortex of summons and repulsion. It is an outside/inside image, an outside (a corpse representative of a particular life that has been and that we cannot even honor properly as we do not even know his name) and an inside (a movement inward by way of a corpse of a stranger in pure abjection that points to an experience of war that both affirms and denies my identity), both leading to the utter ambiguity of the in-between and to my own corporeal excess. While Barthes allows me to connect the photograph to fulguration and to photographic incandescence—the carnality of the photograph that takes us to the limits of our self, to the undoing of the "I" and to loss of meaning—Kristeva's reflections on abjection allow me to consider my experience of fulguration prompted by *Cuesta del Plomo* in connection with the image of the corpse itself.

For Kristeva, suffering is the "place of the subject . . . an incandescent, unbearable limit between inside and outside, ego and other."[19] In Louis-Ferdinand Céline's narrative *Journey to the End of the Night*, Kristeva finds an incandescence that coincides with "the crying-out-theme of suffering-horror," the "violence of poetry, and silence" that has the intimate side of suffering and the public feature of horror.[20] In this reading of abjection, ecstasy before the corpse takes identity to the point in which it turns into something undecidable.[21] While in her explorations on the incandescence of abjection Kristeva centers Céline's narrative, here I explore the point at which identity turns into something undecidable through the writing with light, through the way *Cuesta del Plomo* fulgurates *me* and thus both confirms and disturbs my identity, prompting *exilic incandescence* within me, the fire arising out of an unbearable limit between a place of origin that is no longer mine and a present filled with melancholia—a burning light of time taking me to a different me in a mostly forgotten life in a small country. *Cuesta del Plomo* transports me to the incandescence of abjection, the "crying-out-loud theme" of suffering and horror that both summons and repels.

In Kristeva's view, abjection constitutes a liminal opposition to an "I" and a "dark revolt of being" from an "exorbitant" outside or inside.[22] Abjection is a necessary excess—my necessary excess, your necessary excess. A weight of meaninglessness comes along with the abject, rupturing our everydayness and taking us to a place of uncanniness that both calls us and negates us. In this liminal space, the self finds the border between human and animal.[23] Yet the abject does not take away the subject from what threatens it; rather, it places her in perpetual danger, giving rise to ambiguity, a radical ambiguity in which horror is both compelling and repulsing. Here the threatened, ambiguous, and abject self comes face to face with the corpse all of us are to become.

Regarding the corpse as "the most sickening of wastes," Kristeva takes waste as improper and unclean—what the self must expel. Through the uncleanliness and waste of the body, the self both is othered and gives birth to itself:

As in true theater, without makeup or masks, refuse and corpses show me what I permanently thrust aside in order to live. These bodily fluids, this defilement, this shit are what life withstands, hardly and with difficulty, on the

part of death. There, I am at the border of my condition as a living being. My body extricates itself as being alive, from that border. Such wastes drop so that I might live, until from loss to loss, nothing remains in me and my entire body falls beyond the limit—*cadere*, cadaver . . . the corpse, the most sickening of wastes, is a border that has encroached upon everything.[24]

The "I" is expelled in a final expulsion—the "I" turned waste; the "I" at a point of no return. The self is "pulverized" and the corpse remains the "utmost abjection," because it calls and engulfs us, disrespecting borders, identity, system, and leaving us in an ambiguous "in-between."[25] The corpse, then, constitutes a direct encounter with in-betweenness, liminality, and ambiguity. As Kristeva states, "Abjection is above all ambiguity."[26]

I am interested in Kristeva's attention to this ambiguity insofar as it is connected to the utterly corporeal and to affect. I follow the corpse in *Cuesta del Plomo* that paradoxically directs me to my own ambiguity—to my own pus, blood, and my own waste. I follow that image of that corpse that engulfs me into abjection, the abjection of ultimate ambiguity in which my I becomes *not I*—as I am undone by this image of this corpse, of this waste that even if it is not my own waste takes me to myself and fulgurates me. For Kristeva, one's own waste is connected to abjection. In my view, because of the photograph's carnality, its ability to *affect* us, the photograph can carry with it the possibility of fulguration and incandescence of the type that Kristeva finds in corporality, in bodily waste. I am taken to my own self and limits by way of the rays emanating from this half-eaten corpse written by light. As opposed to Siegfried Kracauer's noted interpretation of a photograph as merely capturing a spatiotemporal continuum, I understand the photograph as an aperture to incandescence of the type that is connected to abjection in the sense of corporeal excess.[27]

The carnality of the photograph, then, has not only the possibility to affect us and to disclose the intertwining between the self as well as earth- and spirit-bodies, but also to take the self to her very limits. That is to say, the carnality of the photograph may prompt a *photographic incandescence* in which the viewing of the photograph leads to a falling into a space of ambiguity, liminality, as well as meaninglessness, as the self is confronted with its limits of being—what Kristeva takes to be the function of corporeal excess or that which, in her view, needs to be expulsed in order to live. This photographic incandescence arises as the rays of the photograph burn us with deep feeling given our particular contexts, histories, desires, and fears. For me, *Cuesta del Plomo* also prompts *exilic* incandescence or the destabilization of myself in light of the experience of loss of "home." In this particular instance, the photograph affects me not only because of my own entwinement with the violence connected to the history of Nicaragua that led to a *cross*ing-turned-uprooting in my life and so many other people's lives, but also because of the disclosure of the corpse itself in the photograph. In its carnality *Cuesta del Plomo* can fulgurate me acutely because of the many relations informing my experience of the photograph. This horrific photograph also captures, among other things, the relation between that mutilated corpse and that shadow ground, the relation of Meiselas to the events she is photographing, and the experience of those who resisted the dictatorship. Yet what remains vivid for me is my nausea and urge to vomit upon looking at *Cuesta del Plomo*—the shock, turmoil, disruption, and upheaval, even if caused by emanations of light from a piece of paper.

With Barthes, I can say that *Cuesta del Plomo*, this photograph that has *haunted* me since I first saw it years ago, fulgurates me, individualizes me—it points to both a there-has-been but also to my own relation to that which is there and is now a corpse.[28] With Kristeva, I can say that the image sends me to "a twisted braid of affect" that constitutes a revolt of being against a threat from the exorbitant outside *and* inside "ejected beyond the scope of the possible, the tolerable, the thinkable."[29] In the complicated play of summons and repulsion (and banishment), the abject seeps in and takes me to the edge of myself. Like the unclean—blood, pus, shit—this photo is what I throw aside in order to live. Following Kristeva I can say, "I am at the border of my condition as a living being."[30] This corpse is death written with light infecting life at the in-between.

PUTTING COYOLXAUHQUI TOGETHER OR "RE-MEMBERING" IN THE IN-BETWEEN

When this represented fragment of a corpse in *Cuesta del Plomo* takes me to an incandescence of abjection, to the crying-out-theme of suffering and horror which is itself connected to border subjectivity and the in-between, I think of Anzaldúa's reflections on Coyolxauhqui, the dismembered moon goddess. I thus return to Anzaldúa's carnal aesthetics and her reflections on Coyolxauhqui. As we saw in chapter 2, Anzaldúa writes about this goddess as exemplifying "women as conquered bodies."[31] For Anzaldúa, Coyolxauhqui symbolizes both fragility and strength; dismemberment becomes a source of pain but also of knowledge. Let us return to Anzaldúa's words on Coyolxauhqui: "I disintegrate into hundreds of pieces, hundreds of separate awarenesses. A plurality of souls splits my awareness so that I see things from a hundred different viewpoints, each with its own intelligence that can 'do' a hundred different things (think, feel, sense, observe) in a continuously changing consciousness moment to moment. Yet while experiencing the many, I cohere as the one reconstituted and restructured by my own unconscious urge toward wholeness. Coyolxauhqui represents the psychic and creative process of tearing apart and pulling together."[32] Coyolxauhqui stands for embodied but dismembered in-betweenness or nepantla, what Anzaldúa describes as the place where "at once we are detached (separated) and attached (connected) to each of our several cultures. Here the watcher on the bridge (nepantla) can 'see through' the larger symbolic process that is trying to become conscious through a particular life situation or event."[33] Similar to abjection in the Kristevan sense, this is a state of contradiction (of "I" and "not-I"), of chaos. While Anzaldúa's description of this dismemberment is connected to the lived experience of living in-between cultures, it also has a deeply corporeal element that points to that which is expelled from the body, especially blood. As she states, "This work, these images, piercing tongue or ear lobes with cactus needle, are my offerings, are my Aztecan blood sacrifices."[34] Anzaldúa also considers the blood coming out of her own body as she discusses her hormonal imbalance, which leads to bleeding from an early age. Metaphorical wounds, actual wounds, and a self that is an herida abierta, "an open wound," just as she says the Mexico-US border is, inform Anzaldúa's own sense of abjection. In her early piece "La Prieta" Anzaldúa states, "The bloodshed on the highway had robbed my adolescence from me like the blood on my diaper had robbed childhood from me."[35] In this early piece she also already understands her dismemberment: "How to turn away from the hellish journey that the disease has put me through, the alchemical nights of the soul. Torn limb from limb, knifed, mugged, beaten. My tongue (Spanish) ripped from my mouth, left voiceless. My name stolen from me. My bowels fucked with a surgeon's knife, uterus and ovaries pitched into the trash. Castrated. Set apart from my own kind, isolated. My life-blood sucked out of me by my role as woman nurturer—the last form of cannibalism."[36] La Prieta, like Coyolxauhqui, is torn apart, body parts dispersed in the borderlands.

Anzaldúa cannot take the dismemberment. As we have seen, in the fifth stage of conocimiento she calls for the "Coyolxauhqui imperative" so that chaos and disintegration will be reorganized and create order and a new kind of being in the world. She finds the need for a reintegration of the fragments/pieces of our souls and divided selves.[37] Aware of the physical and psychic unrest of fragmentation, she calls for the creation of order out of chaos. Through her carnal writing she tries to put herself together. Yet Anzaldúa states that the "deep dive scares," because "there is always a monster in the cave."[38] As we have seen, through a deeply embodied process of pulling entrails from her mouth and in which she confronts monsters, fears, dreams, and anxiety, she finds a way to incorporate her "inner struggle and pain to cannibalize and incorporate into the text."[39] She calls forth her naguala self or her shapeshifting self in order to reenvision different possibilities for her story and characters. Anzaldúa suffers through the creative process in order to create a backbone of the story. She beautifully explains that she assembles los huesos (bones) in a way that all the story's elements add up to more than the sum of the bones: "A story possesses a body: Its skeleton is the framework; the bones, its armature. All the bones are connected to the backbone, a single linchpin that holds the story's tension and contains the crucial threads running throughout the work. The story's ideas—including the most important organ, the heart—are held, encased, and protected by the skeleton."[40] In her move to re-member Coyolxauhqui, Anzaldúa effectively engages the possibility of creativity in the face of the ambiguity produced in the plight of living in the borderlands, in the face of self-disruption and fragmentation. In a seemingly Nietzschean move, Anzaldúa appeals to the creative process as both an expression of will and a possibility of self-making, self-transformation, self-re-membrance.

In a similar vein, although primarily informed by psychoanalytic theory, Kristeva's analysis of depression and melancholia examines the function of the beautiful for the depressed, wounded self that has experienced a loss. She asks, "Might the beautiful be the ideal object that never disappoints the libido? Or might the beautiful object appear as the absolute and indestructible restorer of the deserting object? . . . In the place of death and so as not to die of the other's death, I bring forth—or at least I rate highly—an artifice, an ideal, a 'beyond' that my psyche produces in order to take up a position outside itself—ek-stasis."[41] Kristeva is concerned with the question of whether the beautiful is inseparable from mourning and melancholia. In her analysis of Hans Holbein the

Younger's *The Body of the Dead Christ in the Tomb*, in which Kristeva finds *eros*, invisibility, loneliness, competition between form and death, pain, and melancholia, we are "to be swallowed up by death, or perhaps to see it in its slightest, dreadful beauty, as the limit inherent in life."[42] Images and identities, Kristeva says, are here ultimately "imprinted with inaccessible sadness."[43] In a more recent study of artistic works, she meditates on decapitation or the "sacred slash."[44] She discusses writings as well as paintings about decapitation as transformations of melancholia and asks whether decapitation is emblematic of social and historical divisions and the "brutal admission of our internal fractures."[45] Nevertheless, she exalts our creative capacities and says of Acéphale (a being without a head) that it is a "fertile dead end, whose open wound will never stop being examined by those who like to meditate on the dangers of being alive."[46]

Through storytelling, through painting, through the artistic process, body parts can be re-membered as Anzaldúa calls for, or heads can be slashed as we learn from Kristeva, captured with oil and pigment so as to produce a dreadful beauty that encompasses both the horror of melancholia and also the possibility of transformation. This is decapitation as meditation on melancholia, "and therefore a rebirth," or what Elaine P. Miller in her development of a Kristevan melancholic aesthetics calls spiritual inoculation, "the intentional exposure to a small dose of an otherwise lethal malady (in this case, melancholia or depression), in order to stave off a more disabling form of the same woe."[47] Such spiritual inoculation then becomes a gesture of resistance to the depressive position that "there is meaning only in despair."[48] Whether individual or collective, depression, the condition of modernity, appeals to the very melancholia that undermines it so as to be able to live with the incandescence of abjection that, as carnal beings, arises from the very depths of our blood and guts.

Yet there is the excess, the haunting and sickening excess. How does one put together that which cannot be put together, that resists being put together? I go back to the photographic incandescence that the photograph *Cuesta del Plomo* produced within me, to the fragment of the corpse written with light. That backbone exposed. No attachment to limbs. No possibility of being put together—ever—as historical, political, and cultural forces create an irredeemable excess. It is striking that even with the understanding that "the specter of death always haunts the backgrounds in border art," Anzaldúa longs to put Coyolxauhqui together, even if it is a holding together that can be reconfigured—after all, stories can be retold and reshaped.[49] As Anzaldúa says, "My 'stories' are acts encapsulated in time, 'enacted' every time they are spoken aloud or read silently. . . . The work manifests the same needs as a person, it needs to be 'fed,' la tengo que bañar y vestir [I have to bathe and dress the work]."[50] The gathering of pieces, the re-membering suggested by Anzaldúa is an active one like the Barthesian *punctum* that *punctuate*s the self, that moves and flows with the viewer's desires, needs, wants, and particular histories as photographs are "in effect punctuated, sometimes even speckled with these sensitive points; precisely, these marks, these wounds are so many *points*."[51] But do these pointed wounds of the photograph that are themselves fragments of the fulgurating incandescence of photography lose their sharp edge? Can *Cuesta del Plomo* be bathed and dressed?

Despite the possibility of Anzaldúan re-membrance, as well as of Kristevan spiritual inoculation as suggested by Miller, I find myself burnt by the incandescence of *Cuesta del Plomo* and the manner in which the incandescence of abjection, as Kristeva suggests, takes the self to a boundary subjectivity in which identity, *my* identity, is confirmed, disturbed, and taken to its uttermost limits. Indeed, it is a question of limits, the limits of my own self as well as the limits of an aesthetics forged under conditions of trauma. When thinking about the relation between the fragmented corpse written with light and Anzaldúa's notion of writing as the creation of a backbone, even if a shifting backbone, there may remain a rupture so deep, a corporeal excess so nauseating within the self that no words, paint, or light could make a difference. And then, there is the unexplainable longing to put all the fragments together despite the knowledge that it is a Sisyphean task. Yet it is a longing that might also be reflected in Barthes's affective fulguration when looking at the Winter Garden Photograph of his mother, that one photo that ultimately leads him to the essence of photography but that, at the same time, ruptures him and puts him face to face with his own mortality and individuality.

I understand this longing that looks for some kind of homelike unity, of putting detached, abandoned parts back together despite the knowledge that there is no going back to an original state. While mindful of that longing, following Albert Camus, I wish to keep the "lucidity" of "metaphysical revolt" in the face of absurdity—an understanding of the nonsensical nature of our need for knowledge, for healing, and for hope given the silence of the universe when we desperately look for answers to our deepest questions.[52] There is no room for optimism here, even "cruel optimism."[53] As we learn from Camus, confronted with certain questions and with the ineffable, there is no hope that we will ever understand. Nevertheless, this metaphysical and existential absurdity does not mean that one cannot understand the power of art as it paradoxically inhabits the world alongside abjection and horror. Kristeva recognizes this power as she sees the necessity of the aesthetics of the "sacred slash," all those written and painted works in which melancholy and art unite to provide even a small dose of spiritual inoculation.

Before concluding, let's consider *Cuesta del Plomo* again. In my concern to highlight the fragment of the corpse, I overlooked the background—its beauty—the beauty of Lago Managua. The landscape is a side of the Isla del Amor (Love Island) in Lake Managua. Following Kristeva, can I appeal to abject beauty? When describing the photograph, Meiselas herself states,

> I used to get in the car as early in the morning as I could and just drive, looking for things that seemed unusual. One day I was driving on the outskirts of Managua when I smelled something. It was a very steep hill, and as I got closer to the top the odor overwhelmed me. I looked out and saw a body and stopped to photograph it. I don't know how long it had been there, but long enough for the vultures to have eaten half of it. I shot two frames, I think, one in color and one in black and white, then got out.
>
> The images I made of the body were powerful partly because of the contrast with the beauty of the landscape. For me [the photo] was the link to understanding why the people of Nicaragua were so outraged. [On the other hand] the American public could not relate their reality to this image. They simply could not account for what they saw.[54]

And who can account—I cannot—for what the ravages of war do to the self, for the nauseating incandescence of *Cuesta del Plomo,* for those who were pierced by that 1979 revolution that offered both liberation from brutal dictatorship but also intimacy with the horror of war? The photographer can tell many stories with light and even come back to deal with the pain of the past by way of more art. Meiselas goes back to the shadow ground of *Cuesta del Plomo* and takes another shot (fig. 6.3) for another project, *Reframing History,* marking the twenty-fifth anniversary of the overthrow of the Somoza dictatorship. In this project, she returns to the sites of nineteen previously taken photographs from her 1978–79

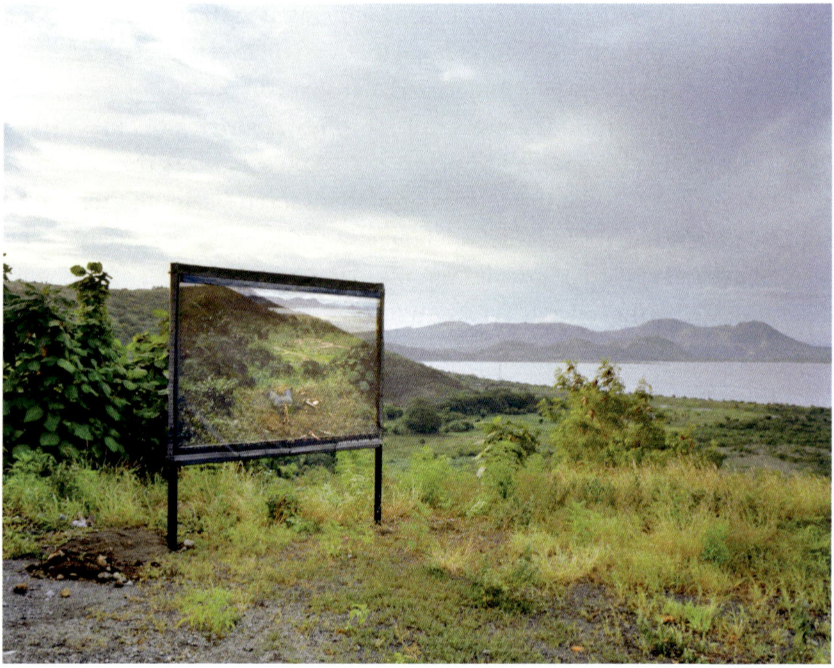

6.3 Susan Meiselas, *Cuesta del Plomo* (*Reframing History* series), 2004. Copyright Susan Meiselas / Magnum Photos.

Nicaragua series to allow for collective memory. But what does she wish with this reframing of abject beauty?[55]

While Meiselas intends to promote collective memories about the events of the revolution by placing the photographs where they were originally taken, and discussing them with Nicaraguans, she may also be reinscribing painful individual memories and not considering the possibility of the incandescence of abjection that these large-scale photographic reproductions may carry within them even in the context of the present. In the doubling of *Cuesta del Plomo*, in the reinscribing of the violence in that ground that remains shadow ground, Meiselas both reifies and reframes abject beauty in a photographic context. The incandescence of abjection, then, may spill out of the confines of photographic paper to the organs, joints, flesh, to all body parts such that no matter the attempts at putting Coyolxauhqui together, the liminal state of the I and the not I, the incandescent states of boundary subjectivity, may arise for so many who view the photographs.[56]

Moreover, in her attempt to address collective memory regarding Nicaragua's revolution, Meiselas runs the risk of reinserting a photograph of the past into a narrative of the present—thus problematically imposing a temporal linearity to historical and personal events related to the 1979 Nicaraguan Revolution. Nevertheless, these photographs that Meiselas brings back to Nicaragua do not merely mark spatiotemporal points in a linear historical and personal sequence but, following Walter Benjamin, they are "flashlike."[57] These flashlike images of the past encompass both the what-has-been and the now. They may serve as sparks of the past that carry with them the futural possibilities that can be understood within the present context—that instant of the past within the photograph that could illuminate the present situation in productive ways. But such illumination becomes a possibility *if* the incandescence in the photograph does not first fulgurate the viewers in such a way that the subject is left in corpse-like utter abjection. For me, though, the one called the exile, "the foreigner," the incandescence of abjection emanating from *Cuesta del Plomo* has not lost its piercing, fulgurating fire or its nauseating hold. *Cuesta del Plomo* is like the piss, blood, vomit, and guts, the corporeal excesses that I need to expel in order to live. When Kristeva describes "the foreigner" and the exile she says, "settled within himself, the foreigner has no self. Barely an empty confidence, valueless, which focuses his possibilities of being constantly other, according to others' wishes and to circumstances. I do what *they* want *me* to, but it is not 'me'—'me' is elsewhere, 'me' belongs to no one, 'me' does not belong to 'me.' . . . Does 'me' exist?"[58] I reply to Kristeva:

> I am and I am not a dreamer making love to absence.[59]
> I am and I am not exquisitely depressed.[60]
> I do and do not wrap myself in an anesthetized skin.[61]
> I am a multiplicitous self.

———

The carnality of the photograph is a source of deep sensation that, as we have seen in previous chapters, is connected to a carnal aesthetics that those whose lives are permeated by being-in-sorrow—due to perverse operations of those dominated by colonial eyes—can engage for the purposes of self-care, self-making, and self-transformation, quiet and resonant ways of being, mourning and carrying our dead. As we have seen, however, an aesthetics informed by the carnality of the photograph needs to concede that as much as the carnality of the photograph may enrich our lives as we continually face the many indignities, bruises, and lesions of a life marked by feeling brown, it can also take us to a frightening limit of subjectivity, to an abjection and unmaking of the self. *Cuesta del Plomo*, whose carnal power was so deep so as to prompt me to vomit and to feel pierced in the deepest part of my being, has taken (and continues) to take me to the edge, so as to remind me about the precarity and vulnerability of being, and about the need to remain cautious, vigilant about the existential and political power of carnalities.

How the rays emanating from a photograph can create this incandescence that negates and fulgurates the self is something that remains a mystery. Barthes's reflections in *Camera Lucida* have helped me get a sense of this carnal power of photography. He understood it—felt it—in his relation to that revealing and crushing photograph of his dear mother, as the rays from her photograph created a shock of such intensity that took him to an existential limit. I do not exaggerate when I say I have carried *Camera Lucida* within me for so long—so much have I learned from it about the power and tenderness of photography, but also about the carnality of aesthetics in general. In my mind I have renamed his text *Carnal Camera*. *Lucida* is a beautiful word, and, indeed, Barthes's words reveal the brightness of the camera and the camera as brightness. Yet it is a word too connected to rational knowledge in philosophy and to that which is apprehended by the eye. In *Carnalities* I have sought a movement toward operations of mouthly, multisensory perception. The incandescence of photography, being taken to the limits of the self by way of the rays emanating from the photograph, is yet another one of these operations. With Barthes, I follow these deep but wounding rays; with Kristeva I recognize that the carnality of the photograph, in particular of *Cuesta del Plomo* as I experience it, is also about the excess of the carnal understood as corporeality. It is about being taken to the boundary of the in-between subjectivity that we are, of the corpses that we are to become. It is about the excess that we are and need to expel in our everydayness. It is about the blood that unhinges Anzaldúa. With her, however, I can recognize the need for some kind of re-membering, of using blood to remake oneself as she does with her ink. This is the work of carnal aesthetics, the work of deep re-membering—an unfolding and learning of our senses at the nexus between the visible and the invisible. I remain vigilant, knowing better than to make false promises about the power of carnalities but also aware of how those who feel brown draw life from them, even when carrying our dead.

Coda

On the week of June 4, 2018, the corpse of Keller Pérez Duarte, a twenty-three-year-old protester against the current Ortega government in Nicaragua, was found in Cuesta del Plomo.[62] Cuesta del Plomo continues to be shadow ground.

"NOTHING VERY EXTRAORDINARY"

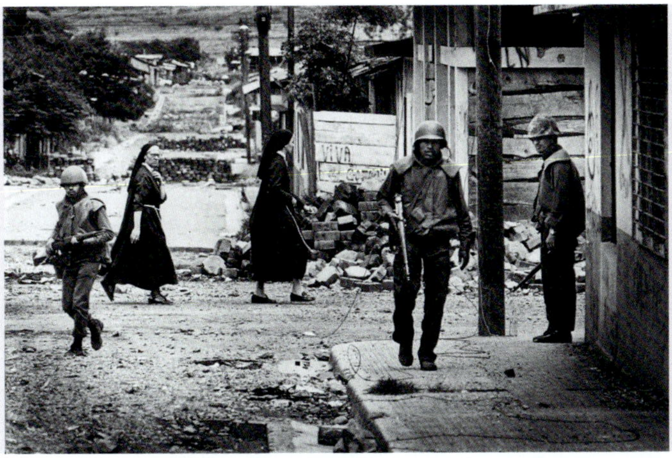

6.4 Koen Wessing, *Nicaragua*, 1978. Gelatin silver print, 16 × 12 in. Courtesy of the Stedelijk Museum of Modern and Contemporary Art and Design.

I was glancing through an illustrated magazine. A photograph made me pause. Nothing very extraordinary: the (photographic) banality of a rebellion in Nicaragua: a ruined street, two helmeted soldiers on patrol, behind them, two nuns. Did this photograph please me? Interest me? Intrigue me? Not even. Simply, it existed (for me). I understood at once that its existence (its "adventure") derived from the co-presence of two discontinuous elements, heterogeneous in that they did not belong to the same world (no need to proceed to the point of contrast): the soldiers and the nuns.
ROLAND BARTHES, *Camera Lucida*

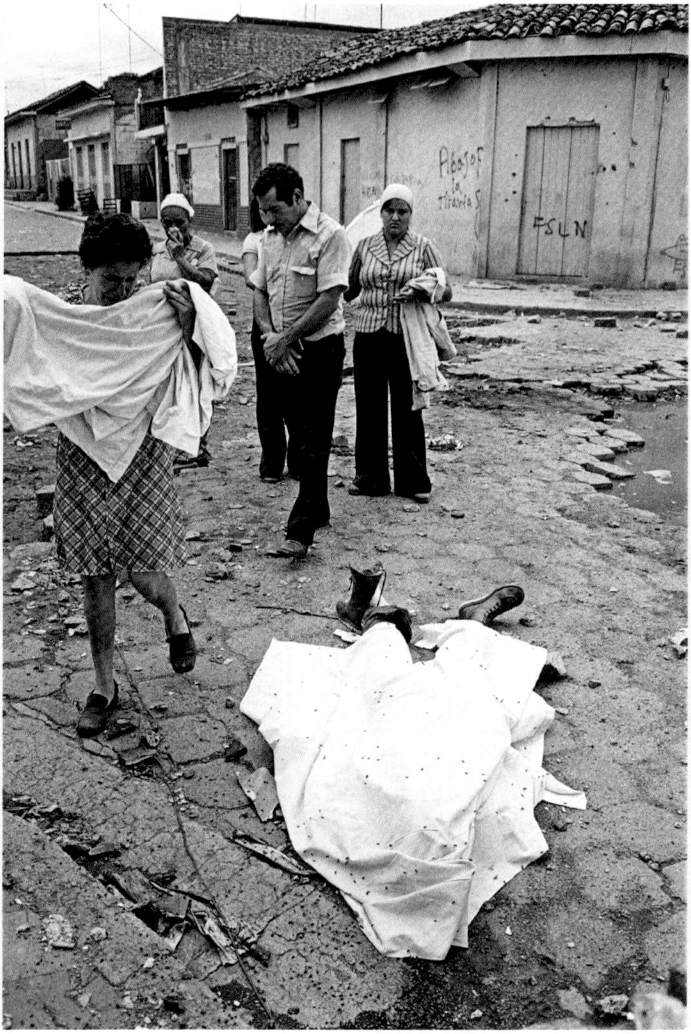

6.5 Koen Wessing, *Estelí, Nicaragua*, 1978. Gelatin silver print, 12 × 16 in. Courtesy of the Stedelijk Museum of Modern and Contemporary Art and Design.

Here, on a torn-up pavement, a child's corpse under a white sheet; parents and friends stand around it, desolate: a banal enough scene, unfortunately, but I noted certain interferences: the corpse's one bare foot, the sheet carried by the weeping mother (why this sheet?), a woman in the background, probably a friend, holding a handkerchief to her nose.
ROLAND BARTHES, *Camera Lucida*

DEAR ROLAND (IF I MAY),

In *A Lover's Discourse*, which I have read with great interest, you say that the love letter has a special dialectic. I would like my letter to you to be expressive, longing to signify desire. I do not want it to be mere correspondence. You are not my lover, but I am thinking you, not of you, even when you are not going to write back. So, this will be one of those letters that remains a love letter that waits for an answer (it will remain a perpetual monologue). And yet. I must write.

I have been wanting to write to you for a long time. Your work has taken me to a not-so-subtle beyond. I do not exaggerate when I say that your *Camera Lucida* pierced me in such a way that it became a book-*punctum* in my life. Yes, I am using your idea. I like that you describe it as a piercing but also a bruising. Piercing is quick, too quick. Bruising lingers.

Indeed, something painful has stayed with me from your beautiful *Camera Lucida*. Well, so much has stayed with me that I love, but then there is your comment "Nothing very extraordinary." These are your words—that are also piercing but in an altogether different way, in the way that hurts, offends, and angers at the same time, the more so because I love your work, which in a sense means that I love you. You were worried about your total undialectical death, but you remain in your work. And I continue to think and feel you.

"Nothing very extraordinary." Would you even remember when you wrote these seemingly innocuous three words? This was your comment on one of Koen Wessing's photograph of armed conflict in Estelí, Nicaragua. But first, let me point out that Wessing took the Estelí photographs in 1978, not 1979 as you write in your book. By July 1979 the revolution had succeeded. Yet it took a long time, with terrible fighting in smaller towns such as Estelí, eventually reaching Managua in June. I remember it well, because my birthday is in late June and we were afraid, thinking we would have to flee our home that day, as the fighting kept getting closer, bullets were landing by the back wall, and the plane was bombing homes near our block.

Details aside, what I really care about is that all you see in the photograph of the guards and nuns is photographic banality. I understand. It is stadium to you, except of course for that copresence of discontinuous elements, nuns and guns. And then there are your observations on the image of the covered dead child (is it a child? Did the magazine you were reading describe it so? I see boots. It doesn't matter. It is still death)—your interest is in the sheet? And in the woman "holding a handkerchief to her nose"?

Please do not come to quick conclusions. I understand your views on connotation and denotation and the deeply subjective aspect of the *punctum*. I don't fail to see your methodology—that you dedicate the book to Jean-Paul Sartre, that you seek the general by way of your own experience of those photographs that interest you. The rays of the photograph will touch you differently than they will touch me. Yet I find myself unable to understand what moves (or doesn't move) you in Wessing's photographs, just as I continue to wonder about your comments about James Van Der Zee's 1926 *Family Portrait*, which are punctuated by a pair of strapped pumps and seem to mock this Black family. But Shawn Michelle Smith already discloses your racial anxieties in her *At the Edge of Sight*. I wish you had read her chapter on your work.

I just needed to let you know that these words you wrote—"nothing very extraordinary"—stayed with me. They almost broke the umbilical cord that connects me to your work. Not that I expect you to be perfect. I know better. It is just that I have learned from you about the carnality of the photography, about its wounding and woundedness, and somehow expected you to have the sensibility that you have in so many of your works to appear in your interpretations of photographs, of these photographs that are carnal daggers for me. But perhaps you think pain is something that just happens there (in those little countries), as Susan Sontag so perceptively tells us about interpretations regarding the pain of others.

In the end, limits always show up. Your own carnal writing might take me to a subtle beyond as you say or it may simply hurt, and take me to a realm of difference, and of a gaze, that is simply not mine but through which I have had to learn to see this world and myself. This is the seemingly impossible-to-get-away-from gaze that I am trying to get away from with this book (you probably would not have taken the time to read my book had it been possible). The otherwise is already here—when I and those like me, those who share feeling brown (which I'm not sure you would have understood) create, even if for an instant.

Sincerely,
Mariana Ortega

NOTES

PREFACE

1 From 1973 to 1978 the Cuban artist Ana Mendieta made the *Silueta* series by leaving her silhouette on water, land, wildflowers, and fire, thus creating ephemeral traces of her exilic self and then photographing them. See Viso, *Ana Mendieta*. For an analysis of the exilic spatiality of the siluetas, see Ortega, "Exiled Space, In-Between Space."

INTRODUCTION

1 This refusal becomes even more poignant given the investigation of the role of her husband Carl Andre in her tragic death.
2 Barthes, *Camera Lucida*, 81.
3 Elizabeth Edwards calls the photograph an "object of affect," arguing that an understanding of the photograph "cannot be contained in the relation between the visual and its material support but rather through an expanded sensory realm of the social in which photographs are put to work." Edwards, "Objects of Affect," 228. An early theorization of this affective, sensuous, embodied dimension of the visual in the context of the phenomenology of film is Vivian Sobchack's *Address of the Eye*. See also her *Carnal Thoughts*, in which she elaborates on the relationship of bodily sense and meaning.
4 Barthes, *Camera Lucida*, 81. Despite her incisive criticisms of photography, Susan Sontag recognized the capacity of the photograph to take us to the realm of feeling. As Sarah Parsons notes, "*On Photography* is a passionate and brave effort to think through photography as an affective and effective medium, to understand how and why it impacts us so deeply." Parsons, "Sontag's Lament," 290.
5 I take "affect" as denoting the sense of immediately being affected by, being moved or touched by something. I do not follow a strict division between affect and emotion in terms of a connection to a cognitive state, as theorized by Brian Massumi in "The Autonomy of Affect," 88. I understand both as having various levels of intensity as they are felt. Moreover, I take

emotions as not necessarily confined within the subject as if the subject were a cabinet of affect. While I may feel affect and emotions as mine, they "emerge," as Edward S. Casey argues, "at the outer edges of our experience." Casey, *Turning Emotion Inside Out*, 9. Yet I am still interested in how affect is registered as deeply intimate and personal.

6 For "bodysoulmind," see Anzaldúa, *Light in the Dark*, 133; for "Earth's-body," see Anzaldúa, *Borderlands / La Frontera*, 75.

7 Anzaldúa, *Borderlands / La Frontera*, 75.

8 M. Rivera, *Poetics of the Flesh*. Rivera explains the Christian notion of flesh as "notoriously susceptible to metamorphosis" (54). She analyzes religious views aiming to liberate themselves from the notion of flesh. She also analyzes understandings of flesh as having opacity, weight, and connection to human communities, earth, water, and bread.

9 Spillers, "Mama's Baby, Papa's Maybe," 67.

10 Weheliye, *Habeas Viscus*, 44.

11 Moraga and Anzaldúa, *This Bridge Called My Back*, 23. I consider Latina/x theories "in the flesh" as offering theories of affect. It is unfortunate that those working on affect theory have not engaged these writings. Like the work of recognized affect theory scholars such as Sara Ahmed, Lauren Berlant, and Brian Massumi, Latina/x theories in the flesh disclose how an embodied dimension of existence attuned to affectivity informs not only our very sense of belonging or not belonging but also the various types of relationalities, whether political, communal, personal, intimate, that are part of daily existence. For discussions on queer women of color and theorizations of affect, see Carrillo Rowe, "Loving Transgressions."

12 Moraga and Anzaldúa, *This Bridge Called My Back*, 23.

13 Anzaldúa, *Borderlands / La Frontera*, 67.

14 Anzaldúa, *Borderlands / La Frontera*, 73.

15 Anzaldúa, *Light in the Dark*, 67. Anzaldúa takes this image from Nahua mythology. The tree of life represents the tripartite intertwining of the underworld (world of spirits), the physical plane, and the world of noncorporeal energies. Anzaldúa, *Light in the Dark*, 232.

16 My translation. Anzaldúa, *Borderlands / La Frontera*, 71.

17 Merleau-Ponty, *The Visible and the Invisible*, 132. As Rawb Leon-Carlyle notes, for Merleau-Ponty color is not to be translated into a reductionistic scientific account of qualia or into "being as Object." Rather, for Merleau-Ponty color is "wild," announcing a host of relationships as well as other sensory sensations beyond the visual and disclosing the intertwining between the visible and the invisible. See Leon-Carlyle, "Wild Red." I am inspired by Merleau-Ponty's example of perceiving red as disclosing the intertwining between perceiver and perceived, and in "Perceiving in Red" I connect this perception with Lugones's notion of resistant trespassing and with Anzaldúa's view of conocimiento.

18 Merleau-Ponty, *The Visible and the Invisible*, 132.

19 Merleau-Ponty, *The Visible and the Invisible*, 130.

20 A sustained discussion of "flesh" appears in Merleau-Ponty's last unfinished work *The Visible and the Invisible*. Lawrence Hass explains that "flesh" is one of Merleau-Ponty's most difficult concepts. He finds three meanings of the term: (1) carnality in connection primarily with corporality; (2) reversibility or the ability of being both a subject and an object; and (3) general principle. Hass, *Merleau-Ponty's Philosophy*, 201–3. I understand flesh in terms of *incarnate possibility*, which encompasses Hass's meanings: flesh is not a mere logical possibility but embodied; it allows for reversibility; and it sees the possibility that incarnate possibility is elemental in the sense that it is what allows for multiple possibilities of interaction or communication between all that there is. Yet this communication by way of reversibility is, in my view, not necessarily equal.

21 Merleau-Ponty, *The Visible and the Invisible*, 152.

22 L. E. Pérez, *Chicana Art*, 23. In a recent work, Pérez theorizes the interconnectedness between humans and other life-forms based on "healing practices of loving awareness and respect for self" as "eros ideologies." See L. E. Pérez, *Eros Ideologies*, 15–16.

23 Merleau-Ponty's ontology of the flesh with its chiasmatic interlacing and reversibility of the perceiver and the perceived has raised difficult questions about its ability to give an account of difference in its many forms. Luce Irigaray, in *An Ethics of Sexual Difference*, faults the philosopher for forgetting the maternal-feminine. Gail Weiss makes clear in her analysis of "urban flesh" that there is deep differentiation and violence that happens when flesh stylizes being (*Refiguring the Ordinary*, 128). Beata Stawarska, in "From the Body Proper to Flesh," faults Merleau-Ponty for understanding the experience of one's own body as the basis for intersubjectivity. Shannon Sullivan, in "Domination and Dialogue in Merleau-Ponty's Phenomenology of Perception," critiques his account as positing an anonymous subject not capable of handling any type of difference. For responses to critiques, see Stoller, "Reflections on Feminist Merleau-Ponty Skepticism"; and Weiss, "The Anonymous Intentions of Transactional Bodies." More recently, disability scholars offer important criticisms of Merleau-Ponty's ableism and of his assumption of normalcy as connected to the white male body. See Reynolds, "Merleau-Ponty, World-Creating Blindness"; and Wieseler, "Challenging Conceptions of the 'Normal' Subject in Phenomenology." When discussing the issue of race in the context of Merleau-Ponty's ontology of chiasm, Andrea Warmack argues that given Merleau-Ponty's account, Black people can be considered *Homo sapiens* but excluded from subjectivity. Warmack, "We Flesh."

24 I am aware of the importance of the figure of the lips in Continental feminism given Luce Irigaray's influential text "When Our Lips Speak Together." Yet my appeal to the figure of the mouth is not a call to female-centered signification. I aim to capture the perceptual multiplicity and relationality in Anzaldúa's creative practice as mouthly and thus carnal. For an anthology inspired in part by the work of important media and film critics Vivian Sobchack and Laura U. Marks, who highlight embodied perception and a new kind of spectatorship, especially in film, see Papenburg and Zarzycka, *Carnal Aesthetics*. Papenburg and Zarzycka recognize the importance of the affective dimension between perceivers and perceived in the context of (anti-)aesthetics and cultural politics.

25 My translation. Anzaldúa, *Borderlands / La Frontera*, 74.

26 According to Michael Kelly, "In its original usage, the word [*aisthesis*] was related to perceptual or sensory knowledge, usually in contrast to conceptual or rational knowledge, but had little or no specific relevance to art." It was not until the eighteenth century that "aesthetics" became connected to art. Kelly, *Encyclopedia of Aesthetics*, ix. In their attempt to provide a decolonial account of artistic practices, Walter Mignolo and Rolando Vázquez have introduced the term *aestheSis*. It is meant to supplant *aesthetics* and to undermine the connection that this latter term has to Kantian philosophy and to Eurocentrism. See Mignolo and Vázquez, "Decolonial AestheSis."

27 In previous writings, I have used *aesthesis* to highlight the decolonial possibilities of the term. See Ortega, "Queer Autoarte" and "Spectral Perception and Ghostly Subjectivity." After much thought, in this work I keep the term *aesthetics*, as in everyday use it points to artistic practices or art in general. Paradoxically, while using *aesthesis* or *aestheSis* is meant to capture a decolonial shift in philosophical aesthetics, it is not a familiar term, thus undermining the possibility of making the work accessible beyond philosophical circles.

28 Anzaldúa, *Borderlands / La Frontera*, 67.

29 Anzaldúa, *Borderlands / La Frontera*, n.p.

30 Campt, *Listening to Images*, 45.

31 Campt, *Listening to Images*, 17.

32 Campt, *Listening to Images*, 5.

33 Quashie, *The Sovereignty of Quiet*, 6.

34 Quashie, *The Sovereignty of Quiet*, 21.

35 Quashie, *The Sovereignty of Quiet*, 23.

36 Quashie, *The Sovereignty of Quiet*, 45.

37 That which is quiet or silent is not always to be thought of as necessarily nonresistant. I thus do not wish to propose a strong dichotomy between the quiet and the resonant in the context of resistance. As we will see,

Anzaldúa's creative practice of border arte has quiet and more resonant elements. For a theorization of "deep silence" that challenges standard conceptions of voice as emancipatory, see Ferrari, "Questions of Silence."

38 As I write from and about the wound, I recognize the dangers of reifying pain and victimhood, especially as it concerns bodies of color. As Amber Jamilla Musser notes, "The spectacle of the black body in pain mobilizes empathy and sympathy, but also passivity." Musser, *Sensual Excess*, 98. It is certainly not my aim here to cater to empty, useless empathy or sympathy or to add to the other side of the spectacle of race, the one in which bodies of color are not to be paraded as angry, savage, dangerous but as damaged, bruised, and victimized and in need of white saviors. *Carnalities* discloses the pain and sorrow of Latinidad as well as the manner in which Latinx life persists, finding moments of self-care, nurture, love, joy, refusal, transformation, and resistance. For an important account of "benevolent violence" as an affective disposition to the perceived vulnerability of marginalized individuals that is part of neoliberal, ornamental multiculturalism, specifically in the context of trans* justice, see DiPietro, "Beyond Benevolent Violence."

39 Cvetkovich, *An Archive of Feelings*, 7.

40 Vázquez, *Vistas of Modernity*, 14.

41 Muñoz, *The Sense of Brown*, 39.

42 Diaz, *Postcolonial Love Poem*, 6.

43 Barthes, *Camera Lucida*, 21.

44 Barthes, *Camera Lucida*, 76. While Barthes theorizes the essence of photography in terms of indexicality, for me the key to his account is his recognition of the photograph's ability to affect or touch the perceiver, hence they invite embodied or "haptic visuality." For an account of "haptic visuality" specifically in film, see Marks, *The Skin of the Film*, chap. 3.

45 Sontag, *On Photography*, 20.

46 Johnson, *The Merleau-Ponty Aesthetics Reader*, 144.

47 Etymologically, *photography* means "writing or drawing with light": from the Greek *photos*, meaning "light," and *graphos*, meaning "writing, delineation, or painting." The term is supposed to have been coined by Charles Wheatstone and Sir John Herschel independently. Hershel's usage of the term in 1839 became the catalyst for its general adoption. Lenman and Nicholson, *The Oxford Companion to the Photograph*.

48 According to André Bazin, photography embalms time. Interestingly, Bazin thought that all the plastic arts suffered from a "mummy complex," the fundamental need to embalm the dead and counter the flow of time. Bazin, "The Ontology of the Photography Image," 4–8.

49 As we will see throughout this book, the "embalming" of time that takes place in photography, which as I have noted was of concern for

Merleau-Ponty as well as photographic theorists such as Barthes and Sontag, need not take away what I am calling the carnal possibilities of the photograph.

50 I now opt to use *othered beings, other,* or *othering* rather than *the other, Other,* or *the Other,* which are surprisingly still very common in philosophical analyses. While the term is used in various texts concerned with showing how one subject can reach another subject (regardless of social identities) or with bringing to light the importance of selves that have been othered due to their social identities, it is time to retire the term. In its capitalized form and in its standing for any other person or for persons who are marked by race or any other social identity considered marginal, it dangerously performs both an abstraction and a reification of these selves. Moreover, it revitalizes a dichotomy of self/other in which self is understood as the white European subject that is to serve as the point of reference, the point from which all perspectives must be explained.

51 For a fascinating account of the formation of new types of beings such as the "savage" in connection with medieval and Renaissance images of the "wild man" and "monstrous races," see Velazco y Trianosky, "Savages, Wild Men, Monstrous Races." For classical phenomenological discussion on the imaginary, see Sartre, *The Imaginary.* For the influential psychoanalytic account of the formation of the imaginary order by way of the ego in the mirror stage, see Lacan, "The Mirror Stage as Formative of the Function of the I." For a key analysis of the role of the social imaginary, see Castoriadis, *The Imaginary Institution of Society.* For recent analysis of the distinction between the imaginary and the imaginal and the political possibilities of the imaginal, see Bottici, *Imaginal Politics.* Moreover, we must not forget that Latina/x theorists have also provided key discussions on the notion of the imaginary. For example, in the 1999 text *The Decolonial Imaginary: Writing Chicanas into History,* Emma Pérez offers an important problematization of the colonial imaginary in historiography that leaves out the history of Chicanas. Moreover, Anzaldúa provides a key theory of the imaginary that highlights images and the unconscious in *Light in the Dark,* esp. chap. 2, "Flights of the Imagination."

52 When discussing the role of photography in the production of new sexual subjects in the nineteenth century, Paul Preciado states, "The truth of sex takes on the nature of a visual disclosure, a process in which photography participates like an ontological catalyst, making explicit a reality that wouldn't be able to emerge any other way." Preciado, *Testo Junkie,* 112. This understanding of photography as "ontological catalyst" is key to photographic projects in the nineteenth century that create different types of beings.

53 Photographic techniques accompanying early alleged "sciences" such as physiognomy aimed at identifying difference and deviancy. From early on, photography became enlisted for practices of othering. See Sekula, "The Body and the Archive"; Kemp and Wallace, *Spectacular Bodies*; Hight and Sampson, *Colonialist Photography*; Maxwell, *Picture Imperfect*; Morris-Reich, *Race and Photography*; Pinney and Peterson, *Photography's Other Histories*; and Morris Hambourg et al., *The Waking Dream*. For an account of "photographic subjection" and modern seeing inspired by Michel Foucault, see Armour, *Signs and Wonders*.

54 Barthes, *Camera Lucida*, 80–81. While Barthes is clearly referring to print photographs here, we can think of digital photographs as also affectively touching those who experience them. Whether taken by a Kodak Brownie or our cell phones, photographs continue to pull at our heart strings. There are important distinctions between the affective impact of analog and digital photographs, yet a comparison of analog versus digital photography is beyond the scope of this discussion. For an interesting discussion that engages the resistant power of digital images, see Armour, *Seeing and Believing*.

55 See Lugones, "Heterosexualism and the Colonial/Modern Gender System" and "Toward a Decolonial Feminism." In these important texts, Lugones introduces the notion of the "coloniality of gender," a view that analyzes gender as a colonial imposition and introduces the "light" and "dark" sides of the coloniality of gender.

56 See Pelaez Lopez, "The X in Latinx Is a Wound Not a Trend."

57 Claudia Milian offers a rich discussion of the problems as well as tremendous possibilities entailed by the *X*. She states, "If we thought we knew all too well the o/a of the familiar Latino/a, LatinX tells us that things are no longer the same, that there is no secure footing, that the X—an expounding concept—is bound to new bodies and new schools of thought." Milian, *LatinX*, 6.

58 See Aparicio and Chávez-Silverman, *Tropicalizations*; Dávila, *Latinos, Inc.*; Laó-Montes and Dávila, *Mambo Montage*; R. Rivera-Servera, *Performing Queer Latinidad*; and Salazar, "The Problem with Latinidad."

59 One of the most difficult aspects of the experience of those at the margins is the exclusion that takes place within their communities due to a perceived lack of sameness or solidarity in the group. I call this experience of marginalization within one's own group "internal exclusions." Such exclusions have been an important topic of discussions for scholars of color. Chicana thinkers such as Mirta Vidal, Bernice Rincón, Enriqueta Longeaux Vasquez, and others provided an early critique of the exclusion of Chicanas in the movement of *La Raza*. See Alma García, *Chicana Feminist Thought*. For an important discussion of exclusions in

the context of nineteenth-century Black women thinkers, see Bell, "Black Feminism and Intersectional Analyses."

60 Beltrán, *The Trouble with Unity*, 162.

61 Beltrán, *The Trouble with Unity*, 18, 19. In a similar vein, Juana María Rodriguez ties Latinidad to Deleuze's nonlinear notion of the rhizome that allows for multiple directions; hence she claims that Latinidad is "about the 'dimensions' or 'the directions in motion' of history and culture and geography and language and self-named identities." Rodriguez, *Queer Latinidad*, 22.

62 Milian, *Latining America*, 4.

63 Milian quotes Morales as foreseeing the coming of this Latinity when he states that "there may be more styles and variations of being Latino than there are different Latin America countries." Milian, *Latining America*, 3.

64 Milian, *Latining America*, 4.

65 Milian, *Latining America*, 4.

66 Muñoz, *The Sense of Brown*, 39.

67 When describing the *punctum*, Barthes states that it "is this element which rises from the scene, shoots out of it like an arrow, and pierces me." Barthes, *Camera Lucida*, 26.

68 Muñoz, *The Sense of Brown*, 121.

69 Muñoz, *The Sense of Brown*, 10, 3, 39.

70 In *Being and Time* Heidegger famously offers an analysis of the existential or ontological characteristics of being human. One of these characteristics is "being-with," or *Mitsein*, what makes it possible for the self to connect or be with others. See Heidegger, *Being and Time*, sec. 26.

71 Ortega, *In-Between*, 61. Following Lugones, I define "being-at-ease" as a function of one's ability to be nonreflective about everyday norms and linguistic practices as well as a sense of sharing a history with people.

72 My view of multiplicitous subjectivity in *In-Between* is part of this attempt. I also offer a coalitional politics that takes into consideration the importance of naming oneself as part of a community while, at the same time, honoring relationality and coalitions across differences. See Ortega, *In-Between*, 159–69.

73 Muñoz, *The Sense of Brown*, 15. Here Muñoz is quoting Cherríe Moraga.

74 See Mitchell, *What Do Pictures Want?*

75 Sandoval, *The Methodology of the Oppressed*, 2.

76 Sandoval, *The Methodology of the Oppressed*, 57–58.

77 Following Anibal Quijano and other decolonial theorists, I see a distinction between coloniality and colonialism. While colonialism refers to past violent processes of the European colonization of the Americas that emerged in 1492, coloniality, specifically "the coloniality of power" points to ongoing structures of power and hegemony that are the result of colonialism. See Quijano, "Coloniality of Power."

78 Sandoval, *The Methodology of the Oppressed*, 140.

79 Sandoval, *The Methodology of the Oppressed*, 141, 147.

80 As Audre Lorde states, "For the erotic is not a question only of what we do; it is a question of how acutely and fully we can feel in the doing." Lorde, *Sister Outsider*, 54.

81 Sandoval, *The Methodology of the Oppressed*, 142–43. An interesting issue here is the extent to which Sandoval's notion of the erotic compares to Lorde's famous account of it. While Sandoval would not disagree about the erotic's potential for intensity of feeling, or the erotic's potential for joy, she also follows Barthes in the theorization of love as the condition of a no place, or third space, where that which is not possible becomes possible, where meanings shift, where selves disintegrate and become otherwise, and where they "pick, graze, convert, cruise, low-ride through meanings." Sandoval, *The Methodology of the Oppressed*, 145.

82 For elaborations of "critical" phenomenological approaches before an explicitly named "critical phenomenology," see Fanon, *Black Skin, White Masks*; Beauvoir, *The Second Sex*; J. M. Martinez, *Phenomenology of Chicana Experience and Identity*; L. R. Gordon, *Bad Faith and Anti-Black Racism*; Yancy, *Black Bodies, White Gazes*; Ahmed, *Queer Phenomenology*; and my own work *In-Between*. For analysis of an explicit elaboration of critical phenomenology, see Salamon, "What's Critical about Critical Phenomenology?"; Ferrari et al., "Editor's Introduction"; and Guenther, "Critical Phenomenology" and "Six Senses of Critique for Critical Phenomenology." For a sustained analysis of the notion of critique as central to phenomenology, see Marder, *Phenomena—Critique—Logos*. For a recent anthology dedicated to the importance of Husserlian phenomenology for critical phenomenology, see Heinämaa, Carr, and Aldea, *Phenomenology as Critique*. As I finish this manuscript, a new work on phenomenology and race that constitutes a critical phenomenology has been published, Lee's *A Phenomenology for Women of Color*.

83 See Ahmed, "A Phenomenology of Whiteness," 152–56. Importantly, in this piece Ahmed does not assume whiteness as an ontological given but as the inheritance of certain orientations that put some things within reach of certain subjects and not others.

84 Guenther, "Critical Phenomenology," 12. While transcendental structures are understood to be structures that make experience possible and are understood to be a priori (before experience) and operative in the same manner in all contexts, Guenther's quasi-transcendental structures are not a priori but "they play a constitutive role in shaping the meaning and manner of our experience" (12).

85 Salamon, "What's Critical about Critical Phenomenology?," 15.

86 While there are various phenomenological analyses of the aesthetic, most notably by Heidegger, Sartre, and Merleau-Ponty and scholars of these

thinkers, they center artistic works by European artists such as Vincent Van Gogh, Alberto Giacometti, and Paul Cézanne. There is surprisingly little work on critical phenomenological aesthetics that also engages work by artists beyond Europe and that takes into consideration the photograph. For a recent important critical, feminist, phenomenological aesthetics that develops the notion of "embodied perceptual cognition" and provides powerful interpretations of a range of different artworks, see Fielding, *Cultivating Perception through Artworks*. For a key phenomenological analysis of racialization through artworks, see Al-Saji, "Glued to the Image."

87 Ortega, *In-Between*, 10.

88 The plural form, *phenomenologies*, seems apt here, as there may be room for different critical phenomenological approaches.

89 According to Dan Zahavi, the most worrisome understanding of phenomenology is one that equivocates phenomenology with phenomenality. Zahavi writes, "My claim, however, is not that phenomenologists are not interested in the phenomenality of experience, my claim is that phenomenology cannot be reduced to a concern with that topic." See Zahavi, "Getting It Quite Wrong," 902.

1. AFFECTED BY THE EYE

1 The mythology of the "evil eye" spans various centuries across varied cultures and epochs. The evil eye is supposed to ward off the curse initiated by a malevolent stare. Campos-Pons has various versions of this image, including one where brown eyes have been drawn on her back, as well as a triptych called "Sagrada Familia (Holy Family)" of photos of her back, her son's back, and her husband's back, all with eyes drawn on them. In a 2013 conversation with Terrence Dempsey, SJ, and Dr. Olubukola Gbadegesin introducing her work for an exhibit at the Museum of Contemporary Religious Art (MOCRA), Campos-Pons explains that when she was very young, her father told her that she had eyes on her back, that she could perceive things even when they were not in front of her. She adds that she thought her father's comment was a beautiful way to describe other sensorial capacities of the body and spirituality, noting that drawing these eyes is about the capacity of compassion, perceiving ahead of time, and perceiving deeply, which the body expresses in a "quiet manner." For her, the eyes point to alertness, to the fact that the body is full of energy and in tune with oneself, the world, and one's art. The conversation can be found on the MOCRA podcast website *MOCRA Voices* (see Campos-Pons, interview). As we will see, given the workings of coloniality, another interpretation of "Untitled" becomes possible, one in which

the colonial eye fixes and invades the racialized self. However, Campos Pons's comments on her work and her understanding of the eyes drawn on her back anticipate various themes in *Carnalities*.

2 Martín Alcoff, *Visible Identities*, chap. 7.

3 It is also an apt description insofar as we are finding ourselves having survived a global pandemic, pushed to return to a "normal" that never was, especially for bodies of color who suffer daily indignities of racism, but, most importantly, for those deemed "essential workers" who were for the most part in service labor and had to face the risk of losing their breath as they worked to make all of our lives more comfortable.

4 Al-Saji, "Glued to the Image," 487, and "Hesitation as Philosophical Method," 342.

5 Quashie, *The Sovereignty of Quiet*, 6, 21.

6 As noted, Anzaldúa states that she writes in "*Tlilli, Tlapalli*," *tlilli*, Nahuatl for charcoal, soot, or black ink, and *tlapalli*, Nahuatl for blood, red, or something dyed. Together these two terms mean wisdom and writing.

7 For various critiques of visuality and ocularcentrism, see Mulvey, "Visual Pleasure and Narrative Cinema"; Sekula, "The Body and the Archive"; Foster, *Vision and Visuality*; Jay, *Downcast Eyes*; Tagg, *The Burden of Representation*; Crary, *Techniques of the Observer*; and Mirzoeff, *The Right to Look*.

8 Mitchell, *What Do Pictures Want?*

9 As already noted, the phrase *the Other* has been widely understood as denoting others in general and those who are racially other or are differently marked than the dominant group. This notion unfortunately continues to be very much part of academic analyses on difference, especially in traditional phenomenological approaches such as those of Merleau-Ponty, Heidegger, and Sartre, and in contemporary analyses of these texts. Not only does it turn particular human beings with different social identities into a general, abstract entity; it also homogenizes particular differences. It is thus time that we avoid using such a notion as equivalent to "another person" or "those who are racially different." Here I use the term *othering* to emphasize the active production of difference for the purposes of categorization, alienation, and abjection.

10 There are various examples of visual practices that counter normative, colonialist visions, even in photography, the visual technology that has been closely connected to practices of othering. Important examples of figures who engaged the photograph to fight the racist, violent gaze are Frederick Douglass, Sojourner Truth, and W. E. B. Du Bois. For an important short piece regarding the resistant power of photographs for African Americans, see hooks, "In Our Glory." For a key collection of the resistant use of photography and African American identity, see Wallace

and Smith, *Pictures and Progress*. See also Smith, *American Archives*; *Photography on the Color Line*; and *Photographic Returns*. In addition to these texts showing how the photograph can be used by racialized selves for purposes of countering and dislodging the colonial, racist self, Smith, inspired by Benjamin's notion of the "optical unconscious," also shows how the photograph may reveal that which is beyond the visible. In *At the Edge of Sight*, Smith provides deeply insightful and novel readings of work by key photographers that capture the "invisible" anxieties, prejudices, and desires connected to social identities such as sexuality, gender, race, and class.

11 Martín Alcoff, *Visible Identities*, 187.

12 Martín Alcoff, *Visible Identities*, 194.

13 Lee, *A Phenomenology for Women of Color*, chap. 1.

14 Lee, *A Phenomenology for Women of Color*, introduction.

15 Ngo, *The Habits of Racism*, 66, 125.

16 Ngo, *The Habits of Racism*, 136.

17 By a background of intelligibility and sensibility, I mean what makes it possible for us to have an understanding of something and what allows affectivity to come to the fore when we are perceiving. That is, concepts or affects do not arise out of the blue. They arise within particular contexts of understanding or of perception. As we will see in the discussion of the figure/ground, a figure always stands out of a ground that makes it possible for us to differentiate the figure.

18 Martín Alcoff, *Visible Identities*, 188.

19 Fanon, *Black Skin, White Masks*, 91. In other words, bodily habituations are informed by particular historical and racial formations—for example, the historico-racial schema in which whiteness becomes the norm.

20 Al-Saji, "A Phenomenology of Hesitation," 139.

21 Al-Saji, "A Phenomenology of Hesitation," 138.

22 Al-Saji, "A Phenomenology of Hesitation," 140.

23 Al-Saji, "A Phenomenology of Hesitation," 134.

24 Al-Saji, "Frantz Fanon," 207.

25 Al-Saji, "A Phenomenology of Hesitation," 141.

26 See Lee, "A Phenomenology of Seeing and Affect in a Polarized Climate." For Lee, the possibility of perceiving otherwise is a function of emotion, which "demonstrates the subject and the world as chiasmatically intertwined" (114); they are between selves and world rather than internal to subjects. For Lee, emotions color the way we perceive the world and others. She is thus interested in the possibility of how shifting emotions might help us deal with those whose politics we do not agree with.

27 Fielding, *Cultivating Perception through Artworks*, 111. Fielding provides a rich, multilayered account of "embodied perceptual cognition" that opens possibilities for ethical, political, and cultural transformation.

See also "White Logic and the Constancy of Color," in which Fielding suggests the destabilization of representation and signification in order to deal with racism. She analyzes Bruce Nauman's films *White, Pink, Green,* and *Black* in the context of Merleau-Ponty's appeal to constancy, revealing the normative influence of a single lighting level that effectively prioritizes whiteness.

28 Al-Saji, "A Phenomenology of Hesitation," 143.

29 Sartre, *Existentialism Is a Humanism*, 35.

30 Interestingly, this photo was taken eight years before Glenn Ligon's important photograph *Self-Portrait Exaggerating My Black Features / Self-Portrait Exaggerating My White Features* (1998), which I read as disturbing the indexicality of the photograph in order to point to ideas, assumptions, racial constructions, and power relations that exceed the image. See Ortega, "Photographic Representations of Racialized Bodies," 166.

31 Jones, "Clothed/Unclothed," 39.

32 My point here is not to say that everyone will have the experience that I have when encountering Aguilar's work. I am describing my experience of the photograph in order to show an example of how elements in a photographic work may prompt a slowing down of one's perceptual experience of it, which may lead to further attention to one's affective experience and more discursive considerations regarding our expectations, et cetera.

33 So important is this notion of affective hesitation for Al-Saji that she takes it to be "a necessary condition for critical and ethical seeing." Al-Saji, "A Phenomenology of Hesitation," 136.

34 Al-Saji, "A Phenomenology of Hesitation," 145.

35 Al-Saji, "A Phenomenology of Hesitation," 148.

36 Al-Saji, "A Phenomenology of Hesitation," 149.

37 See Sullivan, *Revealing Whiteness*. For Sullivan's important discussion of "ontological expansiveness" or the view that people with privilege have the unconscious habit of assuming that they belong in all spaces, see also Sullivan, "Ontological Expansiveness."

38 Al-Saji, "A Phenomenology of Hesitation," 150. One of the many strengths of Al-Saji's account of critical memory in the context of hesitation is precisely the importance of taking into consideration the working together of past, present, and future within normative relational networks.

39 Al-Saji, "A Phenomenology of Hesitation," 155.

40 Al-Saji, "A Phenomenology of Hesitation," 149. The reason for Al-Saji's call for "indirect" strategies to foster hesitation is that hesitation cannot be willfully enacted. Hesitation prompts openings within particular contexts that have yet to be taken up (149). I agree with Al-Saji that hesitation cannot be willfully enacted as it is dependent on multiple

factors that cannot be controlled (both in terms of the context in which hesitation may happen and in terms of the selves that may experience hesitation). This poses problems particularly for those who are interested in changing the habits of those who have white privilege, as those are the selves that do not have a disposition to be attuned to the possibilities of the otherwise that are in their environments. Nonetheless, it is of the utmost importance to provide phenomenological analyses that highlight the affective dimension of racialization so as to find ways to address it.

41 Ngo, *The Habits of Racism*, 30–31.

42 Husserl, *Logical Investigations*, 168.

43 One of the most interesting, important as well as controversial aspects of transcendental phenomenology as practiced by Husserl is the need to perform this "reduction" or a suspension or bracketing of what is regarded as the "natural attitude" or our unphilosophical, commonsense understanding of the world that is generally informed by various unexplored assumptions. The aim in bracketing the natural attitude is precisely to move aside any presupposition so as to reach "the things themselves," the very structures of consciousness that make it possible for us to experience the world in the way that we do. Husserl, *Logical Investigations*, 168. For an account of the complexity of this reduction and a classic commentary on the history of the phenomenological movement, see Spiegelberg, *The Phenomenological Movement*, 118.

44 Al-Saji, "Frantz Fanon," 200.

45 Al-Saji, "Frantz Fanon," 211.

46 Al-Saji, "Frantz Fanon," 211.

47 Al-Saji, "A Phenomenology of Hesitation," 140.

48 Ortega, *In-Between*, 60b. In *In-Between* I introduce the notion of the multiplicitous self as a self in process occupying multiple positionalities or social identities, a self that is being-in-worlds and being-between-worlds (chap. 2).

49 Al-Saji, "Frantz Fanon," 211.

50 Al-Saji, "Hesitation as Philosophical Method," 342, 348.

51 Ngo, *The Habits of Racism*, 66.

52 Yancy, *Black Bodies, White Gazes*, chap. 1.

53 See Ngo, *The Habits of Racism*, 15–22, for a detailed analysis of the complication that arises when gender is brought in as an explanation for the white woman's reaction and Yancy's response that white women may be using gender to cover up their racism. Ngo effectively discusses the difficulties that arise when the intersection of gender and race is not analyzed in a nuanced way.

54 For a moving discussion anchored in the work of Sara Ahmed and Julietta Singh, as well as in Ngo's phenomenological analysis of the racialized body, see Fong, "Forgive Me for So Speaking." Fong seeks to

construct an intimate body archive of wounds with the aim of living otherwise and forging relations.

55 Al-Saji, "Glued to the Image," 483.

56 Al-Saji, "Glued to the Image," 481.

57 It is interesting to think whether this example, the sculpture *This Is General Gordon* by Bob and Roberta Smith, can be considered an indirect strategy for hesitation. This opens room for thinking about different media and different artists' intentions in producing the work. That is, how can an artistic object that has been explicitly designed to disorient be regarded as prompting hesitation in an indirect way? Al-Saji notes that situations can be created so as "to bring hesitation about, as well as attention to ways of holding hesitation open and allowing it to become productive." Al-Saji, "A Phenomenology of Hesitation," 149.

58 The material of the "medium-affect nexus" is meant to capture the idea that there is some material or something beyond matter touching or inspiring the beholder. As such, it can inspire in both bounded and unbounded ways. In other words, it may add some constraints but also room for play in terms of what can be done creatively.

59 Here I am thinking of "material" in terms of how specific materials, elements, or media may inspire a perceiver. I think of the different ways that something like a piece of iron, a sound, an image, words, light, et cetera, may affect or inspire someone. Recent discussions of contemporary art highlight the role of the immaterial in art but conceived in terms of rules of display, conservation, and participation associated with particular artworks; see Irvin, *Immaterial*.

60 Al-Saji, "Hesitation as Philosophical Method," 339.

61 Al-Saji, "A Phenomenology of Hesitation," 155.

62 Al-Saji, "Frantz Fanon," 212. It is important to note that while phenomenological reflection has different meanings in the various traditional phenomenological accounts, it is clear that it does not entail a purely thematic or reflective understanding. In terms of various ways that subjects understand being-in-the-world, to use Heidegger's term, the self is neither reflective nor unconscious but has a prereflective understanding of the world (i.e., the subject is not thematically thinking about the action when performing it but can nevertheless be able to tell what she is doing if prompted to do so). Al-Saji's discussion on hesitation seems to involve various levels of reflection. Gayle Salamon's critical phenomenology is more explicit about the role of reflection in a critical phenomenological approach capable of taking into consideration the lived experience of trans and other marginalized individuals. She appeals to the idea of "shock" that leads to *thinking* and *rethinking* (Salamon, "What's Critical about Critical Phenomenology?," 64–65, my emphasis) of entrenched racist, transphobic, homophobic practices.

63 Barthes, *Camera Lucida*, 80.
64 Al-Saji, "Glued to the Image," 481.
65 Al-Saji, "Glued to the Image," 481.
66 Quashie, *The Sovereignty of Quiet*, 26.
67 In addition to Quashie's view that Blackness is tied to a public demand for resistance, I would like to suggest another reason as to why quiet may be undertheorized, the history of overtheorizing individuality and interiority in philosophical theories of subjectivity. That is, traditional theories such as the Cartesian epistemic subject rely on a subject/object or inner/outer distinction and an underscoring of individuality that translates to highly influential theories of autonomy and sovereignty. It thus becomes necessary to disarm overly individualistic understandings of selfhood as they undermine the self's relationality. Doing so, however, may lead to the other extreme, where there is no room for theorizing about deeply intimate moments of the marginalized self. Undertheorization or missing the importance of quiet can be understood as a result of appeals to identification that are politically essentializing (as Quashie shows) as well as critiques of overly individualistic philosophical notions of selfhood and subjectivity.
68 Quashie, *The Sovereignty of Quiet*, 6.
69 Quashie, *The Sovereignty of Quiet*, 119.
70 See Quashie, *Black Aliveness*.
71 Quashie, *The Sovereignty of Quiet*, 120.
72 Stewart, *The Politics of Black Joy*. Stewart calls for a more nuanced understanding of the complex relations between Black joy and suffering and their deployment. Indeed, by paying close attention to the being-in-sorrow of Latinxs, I do not wish to reify such suffering or to play into the hands of both liberal and conservative racism.
73 I thank Yi-Ting Chang for pointing out that this emphasis on quiet also affects an understanding of scale, as it prompts a recalibration of the impact of protests or other resistant acts.
74 Anzaldúa, *Borderlands / La Frontera*, 87.
75 Anzaldúa, *Borderlands / La Frontera*, 47.
76 Lugones understands resistance to be connected to response. She states, "But resistance is not reaction but response—thoughtful, often complex, devious, insightful response, insightful into the very intricacies of the structure of what is being resisted." Lugones, *Pilgrimages/Peregrinajes*, 29.
77 Lugones, "Motion, Stasis, and Resistance," 50. It is interesting to note that in her first reading of Anzaldúa's *Borderlands / La Frontera*, Lugones takes Anzaldúa as providing a psychological account too concentrated on the inner life without possibility of a politics of sociality. Lugones, "On *Borderlands / La Frontera*." Nevertheless, later Lugones recognizes the

tremendous potential of "germination" in Anzaldúa's work. See Lugones, "From within Germinative Stasis."

78 Lugones, "Motion, Stasis, and Resistance," 49. Importantly, Lugones notes that depending on the context, stasis may be liberatory or oppressive.

79 Quashie, *The Sovereignty of Quiet*, 22.

80 Moraga and Anzaldúa, *This Bridge Called My Back*, 173.

2. TO BE A MOUTH

1 Coyolxauhqui is the Aztec moon goddess, daughter of Coatlicue (serpent skirt), that as we will see greatly inspires Anzaldúa. According to Aztec mythology, Coyolxauhqui was decapitated by her brother Huitzilopochtli after he learned of her plot to kill their mother, who had been impregnated by a floating ball of feathers. According to Susan Milbrath, there are three variations of this myth: two of them do not specify that Coyolxauhqui is Huitzilopochtli's sister, and the third takes Coyolxauhqui to be Huitzilopochtli's mother. See Milbrath, "Decapitated Lunar Goddesses," 185.

2 Anzaldúa, *Borderlands / La Frontera*, 74. A cenote is a deep sinkhole in limestone that contains permanent water. Cenotes are found especially in the Yucatán Peninsula. They were particularly important in the region: ancient Mayas used them as their main water source but also as sacred wells that were considered entrances to the underworld. The cenote, then, can be thought as a liminal, in-between space that for Anzaldúa holds the possibility of connecting to other worlds.

3 As noted in the introduction, the figure of the mouth in this work is not aimed at theorizing a particular feminine way of being, as in the work of Luce Irigaray. Rather, it points to the mouth as symbolic of perceptual openness in terms of all the senses. I also interpret this figure in terms of its possibility for erotic potential when the erotic is understood in terms of Audre Lorde's vision in which the erotic is connected to intensity of feeling. See Lorde, "Uses of the Erotic: The Erotic as Power," in *Sister Outsider*. See also Roelofs, "Navigating Frames of Address," for an interesting discussion of the importance of corporeal modes of address, specifically the way Lugones uses the figure of the tongue to theorize multiple lines of meaning in connection to unruliness, lesbian identity, sexuality, and politics.

4 "I write with the ink that is my blood" (my translation). Anzaldúa, *Borderlands / La Frontera*, 71. Recall that Anzaldúa says that she writes in "*Tlilli, Tlapalli*," Nahuatl for "black ink and red paint."

5 Anzaldúa, *Light in the Dark*, 40.

6 For Sarah Ohmer, conocimiento is a notion that "seams" together many concepts from Nahuatl, Spanish, English languages and epistemologies,

and various religious traditions. She reads the process in term of a shamanic ritual as well as a rewriting of Carl Jung's journey of individuation. Ohmer, "Gloria E. Anzaldúa's Decolonizing Ritual de Conocimiento," 150, 148.

7 The process of "inner work" leading to "public acts" of conocimiento is intimately connected to Anzaldúa's views on spirituality and spiritual activism. Attention to Anzaldúa's spirituality is key in Laura Pérez's 1998 article "Spirit Glyphs: Reimagining Art and Artist in the Work of Chicana Tlamatinime" and continues to inform Pérez's later works, such as "Hybrid Spiritualities and Chicana Altar-Based Art," *Chicana Art*, and *Eros Ideologies*. While Anzaldúa does not mention "spiritual activism" in her work until 1996, Keating shows that it was very much part of Anzaldúa's earlier work. See Keating, *The Anzaldúan Theory Handbook*, 203. For other important texts that discuss or are inspired by Anzaldúa's notion of spirituality, see Keating, "Shifting Perspectives" and "'I'm a Citizen of the Universe'"; L. Medina, "Nepantla Spirituality: Negotiating Fluid Identities" and "Nepantla Spirituality: My Path"; Delgadillo, "Forms of Chicana Feminist Resistance" and *Spiritual Mestizaje*; Ohmer, "Gloria E. Anzaldúa's Decolonizing Ritual de Conocimiento"; Schaeffer, "Spirit Matters"; Tirres, "Spiritual Activism and Praxis"; and Zaytoun, *Shapeshifting Subjects*.

8 Anzaldúa, *Light in the Dark*, 182.

9 Here I emphasize the aesthetic aspects of Anzaldúa's writing. For analyses that engage Anzaldúa's writing in the context of epistemology, see Lockhart, "Writing the Self"; and Pitts, "Gloria E. Anzaldúa's *Autohistoria-teoría* as an Epistemology of Self-Knowledge/Ignorance." For a discussion engaging the aesthetic, myth, the cosmological, and ritual in Anzaldúa in connection with Lugones's work, see Meda Calderon, "Cosmologies, Ritual, and Resistance."

10 Anzaldúa, *Borderlands / La Frontera*, 71. A key move in Anzaldúa's creative process is the appeal to Aztec myths—for example, her theorization of the Coyolxauhqui imperative, and, as we will see, the Coatlicue state. This mythico-relational creation shares some characteristics with what Saidiya Hartman names "critical fabulation," or the use of the historical record as well as critical fictional narrative to retell the histories of Black subjects condemned to oblivion within hegemonic, colonial histories. See Hartman, "Venus in Two Acts," 11. While Anzaldúa centers mythologies, she is also engaging in creating stories about her experience (autohistorias) aimed at telling, if not an impossible story, a story that differs from dominant narratives of the type of self that she is supposed to be. To tell her story (as well as that of Chicanas like her) she goes beyond the traditional historical record.

11 Quashie, *Black Aliveness*.

12 As noted in chapter 1, according to Quashie, "Quiet . . . is a metaphor for the full range of one's inner life—one's desires, ambitions, hungers, vulnerabilities, fears. The inner life is not apolitical or without social value, but neither is it determined entirely by publicness." Quashie, *The Sovereignty of Quiet*, 6.

13 Quashie, *Black Aliveness*, 58.

14 Anzaldúa, *Light in the Dark*, 35.

15 Al-Saji, "A Phenomenology of Hesitation," 141; Lee, "A Phenomenology of Seeing and Affect in a Polarized Climate," 118; Fielding, *Cultivating Perception through Artworks*, 111.

16 Anzaldúa, *Borderlands / La Frontera*, 38.

17 Anzaldúa, *Borderlands / La Frontera*, 38.

18 Anzaldúa, *Borderlands / La Frontera*, 2.

19 Anzaldúa, *Borderlands / La Frontera*, 20, 50, preface. For a key analysis inspired by Laura Pérez's reading of Anzaldúa's *Borderlands / La Frontera* as an invitation to delve "into the deeper recesses of the margins" (191), see Alarcón, "Anzaldúan Textualities." Alarcón discusses Anzaldúa's internalized alienation as a source of her trauma and wound. Importantly, Alarcón also points to the decolonial aspects of Anzaldúa's text.

20 Kelli D. Zaytoun reads la naguala as anchored in Nahua metaphysics; see Zaytoun, *Shapeshifting Subjects*, 10. As Zaytoun explains, "la naguala" is "the feminine form of 'nagual,' a Nahuatl concept associated with pre-Classic Olmec-inspired depictions of shapeshifting humans or of animal guardians or companions or spirit guides" (10). To my knowledge, Zaytoun's is the only comprehensive analysis of the key role of la naguala in the work of Anzaldúa. While this notion appears explicitly in Anzaldúa's later work, and is crucial for Anzaldúa's account of conocimiento, Zaytoun traces it back to talks and interviews of the 1990s where Anzaldúa first discusses the idea of a "nagual" (14). In Zaytoun's interpretation, la naguala becomes the master concept and practice through which we can understand the Anzaldúan corpus, in particular Anzaldúa's metaphysics of selfhood and subjectivity characterized by shifting and anchored in Nahua metaphysics. I agree about the important role of the naguala in Anzaldúa's work, although we must proceed with caution regarding a neat alignment of this notion with Nahua metaphysics, not only because of the possible problems connected to translating a contemporary view by way of a complex Indigenous metaphysics but also because of the possibility of essentializing Anzaldúa's work by subsuming her complex position into one metaphysical framework.

21 Anzaldúa, *Light in the Dark*, 119.

22 Anzaldúa, *Light in the Dark*, 118.

23 See Keating's introduction to Anzaldúa, *Light in the Dark*, xxvii.

24 The notion of healing is key in Anzaldúa and needs to be understood in light of the complexity of her account of conocimiento. While a commonsense understanding as well as a neoliberal reading and appeal of the term read it as a making free from injury, the term should not be read in this light in the context of Anzaldúa's work. In *Light in the Dark / Luz en lo oscuro*, Anzaldúa describes the Coyolxauhqui imperative as a "healing of the wound" (9) and takes healing as leading to transformation and vice versa (19) but without any resolution (20). She also states that healing narratives are not just therapy but "actually change reality" insofar as they allow us to change our agreements about what is fair, change our perceptions, and choose a different future (21). In my view, in the context of a history of coloniality, there is no such thing as healing as becoming free from injury.

25 Anzaldúa, *Light in the Dark*, 25.

26 Anzaldúa, *Borderlands / La Frontera*, 38.

27 Anzaldúa, *Light in the Dark*, 122.

28 Anzaldúa, *Light in the Dark*, 125.

29 Cf. Ngo, *The Habits of Racism*, 66; Fanon, *Black Skin, White Masks*, 119; and Al-Saji, "Glued to the Image," 487.

30 Anzaldúa, *The Gloria Anzaldúa Reader*, 38.

31 Anzaldúa, *The Gloria Anzaldúa Reader*, 48.

32 Anzaldúa, *The Gloria Anzaldúa Reader*, 145. For a crucial and still relevant critical discussion on the differences between the preferred subject of feminism and the kind of subjectivity elaborated by women of color, see Alarcón, "The Theoretical Subject(s) of *This Bridge Called My Back*."

33 Anzaldúa, *The Gloria Anzaldúa Reader*, 145.

34 Anzaldúa, *Light in the Dark*, 135. Despite her desire and pride about her Chicanidad, Anzaldúa recognizes the constraints and difficulties that arise from social identities, including nationality. Given the vexed history of Chicanidad in the context of the formation of a notion of Aztlán, she does not advocate for a strong sense of the nation. For an innovative analysis that connects Latina feminism, including Anzaldúa's view, and creolization in order to reimagine the notions of the nation and subjectivity, see Sealey, *Creolizing the Nation*, esp. chaps. 3 and 4.

35 Anzaldúa, *Light in the Dark*, 65.

36 Anzaldúa, *Light in the Dark*, 1.

37 That a trauma is relational does not mean that it is not felt in one's very skin and guts. For an important analysis of the role of rupture/crisis in forging a new type of intellectual within different contexts (natural disaster, forced displacement, political transitions, racism, and colonialism) that is attuned to the entwinement of the embodied, affect, the aesthetic, and sociopolitical events, see Sierra-Rivera, *Affective Intellectuals and the Space of Catastrophe*.

38 A difficult question that we need to consider is whether there is life in which there are so many ruptures and arrebatos that these become the norm, thus lessening the possibility that the arrebato may lead to movements of conocimiento. Moreover, we need to ask whether there are traumas so deep that we cannot find a constructive way to deal with them.

39 In *Borderlands / La Frontera*, Anzaldúa says, "Let the wound caused by the serpent be cured by the serpent" (46). Here the process of construction that will eventually lead to transformation happens in the Coatlicue state.

40 See Pitts, *Nos/Otras*, for a nuanced reading of the notion of "nepantla" that encompasses different interpretations of the term that extends its meaning beyond a spatial mode of being in between. Pitts writes, "Her [Anzaldúa's] framing of nepantla includes both the sense of 'woundedness' from the León-Portilla reading and a sense of novelty or 'tertium quiddities' that arises from being *no one* particular identity positionality alone, but rather *simultaneously all* or *more than* any one specific racialized and gendered/sexualized positionality" (44).

41 Pitts, *Nos/Otras*, 41–44.

42 Zaytoun, *Shapeshifting Subjects*, 37.

43 Anzaldúa, *Light in the Dark*, 36.

44 Zaytoun, *Shapeshifting Subjects*, chap. 1.

45 Coatlicue in Nahuatl means "Snakes-her-skirt." She is the Aztec mother-earth goddess, goddess of fertility, life, and death.

46 Anzaldúa, *Borderlands / La Frontera*, 42. The quotation that forms part of the subhead is from the same source (48).

47 Anzaldúa, *Borderlands / La Frontera*, 48, 45–46.

48 Anzaldúa, *Borderlands / La Frontera*, 25.

49 Anzaldúa, *Borderlands / La Frontera*, 49.

50 Anzaldúa, *Borderlands / La Frontera*, 46.

51 Lugones, "From within Germinative Stasis," 95. In her first interpretation of *Borderlands / La Frontera*, "On *Borderlands / La Frontera*: An Interpretative Essay," Lugones fails to see the resistant political and social potential of Anzaldúa's work and reads Anzaldúa as presenting an overly subjective and psychological account of "solitary rebellion" (36).

52 Anzaldúa, *Light in the Dark*, 128–31.

53 There are various critical discussions of Anzaldúa's appeal to the notion of mestizaje. One of the most damning is an early critique by María Josefina Saldaña-Portillo, "Who's the Indian in Aztlán?" For discussions of problematic issues regarding Anzaldúa's engagement with the notion of mestizaje and use of Indigenous mythology, see Ortega, *In-Between*, 29–39; Pitts, *Nos/Otras*, 130–40; and Zaytoun, *Shapeshifting Subjects*, 49–53. For a discussion of the problematic connection between the notion of

Latinidad and mestizaje, see Flores, "Latinidad Is Cancelled," 68–75. See also *Aztlán*'s special issue (Saldaña-Portillo, "Dossier: Revisiting Mestizaje Twenty Years Later") on mestizaje after twenty years of the influential essay by Saldaña-Portillo, "Who's the Indian in Aztlán?"; and Saldaña-Portillo and Trujillo, "Introduction: What Does Mestizaje Name?" See also Delgadillo, "Enacting Decoloniality," for a discussion of how Latin American contexts have been imposed on Anzaldúa's use of mestizaje.

54 See Pitts, *Nos/Otras*, for a rich and important reading of *nos/otras*, one of Anzaldúa's later terms of identification. Pitts astutely theorizes *nos/otras* in terms of its possibilities of coalitions across difference while at the same time recognizing the impediments to such coalition. They read *nos/otras* as a "way of describing conflicting patterns of group identification, and experiential belonging that create deep rifts among differing political projects" (24).

55 Anzaldúa, *Light in the Dark*, 131.

56 J. M. Martinez, "Culture, Communication, and Latina Feminist Philosophy," 226.

57 For an interesting reading of Martinez's claim about the borderlands prompting an "involuntary suspension," see Grimm, "Linguistic Rupture, Racialization, and Resistance." Grimm explains the difficulties of Martinez's claim but also its importance. She takes Martinez as proposing that the borderlands prompt an "involuntary suspension" of the natural attitude in the sense that it has the potential to bring the unexpected into consciousness (120) and to destabilize "any particular set of theses that structure any *particular* world" (125).

58 Anzaldúa, *Borderlands / La Frontera*, 80.

59 Zaytoun, *Shapeshifting Subjects*, 39.

60 Anzaldúa, *Light in the Dark*, 118–19.

61 Anzaldúa, *Light in the Dark*, 120.

62 Delgadillo, *Spiritual Mestizaje*, 6.

63 "Spirit is live flesh" (my translation). Anzaldúa, *The Gloria Anzaldúa Reader*, 70. In this text, Anzaldúa also says, "Spirit is spirit only if it lives in mass, in flesh" (70).

64 Ngo, *The Habits of Racism*, 39.

65 Anzaldúa, *Light in the Dark*, 135–37. It is interesting here that this idea of a call preceding self-attunement and change away from the normative also appears in traditional existential phenomenological views such as Heidegger's when he describes a call to conscience connected to the possibility of authentic life. Heidegger, *Being and Time*, 314.

66 Anzaldúa, *Light in the Dark*, 137.

67 According to Susan Milbrath, Coyolxauhqui is difficult to translate. However, it is clear that her name incorporates the Nahuatl word for "bells." Milbrath, "Decapitated Lunar Goddesses," 185.

68 Anzaldúa, *Light in the Dark*, 49.

69 Anzaldúa, *Light in the Dark*, 50.

70 Anzaldúa, *The Gloria Anzaldúa Reader*, 279.

71 Anzaldúa, *Light in the Dark*, 98.

72 Rivera Berruz, "Extending into Space," 28.

73 I should add here that what I am calling the "spirit-body" is very much part of the "earth-body" and what Anzaldúa refers to the "bodymindsoul" or human being. They are all intertwined. I add the notion so as to highlight that a spiritual incarnate is key in her account.

74 Anzaldúa, *Light in the Dark*, 108.

75 Anzaldúa, *Light in the Dark*, 102.

76 Anzaldúa, *Light in the Dark*, 143.

77 Anzaldúa, *Borderlands / La Frontera*, 71; Anzaldúa, *Light in the Dark*, 104.

78 AnaLouise Keating explains these terms in the following way:

> AUTOHISTORIA: Anzaldúa coined this term, as well as the term *autohistoria-teoría*, to describe women-of-color interventions into and transformations of traditional western autobiographical forms. Deeply infused with the search for personal and cultural meaning, or what Anzaldúa describes in her post-*Borderlands* writings as "putting Coyolxauhqui together," both autohistoria and autohistoria-teoría are informed by reflective self-awareness employed in the service of social-justice work. Autohistoria focuses on the personal life story but, as the autohistorian tells her own life story, she simultaneously tells the life stories of others.
>
> AUTOHISTORIA-TEORÍA: Theory developed by Anzaldúa to describe a relational form of autobiographical writing that includes both life story and self-reflection on this storytelling process. Writers of autohistoria-teoría blend their cultural and personal biographies with memoir, history, storytelling, myth, and/or other forms of theorizing.

AnaLouise Keating, "Appendix 1: Glossary," in Anzaldúa, *The Gloria Anzaldúa Reader*, 319. For a very interesting analysis of Anzaldúa's writing practice that inspires a discussion of "autohisteoría," a practice blending fiction, story, theory, and autohistoria for the purposes of making a queer Chicana home, see Danielson, "Anzaldúan Autohisteoría."

79 Anzaldúa, *Borderlands / La Frontera*, 71.

80 Anzaldúa, *Light in the Dark*, 28.

81 "With images I conquer my fear, I cross the abysses that I have within me" (my translation). Anzaldúa, *Borderlands / La Frontera*, 71.

82 Anzaldúa, *Light in the Dark*, 100.

83 Anzaldúa, *Borderlands / La Frontera*, 69.

84 Anzaldúa, *Light in the Dark*, 97. Anzaldúa's understanding of the relationship between image and knowledge opens the possibility for an

anticolonial approach to image and imaginaries. For an excellent discussion of the central role of images in the development of knowledge that counters coloniality, see Vallega, "Displacements."

85 Anzaldúa, *Light in the Dark*, 108.

86 Anzaldúa, *Light in the Dark*, 102.

87 Anzaldúa states, "I use the word 'ensueño' as an "illusion and fantasy, as un sueño que se hace realidad, a dream that becomes reality; as a way to bridge the reality of the dream with the reality of the non-dream; and as a type of lucid dreaming." Anzaldúa, *Light in the Dark*, 35. While ensueños are also connected to the overall creative process she is describing, these ensueños are in her view more "willed" and a type of lucid dreaming.

88 Anzaldúa, *Light in the Dark*, 62.

89 Anzaldúa, *Light in the Dark*, 105. For an interesting discussion of "poet-shamanic aesthetics" that engages the important role of imagery in alternative ways of knowing and compares the work of Anzaldúa with that of Wilson Harris, see Otto, "Poet-Shamanic Aesthetics in the Work of Gloria Anzaldúa and Wilson Harris." For an analysis of Anzaldúa's writing in the context of shamanism, see Dahms, "Shamanic Urgency and Two-Way Movement."

90 Anzaldúa, *Light in the Dark*, 36.

91 Anzaldúa, *Light in the Dark*, 36.

92 I read Anzaldúa's notion of self as encompassing a sense of the one and the many. See Ortega, *In-Between*, chap. 1.

93 Anzaldúa, *Light in the Dark*, 142.

94 Anzaldúa, *Light in the Dark*, 148.

95 Anzaldúa, *Light in the Dark*, 148.

96 Anzaldúa, *Light in the Dark*, 153.

97 Anzaldúa, *Light in the Dark*, 151.

98 Anzaldúa, *Light in the Dark*, 153.

99 Anzaldúa, *Light in the Dark*, 154.

100 Anzaldúa, *Light in the Dark*, 153.

101 For a discussion of Anzaldúa's poetics, see Vivancos, *Radical Chicana Poetics*.

102 Anzaldúa, *Light in the Dark*, 157.

103 Anzaldúa, *Light in the Dark*, 157–59.

104 Lorde, *Sister Outsider*, 55.

105 Lorde, *Sister Outsider*, 54.

106 Lorde, *Sister Outsider*, 57.

107 Anzaldúa, *Borderlands / La Frontera*, 73.

108 Anzaldúa, *Borderlands / La Frontera*, 74.

109 Anzaldúa, *Borderlands / La Frontera*, 71.

3. SPILLING HERSELF IN TREES

1 Anzaldúa, *Light in the Dark*, 56.

2 The importance of inner work in Anzaldúa's writing is also recognized by Chela Sandoval in her important text *The Methodology of the Oppressed*, in which she theorizes both the "inner and outer technologies" necessary for those she considers practitioners of differential social movement. Sandoval, *The Methodology of the Oppressed*, 3.

3 Anzaldúa, *Light in the Dark*, 193.

4 Under the title "Chicana Artists: Exploring nepantla, el lugar de la frontera," the essay was reprinted in NACLA *Report on the Americas* (27, no. 1); in Darder and Torres, *The Latino Studies Reader*; and in Anzaldúa, *The Gloria Anzaldúa Reader*.

5 Note that Anzaldúa makes a distinction between borderlands—the actual, material, geographic borders, "the region on both sides of the Texas-Mexico borderland"—and Borderlands, a metaphorical term that encompasses "psychic, sexual, and spiritual Borderlands." Anzaldúa, *Light in the Dark*, 242.

6 Anzaldúa, "Chicana Artists," 164, 165.

7 Anzaldúa, "Chicana Artists," 165.

8 Anzaldúa, "Chicana Artists," 166.

9 In the 2015 version of the article, Anzaldúa mentions Chicana artists Santa Barraza, Yolanda M. López, Marsha Gómez, and Carmen Lomas Garza as well as Chilean artist Liliana Wilson, whom Anzaldúa describes as "caught in a state of nepantla" (*Light in the Dark*, 56). She also mentions those who make "arte de la frontera," such as Malaquís Montoya and Irene Pérez, as border artists creating "counter art" (53–57). The 1998 version includes some of these artists above as well as Chilean-born artist Juan Dávila and Rafael Barajas.

10 Anzaldúa, *Light in the Dark*, 47.

11 Anzaldúa, *Light in the Dark*, 52.

12 While here I note the liberatory potential of border arte, not all border arte carries this potential. Anzaldúa analyzes the liberatory potential of border arte by way of a consideration of the very naming of art as "border art" and of artists as "border artists." She states, "'Chicana' artist, 'border' artist: These adjectives label identities. Labeling affects expectations. A white poet doesn't write 'white' in front of his name, nor is s/he referred to as 'white' by others. . . . Is 'border' artist just another label that strips legitimacy from the artist, signaling that s/he is inferior to the adjective-less artist? Is 'border' a label designating that s/he is capable only of handling ethnic, folk, and regional subjects and art forms?" Anzaldúa, *Light in the Dark*, 59. Anzaldúa answers the question by saying that we will need these labels in order to resist the pressure to assimilate.

For a more sustained engagement with the issue of designating artists by way of their racial and other identities, see Anzaldúa, "To(o) Queer the Writer." For an account positing a vision of liberatory philosophy anchored in Anzaldúa's view of border arte, see Tuana and Scott, "Border Arte Philosophy."

13 Al-Saji, "A Phenomenology of Hesitation," 141.

14 Importantly, here I am not developing a political aesthetics, a politics of resistance, or a theory of liberation. While there is certainly need for such projects, here I concentrate on finding practices of survival, self-naming, self-transformation at the edges, in the least likely places and to show how Latinx artists are already engaging in these practices through their aesthetic endeavors. I wish to disclose how creative practices allow marginalized selves to survive and navigate hostile worlds but also to redirect, transform, and revise dominant and internalized negative racialized perception.

15 Anzaldúa, *Light in the Dark*, 56.

16 Anzaldúa, *Light in the Dark*, 53.

17 Zaytoun, *Shapeshifting Subjects*, chap. 2.

18 Anzaldúa, *Light in the Dark*, 48–49.

19 Anzaldúa, *Light in the Dark*, xxi. As we will see, Anzaldúa's understanding of wholeness entails not a finished, complete self but a self that is in process.

20 Anzaldúa, *Light in the Dark*, 48.

21 Anzaldúa, *Light in the Dark*, 49–50.

22 The museum catalogue points out that the skeleton with a greenstone in the jaw is a puma rather than a jaguar. Day, *Aztec*, 71. It is not clear whether Anzaldúa assumed it was a jaguar given the importance of this animal for the Aztecs or whether it was mislabeled.

23 Anzaldúa, *Light in the Dark*, 55.

24 Anzaldúa quoted in Zaytoun, *Shapeshifting Subjects*, 55.

25 When thinking about creative production originating in nepantla, I am led to think of Mary Louise Pratt's understanding of the arts of the contact zone. She defines a "contact zone" as referring to "social spaces where cultures meet, clash, and grapple with each other, often in contexts of highly asymmetrical relations of power, such as colonialism, slavery, or their aftermaths as they are lived out in many parts of the world today." Pratt, "Arts of the Contact Zone," 34. She further states, "Autoethnography, transculturation, critique, collaboration, bilingualism, mediation, parody, denunciation, imaginary dialogue, vernacular expression—these are some of the literate arts of the contact zone. Miscomprehension, incomprehension, dead letters, unread masterpieces, absolute heterogeneity of meaning—these are some of the perils of writing in the contact zone" (37). While for Pratt contact zones are particular spatialities holding

difficult and violent encounters between different cultures, the arts of the contact zone constitute creative, although difficult, intertwinings. I take nepantla as a contact zone that is both material and imaginary where creative praxis holds the possibility of intertwining not just different cultures but also different ways of being and sensing.

26 The museum is particularly important given that in this space the way that objects "address" humans and vice versa is constrained. Yet even within this space, Anzaldúa addresses objects and they address her in transformative ways.

27 Zaytoun points out that my phenomenological reading of Anzaldúa does not do enough to capture the shapeshifting activity that happens through la naguala given that I confine my discussion of la naguala to la facultad. Doing so provides narrow possibilities in terms of shifting and coalitions with beings beyond the human. Zaytoun, *Shapeshifting Subjects*, 18–19. I agree with Zaytoun that the role of la naguala is well beyond what I describe in my reading of Anzaldúa in *In-Between*. I welcome a deeper discussion of the role of la naguala in Anzaldúa's corpus, especially beyond *Borderlands / La Frontera*. As I ponder about this issue with the help of Zaytoun's detailed new work, I wonder about the ontological claims regarding shapeshifting in Anzaldúa's work. For Zaytoun, shapeshifting is not merely metaphoric or symbolic but ontological and connected to a Nahua metaphysics informed by a process of becoming (a process metaphysics guided by teotl, a "self-generating energy-in-motion"). Zaytoun, *Shapeshifting Subjects*, 32. This is a difficult issue in Anzaldúa's writings, as she describes shapeshifting in different ways. She says that it is a process that happens in the imagination: "This is why shamanism is so intriguing to people and so intriguing to me, because you can move yourself through your imagination, through your soul. Your soul is actually there." Anzaldúa, *Interviews/Entrevistas*, 159. Yet when asked by AnaLouise Keating whether she believed "that people can literally transform into other shapes—into animals for example," Anzaldúa discusses the importance of shamanism in other cultures and states: "It goes back to the three bodies which I think people have. This other body, the second, or the third body, can leave my physical body and become a jaguar. . . . I don't think that my hands can become flesh-and-blood claw and my mouth a jaguar mouth. I can't do it in my flesh-and-blood but in my other body, I can. I also think that you can lose that body, just like people can misplace their souls. It can stay in the jaguar reality, in the jaguar form" (283–84). In the discussion, one of these three bodies is the soul. She finishes her comment by going back to the idea of shifting as happening through the imaginal but points to the future possibility of literally transforming her body into a jaguar (285). Whether Anzaldúa's understanding of shamanic experiences are metaphorical, connected to

the imaginal, actual transformations of the body, connected to the self's other bodies, including the soul, or thoroughly explainable by Nahua metaphysics is a difficult question, especially given that she is appealing to various spiritual, epistemological, and psychological views throughout her work.

28 In chapter 1 of *The Cultural Promise of the Aesthetic*, "The Aesthetic, the Public, and the Promise of Culture," Roelofs offers a beautiful reading of Neruda's odes (also beautiful) that illustrates her multimodal vision of an aesthetic suffused with promises/threats, modes of address, and aesthetic relationality. In the poems she finds a series of quotidian intersubjective connections that open up a number of patterns of address between people and objects. Such a web of interconnectedness points to shared culture and hence to the cultural promise of the aesthetic. Yet it is also flawed. After all, we need to consider not just the objects but who makes them, who gets to have them; not all of us will get a spoon and get to sit at the table. Lovingly, Roelofs describes the beauty with which in few verses Neruda can remind us of the possibility of shedding light where once there was darkness and of, as Neruda puts it, "a total mobilization of spoons," of food for all (14). Nevertheless, Roelofs also recognizes the arrogance of the poet who may have understood himself as the voice of the people, as the universal voice, when, in reality, he may be merely uplifting his own voice. For our purposes, it is important to see how Anzaldúa's very enactment of border arte and her theory of border arte are caught in a web of relations and webs of address that ultimately point to promises for marginalized multiplicitous selves but also the threats that may always lurk in the limen for those who are atravesados.

29 Roelofs, *Arts of Address*. In this text Roelofs provides an extensive explanation of the meaning of address and the different ways it informs our everyday as well as aesthetic experiences.

30 Roelofs, *Arts of Address*, 7.

31 Roelofs, *Arts of Address*, 6.

32 As Roelofs states, "In designing my mode of address to my material, I have attempted to nourish our being alive to language in the world." Roelofs, *Arts of Address*, 250. Roelofs's understanding of the importance of the aesthetic for being alive to language and the world informs my view and Quashie's notion of aliveness. Quashie, *Black Aliveness*, 57.

33 In *Arts of Address*, Roelofs states that modes of address may be linguistic or nonlinguistic (i.e., looking, reading, and voting). There are five interrelated constitutive elements of modes of address: norms (what counts as appropriate, efficacious, or even legible modes of address—i.e., criteria and codes governing visual display, verbal expression, deliberate processes) (152, 7); forms (linguistic and nonlinguistic addresses that include all sense modalities) (147); structures (distinctive sets of institutionalized

norms of address—e.g., cinemas, school, electorates) (180, 7); scripts (particular ways that modes of address are deployed; i.e., comportment upon entering a classroom or a voting booth) (7); and scenes (different scenarios of particular modes of address). According to Roelofs, norms and forms of address govern scenes and scripts of address within structures (151). Ultimately, all of our interactions are involved in different modes of address leading to multiple relations, directions, and orientations. Here I take it that within this expansive web of relationalities that is created by address there is room for alternative modes that do not conform to Western scripts.

34 Anzaldúa, *Light in the Dark*, 50.

35 Anzaldúa, *Light in the Dark*, 64.

36 Anzaldúa, *Light in the Dark*, 60.

37 Anzaldúa, *Light in the Dark*, 61.

38 Anzaldúa, *Light in the Dark*, 63.

39 Anzaldúa, *Light in the Dark*, 63. For an important theorization of *nos/otras* that discusses possibilities of coalitions across differences in the context of multiplicitous agency, see Pitts, *Nos/Otras*. Pitts adroitly shows how Anzaldúa's account of agency in a plural register rejects agential models reliant on insularity, isolationism, individualism, and imperialism.

40 Anzaldúa, *Light in the Dark*, 63.

41 See my discussion of Anzaldúa's complex notion of subjectivity, one that encompasses a mestizaje of multiplicity and oneness. Ortega, *In-Between*, chap. 1.

42 We can say that the operations of border arte allow for the "distribution of the sensible." See Rancière, *The Politics of Aesthetics*. After parceling out the history of art into three regimes (the ethical, the representative, and the aesthetic), Jacques Rancière claims that the distribution of the sensible becomes possible during the dissensus that takes place in the aesthetic regime. David Lloyd, however, faults Rancière for providing a problematic reinscription of a hegemonic aesthetic regime that made possible the modern racial regime. For Lloyd, representation does not belong to an earlier aesthetic regime, as it does for Rancière, and is not associated only with mimesis. Rather, Lloyd argues that racial judgments have a constitutive role in aesthetic theory since its inception in the late eighteenth century, aesthetics thus instituting a racial regime of representation that regulates discourses of the human informing modernity. Lloyd, *Under Representation*, 9, 38–43.

43 I take it that not all instances of border arte may lead to moments of self-forging, self-transformation, and resistance, as there are differences in degree and intention in terms of the relational, communal aspects of the practice. All of them, however, encompass a perceptual and thus affective attunement to worlds.

44 Anzaldúa, *Borderlands / La Frontera*, 73.

45 Anzaldúa, *Borderlands / La Frontera*, 73.

46 Anzaldúa, *Borderlands / La Frontera*, 75.

47 While here I connect autoarte to Anzaldúa's aesthetics, it may also be theorized beyond this framework. I thus invite the reader to see how autoarte is linked beyond the aesthetic realm.

48 Anzaldúa, *Borderlands / La Frontera*, preface.

49 Anzaldúa, *Borderlands / La Frontera*, 60, 70.

50 Anzaldúa, *Borderlands / La Frontera*, 67.

51 Anzaldúa, *Light in the Dark*, 86, 153–54.

52 Anzaldúa, *Light in the Dark*, 154.

53 Anzaldúa, *Light in the Dark*, 153.

54 With Amber Jamilla Musser, I wish to think of the brown jouissance that is possible within the life of in-betweenness, the excess that is not always captured but that is there, hungry, latent, ready to come out. Musser analyzes the type of hunger associated with abjected Black and brown flesh and says that it is "an embodied hunger that takes joy and pain in this gesture of radical openness toward otherness." Musser, *Sensual Excess*, 5. This description very much captures Anzaldúa and that "precocious girl-child" that is *Borderlands / La Frontera*. Anzaldúa, *Borderlands / La Frontera*, 66.

55 For a discussion of *autopoiesis* in the context of biological systems theory, see Maturana and Varela, "Autopoiesis and Cognition." Importantly, Sylvia Wynter rethinks the notion of *autopoiesis* in the context of her discussion of the genres of being human. This notion allows her to explain how stories have helped our species "autopoetically to institute itself as a now symbolically encoded mode of living." Wynter, "The Ceremony Found," 217. Consequently, for Wynter stories are as much what makes us human as biological processes. My notion of autoarte may be read by some as similar to Wynter's thinking on the autopoetic in the sense that stories become vital for the creation of the self. However, my account of autoarte does not have the wider aim of theorizing the development of the human species and does not make metaphysical claims regarding cognitive and aesthetic closure. Wynter, "The Ceremony Found," 221.

56 Quashie, *The Sovereignty of Quiet*, 22.

57 Quashie, *The Sovereignty of Quiet*, 22.

58 I define *hometactics* as "practices that allow for a sense of familiarity with and a particular sense of 'belonging' to a place, space, group, or world while avoiding the restrictive, exclusive elements that a notion of belonging might carry with it." Ortega, *In-Between*, 194.

59 Another possible complication in connection to the appeal to tactics is that given their mobile nature, they can easily be appropriated. Nonetheless, to think of autoarte in terms of tactics of self-making, naming, and

transformation does not mean that this practice is one that can be easily taken up or exploited. My point is precisely to show that it is an intimate, subjective practice that is dependent on a self's deep perceptual attunement and a self's experience as she navigates different environments. In addition, as we will see, it is also a process that is not always intentional or agential.

60 Although, as noted, it is difficult to appropriate tactics, we unfortunately must think of the ways the creations that arise through autoarte can become public; whether stories or photographs, they may be co-opted by dominant individuals or normative artistic structures. The work of Anzaldúa is a case in point here, as it is sometimes taken up without regard to its depth, context, and connection to Chicana thought, or without attention to her many other writings.

61 Anzaldúa, *Light in the Dark*, 56.

62 While writing her autohistorias and autohistoria-teorías, Anzaldúa is guided by multiple perceptions and intuitions, both conscious and unconscious, as well as multiple relationalities—yet she ultimately translates these processes into writing.

63 Roelofs, *The Cultural Promise of the Aesthetic*, 25.

64 Venegas, "Take Me to the River," 16.

65 For details about Aguilar's life, see Venegas, "Take Me to the River."

66 Lorde, *Sister Outsider*, 54.

67 Sandoval, *The Methodology of the Oppressed*, 4.

68 Sandoval calls for technologies that provide "the skills necessary for accomplishing sign reading across cultures; identifying and consciously constructing ideology; de-coding languages of resistance and/or domination; and for writing and speaking a neorhetoric of love in the postmodern world." Sandoval, *The Methodology of the Oppressed*, 3. Love has a crucial role in Latina/x feminisms, especially in the writings of Sandoval, Anzaldúa, and Laura Pérez. For a recent Chicana theorization of the decolonial in light of the power of the spiritual and of love, see L. E. Pérez, *Eros Ideologies*.

69 Sandoval, *The Methodology of the Oppressed*, 29.

70 Sandoval, *The Methodology of the Oppressed*, 67–79.

71 Sandoval, *The Methodology of the Oppressed*, 7.

72 Sandoval, *The Methodology of the Oppressed*, 11. In this desire to find new ways of imagining, Sandoval has always had an interest in artistic forms. See her early article "Video Production, Liberation Aesthetics, and U.S. Third World Feminist Criticism" and her coauthored work on artivism: Sandoval and Latorre, "Chicana/o Artivism."

73 Sandoval, *The Methodology of the Oppressed*, 4.

74 Here we can think of Lugones's notion of *tantear*, feeling one's way through a situation in terms of perceptual possibilities. As Lugones

states, "The 'pilgrimage' that the title of the book calls forth moves through different levels of liberatory work in company forged through a practice of tantear for meaning, for the limits of possibility; putting our hands to our ears to hear better, to hear the meaning in the enclosures and openings of our praxis." Lugones, *Pilgrimages/Peregrinajes*, 1.

75 Sandoval, *The Methodology of the Oppressed*, 11.

76 Notably, Aguilar's work was part of the 1990 exhibition *Image and Identity: Recent Chicana Art from La Reina del Pueblo de Los Angeles de la Porciúncala* at the Laband Art Gallery of Loyola Marymount University, curated by Sybil Venegas. Karen Mary Davalos notes the importance of this exhibition as it aimed at repairing the gender imbalance from previous exhibitions of Chicano art. See Davalos, *Chicana/o Remix*, 34–35. In this important text, in which Davalos provides nuanced readings of Chicana/o art in Los Angeles since 1963, Davalos opens room for a rethinking and reframing of Chicana/o art that deviates from standard understandings of this movement that do not reflect its complexity and multiplicity. For another important text that opens up discussion on Latinx visuality, in this case on photography, see Ferrer, *Latinx Photography in the United States*. Ferrer reads Aguilar's later work as "a political response to the tradition of modernist nude photography, dominated by the objectifying male gaze" (80). For a discussion that situates Aguilar's self-portraiture within a Western fine art context and compares her photographs to traditional Western depictions of the female reclining nude, see Villaseñor Black, "Reflections on Laura Aguilar."

77 Aguilar's comment is reminiscent of Anzaldúa's in her essay "To(o) Queer the Writer—Loca, escritora y chicana": "For me the term lesbian es un problema. As a working-class Chicana mestiza—a composite being, amalgama de culturas y de lenguas—a woman who loves women, 'lesbian' is a cerebral word, white and middle class" (163). In this text Anzaldúa states that she wishes to choose what to name herself and is uncomfortable with the very process of naming as it might lead to fragmentation and exclusion (166).

78 Ortega, "Queer Autoarte." In this work I analyze Zenil's ex-votos in order to show how his practice allows him to self-define and to defy colonialist modes of perception and understanding. In this piece I connect queer autoarte to a Sandovalian-inspired account of "differential aesthesis of the limen." Since writing this piece I have decided to return to the use of the term *aesthetic*, as I explain in the introduction.

79 A project of using creative practices to put oneself and one's marginalized group in the map answers to a longing to find a visual history of one's group. I discuss this longing in "Cámara Queer."

80 See Estrella, "The *Plush Pony* Series."

81 Estrella, "The *Plush Pony* Series," 57.

82 Estrella, "The *Plush Pony* Series," 57.

83 Estrella, "The *Plush Pony* Series," 61.

84 Estrella, "The *Plush Pony* Series," 57.

85 Estrella, "The *Plush Pony* Series," 61.

86 Gómez-Barris, "The Plush View," 395.

87 Anzaldúa, *Borderlands / La Frontera*, 74.

88 Given my view of the photograph as carnal, the photograph can be understood as a relational surface, a skin of light. For an interesting analysis of another medium, intercultural cinema, understood in terms of it being able to generate multisensory experience, as skin does, see Marks, *The Skin of the Film*. For an early theory of embodied film spectatorship, see Sobchack, *The Address of the Eye*.

89 Zuniga, "Daring to Be More Honest," 67.

90 Epstein, *Laura Aguilar*, 115.

91 Sandoval, *The Methodology of the Oppressed*, 35.

92 Lugones, "From within Germinative Stasis," 94.

93 Lugones, "On *Borderlands / La Frontera*," 36.

94 Lugones, *Pilgrimages/Peregrinajes*, 29. Omar Rivera, in "Stillness, Aesthesis, Resistance," recognizes the importance of stillness in the context of possibilities of resistance.

95 Anzaldúa, *Borderlands / La Frontera*, 45.

96 In her important analysis of place in Chicana photography, Ann Marie Leimer reads Aguilar's later series as showing the fusion of Aguilar and the landscape and the transformation of space to place, which points to intimacy with a geographic location. See Leimer, "Chicana Photography," 28, 31. According to Macarena Gómez-Barris, this intimacy needs to be understood in a historically situated context. As Gómez-Barris explains, Aguilar's "self-portraits are indeed bound by the specificities of American colonial history, the Indigenous relation to geography, and mestizaje. By introducing her body into the landscape, Aguilar forces the viewer to consider the specific histories of violence of American colonization." Gómez-Barris, "Mestiza Cultural Memory," 83.

97 "Becoming-with" entails a change or alteration, a becoming other through relations and communications with others, even when not sharing the same social identity. Ortega, *In-Between*, 168.

98 Sandoval, *The Methodology of the Oppressed*, 6.

99 See Roelofs, *Arts of Address*, 181–84, for a wonderful analysis of how Barthes's account of playful address grounds aesthetic desire. Through her multilayered theory of address, Roelofs explains how various elements of address within Barthes's text and the readers of his text are involved in a sensuous encounter with his writing. As she states, "His notions of the intertext, the stadium, and the punctum locate the pleasure of the text in forever-morphing webs of address that enable the reader to

enjoy intermittently the allegedly self-affirming pleasures of culture, taste, and language, and, in countervailing movements, to disrupt her position in relation to language, and culture more broadly" (183). An important point that Roelofs makes is how the "vulnerability of the touch of the punctum" allows for desire that is uncontrollable and unpredictable.

100 One of the most interesting and perhaps controversial aspects of Sandoval's analysis is her claim that European theorists such Barthes, Gilles Deleuze, and Michel Foucault; American thinkers such as Fredric Jameson and Hayden White; and those she calls "decolonial thinkers," such as Gloria Anzaldúa, Audre Lorde, Frantz Fanon, Aimé Césaire, Merlee Woo, Leslie Marmon Silko, and others, are "aligned." As Sandoval states, "A central argument of this book is that the primary impulses and strains of critical theory and interdisciplinary thought that emerged in the twentieth century are the result of transformative effects of oppressed speech upon dominant forms of perception—that the new modes of critical theory and philosophy, the new modes of reading and analysis that have emerged during the US post–World War II period, are fundamentally linked to the voices of subordinated peoples." Sandoval, *The Methodology of the Oppressed*, 7.

101 In Sandoval's view these forms of oppositional ideologies were used by all kinds of liberation movements in their resistance to capitalism; they constitute "a topography of consciousness in opposition." See Sandoval, *The Methodology of the Oppressed*, 54–57, for a description of each ideology.

102 Sandoval, *The Methodology of the Oppressed*, 58.

103 Sandoval, *The Methodology of the Oppressed*, 183, 61.

104 Sandoval, *The Methodology of the Oppressed*, 63.

105 Sandoval, *The Methodology of the Oppressed*, 95.

106 Sandoval, *The Methodology of the Oppressed*, 95.

107 Anzaldúa, *Borderlands / La Frontera*, 75.

108 Sandoval, *The Methodology of the Oppressed*, 96.

109 Sandoval, *The Methodology of the Oppressed*, 141.

110 Sandoval, *The Methodology of the Oppressed* (quoting Barthes), 141.

4. SORROW, AESTHETIC UNSETTLEMENT, AND SONIC RUPTURE IN THE MEXICO-US BORDERLANDS

1 Anzaldúa, *Borderlands / La Frontera*, 2. The US Customs and Border Protection (CBP) reported a total of 181,059 people apprehended by the Border Patrol in August 2023, a 36 percent increase over July 2023. While previously, those crossing were mostly from Mexico and the Northern Triangle (El Salvador, Guatemala, and Honduras), in 2022 there was an increase from countries such as Colombia, Cuba, Nicaragua, Peru, and

Venezuela. See Gramlich, "Migrant Encounters at the U.S.-Mexico Border." As we will see in the next chapters, migrants are not only crossing on their own or with the help of a coyote, someone who helps to smuggle migrants into the United States, but they have also resorted to moving together in large caravans in a flow of bodies of color trekking to the Mexico-US border. While here I concentrate on crossings into the United States, we cannot forget the countless number of refugees traversing land and sea in order to reach European shores. For an insightful analysis of the way a "refugee crisis" was constructed by hegemonic nationalist and capitalist entities as well as how such a crisis has been spectacularized via the photograph, see Carastathis and Tsilimpounidi, *Reproducing Refugees.*

2 Anzaldúa, *Light in the Dark*, 132.

3 Hartman, "Venus in Two Acts," 13; Sharpe, *In the Wake*, 13, 17.

4 According to Lorgia García Peña, *vaivén* (the coming and going of migrant existence) and El Nié (neither here nor there) characterize a liminal state: not the border that the subject inhabits (as in Anzaldúa's borderlands) but "the body that carries the violent borders that deter them from entering the nation, from access to full citizenship and from public, cultural, historical, and political representation." García Peña, *The Borders of Dominicanidad*, 4. She uses the term *vaivén* to theorize the multiple movements of Black Latinidad, the comings and goings to and from hegemonic notions of belonging to challenges of the social order (20).

5 Inspired by W. E. B. Du Bois, Muñoz theorizes feeling brown as feeling like a problem. It entails a conceptualization of Latinidad away from the notion of identity. As we will see in more detail in the next chapter, it is a structure of feeling, a manera de ser (a way of being). Muñoz, *The Sense of Brown*, 38.

6 Walker, *After the Deluge.*

7 For a discussion of how Mexican migrants were racialized into "illegality" in the early twentieth century in the United States, see Flores, *Deportable and Disposable*. For an analysis of the reproduction of heteronormativity by United States immigration controls and the production of the "illegality" of queer and trans migrants, see Luibhéid, "Treated Neither with Respect nor with Dignity." For a discussion of the term *illegal* in the context of Latino/a immigration, see Rubio, "Undocumented, Not Illegal." Immigration reformers consider the term racist and dehumanizing. In 2021, President Joe Biden's administration banned the use of *illegal alien* to describe undocumented migrants. See Rose, "Immigration Agencies Ordered Not to Use Term 'Illegal Alien.'" For a most interesting discussion of the production of an "illegal imaginary" informed by a deportation regime that calls for aesthetic practices not sanctioned

by legality, see Armando García, "Disposable Subjects." Kency Cornejo, in "Visual Counter Narratives," discusses the importance of the creation of an imaginary of Central American criminality, and the visual tactics and aesthetics of violence used to deem certain Central American bodies as disposable. Importantly, Cornejo explains how Central American artists such as Regina José Galindo, Danny Zavaleta, Simón Vega, Ronald Morán, and Gabriel Galeano counter this criminalization of Central Americans.

8 Nash, *The Black Body in Ecstasy*, 25.

9 See París Pombo, "Violence at the US-Mexico Border"; Rosenberg, Cooke, and Trotta, "The Border's Toll"; and the website for WOLA (Washington Office on Advocacy for Human Rights in the Americas), https://www.wola.org/.

10 See Beltrán, *Cruelty as Citizenship*. For an analysis of racialization of Mexicans in the context of US immigration and Mexican society, see S. Zamora, *Racial Baggage*.

11 For an interesting and important elaboration of the body as an "acoustic box" receptive to different echoes that open the possibility for nondialogical decolonial communication, see Veronelli, "A Coalitional Approach to Theorizing Decolonial Communication."

12 For information on migrant deaths in southern Arizona, see the report produced by the University of Arizona Binational Migration Institute in collaboration with the Pima County Office of the Medical Examiner: D. E. Martínez et al., "Migrant Deaths in Southern Arizona." For information on the continuing humanitarian crisis at the border, see Miroff, "Arrests along US-Mexico Border Top 2 Million a Year"; and Rubio-Goldsmith et al., *Migrant Deaths in the Arizona Desert*. For a discussion of the border zone as a space of exception and a scathing critique of the US government's policy of "Prevention through Deterrence" that is seen as complicit in the death of thousands of border crossers, see De León, *The Land of Open Graves*. For a philosophical discussion on immigration that includes a discussion of this prevention through deterrence policy, see Mendoza, *The Moral and Political Philosophy of Immigration*. For a key analysis that considers the ecological impact of the Trump Wall through an analysis of "border thinking," see Wright, "Border Thinking, Borderland Diversity, and Trump's Wall." See also Sundberg, "Diabolic Caminos in the Desert and Cat Fights on the Río," for an analysis of the political ecology of US border security. For a promising analysis that rejects a colonial, imperialist imaginary of the Great Wall and calls for a "care-ful geopolitics" of the border, see Velez, "Towards a 'Care-ful Geopolitics' of La Frontera in the Era of Trump." For an important analysis that discusses a most-needed coalition between LGBT politics and migration politics, see Chávez, *Queer Migration Politics*. For recent analyses that take a

phenomenological approach to undocumented life and thus go beyond legal understanding of those who are undocumented, see Reed-Sandoval, *Socially Undocumented*; and Sánchez, "Towards a Phenomenology of Undocumented Immigrant Reason." See also Urrea, *By the Lake of Sleeping Children* and *The Devil's Highway*, for deeply influential narratives on borders and border crossing. For an informative documentary engaging the situation at the Mexico-US border and the reasons that have led to the continuing immigration crisis, see De La Torre, *Trails of Hope and Terror*.

13 Omi and Winant, *Racial Formation in the U.S.*, 56.

14 Frankowski, *The Post-racial Limits of Memorialization*, 55.

15 Muñoz, *The Sense of Brown*, 121.

16 See Hartman, *Scenes of Subjection* and *Lose Your Mother*; and Sharpe, *In the Wake*.

17 There are various ways to think about invisibility in the context of Black life. Paul C. Taylor explains four main varieties of Black invisibility: presence (the white gaze completely disregards Black bodies even when they are present); personhood (Black subjects are seen as stereotypes and stock figures); perspectives (the multiplicity and heterogeneity of Black perspectives are denied); and plurality (intraracial diversity is obscured). Taylor, *Black Is Beautiful*, 34, explicitly discusses Black invisibility as a "matter of multi-level racial disregard."

18 A key point to remember is that the numerous South-to-North migrations, specifically migrations from Mexico and Central America, are a result of complex historical and economic factors prompted by various US interventions—political, military, and economic—that have had atrocious consequences for these areas and thus have contributed to the waves of migrations to the North. For an important discussion of how US involvement in Central America has led to instability, violence, poverty, and US domination in the area, see LaFeber, *Inevitable Revolutions*. For a discussion of Central American migration to Mexico and the United States as a result of political and economic unrest in the 1980s and 1990s, see M. C. García, *Seeking Refuge*. For information on the Central American refugee crisis, see the American Immigration Council's report on the issue: Hiskey et al., "Understanding the Central American Refugee Crisis." For a historical account of the Mexico-US border, see St. John, *Line in the Sand*. For a narrative of asylum that includes first-person perspectives, see Truax, *We Built the Wall*. For understanding the impact of NAFTA (North American Free Trade Agreement) on various facets of the lives of Mexicans, including migration practices to the United States, see Gálvez, *Eating NAFTA*. For a particularly interesting analysis of the invisibility of Central American refugees in the United States as a "strategic non-identity" partially connected to Central Americans' subordination to Mexico, see Arias, "Central American-Americans."

19 For a particularly influential critical account of US interventions in Central America, see Chomsky, *Turning the Tide.*
20 Campt, *Listening to Images,* 5.
21 Campt, *Listening to Images,* 31.
22 Campt, *Listening to Images,* 31.
23 Campt, *Listening to Images,* 32.
24 Campt, *Listening to Images,* 32.
25 One of the most powerful aspects of Campt's analysis is her being moved by her father's quiet hum during the night of her mother's funeral. Her father hummed to the sound of her mother's favorite Roberta Flack song. As Campt states in *Listening to Images,* "A hum can be mournful; it can be presence in absence or can take the form of a gritty moan in the foreground or a soothing massage in the background" (4). This experience leads Campt to discover the "affects of quiet" (4).
26 An important point to consider here is whether with the aid of these objects border crossers can be identified. Should there be a sustained effort to identify them in order to mourn them properly? This is a difficult question, as finding their names may allow families to stop waiting for their loved ones and to mourn them, but it may also focus on identification without a proper acknowledgment of the reasons that led them to their deadly crossings in the first place. See Edkins, "Missing Migrants and the Politics of Naming," 366.
27 Frankowski, *The Post-racial Limits of Memorialization,* 54.
28 Du Bois, *The Souls of Black Folk,* 253.
29 Frankowski, *The Post-racial Limits of Memorialization,* chap. 1.
30 Frankowski, *The Post-racial Limits of Memorialization,* 55.
31 Consider Mark Lilla's *The Once and Future Liberal,* which provides a simplistic understanding of identity politics as a fixation on diversity and a pathway to group essentialism and nationalism. Nevertheless, a cursory look at feminist theorizing reveals that the notion of identity politics has had an extensive history that includes early, overly nationalistic understandings of identity as well as broader, more inclusive understandings of it. For an analysis of the complexity of the notion of identity and identity politics, see Ortega, *In-Between,* chaps. 1, 5.
32 A. F. Gordon, *Ghostly Matters,* 25. I take this haunting in the sense that Gordon proposes, as having the task of "conjuring" up something that is absent, in this case something that is relegated to forgetting but that needs to be called forth.
33 Cvetkovich, *An Archive of Feelings,* 7. Cvetkovich sees cultural texts as "repositories of feelings and emotions, which are encoded not only in the content of the texts themselves but in the practices that surround their production and reception." In the case of the photographs from the medical examiner, it is their reception that turns them into an archive of sorrow.

34 Barthes, *Camera Lucida*, 80–81. Elspeth H. Brown and Thy Phu read Barthes as developing a "theory of feeling photography." Brown and Phu, *Feeling Photography*, 5. This is an important collection of essays on feeling photography. Margaret Olin, for her part, states that photography is not only a visual practice; it also touches us. See Olin, *Touching Photographs*.

35 Roelofs, *The Cultural Promise of the Aesthetic*, 25.

36 Roelofs, *Arts of Address*, 7. I engaged this line of thought in chapter 2 to explain Anzaldúa's relation to objects in a museum in her narrative "Border Arte." As Roelofs states, "On a daily basis, lines of address link us to diverse entities: tunes, screeches, clicks, beeps, cracks, theories, poems, photographs, colors, bicycles, lakes, brooms, effigies, bells, computers, pillows, skyscrapers, trash." Roelofs, *Arts of Address*, 6.

37 Roelofs, *The Cultural Promise of the Aesthetic*, 2.

38 Roelofs, *The Cultural Promise of the Aesthetic*, 28.

39 Roelofs, *The Cultural Promise of the Aesthetic*, 108.

40 Roelofs, *The Cultural Promise of the Aesthetic*, 108.

41 For an elaboration of the notion of aesthetic injustice as "harm done to someone specifically in her capacity as an aesthetic being," see Dalaqua, "Aesthetic Injustice."

42 This analysis of the relationship of how the aesthetic is thoroughly involved in the sustaining of various modes of ignorance is one of the most important contributions of Roelofs's text. In "Aesthetic Injustice, Practices of Othering, and Ignorance," I engage Roelofs's work in connection to work on epistemic injustice by Kristie Dotson ("A Cautionary Tale") and José Medina ("Epistemic Justice and Epistemologies of Ignorance"). I analyze the aesthetic as a crucial site for the interrogation of practices of ignorance and call for further analyses on aesthetic injustice in connection to these practices of ignorance.

43 Roelofs, *Arts of Address*, 261.

44 A further movement in terms of what José Medina calls beneficial epistemic friction may follow. This friction, in his view, forces one to be self-critical to recognize cognitive gaps, and to compare and contrast one's beliefs that can aid in the construction of what Medina calls a resistant social imagination. J. Medina, *The Epistemology of Resistance*, chap. 6. This notion of resistant social imagination has recently been connected by Medina to an account of "epistemic activism" composed of "practices of interrogation and resistance that unmask, disrupt, and uproot forms of epistemic insensitivity, that is, ways in which our epistemic capacities and activities (perception, memory, understanding, interpretation, imagination, etc.) have become uncritical and numbed to challenge and interrogation." J. Medina, "Resisting Racist Propaganda," 59. Though his account was initially centered on an "epistemic insensitivity," Medina

has modified it to include the notion of “positive emotional friction” or the “emotional attitudes and responses that need to be mobilized to resist oppression such as empathy, grief, and anger.” J. Medina, “Racial Violence, Emotional Friction, and Epistemic Activism,” 26. See also J. Medina, *The Epistemology of Protest*, chap. 6. For another discussion of how imagination (sympathetic, aesthetic, epistemic, and narrative) may aid in the quest for social justice, see Moody-Adams, *Making Space for Justice.*

45 Barthes, *Camera Lucida*, 40.

46 Azoulay, *Civil Imagination*, 222.

47 Azoulay, *Civil Imagination*, 223. Importantly, according to Azoulay, in an encounter with the photograph, there is an underlying agreement, even if tacit. Those who view a photograph taken on the verge of catastrophe form a relation with each other, a kind of citizenry not mediated by a sovereign power, as is usually demanded by contract theory. This is another sense of political community with obligation to help those who are treated unjustly. Azoulay is thus proposing not an “ethics of seeing” but a civil contract of photography. See Azoulay, *The Civil Contract of Photography*, chap. 2.

48 Photographs by Tom Kiefer can be found on his website, https://www.tomkiefer.com/el-sueno-americano.

49 L. E. Pérez, *Chicana Art*, 50.

50 Artist Susan Harbage Page, who has been traveling to the Mexico-US border to photograph objects left by border crossers since 2007, has created what she calls an “anti-archive” of trauma; see https://susanharbagepage.com/u-s-mexico-border-project/. She takes photos of the objects as found in the landscape and then rephotographs them against colorful backdrops. Her claim is that rephotographing these objects away from the landscape and against these colorful backgrounds takes away their status as evidence. I appreciate the gesture she makes to decriminalize the objects. However, similarly to Kiefer’s work, the presentation of the objects against these lively, colorful backgrounds has the effect of turning them into a new type of representational, indexical work that immerses them within the capitalist, specular practices of the art world.

51 *State of Exception*, featuring photographs and objects collected at the border, has traveled to various museums across the country. See Barnes’s website, http://www.richardbarnes.net/projects#/state-of-exception-1/.

52 De León, *The Land of Open Graves.*

53 The website from the Undocumented Migration Project indicates:

> Started in 2009, the Undocumented Migration Project [UMP] is a long-term anthropological analysis of clandestine border crossings between Latin America and the United States directed by UCLA Anthropology Professor Jason De León.

The UMP uses a combination of ethnographic, archaeological, forensic, and visual anthropological approaches to understand various aspects of unauthorized border crossings including the many forms of violence and suffering that characterize the process, the distinct experiences of migrant sub-populations (e.g., women, children, LGBT, non-Mexican nationals), and the evolving material culture associated with crossing.

By combining ethnographic work in Mexico with forensic and archaeological research in Arizona, Mexico, and Honduras, the UMP has improved our knowledge of this highly politicized and poorly understood process and demonstrated how an archaeological approach can provide new insight into a contemporary social phenomenon. The research being conducted by the UMP is interdisciplinary, a fact reflected by the project's diverse theoretical and methodological approaches, the wide range of venues where this work is being published, and the ethnographic-archaeological field schools that have been running in Arizona and Mexico since 2010.

Undocumented Migration Project, "Background."

54 See my commentary on the spectacle of race in the context of Hurricane Katrina in "Othering the Other."

55 It is interesting to consider the sound of photographs. To me this photograph of backpacks has a certain loudness to it, an overtaking of the senses that might actually have the opposite effect than was intended. That is, it might undermine its affective power as the sheer number of the backpacks is transformed into this big mass, losing the specificity of each backpack and thus the connection to particular human beings carrying them.

56 Alexander, *Pedagogies of Crossing*, 278.

57 For a particularly interesting analysis of the Mexico-US border as an "aural border" or "a field of sound" concerned with disclosing the "audio-formation of national and social identities," see Kun, "The Aural Border."

58 Anzaldúa, *Borderlands / La Frontera*, 50.

59 I attended the exhibition at the Samek Art Museum at Bucknell University in March 2019. I thank Richard Rinehart, the museum's director, for gifting me a copy of the exhibition catalogue. The description of the exhibition is as follows: "*Border Cantos* presents a unique collaboration between photographer Richard Misrach and composer Guillermo Galindo. Misrach has been photographing the two-thousand-mile border between the US and Mexico since 2004, with increased focus starting in 2009—resulting in a distinct melding of the artist as documentarian and interpreter. The latest installation in Misrach's ongoing Desert Cantos series, this project includes eight suites of photographs—some made with a large-format camera and others that have been captured with an iPhone. Misrach and Galindo have worked together to create pieces that

both report on and transform the artifacts of migration: water bottles, clothing, backpacks, Border Patrol 'drag tires,' spent shotgun shells, ladders, and sections of the Border Wall itself, which Galindo then fashions into instruments to be performed as unique sound-generating devices." Misrach and Galindo, *Border Cantos*, n.p.

60 See Fielding, *Cultivating Perception through Artworks*, 14.

61 While an interest in sound usually moves toward an understanding of what Jacques Attali names "the political economy of music," and in this exhibition there is much to say about the political economy of Galindo's compositions, here I am interested in discovering the affective modalities of sounds. See Attali, *The Political Economy of Music*.

62 To listen to *Efigie/Effigy* by Galindo, go to https://vimeo.com/154369901. While the experience that I am describing is my own, I invite you to listen to it while looking at some of Misrach's images. Where does the experience take you?

63 Given the coldness of detention centers, immigrants refer to the cages in which they are held as *hieleras* (coolers).

64 See Ortega, *In-Between*, chap. 2, for an account of a multiplicitous self that is being-in and between-worlds.

65 Al-Saji, "Glued to the Image."

66 Anzaldúa, *Light in the Dark*, 41.

67 Anzaldúa, *Light in the Dark*, 120.

68 Anzaldúa, *Light in the Dark*, 69.

69 Anzaldúa, *Light in the Dark*, 131.

70 The experience of disruption, depression, fear, blocks, and chaos that happens in the Coatlicue state is interpreted by Lugones as a necessary state of germination from which communal political possibilities of resistant arise. As noted, Lugones first criticizes Anzaldúa's view for being too individualistic and psychological, but she later realizes the political potential of germination. See Lugones, "On *Borderlands / La Frontera*" and "From within Germinative Stasis."

71 Anzaldúa, *Borderlands / La Frontera*, 46.

72 Anzaldúa, *Light in the Dark*, 120.

73 Anzaldúa, *Light in the Dark*, 117.

74 Anzaldúa, *Light in the Dark*, 127.

75 Anzaldúa, *Light in the Dark*, 126, 128.

76 Voegelin, *Listening to Noise and Silence*. I thank Helen Fielding for introducing me to Voegelin's work.

77 Anzaldúa, *Light in the Dark*, 133.

78 Muñoz, *Disidentifications*, 63.

79 Muñoz, *Disidentifications*, 58, 207.

80 Muñoz, *Disidentifications*, 74.

81 Muñoz, *Disidentifications*, 71.

82 Muñoz, *Disidentifications*, 72.

83 Muñoz, *Disidentifications*, 73.

84 Muñoz, *Disidentifications*, 74.

85 See Cheng, *The Melancholy of Race*; and Eng and Han, *Racial Melancholia, Racial Dissociation*. Taking up a racial identity as a melancholic act is a complex process that cannot be easily reduced to merely positive or merely negative consequences and modes of being. Here I wish to highlight the possibility for melancholia beyond the pathological and to point to its possibility for movements of the otherwise.

86 My position is not far from Judith Butler's analysis of our precarity, grievability, and vulnerability to others in Butler, *Precarious Life*, chaps. 2 and 5. Nevertheless, I am interested in the phenomenological experience of bodies that are more vulnerable than others due to racism and xenophobia.

87 Muñoz, *Cruising Utopia*, 185.

5. *CROSSING* AND FEELING BROWN

1 Muñoz, *The Sense of Brown*, 8.

2 Muñoz, *The Sense of Brown*, 121.

3 Muñoz, *The Sense of Brown*, 39.

4 See Cárdenas's website, https://veronicagabriela.com/migrant-caravans/.

5 An estimated 85,000 Haitians arrived in Brazil between 2010 and 2017 as Brazil promised construction jobs ahead of the 2014 World Cup and the 2016 Summer Olympics. By 2020 there were an estimated 143,000 Haitians in Brazil. Once the games were over, and with increased anti-immigrant sentiments and racism at the time of the 2018 election of President Jair Bolsonaro, Haitians were driven out and went to Chile (more than 12,000 Haitians arrived in 2005, and more than 103,000 in 2017), where they also faced anti-immigration sentiments and racism. They thus started migrating north. To reach the Mexico-US border, some of these migrants cross multiple borders and face difficult and violent conditions. Part of their journey includes trekking through the Colombia-Panama border, in the infamous Darién Gap, a ninety-three-mile jungle that takes four to eleven days to cross. See Yates, "Haitian Migration through the Americas." For a photo essay of the difficult journey of Haitian migrants, see A. Taylor, "Photos: The Arduous Journey of the Haitian Migrants."

6 Rizzo Lara, "La Caminata del Migrante," 3895.

7 Rizzo Lara notes that a few days later four more groups had formed in El Salvador and Honduras with the same intention of reaching the Mexico-US border. On November 28, after traveling 1,864 miles, the first group

arrived in Tijuana. Throughout 2019–21, thousands more arrived seeking asylum in the United States. Rizzo Lara, "La Caminata del Migrante," 3895.

8 Rizzo Lara, "La Caminata del Migrante," 3895.

9 According to Amelia Frank-Vitale, the violence that migrants endure is not only connected to coyotes or smugglers. It is in great part the result of the state apparatus. As she notes, "Smugglers are not exclusively victimizers from whom migrants need to be saved; the state apparatus and its tentacles, the laws that make their migration illicit, are what structurally victimizes migrants." Frank-Vitale, "Coyotes, Caravans," 8. For an analysis connecting the state apparatus and the complex interaction between gendered violence and narcopolitics through a lens of necropolitics, see Wright, "Necropolitics, Narcopolitics, and Femicide." As noted in the previous chapter, the "Prevention through Deterrence" (PTD) policy has proven deadly for migrants. First implemented in 1993 in El Paso, Texas, the strategy aims at funneling border crossers into remote, inhospitable areas, where the cruelty of a harsh terrain will take care of the problematic intruder. See De León, *The Land of Open Graves*, 2–5.

10 Here I do not wish to oversimplify the religious character of the migrants' processions. I cannot portray their religious character only in positive terms, as the role of religiosity in the lives of those in poverty especially in the context of Latin America is complex.

11 Cordero Díaz and Garibo García, "Las caravanas de migrantes centroamericanos," 254. For an in-depth analysis of the right to flee of migrants that informs their analysis, see Mezzadra, *Derecho de fuga*.

12 Barthes, *Camera Lucida*, 81.

13 Muñoz, *The Sense of Brown*, 39.

14 Death by drowning and other reasons continues at the Mexico-US border; 2022 was the deadliest year so far, with 895 people dying at the border. See Razek and Wolfe, "Four Migrants, Including an Infant, Drowned." While we consider the Rio Grande, we must remember the deaths of Salvadorian migrant Oscar Alberto Martinez Ramirez and his daughter Valeria, who drowned in the Rio Grande in Matamoros and whose bodies were photographed by Julia Le Duc for the Mexican newspaper *La Jornada*. The photo of father and daughter holding each other created an uproar and was compared to the 2015 photograph of the dead body of Aylan Kurdi, a three-year-old Syrian boy who drowned while he and his family sought to reach Greece. While the photograph alerted many people about the perilous situation of migrants trying to reach the United States, it, just like the photo of Aylan Kurdi, unfortunately also became the perfect fodder for the spectacle of race that serves to satisfy the constant need to sensationalize the pain and death of bodies of color without a commitment to change the structures that exacerbate that pain. See Ahmed and Semple, "Photo of Drowned Migrants." For a dis-

cussion of photography and the spectacle of race in the context of Hurricane Katrina, see Ortega, "Othering the Other." Of course, the role of photographs of pain and suffering is a difficult one. Even Susan Sontag, who first sharply denounced photographs in her essays in *On Photography*, states in *Regarding the Pain of Others*, "Let the atrocious images haunt us. Even if they are only tokens, and cannot possibly encompass most of the reality to which they refer, they still perform a vital function. The images say: This is what human beings are capable of doing—may volunteer to do, enthusiastically, self-righteously. Don't forget" (115). In the case of the photograph of Oscar Alberto Martinez and his daughter Valeria, the image says: This is what is happening to migrants at the Mexico-US border in their search for survival and better lives. Please don't forget.

15 Muñoz, *The Sense of Brown*, 2.

16 Muñoz, *The Sense of Brown*, 2.

17 As noted in the introduction, Muñoz is highly skeptical of categories of identity such as "Hispanic" or "Latino" and even "Latinidad." This is precisely the reason why he is in a quest to find an alternative notion that captures the experience of being Latinx without being exclusive and essentialist as well as allowing for possibilities of coalitions across differences.

18 As he states, "The world is and has been brown and has been so despite the various blockages that keep us from knowing or being attuned to brownness." Muñoz, *The Sense of Brown*, 5.

19 Muñoz, *The Sense of Brown*, 3.

20 Muñoz, *The Sense of Brown*, 4. Admittedly, the Rio Grande might not be the commons that Muñoz has in mind, since, despite his desire to include the natural world and the nonhuman, he does not engage these aspects of the brown commons. His vision of the brown commons ends up being more connected to a political and cultural commons. As he says, "While I am narrating an expansive brown commons that traverses the regime of the human, the politics that organize this thought experiment are primarily attached to the lives of human actants in larger social ensembles" (2).

21 Chappell, "U.S. Border Agents Chased Migrants on Horseback."

22 F. Martinez, "Latinx Files."

23 According to Beltrán, "For citizens who long to revisit the politics of whiteness standing, the practices of ICE and CBP offer the right to use the law to police other populations, to impose tyranny while participating in forms of violence that feel like freedom—economic freedom, the freedom to enforce the law, and the frontier freedom of engaging in practices of settler sovereignty characterized by forced removal and transfer." Beltrán, *Cruelty as Citizenship*, 104. See also K. L. Hernández, *Migra!*

24 For "abjection machine," see Brady, *Extinct Lands*, 52; for "genocidal machine," see Mendieta, "Lethal Borders and Mobile Panopticons," 44.

25 Muñoz, *The Sense of Brown*, 121.

26 Piñeiro Aguiar and Diaz, "Muros, racism y resistencias," 3728. See also Dominguez Villegas, "Central American Migrants and 'La Bestia.'" For a Salvadorian journalist's description of two years of immersion on the migrant trail from Chiapas to the Mexico-US border, see O. Martínez, *The Beast*.

27 For an important rendition of Mexican immigrant workers in New York as superheroes, see Mexican-born artist Dulce Pinzón's series *The Real Story of the Superheroes* (2004–5), inspired by the important work that Mexican immigrants were doing before and after the September 11 attacks. To see this series, go to the website of Alida Anderson Art Projects, Pinzón's representative (https://alidaanderson.com/Artists/DulcePinzon/DulcePinzon.html). For a rich analysis of this series, see Mata, "Calling All Superheroes." If we move forward in time and consider how much work Mexican, other Latin American, and Latinx peoples did during the pandemic as "essential" workers, we can only regard those who survived and the many who perished as admirable yet vulnerable superheroes. The UCLA Latino Policy and Politics Institute's May 2023 report on the impact of the pandemic on the Latinx population states that during the first year of the pandemic, Latinxs experienced a disproportionate rate of cases, hospitalizations, and deaths across the United States, California, and Los Angeles County relative to their share of the population. See Majano et al., "The Impact of COVID-19 on Latinos." Overall, reports show that the color of death by COVID-19 was Black and brown. See Jason et al., "The Impact of the COVID-19 Pandemic on Black and Hispanic Americans' Work Outcomes."

28 Muñoz, *The Sense of Brown*, 42.

29 Lugones, "On Complex Communication," 78.

30 Muñoz, *The Sense of Brown*, 43.

31 Muñoz, *The Sense of Brown*, 16.

32 García Peña, *The Borders of Dominicanidad*, 5. For another key discussion that reframes Latinx studies by way of an analysis of Afro-Atlantic Hispanophone diasporic subjectivity and aesthetic creation, see Figueroa-Vázquez, *Decolonizing Diasporas*.

33 García Peña, *The Borders of Dominicanidad*, 8. In her latest work, García Peña states, "Black Latinxs living in the Global North—particularly in the United States and Europe—carry slavery and immigration with them as colonial experiences of unbelonging, often while navigating other forms of internal and transnational colonialities. Their subjecthood and bodies are bordered through palimpsestic colonialisms." García Peña, *Translating Blackness*, 19.

34 García Peña, *The Borders of Dominicanidad*, 11.

35 Muñoz, *The Sense of Brown*, 11. The notion of excess as applied to bodies of color carries ambiguity as it may serve to undermine people of color as well as to provide the possibility of illegibility that is important for people of color. For example, Amber Jamilla Musser interprets this excess as the opacity that is part of feeling brown and that opens a possibility of illegibility that counters a "stabilized notion of resistance." Musser, *Sensual Excess*, 11. Moreover, this excess is also interpreted as subject to commodification and appropriation. See J. Hernandez, *Aesthetics of Excess*.

36 Those of you who are people of color and have been and continue to be read as too loud, too angry, too expressive, not just in the ways that you carry yourself but also in the way you dress, will understand this point well and will understand why this creates constant feelings of anxiety and alienation. Muñoz makes the point that this excess is not liked by whites, as it makes their own affect look underdeveloped and impoverished. On a related note, when considering this aspect of feeling brown, we may also think not only of the affective excess of bodies of color but of the excess that they themselves become in the eyes of dominant groups, white supremacists, and governments that continually enact a necropolitics or a politics of disposability when dealing with them.

37 Despite its wide use, especially as it concerns constructive racial projects, *empathy* is a problematic term, because many times its meaning is taken for granted rather than carefully explained. Within the phenomenological tradition, it is a vexed term, because its need arises from a methodology that starts with a detached individual subject in the first place, hence the need to find a way for this subject to reach other people. Consider Husserl's famous fifth meditation in his *Cartesian Meditations* as he provides an intricate account of experiencing someone else in the context of transcendental phenomenology. See Husserl, *Cartesian Meditations*, 89. Other phenomenologists, such as Heidegger, recognized the problematic position of having to establish a theory of empathy and thus theorize a subject (*Dasein*) that already has the possibility of encountering others as the existential characteristic of being-with.

38 How different racial and ethnic groups within the Latinx, Latin American, and Caribbean communities can "touch" each other to the extent of generating intraracial empathy is a difficult issue. Colorism in the Latinx and Latin American communities is a significant problem. So is anti-Black racism. For a discussion of the difficulties in Black-brown relations, see Ortega, "Photographic Representations of Racialized Bodies." There have been multiple reports of Latinxs choosing "whiteness" as a race despite their mestizaje. The notion of mestizaje itself, which informs a number of projects of nationhood in Latin America, is connected to an

erasure of Indigenous roots and an invisibilizing of Blackness. For an interesting account of race in the context of Mexicans crossing the Mexico-US border, see S. Zamora, *Racial Baggage*. For an important analysis of the difficulty of friendship based on shared brownness between Latinxs and South Asians given the formation of the image of brownness as public enemy after September 11, see Macias, "What Has Brown Done for Me Lately?"

39 The use of shoes placed in strategic spaces for purposes of commemoration, witnessing, mourning, and resistance is a familiar practice. For example, Ekaterina E. Haskins discusses the touring exhibition *Eyes Wide Open*, sponsored by American Friends Service Committee, which placed a collection of combat boots and civilian shoes in specific sites such as Chicago's Federal Plaza (2004) and Washington, DC (2006), in order to memorialize US soldiers and Iraqis who died during the Iraq War. Haskins points to the importance of the exhibition in terms of its ability to open space for civic engagement, to mourn and honor the dead in both sides of the conflict, and to resist war. Haskins, *Popular Memories*, 97, 100, 115.

40 Email correspondence with Cárdenas, January 11, 2019.

41 Margry and Sánchez-Carretero, *The Politics of Memorializing Traumatic Death*.

42 As noted, *coyote* is the term given to one who smuggles undocumented migrants across the US-Mexico border. An ICE agent is a US Immigration and Customs Enforcement officer.

43 In 2011 there were 16,067 children apprehended at the border. By 2014 that number had increased to 68,541, and in 2019 it was 80,634. See Schmidt, "Child Maltreatment and Child Migration," 79. For a revealing, heartbreaking narrative account of questions asked to Central American refugee children in court intake questionnaires, see Luiselli, *Tell Me How It Ends*. For a gripping memoir of a first-person experience of a youth crossing the border, see J. Zamora, *Solito*.

44 De León, *The Land of Open Graves*, 25–28.

45 Dobbins, Goodman, and Sandoval, "The Death Toll Appears to Be One of the Highest in Recent Years"; Ahmed and Semple, "Photo of Drowned Migrants." See also note 14 above.

46 Haney, Leimer, and Lowery, "Spontaneous Memorialization"; Margry and Sánchez-Carretero, *The Politics of Memorializing Traumatic Death*.

47 Bednar, "Killing Memory," 338.

48 Petersson, "The Production of a Memorial Place," 142.

49 Portal, "Las creencias en el asfalto," 67.

50 Reid and Reid, "A Cross Marks the Spot," 344.

51 Lefebvre, *The Production of Space*, 98–99.

52 Lefebvre, *The Production of Space*, 383.

53 With Jennifer Ponce de León, we can think of the creation of these spaces as contributing to an aesthetics of history and an aesthetics of space aimed at creating an altogether different type of memorial, one that, unlike official public monuments, historical markers, and memorials, does not "naturalize a particular historical narrative and the spatial relations to which it corresponds." Ponce de León, *Another Aesthetics Is Possible*, 87.

54 A Chicana artist interested in capturing the importance of the water stations along areas of the desert that migrants cross is Delilah Montoya. Her 2004 series *Sed: A Trail of Thirst* consists of eight photographs taken in the desert in the Tohono O'odham Nation, which used to be one of the most deadly regions for migrants crossing. See Lara, "Living Landscapes," an interview with Montoya regarding the series. One of the most striking photographs in this series is *Humane Borders Water Station, 2004*.

55 A. F. Gordon, *Ghostly Matters*, xvi.

56 A. F. Gordon, *Ghostly Matters*, 63.

57 For Acosta, who provides poignant analyses of the work of Colombian artists engaging death and disappearance, it is important to remember death without having to resolve it. Acosta López, "Las fragilidades de la memoria," 44.

58 Acosta López, "Las fragilidades de la memoria," 45.

59 Patterson, *Slavery and Social Death*. While Patterson develops the notion of social death in the context of slavery, this notion can be extended to lives that have been denied the possibility of identity and freedom within different contexts.

60 For an account of ghostly subjectivity in the context of Lugones's call for decolonial feminism, see Ortega, "Spectral Perception and Ghostly Subjectivity." For an interesting discussion of haunting in the context of the life of world travelers that considers the role of memory and forgetting, see Islekel, "Traveling the Soil of Worlds."

61 As mentioned in chapter 4, the cages in detention centers are called *hieleras* because they are extremely cold.

62 See Gumbel, "'They Were Laughing at Us.'" For information on the "zero tolerance" policy, see Rizzo, "The Facts about Trump's Policy Separating Families at the Border." In a move that resembled the policies of the Trump administration, the Biden administration passed a ruling that denied asylum to migrants who come into the southern border and did not seek protection in the country they passed through, with the exception of children. For up-to-date information regarding changing regulations affecting migrants detained at the Mexico-US border, see Migration Policy Institute, "Research and Initiatives."

63 Gumbel, "'They Were Laughing at Us.'"

64 L. E. Pérez, *Chicana Art*, 91.

65 L. E. Pérez, *Chicana Art*, 100.

66 See Sundberg, "Prayer and Promise along the Migrant Trail." Sundberg notes how migrants create sacred sites, altars, in niches in rocks, where migrants leave intimate possessions such as photographs, rosaries, and prayer cards.

67 As noted, for Barthes, the "essence" of photography consists in pointing to something "that has been." See Barthes, *Camera Lucida*, 76, 80.

68 Saltzman, *Making Memory Matter*, 20.

69 Saltzman, *Making Memory Matter*, 51.

70 For more information on the Central American Refugee Crisis, see Hiskey et al., "Understanding the Central American Refugee Crisis"; and Abrego, "Central American Refugees Reveal the Crisis of the State."

71 For an astute analysis of the deployment of pro-child rhetoric by the immigration movement that reifies heteronormativity and the importance of the white child in the context of the nation's future, see Chávez and Masri, "The Rhetoric of Family in the U.S. Immigration Movement."

72 See Dostoevsky, *The Brothers Karamazov*, book 5, chap. 4. In this text one of the major issues that Dostoevsky brings to light is the problem of evil, and in particular the suffering of children. Whether in a religious or philosophical context, understanding the suffering of children presents a great challenge.

73 Alexander, *Pedagogies of Crossing*, 278. It is a forgetting that we have forgotten. It is also a wanting to forget.

74 For an analysis of "alien sexuality" and the notion of "anchor babies," see Cisneros, "'Alien' Sexuality."

75 Margry and Sánchez-Carretero, *The Politics of Memorializing Traumatic Death*, 20.

76 Ortega, *In-Between*, chap. 7. As noted, hometactics are everyday practices that allow for a sense of familiarity and a sense of "belonging" in various contexts, particularly in spaces in which we find ourselves alienated, othered, or unwelcomed.

77 J. Zamora, *Unaccompanied*, 13.

78 For an important account of the Latinx child as the captive child due to racial capitalism, see Brady, *Racial Capitalism and the Latinx Child*.

6. SOMETHING VERY EXTRAORDINARY

1 Barthes, *Camera Lucida*, 25.

2 According to Barthes a "fulguration" is an "intense mutation of my interest," and a detail that "overwhelms the entirety of my reading." Not "anything whatever. . . . This *something* has triggered me, has provoked a tiny shock." Barthes, *Camera Lucida*, 49.

3 Sontag, *Regarding the Pain of Others*, 71 (my emphasis).

4 It took me a long time to be able to discuss *Cuesta del Plomo*, and I thought that perhaps I would not be able to do it. I did it in 2019 in connection to an intellectual exercise, as so many thinkers do in the face of overwhelming emotion. I knew I would return to this haunting image and my experience of it given that my initial discussion carried with it the early understanding of the view of carnalities proposed in this work. See Ortega, "The Incandescence of Photography." It is important to note that this earlier version has a photograph of the Cuesta del Plomo memorial before it was transformed by the Sandinista government.

5 Kristeva, *Powers of Horror*, 3.

6 The relation between photograph and death is an intimate one. Recall Barthes's characterization of photography as representing "that very subtle moment when, to tell the truth, I am neither subject nor object but a subject who feels he is becoming an object: I then experience a micro-version of death (of parenthesis); I am truly becoming a specter." Barthes, *Camera Lucida*, 14.

7 According to Barthes we can read photographs in terms of their denotative or connotative messages. Denotation refers to what is being photographed, and connotation refers to the response of the viewer in encountering what is photographed, a response informed by the viewer's history as well as ideological factors. Barthes, "The Photographic Message," 524.

8 Meiselas, *Mediations*, 55. This area is famous in Nicaragua due to the many car accidents that occur there given the difficult terrain. Cuesta del Plomo has a complicated political history, as there was first a memorial constructed by the Somoza dictatorship, and it was subsequently refigured and repainted by the Sandinista government as a place to honor all those lost to the violence of Somoza's Guardia Nacional.

9 Barthes, *Camera Lucida*, 49.

10 Barthes, *Camera Lucida*, 49.

11 Barthes, *Camera Lucida*, 49.

12 Barthes, *Camera Lucida*, 77.

13 Barthes, *Camera Lucida*, 82.

14 Barthes, *Camera Lucida*, 72.

15 Barthes, *Camera Lucida*, 72.

16 Barthes, *Camera Lucida*, 73.

17 Barthes, *Camera Lucida*, 81.

18 As we have seen in my discussion of autoarte and my interest in capturing "inner work," there are deeply personal moments that I wish to capture despite the deeply relational character of the self and identity. Thus, here I examine how I was intimately pierced by the photograph. Although this discussion centers my own experience, I understand that

while some that have a painful connection with the events of 1979 in Nicaragua might react similarly as I did, others will have different experiences.

19 Kristeva, *Powers of Horror*, 140.

20 Kristeva, *Powers of Horror*, 141.

21 Kristeva, *Powers of Horror*, 150.

22 Kristeva, *Powers of Horror*, 1.

23 For Kristeva, this liminal space between the human and the animal constitutes a primitive effort to separate from the very being that gave birth to us. Here I do not discuss Kristeva's psychoanalytic claims or her highlighting of the relationship to the mother in our psychic experience. Rather than concentrating on what gives rise to abjection or the specific psychic processes associated with it, I am interested in Kristeva's understanding of abjection as connected to corporeal excess, ambiguity, and in-betweenness.

24 Kristeva, *Powers of Horror*, 3.

25 Kristeva, *Powers of Horror*, 5, 4.

26 Kristeva, *Powers of Horror*, 9.

27 In his famous explanation of photography, Kracauer makes a distinction between photographs and memory-images. As opposed to photographs, which in his view are merely spatiotemporal representations of a subject, memory-images are capable of capturing the subject's "significant" characteristics as well as the subject's ambiguity. Kracauer, "Photography," 425–26. For Kracauer the photograph is less interesting, as it becomes less valuable with time (i.e., an old photograph is emptied of life) and "captures only the residuum that history has discharged" (429). That is, once the subject of the photograph has died, what the photograph indexes is merely a collection of particulars about the person. Here we can thus think about two senses of residue: the excess of the corpse (Kristeva), and the residue of history, what is left imprinted on a piece of paper of a being that once was (429–30). The photograph, then, for Kracauer, becomes merely a ghost (431). In my view, however, the photograph captures more than the residue of history and a spatial configuration of a moment. It discloses the possibility of fulguration and the incandescence of abjection that sends us to the limits of being. As such it is deeply affective, to the point of incandescence.

28 When discussing photographs of corpses, Barthes states, "If the photograph then becomes horrible, it is because it certifies, so to speak, that the corpse is alive, as *corpse*: it is the living image of the dead thing." Barthes, *Camera Lucida*, 79. In its horror, the photograph individualizes in a dangerous way, threatening the very relationality of the self and even her entwinement between earth- and spirit-bodies, as in my case.

29 Kristeva, *Powers of Horror*, 1.

30 Kristeva, *Powers of Horror*, 3.
31 Anzaldúa, *Light in the Dark*, 49.
32 Anzaldúa, *Light in the Dark*, 50.
33 Anzaldúa, *Light in the Dark*, 56.
34 Anzaldúa, *Borderlands / La Frontera*, 97.
35 Moraga and Anzaldúa, *This Bridge Called My Back*, 200.
36 Moraga and Anzaldúa, *This Bridge Called My Back*, 208.
37 Anzaldúa, *Light in the Dark*, 92.
38 Anzaldúa, *Light in the Dark*, 98.
39 Anzaldúa, *Light in the Dark*, 103.
40 Anzaldúa, *Light in the Dark*, 106.
41 Kristeva, *Black Sun*, 98–99.
42 Kristeva, *Black Sun*, 137.
43 Kristeva, *Black Sun*, 138.
44 Kristeva, *The Severed Head*, 87.
45 Kristeva, *The Severed Head*, 105.
46 Kristeva, *The Severed Head*, 130.
47 Kristeva, *The Severed Head*, 120; Miller, *Head Cases*, 22.
48 Miller, *Head Cases*, 25. This is a different approach to melancholia than that of Muñoz, presented in the previous chapter. Both approaches, however, refuse melancholia as merely pathological and destructive.
49 Anzaldúa, *Light in the Dark*, 63.
50 My translation. Anzaldúa, *Borderlands / La Frontera*, 67.
51 Barthes, *Camera Lucida*, 27.
52 Camus, *The Myth of Sisyphus*, 40.
53 Berlant, *Cruel Optimism*.
54 Matos, "Examining Susan Meiselas's *Cuesta del Plomo*."
55 What does it mean for this artist of "cruel radiance" (what "illuminates the unbridgeable chasm that separates ordinary life from extraordinary experiences of political trauma") to travel back to these shadow grounds to prompt collective memorialization? Linfield, *The Cruel Radiance*, xv. Where are we to draw the line between documentation and the suffering of others as a continued spectacle?
56 See Meiselas's website (https://www.susanmeiselas.com/nicaragua-rh) for a video on the project *Reframing History*. Meiselas discusses the project and interviews people about her installations in which she placed large-scale reproductions of some of her photographs from 1978 and 1979 in Nicaragua in places where they were originally taken. While in the video we can see various people engaging with many of the reproductions, there are no discussions about the *Cuesta del Plomo* photograph when placed in the area again. What would it mean for Nicaraguans to engage with such a photo of utter abjection in a way that brings collective memory? Not only does Meiselas not understand the kind of fulguration that this photo may

give rise for an individual whose past has been touched by the revolution that for her has become an aesthetic object; she also does not appreciate the fact that many individuals may not wish to remember that particular image from the past. For example, the video documents a man who does not wish to have a large reproduction of a photograph installed on the wall of his house due to the pain it causes him to remember the past and the loss of various family members, including his daughter. Surprisingly, Meiselas does not at first understand why the man refuses to engage with her aesthetic project, a sign of the problematic relationship that the photographer has to what has primarily become an (her) art object. Perhaps in her own way Meiselas is engaging in a gathering of the temporal moments of a revolution, but they cannot be put together without creating more pain.

57 Benjamin, *Arcades Project*, 246.

58 Kristeva, *Stranger to Ourselves*, 8.

59 Kristeva, *Stranger to Ourselves*, 10.

60 Kristeva, *Stranger to Ourselves*, 10.

61 Kristeva, *Stranger to Ourselves*, 6.

62 For more information on the killing of Keller Pérez, see Nicaragua Investiga, "El Asesinato del estudiante Keller Pérez cumple cinco años de impunidad."

BIBLIOGRAPHY

Abrego, Leisy J. "Central American Refugees Reveal the Crisis of the State." In *The Oxford Handbook of Migration Crises*, edited by Cecilia Menjívar, Marie Ruiz, and Immanuel Ness, 213–28. Oxford: Oxford University Press, 2018.

Acosta López, María del Rosario. "Las fragilidades de la memoria: Duelo y Resistencia al olvido en el arte colombiano (Muñoz, Salcedo, Echavarría)." In *Resistencias al olvido: Memoria y arte en Colombia*, edited by María del Rosario Acosta López, 23–48. Bogota: Universidad de los Andes, 2016.

Ahmed, Azam, and Kirk Semple. "Photo of Drowned Migrants Captures Pathos of Those Who Risk It All." *New York Times*, June 25, 2019. https://www.nytimes.com/2019/06/25/us/father-daughter-border-drowning-picture-mexico.html.

Ahmed, Sara. "A Phenomenology of Whiteness." *Feminist Theory* 8, no. 2 (2007): 149–68.

Ahmed, Sara. *Queer Phenomenology: Orientations, Objects, Others*. Durham, NC: Duke University Press, 2006.

Alarcón, Norma. "Anzaldúan Textualities: A Hermeneutic of the Self and the Coyolxauhqui Imperative." In *El Mundo Zurdo 3: Selected Works from the 2012 Meeting of the Society for the Study of Gloria Anzaldúa*, edited by Larissa M. Merado-López, Sonia Saldívar-Hull, and Antonia Castañeda, 189–203. San Francisco: Aunt Lute Books, 2013.

Alarcón, Norma. "The Theoretical Subject(s) of *This Bridge Called My Back* and Anglo American Feminism." In *Criticism in the Borderlands: Studies in Chicano Literature, Culture, and Ideology*, edited by Hector Calderón, José David Saldívar, and Roberto Trujillo, 28–40. Durham, NC: Duke University Press, 1991.

Alessandri, Mariana. "Gloria Anzaldúa as Philosopher: The Early Years (1962–1987)." *Philosophy Compass* 15, no. 7 (2020): 1–15.

Alessandri, Mariana, and Alexander Stehn. "Gloria Anzaldúa's Mexican Genealogy: From Pelados and Pachucos to New Mestizas." *Genealogy* 4, no. 12 (2020): 1–14.

Alexander, M. Jacqui. *Pedagogies of Crossing: Meditations on Feminism, Sexual Politics, Memory, and the Sacred*. Durham, NC: Duke University Press, 2005.

Al-Saji, Alia. "Frantz Fanon." In *The Routledge Handbook of Phenomenology of Emotion*, edited by Thomas Szanto and Hilge Landweer, 207–14. New York: Routledge, 2020.

Al-Saji, Alia. "Glued to the Image: A Critical Phenomenology of Racialization through Works of Art." *Journal of Aesthetics and Art Criticism* 77, no. 4 (2019): 475–88.

Al-Saji, Alia. "Hesitation as Philosophical Method—Travel Bans, Colonial Durations, and the Affective Weight of the Past." *Journal of Speculative Philosophy* 32, no. 3 (2018): 331–59.

Al-Saji, Alia. "A Phenomenology of Hesitation: Interrupting Racializing Habits of Seeing." In *Living Alterities: Phenomenology, Embodiment, and Race*, edited by Emily S. Lee, 133–72. Albany: State University of New York Press, 2014.

Anzaldúa, Gloria. *Borderlands / La Frontera: The New Mestiza*. San Francisco: Aunt Lute Books, 1987.

Anzaldúa, Gloria. "Chicana Artists: Exploring Nepantla, El Lugar de la Frontera." In *The Latino Studies Reader: Culture, Economy, and Society*, edited by Antonia Darder and Rudolfo D. Torres, 163–69. Malden, MA: Blackwell, 1998.

Anzaldúa, Gloria. *The Gloria Anzaldúa Reader*. Edited by AnaLouise Keating. Durham, NC: Duke University Press, 2009.

Anzaldúa, Gloria. *Gloria E. Anzaldúa: Interviews/Entrevistas*. Edited by AnaLouise Keating. New York: Routledge, 2000.

Anzaldúa, Gloria. *Light in the Dark / Luz en lo oscuro: Rewriting Identity, Spirituality, Reality*. Edited by AnaLouise Keating. Durham, NC: Duke University Press, 2015.

Anzaldúa, Gloria. "Speaking in Tongues: A Letter to Third World Women Writers." In *The Gloria Anzaldúa Reader*, edited by AnaLouise Keating, 26–35. Durham, NC: Duke University Press, 2009.

Anzaldúa, Gloria. "To(o) Queer the Writer: Loca, escritora y chicana." In *The Gloria Anzaldúa Reader*, edited by AnaLouise Keating, 163–75. Durham, NC: Duke University Press, 2009.

Aparicio, Frances R., and Susana Chávez-Silverman, eds. *Tropicalizations: Transcultural Representations of Latinidad*. Hanover, NH: University Press of New England, 1997.

Arias, Arturo. "Central American-Americans: Invisibility, Power, and Representation in the U.S. Latino World." *Latino Studies* 1 (2003): 168–87.

Armour, Ellen T. *Seeing and Believing: Religion, Digital Visual Culture, and Social Justice*. New York: Columbia University Press, 2023.

Armour, Ellen T. *Signs and Wonders: Theology after Modernity*. New York: Columbia University Press, 2016.

Attali, Jacques. *The Political Economy of Music*. Translated by Brian Massumi. Manchester: Manchester University Press, 1985.

Azoulay, Ariella. *The Civil Contract of Photography*. New York: Zone Books, 2008.

Azoulay, Ariella. *Civil Imagination: A Political Ontology of Photography*. London: Verso, 2015.

Barnes, Richard. *State of Exception*. Accessed March 5, 2023. http://www.richardbarnes.net/projects#/state-of-exception-1/.

Barthes, Roland. *Camera Lucida: Reflections on Photography*. Translated by Richard Howard. New York: Hill and Wang, 1981.

Barthes, Roland. "The Photographic Message." In *A Barthes Reader*, edited by Susan Sontag, 194–210. New York: Hill and Wang, 1982.

Bazin, André. "The Ontology of the Photography Image." *Film Quarterly* 13, no. 4 (1960): 4–9.

Beauvoir, Simone de. *The Second Sex*. Translated by Constance Borde and Sheila Malovany-Chevallier. London: Vintage Books, 2011.

Bednar, Robert M. "Killing Memory: Roadside Memorial Removals and the Necropolitics of Affect." *Cultural Politics* 9, no. 3 (2013): 337–56.

Bell, Kathryn Sophia (formerly Kathryn T. Gines). "Black Feminism and Intersectional Analyses: A Defense of Intersectionality." *Philosophy Today* 55 (2011): 275–84.

Beltrán, Cristina. *Cruelty as Citizenship: How Migrant Suffering Sustains White Democracy*. Minneapolis: University of Minnesota Press, 2020.

Beltrán, Cristina. *The Trouble with Unity: Latino Politics and the Creation of Identity*. Oxford: Oxford University Press, 2010.

Benjamin, Walter. *Arcades Project*. Translated by Howard Eiland and Kevin McLaughlin. Cambridge, MA: Belknap Press of Harvard University Press, 1999.

Berlant, Lauren. *Cruel Optimism*. Durham, NC: Duke University Press, 2011.

Border Cantos. *Efigie/Effigy*. Accessed May 10, 2024. https://vimeo.com/154369901.

Bottici, Chiara. *Imaginal Politics: Images beyond Imagination and the Imaginary*. New York: Columbia University Press, 2014.

Brady, Mary Pat. *Extinct Lands, Temporal Geographies: Chicana Literature and the Urgency of Space*. Durham, NC: Duke University Press, 2002.

Brady, Mary Pat. *Racial Capitalism and the Latinx Child*. Durham, NC: Duke University Press, 2022.

Brown, Elspeth H., and Thy Phu, eds. *Feeling Photography*. Durham, NC: Duke University Press, 2014.

Butler, Judith. *Precarious Life: The Powers of Mourning and Violence*. London: Verso, 2004.

Campos-Pons, Maria Magdalena. Interview with Terrence Dempsey, S.J., and Dr. Olubukola Gbadegesin, March 2013. *MOCRA Voices*, episode 7, May 15, 2017. https://mocravoices.libsyn.com/episode-7-maria-magdalena-campos-pons.

Campt, Tina M. *Listening to Images*. Durham, NC: Duke University Press, 2017.

Camus, Albert. *The Myth of Sisyphus and Other Essays*. New York: Vintage Books, 1995.

Carastathis, Anna, and Myrto Tsilimpounidi. *Reproducing Refugees: Photographìa of a Crisis*. New York: Rowman and Littlefield, 2020.

Cárdenas, Verónica Gabriela. *Migrant Caravans*. Accessed February 19, 2023. https://veronicagabriela.com/migrant-caravans/.

Carrillo Rowe, Aimee. "Loving Transgressions: Queer of Color Bodies, Affective Ties, Transformative Community." *Journal of Lesbian Studies* 21, no. 3 (2017): 243–53.

Casey, Edward S. *Turning Emotion Inside Out: Affective Life beyond the Subject*. Evanston, IL: Northwestern University Press, 2022.

Castoriadis, Cornelius. *The Imaginary Institution of Society*. Translated by Kathleen Blamey. Cambridge: Polity Press, 1987.

Chappell, Bill. "U.S. Border Agents Chased Migrants on Horseback. A Photographer Explains What He Saw." NPR, September 21, 2021. https://www.npr.org/2021/09/21/1039230310/u-s-border-agents-haiti-migrants-horses-photographer-del-rio.

Chávez, Karma R. *Queer Migration Politics: Activist Rhetoric and Coalitional Possibilities*. Urbana: University of Illinois Press, 2013.

Chávez, Karma R., and Hana Masri. "The Rhetoric of Family in the U.S Immigration Movement." In *Queer and Trans Migrations: Dynamics of Illegalization, Detention, and Deportation*, edited by Eithne Luibhéid and Karma R. Chávez, 210–25. Urbana: University of Illinois Press, 2020.

Cheng, Anne Anlin. *The Melancholy of Race: Psychoanalysis, Assimilation, and Hidden Grief*. Oxford: Oxford University Press, 2000.

Chomsky, Noam. *Turning the Tide: U.S. Intervention in Central America and the Struggle for Peace*. London: Pluto, 2015.

Cisneros, Natalie. "'Alien' Sexuality: Race, Maternity, and Citizenship." *Hypatia* 28, no. 2 (2013): 290–306.

Cordero Díaz, Blanca Laura, and María Georgina Garibo García. "Las caravanas de migrantes centroamericanos: Acuerpamiento en movimiento." In *Migraciones internacionales en el siglo XXI: Un análisis desde una perspectiva crítica*, edited by Ada Celsa Cabrera García, Gustavo Rodríguez Albor, and Ibelis Blanco Rangel, 253–70. Barranquilla: Universidad Autónoma del Caribe, 2019.

Cornejo, Kency. "Visual Counter Narratives: Central American Art on Migration and Criminality." *Journal of Commonwealth and Postcolonial Studies* 5, no. 1 (2017): 63–82.

Crary, Jonathan. *Techniques of the Observer: On Vision and Modernity in the Nineteenth Century*. Cambridge, MA: MIT Press, 1992.

Cvetkovich, Ann. *An Archive of Feelings: Trauma, Sexuality, and Lesbian Public Cultures*. Durham, NC: Duke University Press, 2003.

Dahms, Betsy. "Shamanic Urgency and Two-Way Movement as Writing Style in the Works of Gloria Anzaldúa." *Letras Femeninas* 38, no. 2 (2012): 9–27.

Dalaqua, Gustavo H. "Aesthetic Injustice." *Journal of Aesthetics and Culture* 12, no. 1 (2020): 1–12.

Danielson, Marivel T. "Anzaldúan Autohisteoría: Queer Chicana Desire at the Intersection of Theory and Story." *Aztlán* 47, no. 2 (2022): 51–79.

Darder, Antonia, and Rodolfo D. Torres, eds. *The Latino Studies Reader: Cultures, Economy, and Society*. Hoboken, NJ: Wiley-Blackwell, 1998.

Davalos, Karen Mary. *Chicana/o Remix: Art and Errata since the Sixties*. New York: New York University Press, 2017.

Dávila, Arlene. *Latinos, Inc.: The Marketing and Making of a People*. Berkeley: University of California Press, 2001.

Day, Jane S. *Aztec: The World of Moctezuma*. Niwot, CO: Roberts Rinehart, 1992.

De La Torre, Vincent, dir. *Trails of Hope and Terror*. V1 Educational Media, Inc., 2017.

De León, Jason. *The Land of Open Graves: Living and Dying on the Migrant Trail*. Berkeley: University of California Press, 2015.

Delgadillo, Theresa. "Enacting Decoloniality." *Aztlán: A Journal of Chicano Studies* 47, no. 1 (2022): 203–15.

Delgadillo, Theresa. "Forms of Chicana Feminist Resistance: Hybrid Spirituality in Ana Castillo's *So Far from God*." *MFS Modern Fiction Studies* 44, no. 4 (1998): 888–916.

Delgadillo, Theresa. *Spiritual Mestizaje: Religion, Gender, Race, and Nation in Contemporary Chicana Narrative*. Durham, NC: Duke University Press, 2011.

Diaz, Natalie. *Postcolonial Love Poem*. Minneapolis: Graywolf, 2020.

DiPietro, PJ. "Beyond Benevolent Violence: Trans* of Color, Ornamental Multiculturalism, and the Decolonization of Affect." In *Speaking Face to Face: The Visionary Philosophy of María Lugones*, edited by PJ DiPietro, Jennifer McWeeny, and Shireen Roshanravan, 197–216. Albany: State University of New York Press, 2019.

Dobbins, James, J. David Goodman, and Edgar Sandoval. "The Death Toll Appears to Be One of the Highest in Recent Years." *New York Times*, June 27, 2022. https://www.nytimes.com/live/2022/06/28/us/migrants-san-antonio-tractor-killed.

Dolezal, Luna, and Danielle Petherbridge, eds. *Body/Self/Other: The Phenomenology of Social Encounters*. Albany: State University of New York Press, 2017.

Dominguez Villegas, Rodrigo. "Central American Migrants and 'La Bestia': The Route, the Dangers, and Government Responses." Migration Policy Institute, September 10, 2014. https://www.migrationpolicy.org/article/central-american-migrants-la-bestia.

Dostoevsky, Fyodor. *The Brothers Karamazov*. New York: Norton, 1976.

Dotson, Kristie. "A Cautionary Tale: On Limiting Epistemic Oppression." *Frontiers: A Journal of Women Studies* 33, no. 1 (2012): 24–47.

Du Bois, William Edward Burghardt. *The Souls of Black Folk: Essays and Sketches.* Chicago: A. C. McClurg & Co., 1903.

Edkins, Jennifer. "Missing Migrants and the Politics of Naming: Names without Bodies, Bodies without Names." *Social Research* 83, no. 2 (2016): 359–89.

Edwards, Elizabeth. "Objects of Affect: Photography beyond the Image." *Annual Review of Anthropology* 41 (2012): 221–34.

Eng, David L., and Shinhee Han, eds. *Racial Melancholia, Racial Dissociation: On the Social and Psychic Lives of Asian Americans.* Durham, NC: Duke University Press, 2019.

Epstein, Rebecca, ed. *Laura Aguilar: Show and Tell.* Los Angeles: UCLA Chicano Studies Research Center Press, 2017.

Estrella, James. "The *Plush Pony* Series: An Untold Story of Hope and Despair." In *Laura Aguilar: Show and Tell*, edited by Rebecca Epstein, 57–65. Los Angeles: UCLA Chicano Studies Research Center Press, 2017.

Fanon, Frantz. *Black Skin, White Masks.* Translated by Richard Philcox. New York: Grove, 2008.

Ferrari, Martina. "Questions of Silence: On the Emancipatory Limits of Voice and the Coloniality of Silence." *Hypatia* 35, no. 1 (2020): 123–42.

Ferrari, Martina, Devin Fitzpatrick, Sarah McLay, Shannon Hayes, Kaja Jenssen Rathe, and Amie Zimmer. "Editors' Introduction: Reflections on the First Issue." *Puncta: Journal of Critical Phenomenology* 1, no. 1 (2018): 1–7.

Ferrer, Elizabeth. *Latinx Photography in the United States: A Visual History.* Seattle: University of Washington Press, 2020.

Fielding, Helen A. *Cultivating Perception through Artworks: Phenomenological Enactments of Ethics, Politics, and Culture.* Bloomington: Indiana University Press, 2021.

Fielding, Helen A. "White Logic and the Constancy of Color." In *Feminist Interpretations of Merleau-Ponty*, edited by Dorothea Olkowski and Gail Weiss, 71–89. University Park: Pennsylvania State University Press, 2006.

Figueroa-Vásquez, Yomaira. *Decolonizing Diasporas: Radical Mappings of Afro-Atlantic Literature.* Evanston, IL: Northwestern University Press, 2020.

Flores, Lisa. *Deportable and Disposable: Public Rhetoric and the Making of the "Illegal" Immigrant.* University Park: Pennsylvania State University Press, 2020.

Flores, Tatiana. "Latinidad Is Cancelled." *Latin American and Latinx Visual Culture* 3, no. 3 (2021): 58–79.

Fong, Cai D. "Forgive Me for So Speaking: Towards a Hermeneutic of Wounded Embodiment and an Ethics of Contingency." *Social Identities* 28, no. 1 (2022): 60–73.

Foster, Hal, ed. *Vision and Visuality.* Seattle: Bay Press, 1988.

Frankowski, Alfred. *The Post-racial Limits of Memorialization.* London: Lexington Books, 2015.

Frank-Vitale, Amelia. "Coyotes, Caravans, and the Central American Migrant Smuggling Continuum." *Trends in Organized Crime*, January 2023, 1–16.

Gálvez, Alyshia. *Eating NAFTA: Trade, Food Policies, and the Destruction of Mexico*. Berkeley: University of California Press, 2018.

García, Alma, ed. *Chicana Feminist Thought: The Basic Historical Writings*. New York: Routledge, 1997.

García, Armando. "Disposable Subjects: Staging Illegality and Racial Terror in the Borderlands." *Critical Philosophy of Race* 7, no. 1 (2019): 160–86.

García, María Cristina. *Seeking Refuge: Central American Migration to Mexico, the United States, and Canada*. Berkeley: University of California Press, 2006.

García Peña, Lorgia. *The Borders of Dominicanidad: Race, Nation, and Archives of Contradiction*. Durham, NC: Duke University Press, 2016.

García Peña, Lorgia. *Translating Blackness: Latinx Colonialities in Global Perspective*. Durham, NC: Duke University Press, 2022.

Gómez-Barris, Macarena. "Mestiza Cultural Memory: The Self-Ecologies of Laura Aguilar." In *Laura Aguilar: Show and Tell*, edited by Rebecca Epstein, 79–85. Los Angeles: UCLA Chicano Studies Research Center Press, 2017.

Gómez-Barris, Macarena. "The Plush View: Makeshift Sexualities and Laura Aguilar's Forbidden Archives." In *Axis Mundo: Queer Networks in Chicano L.A.*, edited by C. Ondine Chavoya, David Evans Frantz, and Macarena Gómez-Barris, 320–33. New York: Prestel, 2017.

Gordon, Avery F. *Ghostly Matters: Haunting and the Sociological Imagination*. Minneapolis: University of Minnesota Press, 2008.

Gordon, Lewis R. *Bad Faith and Anti-Black Racism*. Highlands, NJ: Humanities Press, 1995.

Gracia, Jorge. *Hispanic/Latino Identity: A Philosophical Perspective*. Hoboken, NJ: Wiley-Blackwell, 1999.

Gracia, Jorge. *Latinos in America: Philosophy and Social Identity*. Hoboken, NJ: Wiley-Blackwell, 2008.

Gracia, Jorge, ed. *Race or Ethnicity? On Black and Latino Identity*. Ithaca, NY: Cornell University Press, 2007.

Gramlich, John. "Migrant Encounters at the U.S.-Mexico Border Hit a Record High at the End of 2023." Pew Research Center, February 15, 2024. https://pewrsr.ch/3H5zxNr.

Grimm, Erika. "Linguistic Rupture, Racialization, and Resistance in Latina/x Feminisms: A Critical Phenomenological Approach." PhD diss., Penn State University, 2023.

Guenther, Lisa. "Critical Phenomenology." In *50 Concepts for a Critical Phenomenology*, edited by Gail Weiss, Ann V. Murphy, and Gayle Salamon, 11–16. Evanston, IL: Northwestern University Press, 2020.

Guenther, Lisa. "Six Senses of Critique for Critical Phenomenology." *Puncta: Journal of Critical Phenomenology* 4, no. 2 (2021): 5–23.

Gumbel, Andrew. "'They Were Laughing at Us': Immigrants Tell of Cruelty, Illness, and Filth in US Detention." *Guardian*, September 12, 2018. https://www.theguardian.com/us-news/2018/sep/12/us-immigration-detention-facilities.

Haney, C. Allen, Christina Leimer, and Juliann Lowery. "Spontaneous Memorialization: Violent Death and Emerging Mourning Ritual." *Omega* 35, no. 2 (1997): 159–71.

Hartman, Saidiya. *Lose Your Mother: A Journey along the Atlantic Slave Route*. New York: Farrar, Straus and Giroux, 2007.

Hartman, Saidiya. *Scenes of Subjection: Terror, Slavery, and Self-Making in Nineteenth-Century America*. New York: Oxford University Press, 1997.

Hartman, Saidiya. "Venus in Two Acts." *Small Axe* 26 12, no. 2 (2008): 1–14.

Haskins, Ekaterina V. *Popular Memories: Commemoration, Participatory Culture, and Democratic Citizenship.* Columbia: University of South Carolina Press, 2015.

Hass, Lawrence. *Merleau-Ponty's Philosophy*. Bloomington: Indiana University Press, 2008.

Heidegger, Martin. *Being and Time*. Translated by John Macquarrie and Edward Robinson. New York: Harper and Row, 1962.

Heinämaa, Sara, David Carr, and Andreea Smaranda Aldea, eds. *Phenomenology as Critique: Why Method Matters*. New York: Routledge, 2022.

Hernandez, Jillian. *Aesthetics of Excess: The Art and Politics of Black and Latina Embodiment*. Durham, NC: Duke University Press, 2020.

Hernández, Kelly Lytle. *Migra! A History of the U.S. Border Patrol*. Berkeley: University of California Press, 2010.

Hight, Eleanor M., and Gary D. Sampson, eds. *Colonialist Photography: Imag(in)ing Race and Place*. New York: Routledge, 2004.

Hiskey, Jonathan T., Abby Córdova, Diana Orcés, and Mary Fran Malone. "Understanding the Central American Refugee Crisis." *American Immigration Council*, February 1, 2016. https://www.americanimmigrationcouncil.org/research/understanding-central-american-refugee-crisis.

hooks, bell. *Feminist Theory from Margin to Center*. Boston: South End, 1984.

hooks, bell. "In Our Glory: Photography and Black Life." In *Art on My Mind: Visual Politics*, 55–64. New York: New York University Press, 1995.

Hurston, Zora Neale. *Dust Tracks on a Road*. 1942. New York: Harper Perennial, 2006.

Husserl, Edmund. *Cartesian Meditations: An Introduction to Phenomenology*. Translated by Dorion Cairns. Dordrecht: Kluwer Academic, 1993.

Husserl, Edmund. *Logical Investigations*. Translated by J. N. Findlay. New York: Routledge, 2001.

Irigaray, Luce. *An Ethics of Sexual Difference*. Translated by Carolyn Burke and Gillian C. Gill. Ithaca, NY: Cornell University Press, 1993.

Irigaray, Luce. "When Our Lips Speak Together." Translated by Carolyn Burke. *Signs* 6, no. 1 (1980): 69–79.

Irvin, Sherri. *Immaterial: Rules in Contemporary Art*. Oxford: Oxford University Press, 2022.

Islekel, Ege Selin. "Traveling the Soil of Worlds: Haunted Forgettings and Opaque Memories." *Hypatia* 35, no. 3 (2020): 439–53.

Jason, Kendra, Miguel Wilson, Jamel Catoe, Courtney Brown, and Mayleen Gonzalez. "The Impact of the COVID-19 Pandemic on Black and Hispanic Americans' Work Outcomes: A Scoping Review." *Journal of Racial and Ethnic Health Disparities*, April 28, 2023, 1–16. https://doi.org/10.1007/s40615-023-01594-6.

Jay, Martin. *Downcast Eyes: The Denigration of Vision in Twentieth-Century French Thought*. Berkeley: University of California Press, 1993.

Johnson, Galen A., ed. *The Merleau-Ponty Aesthetics Reader: Philosophy and Painting*. Evanston, IL: Northwestern University Press, 1993.

Jones, Amelia. "Clothed/Unclothed: Laura Aguilar's Radical Vulnerability." In *Laura Aguilar: Show and Tell*, edited by Rebecca Epstein, 39–53. Los Angeles: UCLA Chicano Studies Research Center Press, 2017.

Keating, AnaLouise. *The Anzaldúan Theory Handbook*. Durham, NC: Duke University Press, 2022.

Keating, AnaLouise. "'I'm a Citizen of the Universe': Gloria Anzaldúa's Spiritual Activism as Catalyst for Social Change." *Feminist Studies* 34, nos. 1–2 (2008): 54–55.

Keating, AnaLouise. "Shifting Perspectives: Spiritual Activism, Social Transformation, and the Politics of Spirit." In *Entremundos / Among Worlds: New Perspectives on Gloria E. Anzaldúa*, edited by AnaLouise Keating, 241–54. New York: Palgrave Macmillan, 2005.

Keating, AnaLouise. "Speculative Realism, Visionary Pragmatism, and Poet-Shamanic Aesthetics in Gloria Anzaldúa—and Beyond." *Women's Studies Quarterly* 40, nos. 3/4 (2012): 51–69.

Keating, AnaLouise. *Transformation Now! Toward a Post-oppositional Politics of Change*. Urbana: University of Illinois Press, 2013.

Kelly, Michael, ed. *Encyclopedia of Aesthetics*. New York: Oxford University Press, 1998.

Kemp, Martin, and Marina Wallace. *Spectacular Bodies*. Berkeley: University of California Press, 2000.

Kiefer, Tom. *El Sueño Americano*. Accessed May 30, 2024. https://www.tomkiefer.com/el-sueno-americano.

Kracauer, Siegfried. "Photography." Translated by Thomas Y. Levin. *Critical Inquiry* 19 (Spring 1993): 421–36.

Kristeva, Julia. *Black Sun: Depression and Melancholia*. Translated by Leon S. Roudiez. New York: Columbia University Press, 1989.

Kristeva, Julia. *Powers of Horror: An Essay on Abjection*. Translated by Leon S. Roudiez. New York: Columbia University Press, 1982.

Kristeva, Julia. *The Severed Head: Capital Visions*. Translated by Jody Gladding. New York: Columbia University Press, 2012.

Kristeva, Julia. *Stranger to Ourselves*. Translated by Leon S. Roudiez. New York: Columbia University Press, 1991.

Kun, Josh D. "The Aural Border." *Theatre Journal* 52 (2000): 1–21.

Lacan, Jacques. "The Mirror Stage as Formative of the Function of the I as Revealed in Psychoanalytic Experience." In *Reading French Psychoanalysis*, edited by Dana Breen, Sara Flanders, and Alain Gibeault, 97–104. New York: Routledge, 2014.

LaFeber, Walter. *Inevitable Revolutions: The United States in Central America*. New York: Norton, 1993.

Laó-Montes, Agustín, and Arlene Dávila. *Mambo Montage: The Latinization of New York*. New York: Columbia University Press, 2001.

Lara, Orlando. "Living Landscapes." Accessed November 7, 2023. www.orlandolara.com/thirst/talk.html.

Lee, Emily S. *A Phenomenology for Women of Color: Merleau-Ponty and Identity in Difference*. Lanham, MD: Lexington Books, 2024.

Lee, Emily S. "A Phenomenology of Seeing and Affect in a Polarized Climate." In *Race as Phenomena: Between Phenomenology and Philosophy of Race*, edited by Emily S. Lee, 107–23. Lanham, MD: Rowman and Littlefield, 2019.

Lefebvre, Henri. *The Production of Space*. Translated by Donald Nicholson-Smith. Oxford: Blackwell, 1984.

Leimer, Ann Marie. "Chicana Photography: The Power of Place." In *National Association for Chicana and Chicano Studies 35th Annual Conference Proceedings*, 28–39. San Jose, CA: National Association for Chicana and Chicano Studies, 2008.

Lenman, Robin, and Angela Nicholson, eds. *The Oxford Companion to the Photograph*. Oxford: Oxford University Press, 2005.

Leon-Carlyle, Rawb. "Wild Red: Synesthesia, Deuteranomaly, and Euclidean Color Space." *Chiasmi International* 21 (2019): 355–66.

Lilla, Mark. *The Once and Future Liberal: After Identity Politics*. New York: HarperCollins, 2017.

Linfield, Susie. *The Cruel Radiance: Photography and Political Violence*. Chicago: University of Chicago Press, 2010.

Lloyd, David. *Under Representation: The Racial Regime of Aesthetics*. New York: Fordham University Press, 2019.

Lockhart, Tara. "Writing the Self: Gloria Anzaldúa, Textual Form, and Feminist Epistemology." *Michigan Feminist Studies*, no. 20 (2007). http://hdl.handle.net/2027/spo.ark5583.0020.002.

Lorde, Audre. *Sister Outsider*. Freedom, CA: Crossing Press, 1984.

Lugones, María. "From within Germinative Stasis: Creating Active Subjectivity, Resistant Agency." In *Entre Mundos / Among Worlds: New Perspectives on Gloria Anzaldúa*, edited by AnaLouise Keating, 85–99. New York: Palgrave Macmillan, 2005.

Lugones, María. "Heterosexualism and the Colonial/Modern Gender System." *Hypatia* 22, no. 1 (2007): 186–219.

Lugones, María. "Motion, Stasis, and Resistance to Interlocked Oppressions." In *Making Worlds: Gender, Metaphor, Materiality*, edited by Susan Hardy Aiken, 49–53. Tucson: University of Arizona Press, 1998.

Lugones, María. "On *Borderlands / La Frontera*: An Interpretive Essay." *Hypatia* 7, no. 4 (1992): 31–37.

Lugones, María. "On Complex Communication." *Hypatia* 21, no. 3 (2006): 75–85.

Lugones, María. *Pilgrimages/Peregrinajes: Theorizing Coalition against Multiple Oppressions*. Lanham, MD: Rowman and Littlefield, 2003.

Lugones, María. "Toward a Decolonial Feminism." *Hypatia* 25, no. 3 (2010): 742–59.

Lugones, María, and Mariana Ortega. "Carnal Disruptions." In *Speaking Face to Face: The Visionary Philosophy of María Lugones*, edited by PJ DiPietro, Jennifer McWeeny, and Shireen Roshanravan, 273–84. Albany: State University of New York Press, 2019.

Luibhéid, Eithne. "Treated Neither with Respect nor with Dignity: Contextualizing Queer and Trans Migrant 'Illegalization,' Detention, and Deportation." In *Queer and Trans Migrations: Dynamics of Illegalization, Detention, and Deportation*, edited by Eithne Luibhéid and Karma R. Chávez, 19–40. Urbana: University of Illinois Press, 2020.

Luiselli, Valeria. *Tell Me How It Ends: An Essay in Forty Questions*. Minneapolis: Coffee House Press, 2017.

Macias, Roberto, Jr. "'What Has Brown Done for Me Lately?': The (Im)possibilities of Recuperating Brownness after 9/11." *Aztlán: A Journal of Chicano Studies* 48, no. 1 (2023): 145–56.

Majano, Rosario, Alberto Murillo, Misael Galdámez, and Arturo Vargas Bustamante. "The Impact of COVID-19 on Latinos, 3 Years In: Trends in Health Outcomes and Vaccinations in the U.S., California, and Los Angeles." UCLA Latino Policy and Politics Institute, May 24, 2023. https://latino.ucla.edu/research/the-impact-of-covid-19-on-latinos/.

Marder, Michael. *Phenomena—Critique—Logos: The Project of Critical Phenomenology*. London: Rowman and Littlefield, 2014.

Margry, Peter Jan, and Cristina Sánchez-Carretero, eds. *The Politics of Memorializing Traumatic Death*. New York: Berghahn Books, 2011.

Marks, Laura U. *The Skin of the Film: Intercultural Cinema, Embodiment, and the Senses*. Durham, NC: Duke University Press, 2000.

Martín Alcoff, Linda. *Visible Identities: Race, Gender, and the Self*. New York: Oxford University Press, 2006.

Martínez, Daniel E., Robin C. Reineke, Geoffrey Boyce, Samuel N. Chambers, Sarah Launius, Bruce E. Anderson, Gregory L. Hess, et al. "Migrant Deaths in Southern Arizona: Recovered Undocumented Border Crosser Remains Investigated by the Pima County Office of the Medical Examiner, 1990–2020." Binational Migration Institute, University of Arizona College of Social and Behavioral Sciences, April 2021. https://sbs.arizona.edu/sites/sbs.arizona.edu/files/BMI%20Report%202021%20ENGLISH_FINAL.pdf.

Martinez, Fidel. "Latinx Files: The Photo That Captured the Decades of Failures of U.S. Border Policy." *Los Angeles Times*, September 23, 2021. https://www.latimes.com/world-nation/newsletter/2021-09-23/latinx-files-border-patrol-haitians-latinx-files.

Martinez, Jacqueline M. "Culture, Communication, and Latina Feminist Philosophy: Toward a Critical Phenomenology of Culture." *Hypatia* 29, no. 1 (2014): 221–36.

Martinez, Jacqueline M. *Phenomenology of Chicana Experience and Identity: Communication and Transformation in Praxis*. Lanham, MD: Rowman and Littlefield, 2000.

Martínez, Oscar. *The Beast: Riding the Rails and Dodging Narcos on the Migrant Trail*. Translated by Daniela Maria Ugaz and John Washington. London: Verso, 2013.

Massumi, Brian. "The Autonomy of Affect." *Cultural Critique* 31 (Fall 1995): 83–109.

Mata, Irene. "Calling All Superheroes." In *Domestic Disturbances: Re-imagining Narratives of Gender, Labor, and Immigration*, 127–59. Austin: University of Texas Press, 2014.

Matos, Andrea Sofía R. "Examining Susan Meiselas' *Cuesta del Plomo*." Accessed March 13, 2023. https://www.andreasofiarm.com/writings/susanmeiselas.

Maturana, Humberto, and Francisco Varela. *Autopoiesis and Cognition: The Realization of the Living*. Dordrecht: D. Reidel, 1980.

Maxwell, Anee. *Picture Imperfect: Photography and Eugenics 1870–1940*. Eastbourne, UK: Sussex Academy Press, 2010.

Meda Calderon, Denise. "Cosmologies, Ritual, and Resistance: An Exploration of María Lugones' Decolonial Aesthesis and Coalitional *Movidas*." *Inter-American Journal of Philosophy* 13, no. 1 (2022): 119–39.

Medina, José. "Epistemic Justice and Epistemologies of Ignorance." In *The Routledge Companion to the Philosophy of Race*, edited by Paul C. Taylor, Linda Martín Alcoff, and Luvell Anderson, 247–60. New York: Routledge, 2018.

Medina, José. *The Epistemology of Protest: Silencing, Epistemic Activism, and the Communicative Life of Resistance*. Oxford: Oxford University Press, 2023.

Medina, José. *The Epistemology of Resistance: Gender and Racial Oppression, Epistemic Injustice, and Resistant Imaginations*. Oxford: Oxford University Press, 2013.

Medina, José. "Racial Violence, Emotional Friction, and Epistemic Activism." *Angelaki: Journal of Theoretical Humanities* 24, no. 4 (2019): 22–37.

Medina, José. "Resisting Racist Propaganda: Distorted Visual Communication and Epistemic Activism." *Southern Journal of Philosophy* 56, Spindel suppl. (2018): 50–75.

Medina, Lara. "Nepantla Spirituality: My Path to the Source(s) of Healing." In *Fleshing the Spirit: Spirituality and Activism in Chicana, Latina, and Indigenous Women's Lives*, edited by Elisa Facio and Irene Lara, 167–86. Tucson: University of Arizona Press, 2014.

Medina, Lara. "Nepantla Spirituality: Negotiating Fluid Identities, Faiths, and Practices." In *El Mundo Zurdo: Selected Works from the Meetings of the Society for the Study of Gloria Anzaldúa 2007 and 2009*, edited by Norma E. Cantú, Christina L. Gutiérrez, Norma Alarcón, and Rita E. Urquijo-Ruiz, 223–48. San Francisco: Aunt Lute Books, 2010.

Meiselas, Susan. *Mediations*. Bologna: Damiani, 2018.

Meiselas, Susan. *Reframing History*. Accessed March 11, 2023. https://www.susanmeiselas.com/nicaragua-rh.

Mendieta, Eduardo. "Lethal Borders and Mobile Panopticons: Thanatological Dispositifs." In *Borders and Debordering, Typologies, Praxes, Hospitableness*, edited by Eduardo Mendieta, Lenart Škof, and Tomaž Grušovnik, 70–101. Lanham, MD: Lexington Books, 2018.

Mendoza, José Jorge. *The Moral and Political Philosophy of Immigration: Liberty, Security, and Equality*. Lanham, MD: Lexington Books, 2017.

Merleau-Ponty, Maurice. "Cezanne's Doubt." In *The Merleau-Ponty Aesthetics Reader: Philosophy and Painting*, edited by Galen A. Johnson, 59–75. Evanston, IL: Northwestern University Press, 1993.

Merleau-Ponty, Maurice. "Eye and Mind." In *The Merleau-Ponty Aesthetics Reader: Philosophy and Painting*, edited by Galen A. Johnson, 121–50. Evanston, IL: Northwestern University Press, 1993.

Merleau-Ponty, Maurice. *The Visible and the Invisible*. Edited by Claude Lefort; translated by Alphonso Lingis. Evanston, IL: Northwestern University Press, 1968.

Mezzadra, Sandro. *Derecho de fuga: Migraciones, ciudadanía y globalización*. Translated by Miguel Santucho. Madrid: Traficantes de sueños, 2005.

Mignolo, Walter D., and Rolando Vázquez. "Decolonial AestheSis: Colonial Wounds / Decolonial Healings." *Social Text Online*, July 15, 2013. https://socialtextjournal.org/periscope_article/decolonial-aesthesis-colonial-woundsdecolonial-healings/.

Migration Policy Institute. "Research and Initiatives." Accessed November 7, 2023. https://www.migrationpolicy.org/research-initiatives.

Milbrath, Susan. "Decapitated Lunar Goddesses in Aztec Art, Myth, and Ritual." *Ancient Mesoamerica* 8, no. 2 (1997): 185–206.

Milian, Claudia. “Latin.” In *Keywords for Southern Studies*, edited by Scott Romine and Jennifer Rae Greeson, 179–88. Athens: University of Georgia Press, 2016.

Milian, Claudia. *Latining America: Black-Brown Passages and the Coloring of Latino/a Studies*. Athens: University of Georgia Press, 2013.

Milian, Claudia. *LatinX*. Minneapolis: University of Minnesota Press, 2019.

Milian, Claudia, ed. “Theorizing LatinX.” *Cultural Dynamics* 29, no. 3 (2017): 121–40.

Miller, Elaine. *Head Cases: Julia Kristeva on Philosophy and Art in Depressed Times*. New York: Columbia University Press, 2014.

Miroff, Nick. “Arrests along U.S.-Mexico Border Top 2 Million a Year for the First Time.” *Texas Tribune*, September 19, 2022. https://www.texastribune.org/2022/09/19/u-s-mexico-border-arrests-record-2022/.

Mirzoeff, Nicholas. *The Right to Look: A Counterhistory of Visuality*. Durham, NC: Duke University Press, 2011.

Misrach, Richard, and Guillermo Galindo. *Border Cantos*. With an introduction by Josh Kun. New York: Aperture, 2016.

Mitchell, W. J. T. *What Do Pictures Want? The Lives and Loves of Images*. Chicago: University of Chicago Press, 2005.

Moody-Adams, Michele. *Making Space for Justice: Social Movements, Collective Imagination, and Political Hope*. New York: Columbia University Press, 2023.

Moraga, Cherríe, and Gloria Anzaldúa, eds. *This Bridge Called My Back: Writings by Radical Women of Color*. New York: Kitchen Table Press, 1983.

Morris Hambourg, Maria, Pierre Apraxine, Malcolm Daniel, Jeff L. Rosenheim, and Virginia Heckert. *The Waking Dream: Photography's First Century*. New York: Metropolitan Museum of Art, 1993.

Morris-Reich, Amos. 2016. *Race and Photography: Racial Photography as Scientific Evidence, 1876–1980*. Chicago: University of Chicago Press, 2016.

Mulvey, Laura. “Visual Pleasure and Narrative Cinema.” *Screen* 16, no. 3 (1975): 6–18.

Muñoz, José Esteban. *Cruising Utopia: The Then and There of Queer Futurity*. New York: New York University Press, 2009.

Muñoz, José Esteban. *Disidentifications: Queers of Color and the Performance of Politics*. Minneapolis: University of Minnesota Press, 1999.

Muñoz, José Esteban. *The Sense of Brown*. Edited by Joshua Chambers-Letson and Tavia Nyong'o. Durham, NC: Duke University Press, 2020.

Musser, Amber Jamilla. *Sensual Excess: Queer Femininity and Brown Jouissance*. New York: New York University Press, 2018.

Nash, Jennifer. *The Black Body in Ecstasy: Reading Race, Reading Pornography*. Durham, NC: Duke University Press, 2014.

Neruda, Pablo. *Fully Empowered*. Translated by Alastair Reid. New York: New Directions, 1995.

Ngo, Helen. *The Habits of Racism: A Phenomenology of Racism and Racialized Embodiment*. Lanham, MD: Lexington Books, 2017.

Nicaragua Investiga. "El Asesinato del estudiante Keller Pérez cumple cinco años de impunidad." May 1, 2023. https://nicaraguainvestiga.com/politica/118230-impunidad-estudiante-keller/.

Nuccetelli, Susana, Schutte Ofelia, and Otávio Bueno, eds. *A Companion to Latin American Philosophy*. Hoboken, NJ: Wiley Blackwell, 2009.

Ohmer, Sarah. "Gloria E. Anzaldúa's Decolonizing Ritual de Conocimiento." *Confluencia* 26, no. 1 (2010): 141–53.

Olin, Margaret. *Touching Photographs*. Chicago: University of Chicago Press, 2012.

Omi, Michael, and Howard Winant. *Racial Formation in the U.S. from the 1960s to the 1990s*. New York: Routledge, 1994.

Ortega, Mariana. "Aesthetic Injustice, Practices of Othering, and Ignorance." *Philosopher Blog*, May 26, 2017. https://politicalphilosopher.net/2017/05/26/featured-philosopher-mariana-ortega/.

Ortega, Mariana. "Cámara Queer: Longing, the Photograph, and Queer Latinidad." In *Theories of the Flesh: Latinx and Latin American Feminisms, Transformation, and Resistance*, edited by Andrea J. Pitts, Mariana Ortega, and José Medina, 264–80. New York: Oxford University Press, 2020.

Ortega, Mariana. "Exiled Space, In-Between Space: Existential Spatiality in Ana Mendieta's Siluetas Series." *Philosophy and Geography* 7, no. 1 (2004): 25–41.

Ortega, Mariana. *In-Between: Latina Feminist Phenomenology, Multiplicity, and the Self*. Albany: State University of New York Press, 2016.

Ortega, Mariana. "The Incandescence of Photography: On Abjection, Fulguration, and the Corpse." *philoSOPHIA* 9, no. 2 (2019): 68–87.

Ortega, Mariana. "Othering the Other: The Spectacle of Katrina for Our Racial Entertainment Pleasure." *Contemporary Aesthetics*, special vol. 2 (2009). https://digitalcommons.risd.edu/liberalarts_contempaesthetics/vol0/iss2/2.

Ortega, Mariana. "Perceiving in Red: The Visible, the Invisible, and Aesthesic Trespassing." In *Life in Art: Phenomenology and World-Making*. Bloomington: Indiana University Press, forthcoming.

Ortega, Mariana. "Photographic Representations of Racialized Bodies: Afro-Mexicans, the Visible, and the Invisible." *Critical Philosophy of Race* 1, no. 2 (2013): 163–89.

Ortega, Mariana. "Queer Autoarte: A Differential Aesthesis of the Limen." *Graduate Faculty Philosophy Journal* 41, no. 1 (2020): 207–32.

Ortega, Mariana. "Spectral Perception and Ghostly Subjectivity at the Colonial Gender/Race/Sex Nexus." *Journal of Aesthetics and Art Criticism* 77, no. 4 (2019): 401–9.

Ortega, Mariana, and Helen Fielding, eds. *Life in Art: Phenomenology and World-Making*. Bloomington: Indiana University Press, forthcoming.

Otto, Melanie. "Poet-Shamanic Aesthetics in the Work of Gloria Anzaldúa and Wilson Harris." *C. L. R. James Journal* 23, nos. 1/2 (2017): 135–56.

Page, Susan Harbage. *US-Mexico Border Project*. Accessed March 5, 2023. https://susanharbagepage.com/u-s-mexico-border-project/.

Papenburg, Bettina, and Marta Zarzycka, eds. *Carnal Aesthetics: Transgressive Imagery and Feminist Politics*. London: I. B. Tauris, 2013.

París Pombo, María Dolores. "Violence at the US-Mexico Border." In *The Oxford Handbook of Migration Crises*, edited by Cecilia Menjívar, Marie Ruiz, and Immanuel Ness, 214–38. Oxford: Oxford University Press, 2018.

Parsons, Sarah. "Sontag's Lament: Emotion, Ethics, and Photography." *Photography and Culture* 2, no. 3 (2009): 289–302.

Patterson, Orlando. *Slavery and Social Death: A Comparative Study*. Cambridge, MA: Harvard University Press, 1982.

Pelaez Lopez, Alan. "The X in Latinx Is a Wound Not a Trend." *Color Bloq: The Stories of Us*, September 2018. https://www.colorbloq.org/the-x-in-latinx-is-a-wound-not-a-trend.

Pérez, Emma. *The Decolonial Imaginary: Writing Chicanas into History*. Bloomington: Indiana University Press, 1999.

Pérez, Laura E. *Chicana Art: The Politics of Spiritual and Aesthetic Altarities*. Durham, NC: Duke University Press, 2007.

Pérez, Laura E. *Eros Ideologies: Writings on Art, Spirituality, and the Decolonial*. Durham, NC: Duke University Press, 2019.

Pérez, Laura E. "Hybrid Spiritualities and Chicana Altar-Based Art: The Work of Amalia Mesa-Bains." In *Mexican American Religions, Spirituality, Activism, and Culture*, edited by Gastón Espinosa and Mario T. García, 338–58. Durham, NC: Duke University Press, 2008.

Pérez, Laura E. "Spirit Glyphs: Reimagining Art and Artist in the Work of Chicana Tlamatinime." *MFS: Modern Fiction Studies* 44, no. 1 (1998): 36–76.

Petersson, Anna. "The Production of a Memorial Place: Materialising Expressions of Grief." In *Deathscapes: Places of Death, Dying, Mourning and Remembrance*, edited by Avril Maddrell and James D. Sidaway, 141–59. Farnham, UK: Ashgate, 2010.

Piñeiro Aguiar, Eleder, and Carlos Diaz. "Muros, racism y resistencias: Movilidad humana a lomos de la Bestia." *Revista izquierdas* 49 (2020): 3721–37.

Pinney, Christopher, and Nicolas Peterson, eds. *Photography's Other Histories*. Durham, NC: Duke University Press, 2003.

Pinzón, Dulce. *The Real Story of the Superheroes*. Accessed October 31, 2023. https://alidaanderson.com/Artists/DulcePinzon/DulcePinzon.html.

Pitts, Andrea J. "Gloria E. Anzaldúa's *Autohistoria-teoría* as an Epistemology of Self-Knowledge/Ignorance." *Hypatia* 31, no. 2 (2016): 352–69.

Pitts, Andrea J. *Nos/Otras: Gloria E. Anzaldúa, Multiplicitous Agency, and Resistance*. Albany: State University of New York Press, 2021.

Ponce de León, Jennifer. *Another Aesthetics Is Possible: Arts of Rebellion in the Fourth World War*. Durham, NC: Duke University Press, 2021.

Portal, Ana María. "Las creencias en el asfalto: La sacralización como una forma de apropiación del espacio público en la ciudad de México." *Cuadernos de Antropología Social* 30 (2009): 59–75.

Pratt, Mary Louise. "Arts of the Contact Zone." *Profession* (1991): 33–40.

Pratt, Mary Louise. *Extinct Lands: Temporal Geographies, Chicana Literature, and the Urgency of Space*. Durham, NC: Duke University Press, 2002.

Preciado, Paul B. *Testo Junkie: Sex, Drugs, and Biopolitics in the Pharmacopornographic Era*. Translated by Bruce Benderson. New York: Feminist Press, 2013.

Quashie, Kevin. *Black Aliveness, or A Poetics of Being*. Durham, NC: Duke University Press, 2021.

Quashie, Kevin. *The Sovereignty of Quiet*. New Brunswick, NJ: Rutgers University Press, 2012.

Quijano, Anibal. "Coloniality of Power, Eurocentrism, and Latin America." *Nepantla: Views from South* 1, no. 3 (2000): 533–80.

Rancière, Jacques. *The Politics of Aesthetics*. Edited and translated by Gabriel Rockhill. New York: Bloomsbury Academic, 2006.

Razek, Raja, and Elizabeth Wolfe. "Four Migrants, Including an Infant, Drowned in the Rio Grande River over 3-Day Period, Official Says." CNN, July 4, 2023. https://www.cnn.com/2023/07/04/us/migrant-drownings-texas-mexico-border/index.html.

Reed-Sandoval, Amy. *Socially Undocumented: Identity and Immigration Justice*. Oxford: Oxford University Press, 2020.

Reid, John K., and Cynthia L. Reid. "A Cross Marks the Spot: A Study of Roadside Death Memorials in Texas and Oklahoma." *Death Studies* 25 (2001): 341–56.

Reynolds, Joel Michael. "Merleau-Ponty, World-Creating Blindness, and the Phenomenology of Non-normate Bodies." *Chiasmi International: Trilingual Studies concerning Merleau-Ponty's Thought* 19 (2017): 419–34.

Rivera, Mayra. *Poetics of the Flesh*. Durham, NC: Duke University Press, 2015.

Rivera, Omar. "Stillness, Aesthesis, Resistance." *Critical Philosophy of Race* 8, nos. 1–2 (2020): 84–101.

Rivera Berruz, Stephanie. "Extending into Space: The Materiality of Language and the Arrival of Latina/o Bodies." *Inter-American Journal of Philosophy* 5, no. 1 (2014): 23–41.

Rivera Garza, Cristina. *Grieving: Dispatches from a Wounded Country*. New York: Feminist Press, 2020.

Rivera-Servera, Ramón. *Performing Queer Latinidad: Dance, Sexuality, Politics*. Ann Arbor: University of Michigan Press, 2012.

Rizzo, Salvador. "The Facts about Trump's Policy Separating Families at the Border." *Washington Post*, June 19, 2018. https://www.washingtonpost

.com/news/fact-checker/wp/2018/06/19/the-facts-about-trumps-policy-of-separating-families-at-the-border/.

Rizzo Lara, Rosario. "La Caminata del Migrante: A Social Movement." *Journal of Ethnic and Migration Studies* 47, no. 17 (2021): 3891–910.

Rodriguez, Juana María. *Queer Latinidad: Identity Practices, Discursive Spaces.* New York: New York University Press, 2003.

Roelofs, Monique. *Arts of Address: Being Alive to Language and the World.* New York: Columbia University Press, 2020.

Roelofs, Monique. *The Cultural Promise of the Aesthetic.* London: Bloomsbury, 2014.

Roelofs, Monique. "Navigating Frames of Address: María Lugones on Language, Bodies, Things, and Places." *Hypatia* 31, no. 2 (2016): 370–87.

Rose, Joel. "Immigration Agencies Ordered Not to Use Term 'Illegal Alien' under New Biden Policy." NPR, April 19, 2021. https://www.npr.org/2021/04/19/988789487/immigration-agencies-ordered-not-to-use-term-illegal-alien-under-new-biden-polic.

Rosenberg, Mica, Kristina Cooke, and Daniel Trotta. "The Border's Toll." Reuters, July 8, 2022. https://www.reuters.com/investigates/special-report/usa-immigration-border-deaths/.

Rubio, Angelica. "Undocumented, Not Illegal: Beyond the Rhetoric of Immigration Coverage." *NACLA Report on the Americas* 44, no. 6 (2011): 50–52.

Rubio-Goldsmith, Raquel, Celestino Fernández, Jessie K. Finch, and Araceli Masterson Algar, eds. *Migrant Deaths in the Arizona Desert: La Vida No Vale Nada.* Tucson: University of Arizona Press, 2016.

Salamon, Gayle. *The Life and Death of Latisha King.* New York: New York University Press, 2018.

Salamon, Gayle. "What's Critical about Critical Phenomenology?" *Puncta: Journal of Critical Phenomenology* 1, no. 1 (2018): 8–17.

Salazar, Miguel. "The Problem with Latinidad." *Nation*, September 16, 2019. https://www.thenation.com/article/archive/hispanic-heritage-month-latinidad/.

Saldaña-Portillo, María Josefina, ed. "Dossier: Revisiting Mestizaje Twenty Years Later." *Aztlán: A Journal of Chicano Studies* 46, no. 2 (2021): 145–252.

Saldaña-Portillo, María Josefina. "Who's the Indian in Aztlán? Rewriting *Mestizaje*, Indianismo, and Chicanismo from the Lacandón." In *The Latin American Subaltern Studies Reader*, edited by Ileana Rodríguez, 402–23. Durham, NC: Duke University Press, 2001.

Saldaña-Portillo, María Josefina, and Simón Ventura Trujillo. "Introduction: What Does Mestizaje Name?" *Aztlán: A Journal of Chicano Studies* 46, no. 2 (2021): 149–61.

Saltzman, Lisa. *Making Memory Matter: Strategies of Remembrance in Contemporary Art.* Chicago: University of Chicago Press, 2006.

Sánchez, Carlos Alberto. "Towards a Phenomenology of Undocumented Immigrant Reason." *Puncta: Journal of Critical Phenomenology* 5, no. 3 (2022): 60–71.

Sandoval, Chela. *The Methodology of the Oppressed*. Minneapolis: University of Minnesota Press, 2000.

Sandoval, Chela. "Video Production, Liberation Aesthetics, and U.S. Third World Feminist Criticism." In *Prosthetic Territories: Politics and Hypertechnologies*, edited by Gabriel Brahm Jr. and Mark Driscoll, 151–67. Boulder, CO: Westview, 1995.

Sandoval, Chela, and Guisela Latorre. "Chicana/o Artivism: Judy Baca's Digital Work with Youth of Color." In *Learning Race and Ethnicity: Youth and Digital Media*, edited by Anna Everett, 81–108. Cambridge, MA: MIT Press, 2008.

Sartre, Jean-Paul. *Existentialism Is a Humanism.* Translated by Carol Macomber. New Haven, CT: Yale University Press, 2007.

Sartre, Jean-Paul. *The Imaginary: A Phenomenological Psychology of the Imagination.* Translated by Jonathan Webber. New York: Routledge, 2004.

Schaeffer, Felicity Amaya. "Spirit Matters: Gloria Anzaldúa's Cosmic Becoming across Human/Nonhuman Borderlands." *Signs: Journal of Women in Culture and Society* 43, no. 4 (2018): 1005–29.

Schmidt, Susan. "Child Maltreatment and Child Migration: Abuse Disclosures by Central American and Mexican Unaccompanied Migrant Children." *Journal of Migration and Human Security* 10, no. 1 (2022): 77–92.

Sealey, Kris. *Creolizing the Nation*. Evanston, IL: Northwestern University Press, 2020.

Sekula, Alan. "The Body and the Archive." In *The Contest of Meaning: Critical Histories of Photography*, edited by Richard Bolton, 3–64. Cambridge, MA: MIT Press, 1992.

Sharpe, Christina. "Beauty Is a Method." *e-flux Journal*, no. 105 (December 2019). https://www.e-flux.com/journal/105/303916/beauty-is-a-method/.

Sharpe, Christina. *In the Wake: On Blackness and Being.* Durham, NC: Duke University Press, 2016.

Sierra-Rivera, Judith. *Affective Intellectuals and the Space of Catastrophe in the Americas*. Columbus: Ohio State University Press, 2018.

Smith, Shawn Michelle. *American Archives: Gender, Race, and Class in Visual Culture*. Princeton, NJ: Princeton University Press, 1999.

Smith, Shawn Michelle. *At the Edge of Sight: Photography Unseen*. Durham, NC: Duke University Press, 2013.

Smith, Shawn Michelle. *Photographic Returns: Racial Justice and the Time of Photography*. Durham, NC: Duke University Press, 2020.

Smith, Shawn Michelle. *Photography on the Color Line: W. E. B. Du Bois, Race, and Visual Culture*. Durham, NC: Duke University Press, 2004.

Sobchack, Vivian. *The Address of the Eye: A Phenomenology of Film Experience*. Princeton, NJ: Princeton University Press, 1992.

Sobchack, Vivian. *Carnal Thoughts: Embodiment and Moving Image Culture*. Berkeley: University of California Press, 2004.

Sontag, Susan. *On Photography*. New York: Farrar, Straus and Giroux, 1978.

Sontag, Susan. *Regarding the Pain of Others*. New York: Farrar, Straus and Giroux, 2003.

Spiegelberg, Herbert. *The Phenomenological Movement: A Historical Introduction*. The Hague: Martinus Nijhoff, 1984.

Spillers, Hortense. "Mama's Baby, Papa's Maybe: An American Grammar Book." *Diacritics* 17, no. 2 (1987): 64–81.

Stawarska, Beata. "From the Body Proper to Flesh: Merleau-Ponty on Intersubjectivity." In *Feminist Interpretations of Maurice Merleau-Ponty*, edited by Gail Weiss and Dorothea Olkowski, 91–106. University Park: Pennsylvania State University Press, 2006.

Stewart, Lindsey. *The Politics of Black Joy: Zora Neale Hurston and Neo-abolitionism*. Evanston, IL: Northwestern University Press, 2021.

St. John, Rachel C. *Line in the Sand: A History of the Western U.S. Mexico Border*. Princeton, NJ: Princeton University Press, 2011.

Stoller, Silvia. "Reflections on Feminist Merleau-Ponty Skepticism." *Hypatia* 15, no. 1 (2000): 175–82.

Sullivan, Shannon. "Domination and Dialogue in Merleau-Ponty's Phenomenology of Perception." *Hypatia* 12, no. 1 (1997): 1–19.

Sullivan, Shannon. "Ontological Expansiveness." In *Encyclopedia of Critical Whiteness Studies in Education*, edited by Zachary A. Casey, 432–38. Leiden: Brill, 2021.

Sullivan, Shannon. *Revealing Whiteness: The Unconscious Habits of Racial Privilege*. Bloomington: Indiana University Press, 2006.

Sundberg, Juanita. "Diabolic Caminos in the Desert and Cat Fights on the Río: A Posthumanist Political Ecology of Boundary Enforcement in the United States—Mexico Borderlands." *Annals of the Association of American Geographers* 101, no. 2 (2011): 318–36.

Sundberg, Juanita. "Prayer and Promise along the Migrant Trial." *Geographical Review* 103, no. 2 (2013): 230–33.

Tagg, John. *The Burden of Representation: Essays on Photographies and Histories*. Amherst: University of Massachusetts Press, 1988.

Taylor, Alan. "Photos: The Arduous Journey of the Haitian Migrants." *Atlantic*, September 28, 2021. https://www.theatlantic.com/photo/2021/09/photos-arduous-journey-haitian-migrants/620226/.

Taylor, Paul C. *Black Is Beautiful: A Philosophy of Black Aesthetics*. Malden, MA: Wiley Blackwell, 2016.

Tirres, Christopher D. "Spiritual Activism and Praxis: Gloria Anzaldúa's Mature Spirituality." *Pluralist* 14, no. 1 (2019): 119–40.

Trethewey, Natasha. *Thrall: Poems*. Boston: Houghton Mifflin Harcourt, 2012.

Truax, Eileen, ed. *We Built the Wall: How the U.S. Keeps Asylum Seekers from Mexico, Central America and Beyond*. London: Verso, 2018.
Tuana, Nancy, and Charles Scott. "Border Arte Philosophy: Altogether beyond Philosophy." *Journal of Speculative Philosophy* 32, no. 1 (2018): 70–91.
Undocumented Migration Project. "Background." Accessed May 30, 2024. https://www.undocumentedmigrationproject.org/background1.
Urrea, Luis Alberto. *By the Lake of Sleeping Children: The Secret Life of the Mexican Border*. New York: Anchor Books, 1996.
Urrea, Luis Alberto. *The Devil's Highway: A True Story*. New York: Little, Brown, 2004.
Vallega, Alejandro. "Displacements: Beyond the Coloniality of Images." *Research in Phenomenology* 41, no. 2 (2011): 206–27.
Vázquez, Rolando. *Vistas of Modernity: Decolonial Aesthesis and the End of the Contemporary*. Amsterdam: Mondrian Fund, 2020.
Velazco y Trianosky, Gregory. "Savages, Wild Men, Monstrous Races: The Social Construction of Race in the Early Modern Era." In *Beauty Unlimited*, edited by Peg Zeglin Brand, 45–71. Bloomington: Indiana University Press, 2012.
Velez, Emma. "Towards a 'Care-ful Geopolitics' of La Frontera in the Era of Trump." *Journal of Speculative Philosophy* 34, no. 3 (2020): 339–52.
Venegas, Sybil. "Take Me to the River: The Photography of Laura Aguilar." In *Laura Aguilar: Show and Tell*, edited by Rebecca Epstein, 9–18. Los Angeles: UCLA Chicano Studies Research Center Press, 2017.
Veronelli, Gabriela. "A Coalitional Approach to Theorizing Decolonial Communication." *Hypatia* 32, no. 2 (2016): 404–20.
Villaseñor Black, Charlene. "Reflections on Laura Aguilar." *Aztlán: A Journal of Chicano Studies* 43, no. 2 (2018): 1–16.
Viso, Olga. *Ana Mendieta: Earth Body*. Washington, DC: Hirshhorn Museum and Sculpture Garden, Smithsonian Institution, 2004.
Vivancos, Ricardo F. *Radical Chicana Poetics*. New York: Palgrave Macmillan, 2013.
Voegelin, Salomé. *Listening to Noise and Silence: Towards a Philosophy of Sound Art*. London: Bloomsbury, 2010.
Walker, Kara Elizabeth. *After the Deluge*. New York: Rizzoli, 2003.
Wallace, Maurice O., and Shawn Michelle Smith. *Pictures and Progress: Early Photography and the Making of African American Identity*. Durham, NC: Duke University Press, 2012.
Warmack, Andrea. "We Flesh: Musser, Spillers, and Beyond the Phenomenological Body." *Puncta: Journal of Critical Phenomenology* 5, no. 4 (2022): 106–24.
Weheliye, Alexander G. *Habeas Viscus: Racializing Assemblages, Biopolitics, and Black Feminist Theories of the Human*. Durham, NC: Duke University Press, 2014.
Weiss, Gail. "The Anonymous Intentions of Transactional Bodies." *Hypatia* 17, no. 4 (2002): 187–200.
Weiss, Gail. *Refiguring the Ordinary*. Bloomington: Indiana University Press, 2008.

Wieseler, Christine. "Challenging Conceptions of the 'Normal' Subject in Phenomenology." In *Race as Phenomena: Between Phenomenology and Philosophy of Race*, edited by Emily Lee, 69–85. New York: Rowman and Littlefield, 2019.

Wollheim, Richard. *Art and Its Objects*. Cambridge: Cambridge University Press, 1980.

Wright, Melissa W. "Border Thinking, Borderland Diversity, and Trump's Wall." *Annals of the American Association of Geographers* 109, no. 2 (2019): 511–19.

Wright, Melissa W. "Necropolitics, Narcopolitics, and Femicide: Gendered Violence on the Mexico-US Border." *Signs: Journal of Women in Culture and Society* 36, no. 3 (2011): 707–31.

Wynter, Sylvia. "The Ceremony Found: Towards the Autopoetic Turn/Overturn, Its Autonomy of Human Agency and Extraterritoriality of (Self-) Cognition." In *Black Knowledges / Black Struggles: Essays in Critical Epistemologies*, edited by Jason R. Ambroise and Sabine Broeck, 184–253. Liverpool: Liverpool University Press, 2015.

Yancy, George. *Black Bodies, White Gazes: The Continuing Significance of Race*. Lanham, MD: Rowman and Littlefield, 2008.

Yates, Caitlyn. "Haitian Migration through the Americas: A Decade in the Making." Migration Policy Institute, September 30, 2021. https://www.migrationpolicy.org/article/haitian-migration-through-americas.

Zahavi, Dan. "Getting It Quite Wrong: Van Manen and Smith on Phenomenology." *Qualitative Health Research* 29, no. 6 (2018): 900–907.

Zamora, Javier. *Solito: A Memoir*. New York: Random House, 2022.

Zamora, Javier. *Unaccompanied*. Port Townsend, WA: Copper Canyon, 2017.

Zamora, Sylvia. *Racial Baggage: Mexican Immigrants and Race across the Border*. Stanford, CA: Stanford University Press, 2022.

Zaytoun, Kellie. *Shapeshifting Subjects: Gloria Anzaldúa's Naguala and Border Arte*. Urbana: University of Illinois Press, 2022.

Zuniga, Tracy M. "Daring to Be More Honest." In *Laura Aguilar: Show and Tell*, edited by Rebecca Epstein, 67–72. Los Angeles: UCLA Chicano Studies Research Center Press, 2017.

INDEX